Chiara Gianollo, Agnes Jäger, Doris Penka (Eds.)
Language Change at the Syntax-Semantics Interface

Trends in Linguistics Studies and Monographs

Volume 278

Language Change at the Syntax-Semantics Interface

—

Edited by
Chiara Gianollo
Agnes Jäger
Doris Penka

DE GRUYTER
MOUTON

ISBN 978-3-11-035217-7
e-ISBN (PDF) 978-3-11-035230-6
e-ISBN (EPUB) 978-3-11-039492-4
ISSN 1861-4302

Library of Congress Cataloging-in-Publication Data
A CIP catalog record for this book has been applied for at the Library of Congress.

Bibliographic information published by the Deutsche Nationalbibliothek
The Deutsche Nationalbibliothek lists this publication in the Deutsche Nationalbibliografie;
detailed bibliographic data are available on the Internet at http://dnb.dnb.de.

© 2015 Walter de Gruyter GmbH, Berlin/Munich/Boston
Typesetting: RoyalStandard, Hong Kong
Printing and binding: CPI books GmbH, Leck
♾ Printed on acid-free paper

www.degruyter.com

Preface and acknowledgements

Bringing together diachronic research from a variety of perspectives, this volume focuses on the interplay of syntactic and semantic factors in language change – an issue recently brought into the focus of formal linguistics by grammaticalization theory as well as Minimalist diachronic syntax.

The contributions draw on data from numerous Indo-European languages including Vedic Sanskrit, Middle Indic, Greek as well as English and German, and discuss a range of phenomena such as change in negation markers, indefinite articles, quantifiers, modal verbs, argument structure among others. The papers analyze diachronic evidence in the light of contemporary syntactic and semantic theory, addressing the crucial question of how syntactic and semantic change are linked, and whether both are governed by similar constraints, principles and systematic mechanisms.

This thematic volume grew out of a workshop we organized at the 34th annual meeting of the Deutsche Gesellschaft für Sprachwissenschaft (DGfS) in Frankfurt/Main in March 2012. The workshop brought together researchers interested in diachrony from a variety of perspectives (typological/language- or family-specific, formal/functional), and prompted lively and constructive discussion of the methodological assumptions as well as empirical findings. The present volume collects a selection of the papers presented there, as well as a number of invited contributions complementing the results of the original discussion.

We would like to thank first of all the authors who engaged in this project and submitted contributions for this volume. Without their cooperation at all stages, this book would not have been possible. We furthermore thankfully acknowledge the support of the organisers of the DGfS 2012 in Frankfurt who, in accepting the idea of the workshop, provided us with an optimal venue and allowed us to reach a high number of interested scientists. We also want to thank the speakers and the audience at this workshop for discussion and feedback. Besides those who contributed to this volume, we would in particular like to mention Regine Eckardt, Stefan Evert, Ian Roberts, Ewa Trutkowski, David Willis, Hedde Zeijlstra, and Mirjam Zumstein. We are also indebted to our colleagues, who with their comments and suggestions considerably contributed to the quality of the presented research and reviewed abstracts for the workshop or papers for this volume: Daniel Buncic, Cornelia Ebert, Eric Haeberli, Klaus von Heusinger, Paul Kiparsky, Sveta Krasikova, Chris Lucas, Silvia Luraghi, Jakob Maché, Umut Özge, Frans Plank, Beatrice Primus, Ian Roberts, Maribel Romero, Arnim von Stechow, Ruprecht von Waldenfels, Helmut Weiß, and Eirik Welo.

We also want to express our gratitude to Volker Gast, the main series editor for this volume, and the other editors of the 'Trends in Linguistics' series, as well as Birgit Sievert from Mouton de Gruyter, who supported every step of the project with competence and enthusiasm. Susanne Trissler provided invaluable help with proof-reading and formatting. Finally, we thankfully acknowledge the financial support of the Zukunftskolleg at the University of Konstanz.

Cologne and Konstanz, October 2014
Chiara Gianollo
Agnes Jäger
Doris Penka

Table of contents

Chiara Gianollo, Agnes Jäger and Doris Penka

1 Language change at the syntax-semantics interface. Perspectives and challenges

1 Introduction

The contributions in this volume address, from various theoretical and method-ological perspectives, the interplay of grammatical structure and meaning through time. The "interface" between syntax and semantics is understood here in two different senses, a technical and a methodological one.

In the technical sense, change at the syntax-semantics interface is repre-sented by events targeting both the structural configuration and the meaning of a certain item. This is, for example, the typical situation in grammaticalization phenomena, whose effects range across multiple linguistic modules. All contri-butions in this volume are based on diachronic data attesting this kind of inter-face change, and aim at uncovering temporal and causal relationships between interpretational and structural factors. Besides proposing a detailed reconstruc-tion of their particular case studies, the authors engage in the challenge of precisely modeling – according to their respective theoretical frameworks – the interaction of meaning and form, thus suggesting general formats.

In a more methodological sense, the term "interface" is also understood in this volume as the theoretical comparison and dialogue between syntactic and semantic models of diachronic processes. Traditionally, the investigation of causes and forms of regularity in language change has prompted the formulation of general mechanisms, which guide the reorganization of grammatical systems. Cognitively based frameworks, in particular, have been successful in proposing abstract schemes for processes of syntactic change, which are now widely assumed in current diachronic research. With respect to meaning, historical work has focused especially on lexical semantics, and formal semanticists have only recently taken interest in exploring how truth-conditional models of pro-positional meaning can be fruitfully applied to diachronic problems. The first results of this line of research open exciting perspectives for the study of the syntax-semantics interface: a comparison between abstract mechanisms of change proposed for syntax on the one hand and semantics on the other has the potential of fostering our understanding not only of historical dynamics in language, but also of the general architecture of grammar. Some studies in this volume have in common a marked focus on semantics, as well as the aim of singling out abstract formats of change in the domain of functional meaning.

This kind of work is a natural and necessary prerequisite for the further step of comparing mechanisms of development in syntax and semantics.

In what follows, we give a short overview of the general issues addressed by the contributions in this collection, and of the challenges and open questions that motivate our joint efforts. In Section 2 we present the factors that prompt a renewed attention for the syntax-semantics interface in historical linguistics. In Section 3 we formulate the questions that, in our opinion, should guide research in this area. In Section 4 we review recent advances in the understanding of systematicity in syntactic and semantic change. Section 5 offers an overview of the various studies collected in this volume.

2 Historical linguistics and the syntax-semantics interface

Contemporary historical linguistics has greatly profited from the interaction with synchronic theory building, and, in turn, thanks to its significant results, has contributed in shaping the more general research agenda in linguistics. The syntax-semantics interface has become salient in historical linguistics due to a number of theoretical, empirical and methodological advances. Nonetheless, diachronic syntax and semantics have largely developed as separate disciplines. In particular, formal frameworks have been extended to the investigation of diachrony much earlier in syntax than in semantics. For syntax, Lightfoot (1979) opened the way to the application of generative models of syntactic structure and language competence to historical questions. This research direction gained momentum in connection with the synchronic study of cross-linguistic variation within the Principles and Parameters approach. In semantics, the first ground-breaking work to provide a truth-conditional account of change in functional meaning, and to formalize general principles guiding it, is Eckardt (2006). If theory building by formalization has proceeded separately in syntax and semantics until now, empirical comparative work at the syntax-semantics interface has been experiencing a surge in interest among diachronic linguists of all persuasions in the last decades.

2.1 Grammaticalization

A privileged area of research, where historical syntax and semantics naturally meet, is grammaticalization.[1] In grammaticalization phenomena, new exponents

---

[1] See Hopper and Traugott (2003: 19–38) for the history of the research; Heine and Kuteva (2002) for the cross-linguistic picture.

of grammatical categories ("function words") develop out of pre-existing lexical material, or grammatical elements change their function through time. In the investigation of the lexical development of e.g. complementizers, modal particles, negation exponents, auxiliaries, pronouns, and determiners, syntactic and semantic considerations are necessarily intertwined.

The cross-linguistic investigation of grammaticalization has uncovered a number of interesting generalizations concerning the kind of categories most typically involved, the interaction between phonological, morpho-syntactic, and semantic change, and the types of processes observed. In particular, it has been possible to single out linguistic "cycles", that is, cross-linguistically recurrent developments at the syntax-semantics interface, which remarkably go through similar stages. Perhaps the most famous of such cycles is the one affecting negation (Jespersen's cycle): it has been extensively studied in diachronic syntax, also thanks to the fact that negation is a synchronically well-studied area in current theoretical semantics and syntax.[2] But many other domains have been shown to offer examples of cyclic development too (aspectual forms, modal verbs, indefinite pronouns, among numerous others, cf. van Gelderen 2011 for a recent comprehensive picture).

This substantial body of empirical work has highlighted the necessity to integrate the methods and research questions of historical syntax and semantics.

On the one hand, syntacticians have been confronted with the fact that the input elements getting grammaticalized as exponents for certain functional categories show a remarkable semantic similarity (e.g. minimizers in the case of negation, demonstratives in the case of definite articles) and undergo parallel extensions or restrictions in their contexts of use in a stepwise fashion. This calls for a semantic explanation, which takes into consideration which part(s) of the meaning trigger grammaticalization, and which elements are retained after the category and structure change.

On the other hand, the limits of an exclusively lexical approach to diachronic semantics have become evident, since semantic change in one word is often accompanied by change in the surrounding structure, and thus in the compositional interface with the interpretive mechanism. It is therefore not productive to draw a rigid dividing line between lexical and propositional semantics in diachronic work. The application of modern compositional theories of meaning can be instrumental in pursuing a better understanding of semantic change.

---

2 The volumes edited by Larrivée and Ingham (2011) and by Willis, Lucas, and Breitbarth (2013 and *forthcoming*) present the state of the art on the diachrony of negation.

A number of insights gained from grammaticalization theory have been captured in recent diachronic work within the generative framework (cf. e.g. Roberts and Roussou 2003; van Gelderen 2004, 2011; and Section 4 below). Generative syntactic analyses are usually coupled with a semantic mechanism of "bleaching" or "weakening", which has been first accounted for in a formal framework by von Fintel (1995). However, grammaticalization often brings about the enrichment of some meaning components (cf. Hopper and Traugott 2003; Eckardt 2006; and our Section 4), a process which still awaits a proper syntactic treatment.

2.2 Systematicity in language change

Crucially, research on grammaticalization and on linguistic cycles has provided important support to the idea that a clear systematicity underlies syntactic and semantic diachronic processes, at least in these types of change. This claim has represented an absolute novelty in the field of historical linguistics, where only sound change was considered to be subject to regularity. For syntax, this led to a renewed interest on the part of theoretical linguists in diachronic issues, for the observed systematicity lent itself to formal, cognitively motivated rule-based treatments.

In fact, the investigation of regularity in sound change (the Neogrammarians' formulation of "sound laws", and their application to questions of genealogical relatedness) had been the first empirical field in which linguistics developed into a science.[3] Morphology and the lexicon played a very important role in this enterprise, but mostly in their interface with phonology: meaning was only taken into consideration insofar as it contributed evidence for establishing diachronic and cross-linguistic links between lexical and grammatical items. In the perspective of the classical comparative method, the impression gained from lexical semantics was that semantic change is fairly unconstrained: "By and large, semantic change operates in a rather random fashion, affecting one word here (in one way), and another form there (in another way). Given the 'fuzzy' nature of meaning, this is of course not surprising. What is surprising is that there should be any instances at all in which semantic change exhibits a certain degree of systematicity. But some such cases can be found" (Hock 1991: 305).

As for syntax, a body of important observations had been collected within the comparative framework, and some linguistic cycles, as well as the very

---

3 See Hock (1991: 34–51, 627–661) for an overview of the debate surrounding the Neogrammarians' notion of regularity, and its post-Labovian understanding.

notion of grammaticalization, had already gained the attention of historical lin-guists. The first decisive impulse towards addressing the question of systematicity in syntactic change came, however, with Greenberg's research on language uni-versals (Greenberg 1963, 1966, 1978 a.o.), which inspired a number of studies on the diachronic role of implicational universals (among the earliest Lehmann 1974 and contributions in Li 1975). Since this work dealt with long-term changes, sometimes spanning several centuries, the question arose how to account for the gradual nature of change and for supra-individual forces driving it. A decisive methodological turn, in this respect, was represented by Lightfoot's (1979) appli-cation of the generative approach to syntactic change. Lightfoot argued that a deeper understanding of the principles of change would be attained by analyz-ing in detail single case studies, reconstructing individual grammars, intended as systems of cognitive rules, and looking for local causes of disruption in language transmission during acquisition: he rooted systematicity of syntactic change in the structure of synchronic rules and in the conservative nature of first-language acquisition.

At this point, the investigation of syntactic change came to be tied more and more to synchronic models of competence and of cross-linguistic variation, especially with the rise of the Principles and Parameters framework: the process of parameter-resetting during acquisition came to be considered "the principal explanatory mechanism in diachronic syntax" (Roberts 2007: 121).

In order to better understand diachronic processes, a grasp of the extent of cross-linguistic variation, and of its formalization at a synchronic level, is a necessary prerequisite. It is probably because of the lack of a comparable interest in variation that diachronic research in semantics did not undergo a similar development.

Attempts to formulate general mechanisms involved in meaning change started early, and could build on the vast evidence provided by the lexico-graphic and etymological work in the Indo-European comparative tradition.[4] Paul ([1880] 1995: 87–103), for instance, proposed four basic mechanisms (gener-alization, specification, metaphor, metonymy); within the structuralist tradition, the study of word-fields prompted generalizations concerning the dynamics of meaning systems, sometimes formulated in terms of loss / acquisition of distinc-tive features (cf. e.g. Coseriu 1964). In fact, until very recently, the investigation of semantic change was limited to lexical semantics. As in the case of syntax, a decisive turn towards the investigation of systematicity in structure-sensitive / structure-relevant semantic change came from grammaticalization research. As noted by Eckardt (2006: 28), though, despite the large amount of formal studies

---

4 Fritz (2012) offers an up-to-date overview of theories of meaning change.

on grammaticalization, "this work has, however, so far not been complemented by truth value based investigations into meaning change".

2.3 The textual base: electronic corpora and philological issues

A further fundamental prerequisite for historical research at the syntax-semantics interface is represented by the collection of a broad enough pool of relevant data: this ensures, on the one hand, an empirically adequate description of single diachronic phenomena, on the other hand, the comparison of the form and the course of change across languages, which in turn allows for formulating far-reaching theoretical generalizations.

This is again a point where research in syntax and semantics did not progress at an equal pace in historical linguistics. Most importantly, we believe, diachronic semantics has not yet fully embraced the quantitative methods that substantially improved the quality of the evidence on which current syntactic research is based. Historical corpora are necessarily closed. In the most unfortunate cases, this means that historical stages are only fragmentarily attested, and data allowing for safe syntactic generalizations are scarce. But even where languages are more richly documented, historical linguists still face a special qualitative "poverty-of-the-stimulus" problem: in absence of native speakers' judgments, even the lack of attestation for a certain construction does not constitute unambiguous negative evidence, since it could just be due to chance in text transmission. The possibility of counterbalancing this risk is reached by examining ample portions of text, containing a number of potential contexts of occurrence sufficient to render the lack of occurrence statistically significant (cf. Crisma and Longobardi 2009: 3–4). Syntactically parsed electronic corpora, allowing the retrieval of data by means of (at least partially) automated queries over parsed text, make this kind of progress in empirical coverage feasible, and many studies collected in this volume attest to that. English is in a particularly favorable situation, thanks to the syntactically annotated *York-Toronto-Helsinki* and *Penn-Helsinki* corpora.[5] A similar annotation scheme has also been applied to Old Portuguese, Old French and Icelandic. For languages such as German, in fact, the situation is not quite as good: there are currently no publicly available parsed corpora of historical German, only a few morpho-syntactically tagged corpora, noticeably the *Bonner Frühneuhochdeutschkorpus*, several texts from

---

5 References to these corpora, as well as those mentioned below, are collected in the section "Cited Corpora" preceding the general References.

the *Referenzkorpus Altdeutsch* as well as texts from the early Modern German period in the *GerManC project* corpus and two annotated texts in the *Kali-Korpus*. Further annotated and partly also parsed corpora of Old and Middle High and Low German as well as Early New High German are currently under preparation (see the Section "Cited Corpora"). For languages like Latin and Ancient and Koine Greek morphologically annotated electronic texts are now extensively available. The *Pragmatic Resources in Old Indo-European Languages* (PROIEL) corpus also offers syntactic annotation, whose format is not immediately comparable with the corpora mentioned above. Much still has to be done for the classical languages, as well as for philologically more challenging Indo-European varieties like Vedic (which in our volume is represented by two contributions, Casaretto and Schneider; Condoravdi and Deo), and, of course, for non-Indo-European languages with a long written tradition.[6]

Clearly the kind of annotation scheme devised for the corpora mentioned above has been designed for morpho-syntactic research. A *desideratum* for the study of meaning change is that semantic information too be incorporated in the annotation. We currently witness the incipient incorporation of semantic and pragmatic information into electronic corpora (see, for instance, the *Penn Discourse Treebank*, or the *Groningen Meaning Bank*). For some areas, in particular information structure, schemes have already been developed, not only at the synchronic, but also at the diachronic level. The PROIEL corpus, for instance, contains semantic-pragmatic annotation (a.o. information structure, anaphora resolution) for many ancient Indo-European languages, with the aim of building a parallel corpus of the New Testament translations in these ancient varieties; for Old High German, a smaller corpus annotated for information-structural notions exists (the *Tatian Corpus of Deviating Examples*).

Creating semantically annotated diachronic corpora is clearly not an easy task, and involves a higher level of risk compared to syntactic annotation for a number of reasons, among which the cultural distance, the pervasive ambiguity in the texts, and the interaction between truth-conditional and pragmatic contribution seem to be the most serious. Crisma (this volume) accurately describes the difficulties of reaching a satisfactory semantic annotation in the domain of referential and quantificational categories. With information structure, the task

---

6 The fact that the languages on which the authors in this volume focus are all Indo-European reflects the preponderant role that these languages still have in current historical research. However, non-Indo-European languages are starting to play an increasing role in the general discussion, as mirrored, for instance, by the very popular handbook by Crowley and Bowern (2010). Van Gelderen (this volume) bases her theoretical conclusions also on languages outside Indo-European.

is further complicated by the fact that there is no consensus yet as to how some of the notions adopted have to be defined and tested at a synchronic level. Although diachronic evidence and analysis may help settle some theoretical questions, it is more frequently the case that diachrony applies theoretical models based on solid (experimental or introspective) synchronic evidence as a guide towards formulating hypotheses and selecting supporting evidence.

Before we move to the questions that we would like to pose for research at the syntax-semantics interface, let us conclude this section with a methodological consideration. The parsed and annotated corpora that are available today, being developed over years by teams of trained linguists, and being constantly checked by the scientist users themselves, are extremely accurate. Nonetheless, it is obvious to any historical linguist that the use of such powerful tools does not eliminate the need to give full consideration to the classic philological issues that accompany diachronic work. As many authors in this volume discuss, one is quite normally faced with philological challenges linked to text transmission such as e.g. discrepancies between date of composition and age of written attestation, and existence of different textual traditions. A further pervasive problem has to do with the linguistic interpretation of the variability observed in the corpus (optionality, "intermediate grammars", grammars in competition), which in turn requires a correct evaluation of differences in stylistic registers. The kind of philological competence needed to address these issues results from a profound acquaintance with the texts, and with the culture that produced them. In order for historical linguistics to advance so significantly, as it has been the case in the past decades, and to develop formal methods for the study of meaning change, the systematic teaching of ancient languages, coupled with a sound theoretical background, should be more valued and better integrated into linguistics programs.

3 Diachronic questions concerning the syntax-semantics interface

In this section we present the general questions that the contributions in this volume, more or less directly, address. They aim at both gaining empirical knowledge regarding the syntax-semantics interface and fostering a dialogue between methodological approaches to syntactic and semantic change. As we discuss below, they also include some issues that, we think, "are up next", that is, are not yet addressed by the present contributions, but should guide future research in this direction.

(a) What is the division of labor between syntax and semantics in grammatic-
    alization and other diachronic processes at the syntax-semantics interface?
(b) How do syntactic and semantic change differ in their local causes, their
    actuation, and their spread among communities?
(c) Do the same constraints, principles and mechanisms that govern syntactic
    change also apply to semantic change?

Questions (a) and (b) mainly concern empirical issues, and can be answered
only on the basis of ample comparative evidence. In Section 3.1 we mention
some salient topics related to these two questions, which are variously discussed
by the studies collected here. In Section 3.2 we address more specifically the
scope of question (c). Since we are convinced that answers to this latter question
are of particular import for an improved understanding of language change,
Section 4 is dedicated to laying out more extensively the contribution made by
the present volume in this respect.

3.1 Syntactic and semantic change: triggers and actuation

Question (a) involves the so-called chicken-and-egg problem (Roberts 2007: 125–
127), i.e., distinguishing between cause and effect in processes of grammatical
change. In cases where syntactic and semantic change are interrelated, does
change in the one area presuppose or rather cause change in the other area?
We can well imagine that the process can go either way, but that different
classes of change can be distinguished, according to whether they are syntactically or semantically initiated.

A step towards answering this question consists in individuating the triggering evidence starting the change, and thus the local causes mentioned in question (b), in the specific historical setting in which the change takes place. In this
respect, interesting generalizations have been put forth regarding possible onset
contexts for syntactic and semantic reanalysis.

For syntax, a very influential proposal has been made by Lightfoot (1979:
98–115, 121–141) in terms of his Transparency Principle. Under this view, syntactic
reanalysis occurs as the learners' reaction to opacity, seen as accumulation of
exceptions and structural ambiguity (for instance, Lightfoot argued that such a
situation was the trigger for the grammaticalization of English modals); after
a certain threshold, the learners opt for a less complex representation, which
involves a simpler syntactic derivation.

Scarcity of primary data, due for instance to stylistically based or contact-
induced frequency fluctuations, can also trigger change. Many explanatory accounts of syntactic change in such settings have been based on the acquisition

strategy known as Subset Principle, originally proposed by Berwick (1985): the learner, in trying to conservatively attain the grammar of the previous generation, avoids overgeneralization and adopts the most restrictive grammar compatible with the primary data, revising her hypothesis only in the presence of positive evidence. In the case of scant evidence for a certain phenomenon, the learner may disregard it and maintain the more restrictive hypothesis, thus "ousting" the phenomenon from the grammar.

These approaches raise the problem of how to exactly measure the opacity / paucity threshold, which has occupied syntacticians ever since. Also, opacity as such does not contribute much to the chicken-and-egg problem, since sources of opacity can in principle reside in the semantics as well as in the syntax (not to mention the interface with the phonological system).

For semantics, the source of change has often been recognized at another interface, that is, at the boundary with pragmatics. A general triggering mechanism, which has been proposed in the literature, is Eckardt's (2006: 244–247) Principle of Avoiding Pragmatic Overload: onset contexts for semantic change are those where speakers use items "in a way that charge[s] too much pragmatic accommodation from the listener" (Eckardt 2006: 20). The avoidance of pragmatic overload pushes towards the incorporation of the meaning components in the lexical representation, a change which has been modeled as conventionalization of pragmatic implicatures (see Section 4).

As Eckardt (2006: 247) observes, there is a notable conceptual parallelism between her Principle of Avoiding Pragmatic Overload and Lightfoot's Transparency Principle, since both are driven by optimization strategies. She notes, however, that the two principles require differing assumptions with respect to the actuation of the change (cf. question [b]), and more specifically in terms of its temporal dimension. According to generative treatments of syntactic reanalysis, changes driven by the Transparency Principle (or analogous tendencies) are assumed to take place and be finalized during first-language acquisition. The types of triggers and the actuation dynamics for pragmatically-driven semantic changes seem instead to lie in the adult competence. Semantic change through conventionalization of pragmatic implicatures must occur in the mental lexicon of adult speakers, because only adult speakers are exposed to the communicative situations that trigger such conventionalizations.

Eckardt (2006), however, adds a proviso to this observation: she remarks that the conclusions on the role of adult competence in semantic change have been reached on the basis of diachronic processes concerning single lexical entries. When the attention shifts to whole grammatical systems, "global reorganizations most likely occur in first language acquisition" (Eckardt 2006: 41). The exploration of additional mechanisms of semantic change, as carried out for instance by van Gelderen, Gergel, Condoravdi and Deo (this volume), may help shed light on the debate concerning the role of adult and children speakers in the diachronic process of reanalysis. In the long run, further issues concerning the spread of the change across communities and the form that gradualness takes in syntactic and semantic change will also benefit from this kind of work.

A last point that we would like to mention with respect to question (b) concerns the discussion surrounding Inertia, which has played an important role in recent research on diachronic syntax. In the case of semantics, the widespread impression of randomness concerning change is certainly due to the undeniable fact that "meaning change is driven by language external factors perhaps more than any other mode of language change and therefore has a notoriously contingent quality" (Eckardt 2006: 4). This observation is suggestive of a connection with a research hypothesis proposed for syntax by Keenan (1994, 2009), and Longobardi (2001), namely that syntax *per se* is inert to change, that is, syntactic change is always triggered by change in another module of grammar, i.e., by interface phenomena. Inertia fits very well with two central tenets of current generative theory (see also Section 4): namely, it predicts that change, like cross-linguistic variation (to which it is logically connected), is located at the interfaces and is due to legibility conditions; moreover, Inertia naturally follows from the conservative nature of language acquisition.

Now, since semantic change, too, may be argued to follow from interface dynamics, and is so prone to language-external factors, the question arises whether syntax is demonstrably more inert to change than semantics, or if, at the appropriate level of abstraction, semantics could be argued to be inert as well, and change in general to be an interface phenomenon. If semantic change is structure-sensitive at the level of Logical Form, as has been argued in recent research (Gergel 2009, cf. also Section 4), it is expected to be subject to the conservativity-induced inertial effect of language acquisition. Along this line of investigation, one would possibly have to distinguish between more or less inert sub-modules within syntactic and semantic competence. And surely the Inertia hypothesis has to be weakened to account for endogenous forces like analogical generalizations, which may be very powerful (especially as soon as non-exemplar-based analogy is taken into account, cf. Kiparsky 2012 and Section 4 below). In the domain of syntax, for instance, they may lead to macro-parametric changes in terms of (economy-driven) cross-categorial harmonization (see Section 4).

3.2 Syntactic and semantic change: comparable mechanisms?

Question (c) has a more theoretical and programmatic scope, and presupposes that a certain systematicity, which can be captured by formal abstract mechanisms, characterizes change. While this presupposition has been firmly assessed for syntax, it is still met with scepticism in the field of semantics. More precisely, while the existence of specific trends in the development of meaning is universally acknowledged, the possibility of discovering general formats of change and, especially, of formalizing them in truth-conditional frameworks, is still subject to the burden of proof.

Systematicity in change at the syntax-semantics interface has two main general manifestations: on the one hand, a change targeting a specific grammatical domain may repeat itself within languages (cyclicity proper) and across languages; a further dimension in this respect is possibly the (uni)directionality of such changes. On the other hand, different changes across grammatical domains undergo similar stages, and / or can be shown to be subject to the same formal constraints and evolutionary tendencies.

The prerogative of a certain change to be cyclic points to the tendency of a domain to renew its formal means of expression; this tendency normally has a pragmatic motivation, and has, for instance, been considered responsible for renewal cycles in negation, whose origin can be traced back to emphatic strengthening and subsequent extension to non-emphatic contexts (cf. e.g. Kiparsky and Condoravdi 2006).

Unidirectionality, instead, can yield insights with respect to the internal make-up of certain grammatical categories (e.g. the semantic relationship between deixis and definiteness, or between perfect and perfective aspect), and the implicational relations among formal elements of structure (e.g. algorithm of parameter fixation during acquisition, constraint ranking) and meaning (e.g. subset / entailment relations). Unidirectionality also possibly reflects the structure of the general abstract operations governing change. Grammaticalization research in the typological framework has identified similar stages in various grammaticalization processes, and has proposed general formats of change, like for instance erosion at the phonetic level, morphological condensation and paradigmatic integration, context generalization and desemanticization (see Lehmann 1995 for a systematic presentation of these and other processes). As we will discuss in more detail in Section 4, in the generative framework some of these processes have been interpreted as involving upward reanalysis along the functional architecture, and as being motivated in terms of acquisition strategies, tending towards optimization in terms of economy.

In this respect, it has been repeatedly noticed that the accounts of the structural part of the change in grammaticalization and other systematic processes are more fine-grained than the descriptions and explanations of semantic change. Since empirical and theoretical work on the semantic side starts to accumulate, a comparison between the cognitively based mechanisms giving rise to systematicity in both syntactic and semantic change becomes possible, and raises further questions: are these abstract mechanisms comparable in form? For instance, does something like upward reanalysis also apply at the level of Logical Form? And / or are these mechanisms comparable in their motivation? Do we have economy constraints in semantic change as well?

The studies in this volume innovatively contribute to the current debate on question (c), as will be highlighted in the following section.

4 Systematicity in change at the syntax-semantics interface

The various answers to the crucial question on constraints and mechanisms of change offered by recent research have a common denominator: the hypothesis that grammatical change is characterized by systematicity and regularity, which can be captured by explanations independently grounded in the nature of the language faculty.

Systematicity is expected under restrictive theories of language, since it ultimately follows from the constrained inventory of elements and rules in grammar (be they conceived of as typological universals, or as a system of principles and parameters coupled with a compositional semantics). In fact, in strongly deterministic theoretical models of the language faculty, what is in principle in need of an explanation is change itself, on a par with variation.[7]

4.1 Variation and change

Under the Strong Minimalist Thesis (Chomsky 2000), language is seen as the optimal solution to interface conditions in mapping sound to meaning. Syntax, in particular, is the optimal computational core of this system, and is based on a universal, restricted set of mechanisms. Variation, and hence potential change, is due to legibility conditions at the interface with the conceptual-intentional

---

7 Actually, the study of absence of change, that is, of pertinacity in language histories yields important insights into the structure and the source of cross-linguistic variation, as Nichols (1992, 2003) has shown. See also Breitbarth et al. (2010) on this point. For syntax, the persistence of parametric values has been argued to convey a genealogical signal, which can be used to reconstruct phylogenetic relations among languages, cf. Gianollo, Guardiano, and Longobardi (2008), Crisma and Longobardi (2009: 6–10).

system (meaning) and the sensorimotor system (sound): in other words, interfaces are the loci for Minimalist parameters.[8]

Parameters themselves are conceived of as constrained in their format (if not number): they are understood as residing in the feature composition of lexical items (the so-called "Borer-Chomsky" conjecture, see Baker 2008), as displaying a significant formal parallelism across categories (captured e.g. in terms of parametric schemata by Gianollo, Guardiano, and Longobardi 2008), and as clustering in virtue of their implicational relations (modeled as parametric hierarchies in Roberts 2012a, b).

The form of variation, together with invariant principles, restricts the form of possible syntactic change. Implicational relations among parameter values, in turn, have been argued to have a crucial role in diachrony. On the one hand, they may have a blocking effect on change: parameter values that are intertwined may be more resistant, since the resetting is dependent on a broader set of surface evidence. This may be the case, for instance, with parameters related to agreement, whose manifestations are pervasive in the grammar, as discussed in this volume by Birkenes and Sommer.

On the other hand, implicational relations among parameter values may also trigger optimization mechanisms in language acquisition, which could lead to macro-changes like cross-categorial harmonization. For instance, Roberts' (2012a, b) parametric hierarchies are algorithms mirroring the learning path, that is, they set precedence relations for the parameter-setting operations taking place during language acquisition. They are "defined by complexity relations: the higher settings are simpler, having a shorter description, than the lower ones" (Roberts 2012a: 333).

4.2 Markedness and economy

This view of parameters introduces considerations of markedness into the grammar ("simpler, hence unmarked"), which may prompt analogical extension of the unmarked value (e.g. absence of movement) to categories for which the positive evidence has become scant in the language. The analogy, in such cases, is driven by "exemplars provided by Universal Grammar" (Kiparsky 2012: 15) and is "constrained by the entire grammatical system" (Lahiri 2000: 11–12).

---

8 See Biberauer (2008) for an insightful discussion of the role of parameters in the Minimalist Program. Berwick and Chomsky (2011: 30), on the basis of evolutionary considerations, have argued that, in fact, the interface with 'thought', i.e., the semantic component, might be close to perfect, thus allowing much less space for variation and change than the externalization interface, i.e., the morpho-phonological component.

Considerations of markedness may be, at least partially, language-specific, and depend on the system-internal balance (for instance, a head-final structure will be marked in an overwhelmingly head-initial language, but obviously not in a head-final language, cf. Roberts 2007: 273–274). There are, however, optimization strategies that are arguably driven by universal principles of language acquisition.[9] In Section 3 we already mentioned Lightfoot's (1979) Transparency Principle, which "requires derivations to be minimally complex and initial, underlying structures to be 'close' to their respective surface structures" (Lightfoot 1979: 121). Diachronic syntacticians have been trying to give a precise formalization of the notion of "simplicity" involved in reanalysis. Roberts (1993), with his "Least Effort Strategy", formalizes simplicity in terms of "shortest derivation": "Representations assigned to sentences of the input to acquisition should be such that they contain the set of the shortest possible chains (consistent with (a) principles of grammars, (b) other aspects of the trigger experience)" (1993: 156). This formulation points to a central tenet of generative historical syntax, which clearly has strong ties with analogous synchronic considerations on representational and derivational economy (see Hornstein, Nunes, and Grohmann 2005: 330–365 for a survey): movement is costly, and dispreferred in acquisition. According to the metric of the Least Effort Strategy, this is due to the fact that movement involves at least two instances of the operation Merge, and the ensuing traces / copies in the first Merge position.

More recent proposals have re-formulated the economy metric in terms of features, thus with a more direct impact on the modeling of the syntax-semantics interface. Movement involves an item that spells out the features of (at least) two different projections, resulting in feature syncretism, which is dispreferred due to a general acquisition principle ("Minimize feature content" in Longobardi 2001: 294). Roberts and Roussou (2003) propose, accordingly, a feature-based simplicity metric: given two structural representations R and R' for a given surface structure, R is simpler than R' if R contains fewer formal features than R' (Roberts and Roussou 2003: 201).

The bias against syntactic movement is incorporated in generative treatments of syntactic reanalysis taking place in grammaticalization (Roberts and Roussou 2003; van Gelderen 2004), and features as a prominent theoretical tool in many contributions collected here (Breitbarth, Chatzopoulou, Crisma, van Gelderen). According to the "Merge over Move" constraint (van Gelderen 2004: 11), a syntactic constituent should rather be merged directly into a certain position

---

9 For an approach reconciling markedness and acquisition under an underspecification-theoretic perspective see Jäger (2010).

than being moved there, in order to have an economical derivation. The diachronic effect of this constraint is that elements that used to reach a syntactic position by movement over some period of time may be learned as being first-merged into that position: this results in "reanalysis 'upwards' along the functional structure" (Roberts and Roussou 2003: 71) of lexical items, which thus are analyzed with fewer features (only those pertaining to the higher syntactic position) as exponents of functional categories. The preference for Merge over Move conditions the directionality of grammaticalization processes, and is compatible, by assuming multiple lexical entries, with the frequent situation where the old lexical item survives alongside the new grammaticalized element.

Van Gelderen (2008: 297, 2009: 8) proposes a Feature Economy Principle, which more specifically targets semantic and interpretable features (on which see below): in case of ambiguity, an analysis with fewer interpretable features will be favored in acquisition.[10] Thus, according to van Gelderen, syntactic and semantic change are tightly interrelated: economy leads to diachronic reduction of interpretable features in the derivation, and this, in turn, affects the syntactic status of elements within a projection, since interpretable features may be reanalyzed as uninterpretable. Lavidas (this volume) points out that, in case of language contact, the diachronic pressure on interpretable features resulting from the Feature Economy Principle may be counterbalanced by the protective effect of another acquisitional principle: according to the Interpretability Hypothesis for second language acquisition (Tsimpli and Dimitrakopoulou 2007), interpretable features are more accessible to second language learners and are, thus, expected to be more resistant in case of contact-induced change.

Van Gelderen (2004) has identified further economy principles that are active during syntactic acquisition and may lead to syntactic change: in particular, the Late Merge Principle ("Merge as late as possible", van Gelderen 2004: 12) and the Head Preference or Spec to Head Principle ("be a head rather than a phrase", van Gelderen 2004: 11) have been very influential in guiding subsequent research. As Gergel (this volume) notes, the Head Preference Principle, triggering the reanalysis of specifiers as heads of functional projections, can be rephrased as "be a projecting structure rather than a non-projecting one".

Obviously, saying that principles of simplicity guide learning and, as a consequence, syntactic change, does not amount to saying that change makes

---

10 Van Gelderen (this volume) proposes a reformulation of the Feature Economy Principle in terms of a third-factor (non-language-specific) principle, triggering the grammaticalization (as interpretable and uninterpretable features) of semantic features originating as innate concepts (time, causation, etc.).

grammars simpler: besides the fact that reanalysis processes may cause complications in other areas of grammars (see Roberts 1993: 177–186 for an example from French), the result of parametric change is just another grammar with different properties, as a whole in no way simpler than the former system. In this respect, the considerations on markedness and parametric hierarchies shortly reviewed above are different in nature, because they are based on the assumption that a homogeneous grammar will be a simpler one to learn, thanks to the possibility of across-the-board input generalization. This is, however, at odds with the empirical observation that "pure" linguistic types seldom find instantiation in natural languages. Nonetheless, once appropriately relativized, cross-categorial harmonization has the potential to account for long-range diachronic developments, like the development of analytic structures (see Ledgeway's 2012 recent proposal for the transition from Latin to Romance).

4.3 Models of the interface

We have mentioned that the prevailing economy metric in current studies of syntactic change is based on features. This takes us, again, to the problem of how to model the dynamics at the interface with semantics: namely, while syntacticians widely use features to model the interaction between syntax and semantics (in language change as well as in synchronic accounts), these assumptions have not yet been subject to the scrutiny of truth-conditional analyses. So, in a way, syntacticians are developing a model of the syntax-semantics interface that is not necessarily shared by current semantic approaches.

Features drive syntactic movement. Each feature occurs in an interpretable form (where it is interpreted at the semantic level of Logical Form), and in uninterpretable, merely formal occurrences on other constituents. Uninterpretable features, in a certain syntactic configuration (if necessary achieved by movement), are deleted against the interpretable occurrence of the same feature. To attribute an interpretable feature to some constituent is not merely a syntactic but a semantic statement: questions such as which features should be assumed, or which constituent bears the interpretable variant of the feature should thus be answered on the basis of semantic considerations.

An influential model of the syntax-semantics interface, which rests on a feature system and is adopted by many contributions in this volume, is represented by the Cartographic approach (starting with Cinque 1999): in the Cartographic model, semantics is hard-wired into the syntax in so far as semantic features reside in specific functional projections, along the spine of the clausal architecture. Interpretive properties are encoded in a fine-grained syntactic structure, which mirrors the compositional make-up of meaning; each feature can in principle project a category, giving rise to "lower" and "higher" meanings, according to scopal differences. In such a model, syntactic and semantic change naturally come to be viewed as being linked through the functional architecture of the clause.[11]

Chatzopoulou (this volume), for instance, analyzes the change in the non-veridical negation of Greek, whereby an "intensified predicate negation" becomes a plain propositional negation, as "structural microelevation" along the functional spine, modeled in terms of Cinque's (1999) Cartographic approach, accompanied by semantic bleaching.

Breitbarth (this volume) interprets the development of English conditional *should* as upward reanalysis with loss of movement. By adopting a Cartographic approach, Breitbarth offers a syntactic account for the semantic development of conditional *should*. She puts forward the hypothesis, naturally arising under an "upward-reanalysis" approach to grammaticalization, that the gradualness observed in this and other instances of syntactic change be a reflection of the fine-grainedness of functional categories: multiple successive lexical splits would be needed to "climb up" the functional spine. Breitbarth also discusses the problem of locality in Cartographic approaches, that is, why diachronic reanalysis can skip intervening heads. Her proposed solution, inspired by current synchronic approaches, is that the relevance of features has to be relativized, e.g., as Roberts (2012c) does, by distinguishing between two types of features: substantive features, which are universal, and parametrically activated formal features.

Crisma (this volume) also has to face the problem of how to distinguish between different types of features, in connection with the comparison between a lexical and a syntactic treatment of the mass/count distinction. In the first case, the ±count feature would be stored on the lexical item, in the second it would be encoded as a syntactically active feature in a functional projection. The choice between the two models leads to different predictions in terms of grammaticalization of the indefinite article, as Crisma shows by means of Old English data.

In her contribution to this collection, van Gelderen explores an even more foundational dimension of variation with respect to features, which directly impinges on our understanding of the syntax-semantics interface. She distinguishes

---

11 Roughly similar notions are also incorporated in other frameworks. Thus, Kasper (this volume), working in a Role and Reference Grammar approach, assumes that items with certain semantic features develop the tendency to appear in specific syntactic positions – in his case within the nominal phrase.

between semantic and grammatical features: grammatical features arise evolutionarily as an abstraction of innate semantic features; semantic features also guide the process of language acquisition, in that the learner assumes corresponding functional features. Grammaticalization involves a process of feature change, more precisely a unidirectional cline whereby semantic features realized by lexical items are either lost or reanalyzed as grammatical, i.e., relevant to syntactic computation; in the first grammaticalization stage they start out as interpretable, and they may be further reanalyzed as uninterpretable.

Van Gelderen's scenario is based on the strong hypothesis that semantic features, either as part of UG, or as third-factor principles, are innate, and belong to a restricted universal inventory. In this, they would be very much parallel to syntactic parameters, and they would provide a format to model (syntactically relevant) semantic variation, and hence change at the syntax-semantics interface.

However, as mentioned above, feature-based models have typically been developed within a syntactic framework, and have been systematically investigated in formal semantics only for a restricted subset of phenomena (e.g. negation in Penka 2011 and tense in von Stechow 2009).

Moreover, feature-based models of the syntax-semantics interface such as Cartographic representations largely disregard the fine-grained distinctions between levels of meaning (asserted, presupposed, and conventionally or conversationally implicated content) that have been successfully investigated by contemporary semantic and pragmatic theories. This often leads to an unnecessary proliferation of semantically motivated features in the syntactic representation. As, for instance, Crisma (this volume) concludes with respect to specificity, a deeper semantic analysis may provide a more economical account: in the case of Old English indefinites, a specific interpretation may not result from a syntactically active specificity feature, but rather arise as a by-product of the existential operator taking wide scope.

A deeper integration of these insights into models of the syntax-semantics interface could certainly allow for a more restrictive feature model, encompassing a constrained set of abstract entities and an insightful account of context-dependent meaning effects.

4.4 Bleaching and strengthening

Against the background provided above, it is interesting to see how change at the syntax-semantics interface may be modelled coming from the perspective of approaches to semantic change. Problems of the interface with syntax have been given little attention in historical semantics so far. The rise of compositional theories of meaning, however, has made a strict separation between lexical and propositional semantics impracticable, and historical research, too, has shifted the focus to structure-sensitive semantic change.

Eckardt (2006: 236) has stressed the diachronic importance of compositional principles, which ensure the adaptability of linguistic means to new communicative needs and inextricably tie word meaning to sentence meaning: during the process of semantic reanalysis "the salient overall conveyed information remains the same, but is composed in a different manner. What may have previously been in part assertion, in part implication, turns entirely into a literal assertion after reanalysis". Gergel (2009: 250) has made a similar point: "Developments in terms of meaning change can only be fully understood if we consider them at the propositional level [...] Alongside potential morphological and phonological change, both the surrounding tree geometry of the word (including LF for the purposes of interpretation) and the way its lexical entry combines with the other nodes of the clause can thus typically change."

Two main general mechanisms of semantic change, apparently complementary to each other, have emerged from the body of research on grammaticalization: bleaching or semantic generalization, and pragmatic strengthening.

Bleaching lends itself more easily to an integration with syntactic models, and, in fact, has figured prominently in generative research on grammaticalization. For instance, Roberts and Roussou (2003), following von Fintel (1995), describe bleaching as loss of descriptive content (e.g. predicative properties such as argument structure) and retention of logical content (e.g. modal properties), "logical" being defined as invariant under isomorphism (Roberts and Roussou 2003: 218–224). Directional change in grammaticalization phenomena has been seen as "uniformly generalizing" also by Kiparsky (2012).

Breitbarth (this volume) interprets the semantic change taking place in grammaticalization as "semantic abstraction". Meaning is decomposed into syntactically visible, i.e., potentially active, features; semantic abstraction is understood as loss of features associated with lexical items. In her case study on English *should*, she identifies a mechanism of abstraction from posteriority to hypothetical potentiality; as a consequence of semantic abstraction, movement to higher positions becomes possible. The question remains which semantic mechanisms precisely drive the abstraction: Breitbarth tentatively mentions metaphorical processes or subset relations between meaning ingredients.

Gergel's contribution to this collection also deals with functionalization of lexical material (in his case, the English quantifier *most*). He starts from the assumption that grammaticalization / functionalization may rest not only on structure-based semantic change, but also, in some cases, on lexicon-based semantic change (change in the internal properties of a lexical item). In a process that he calls "ontological semantic functionalization", a semantic property of an originally independent lexical item (*part* in his study) is incorporated into the functional word as a new internal property of its lexical entry (in his case, the partitioning function). Still, lexicon-based change of the type discussed by Gergel has a syntactic structure as input: in the case of *most*, the input structure is a partitive construction, displaying a peculiar internal tightness, i.e. having the properties of a single projection despite containing a second one.

Gergel's account highlights the importance of semi-functional categories in language change: when the border is synchronically "blurry", we can expect this fact to have diachronic effects. This is also apparent in the case of the local particles investigated in Vedic by Casaretto and Schneider (this volume): their flexible syntax, allowing them to occur as modifiers of verbal and nominal heads, is at least partially responsible for their twofold syntactic and semantic development as semi-adpositions and preverbs.

Crisma (this volume) considers semantic bleaching to be involved in the grammaticalization of the indefinite article. She interprets it as the shift from asserted to implied (and thus cancelable) meaning: the "special cardinal" *one*, which is the source of the English indefinite article, encodes the lower as well as the upper bound in the lexical entry yielding the asserted meaning 'exactly one'; the indefinite article, instead, has only the lower bound 'at least one' in the lexical entry and triggers the upper bound 'at most one' as an implicature. Bleaching is thus understood as eliminating the upper bound from the lexicon, and, thus, as affecting the truth-conditional semantics (weakening from subset to superset). At the same time, the grammaticalization shows a decreasing saliency of the existential presupposition.

Condoravdi and Deo (this volume) provide a truth-conditional account of semantic generalization. They analyze aspect shifts (resultative to perfect to perfective aspect) from Early Vedic to Middle Indic as an instance of semantic weakening, analyzed as two-step generalization. According to Condoravdi and Deo, in cases of semantic generalization there is a relation of entailment between the "old" and the "new" meaning, in that the "old" entails the "new": weakening amounts to reduction in the set of entailments, since some semantic entailments become conventionalized in the new meaning. Note that semantic entailments are here clearly distinguished from pragmatically invited inferences, and thus semantic generalization represents a mechanism of semantic change different from the conventionalization of pragmatic implicatures (on which see below). Condoravdi and Deo tentatively suggest that the latter may apply in the grammaticalization of lexical material, while semantic generalization would be typical of grammaticalization clines involving material that is already functional, that is, of changes in grammatical meaning. Interestingly, also in this case, as with syntactic reanalysis, the mechanism rests on non-exemplar-based analogy (cf. Kiparsky 2012), i.e., it is driven by universal constraints on the meaning of operators.

Accounts of grammaticalization based solely on bleaching during reanalysis, however, are difficult to reconcile with the often observed fact that meaning change in grammaticalization does not always amount to loss of semantic content, but can be accompanied by an enrichment of some components. Substantial progress in our understanding of the role of contextual meaning aspects has been made, in this respect, by work in the typological-functional tradition (Sweetser 1988; Traugott 1988; Traugott and König 1991; Hopper and Traugott 2003; Traugott and Dasher 2002). These approaches to semantic change highlight in particular the role of the interaction with pragmatics, and attribute meaning changes occurring during reanalysis to the conventionalization of pragmatic implicatures, thus locating the crucial change-triggering evidence at the propositional level (cf. the Invited Inferencing Theory of semantic change in Traugott and König 1991; Traugott and Dasher 2002, and also the pragmatic implicature approach of Levinson 2000).

Eckardt (2006) casts this approach in a formal semantic framework. She shows, with a number of case studies, that the trigger for a construction's or a word's meaning to shift must be represented by something more than pragmatic inferencing, which is inevitable in some contexts, but nonetheless does not lead to reanalysis in all of them. She argues that reanalysis is further pushed by the unverifiability of the literal meaning in certain contexts of use.

4.5 Concluding remarks

The short overview above has shown that current investigations of diachronic syntax and semantics unfold exciting perspectives for our understanding of systematicity in language change. This line of research raises new questions.

First, does economy, and more specifically, do economy principles, such as those described for syntax in the previous sections, play a role in semantic change, too? In recent literature, there are indications that this may indeed be the case. For instance, Gergel (2009), in his analysis of the diachronic development of English *rather*, argues that a preference for Merge over Move also holds at the level of Logical Form. According to Gergel, *rather* was diachronically reanalysed as being first-merged in a position that it formerly used to reach by Quantifier Raising. It would be interesting to explore whether there are further instances of structure-based economy principles leading to change at the level of Logical Form.

Second, one could ask whether the notion of economy could be extended to cover change induced by pragmatics: one could imagine, for instance, that the conventionalization of a frequently triggered implicature could be captured in terms of economy in the language system, according to principles like Eckardt's (2006) Principle of Avoiding Pragmatic Overload, discussed in Section 3.

Another field of study that could profit from a broader body of empirical studies, and from an enhanced dialogue with diachronic syntax, is the investigation of directionality in meaning change. Numerous cycles or clines have been proposed in the literature. One powerful descriptive tool to model them is represented by the semantic maps used in typological linguistics (e.g. Haspelmath 1997 for indefinite pronouns, van der Auwera and Plungian 1998 for modality, cf. also van der Auwera 2013 for a methodological evaluation). In semantic maps, recurrent directional changes are modeled by means of the arrangement of functions on the maps, which is meant to capture distributional implicational relations that are argued to hold at a diachronic level, too. According to Haspelmath (1997: 63), "where markers gradually acquire new functions, they will first be extended to those functions that are adjacent to the original functions on the map, and only later to functions that are further away". Haspelmath, too, resorts to a notion of bleaching to describe the semantic change leading to shifts or expansions in function: functions in the map can be arranged along a cline, from semantically stronger to semantically weaker; in their development, elements lose features and move towards weaker functions, thus yielding unidirectional developments.

Semantic maps provide a valid link to syntactic research based on feature dynamics, and can also be very useful in representing paradigmatic relations among elements pertaining to the same semantic sphere, thus accounting for competition / blocking effects.

However, in order to attain explanatory power, the systems of features on which they are based should be more fine-grained, and more rigorously formulated. In particular, treatments in terms of implicational relations among functions still lack a precise model of the interaction between basic lexical import and contextually contributed meaning, necessary to account for conditions of use (see Aguilar-Guevara et al. 2011 for an attempt in this sense).

This takes us to our last point: as Condoravdi and Deo (this volume) and Gergel (this volume) stress, a prerequisite for diachronic research is represented by an adequate synchronic analysis of the categories involved, and, thus, by a theory of variation. We have commented above on the relevance of a parametric theory of syntactic variation for the study of change. For semantics, as Gergel states, "compositionality itself restricts some options in change", and a sound decomposition into abstract meaning blocks is the key to understanding variation and change.[12]

Condoravdi and Deo (this volume) argue that an explanatory account of semantic change involves three separate steps. First, one has to approach the problem of singling out the logical relation between ingredients of meaning that is responsible for the directionality observed in "semantic cycles"; in other words, one needs to root the potentiality of the (systematic) diachronic connection between categories in the synchronic relation between their meaning parts. Secondly, one needs to identify the mechanism driving the diachronic connection, i.e. the form that the change takes and its cognitive motivation. Thirdly, one has to face the problem of local causes, i.e., to reconstruct, in the historical data, the trigger that started the mechanism in the particular diachronic setting.

Once we embrace this line of analysis, we are in the position to systematically address in a comparative way triggers, mechanisms of actuation, and constraints of both syntactic and semantic change and the syntax-semantics interface properly.

5 The contributions in this volume

The contributions in this volume are arranged according to the empirical domain on which they focus. Starting with a chapter by Elly van Gelderen, which encompasses a variety of phenomena in order to substantiate more general claims on the organization of the syntax-semantics interface, we proceed to studies on categories related to the nominal phrase (possession, quantification, determination). We then move to types of change involving the nominal as well as the verbal domain (pronominal objects, number agreement), to focus then on the syntax-semantics interface at the propositional level (local particles, aspect, modals, and negation). Below we provide a short summary for each chapter.

With "Semantic and formal features: Feature economy in language change", Elly **van Gelderen** makes a fundamental conceptual contribution to this volume. She analyzes various instances of systematic syntactic change as linked to a reduction in features from semantic to formal, and here again from interpretable

---

12 On the other side, as Gergel (this volume) remarks, synchronic models should take into account diachronic evidence, and ask themselves if there is a plausible way how the proposed representations might have arisen over time. Van Gelderen (this volume) makes a similar point, but based on evolutionary calculations, concerning the re-evaluation of third-factor principles in the modeling of language variation.

to uninterpretable in terms of Minimalism (e.g. semantic features of a noun changing into a pronoun being reduced to interpretable phi-features and becoming uninterpretable as the pronoun is reanalyzed as verbal agreement morphology; interpretable locative/deictic and phi-features of demonstratives being lost or turning uninterpretable depending on the different possible syntactic reanalyses as articles, complementizers or copulas etc.). This sheds light not only on the syntax-semantics interface in language change, but also on the nature of these features and their acquisition.

In his study "Linking syntax and semantics of adnominal possession in the history of German", Simon **Kasper** traces changes in the various syntactic ways of expressing the semantics of possession within the noun phrase, including pre- and postnominal genitive construction, adnominal possessive dative as well as various prepositional constructions grammaticalized from spatial meanings. The developments are explained in a Role and Reference Grammar framework on the basis of a competition between the prenominal position in the German noun phrase being increasingly reanalyzed as a position for article expressions, on the one hand, and the tendency for a linear precedence of the more referential/definite/agentive entity in the relation within the noun phrase, on the other hand.

In his contribution "*Most* historically", Remus **Gergel** investigates the diachronic development of the Present-Day English quantifier *most*. His study of Old and Middle English data shows that *most* originated from a gradable adjective in the superlative meaning 'largest'. Building on recent synchronic work on the semantic composition of *most*, Gergel argues that the crucial change at the syntax-semantics interface involved the incorporation of a formerly independent co-occurring noun *part* into the lexical meaning of the quantifier. This motivates a new mechanism of development he calls "ontological semantic functionalization".

Paola **Crisma** traces the development of "The 'indefinite article' from cardinal to operator to expletive" in the history of English. In a study of Old English, she shows that *an* did not have the same use as the indefinite article of Present-Day English. Rather, two different grammars can be clearly distinguished: In the first, *an* is a cardinal, meaning '(exactly) one', in the second it is a specificity marker. Relating these different semantic functions to different syntactic positions, Crisma argues that the development of *an* in the history of English is a typical case of grammaticalization involving both upward movement and semantic bleaching.

Nikolaos **Lavidas** addresses the effects of acquisition and language contact in "The Greek Septuagint and language change at the syntax-semantics interface: from null to 'pleonastic' object pronouns". His study deals with the loss of referential null objects in the history of Greek, which, traditionally, has been attributed to influence from Hebrew. Lavidas argues that the loss of referential null objects in later Greek is not directly due to Hebrew influence: rather than showing an indiscriminate increase in the overt, "pleonastic", realization that would be expected in that case, biblical translations bear witness to a change in frequency only with 3rd person, and not 1st and 2nd person, pronouns. Lavidas attributes this to the fact that 3rd person pronouns carry uninterpretable features and, thus, according to the Interpretability Hypothesis, are more prone to transfer in second language acquisition. Hebrew influence leads to an interface change in the spell-out of uninterpretable features with 3rd person pronouns, while the complete loss of referential null objects is due to further diachronic processes.

In "The agreement of collective nouns in the history of Ancient Greek and German" Magnus Breder **Birkenes** and Florian **Sommer** deal with the cross-linguistically frequent mismatch in the syntax of number agreement caused by collective nouns, like 'committee', 'crowd', 'people'. Due to their semantic content, these nouns can trigger plural agreement (on the verb, on attributes, in anaphoric reference) despite being morphologically singular. The authors carry out two diachronic corpus studies of Greek and German, and conclude that the parameters of Corbett's (2006) Agreement Hierarchy combined with word order and linear distance can account for the cases of plural agreement. They single out stylistic factors favouring or blocking the mismatches, but also clear structural constraints: for instance, in the history of German, plural agreement on the verb is never really licensed, and results from phenomena like attraction, rhyme, or loan syntax.

Antje **Casaretto** and Carolin **Schneider** address the complex developmental paths of local adverbials in Vedic, which interact both with nominal and verbal constituents, thus undergoing separate semantic-syntactic change processes. In "Vedic local particles at the syntax-semantics interface", they argue that Vedic presents a situation, comparable to the Proto-Indo-European one, where a class of particles is not yet specialized for an adnominal or an adverbal use. They show that in Vedic the grammaticalization of adpositions is not completed, since most of the local functions are expressed by case morphology, whereas the development of preverbs, which they treat as lexicalization of a novel verb, is more advanced. They thus argue against a grammaticalization path adverb > adposition > preverb, where preverbs are supposed to go through the intermediate adpositional stage. Vedic shows that the two processes can happen independently, and that their productivity is constrained by the general structure of the language in which they take place.

In "Aspect shifts in Indo-Aryan and trajectories of semantic change", Cleo **Condoravdi** and Ashwini **Deo** make the new empirical claim that the cross-linguistically observed path of change from resultative to perfect to perfective aspect is attested also in the history of Indo-Aryan. They present a corpus study of deverbal forms in *-ta* across Early and Later Vedic as well as Middle Indo-Aryan, and model the change in terms of truth-conditional semantics, proposing an explicit analysis for the synchronic categories and for the diachronic mechanism involved. The semantic development is analyzed as generalization, starting from the Early Vedic result state reading for the forms in *-ta*, and leading to a principled expansion during subsequent stages.

Anne **Breitbarth** discusses "The development of conditional *should* in English". On the basis of data from Middle, Early Modern and Present-Day English, she argues that in the conditional use of the modal *shall/should* the connection between its morphological and semantic tense is significantly reduced over time. Adopting a Cartographic approach, she proposes an account of the diachronic development of conditional *should* in terms of grammaticalization as upwards reanalysis and concludes that in this case semantic change and syntactic change go hand in hand. It is also proposed that *should* is subject to ongoing grammaticalization resulting in a new pure conditional marker.

In "The Greek Jespersen's cycle: Renewal, stability and structural micro-elevation", Katerina **Chatzopoulou** sheds light on the syntax-semantics interface in the development of negation. Of the two Greek negators, one is subject to Jespersen's Cycle under a new and more inclusive, basically semantic definition of this cycle proposed here. In the analysis of the second negator, which remained a polarity item sensitive to nonveridicality throughout the history of Greek, semantic change, viz. change from intensified negation to plain propositional negation, is linked to structural syntactic change, viz. stepwise diachronic upwards reanalysis ("microelevation") from VP-internal NP to VP-adjoined AdvP to Neg°.

Cited Corpora

Old Indo-European Languages

PROIEL. *Pragmatic Resources in Old Indo-European Languages.* Maintained by Dag Haug (University of Oslo). http://www.hf.uio.no/ifikk/english/research/projects/proiel/.

English

PPCEME. Kroch, Anthony, Beatrice Santorini & Ariel Diertani. 2004. *Penn-Helsinki Parsed Corpus of Early Modern English.* http://www.ling.upenn.edu/hist-corpora/PPCEME-RELEASE-2/index.html.

PPCME2. Kroch, Anthony & Ann Taylor. 2000. *Penn-Helsinki Parsed Corpus of Middle English, second edition.* http://www.ling.upenn.edu/hist-corpora/PPCME2-RELEASE-3/index.html.

YCOE. Taylor, Anne, Anthony Warner, Susan Pintzuk & Frank Beths. 2003. *York-Toronto-Helsinki Parsed Corpus of Old English Prose.* Heslington: University of York. http://www-users.york.ac.uk/~lang22/YcoeHome1.htm.

PDTB. *Penn Discourse Treebank Project.* Maintained by Aravind Joshi (University of Pennsylvania). http://www.seas.upenn.edu/~pdtb/.

GMB. *Groningen Meaning Bank.* Maintained by Johan Bos (University of Groningen). http://gmb.let.rug.nl.

Icelandic

IcePaHC. *Icelandic Parsed Historical Corpus.* Maintained by Joel C. Wallenberg, Anton Karl Ingason, Einar Freyr Sigurðsson & Eiríkur Rögnvaldsson (University of Iceland). http://linguist.is/icelandic_treebank/Icelandic_Parsed_Historical_Corpus_(IcePaHC).

German

Bonner Frühneuhochdeutschkorpus. Maintained by Werner Besch, Winfried Lenders, Hugo Moser & Hugo Stopp (University of Bonn). http://www.korpora.org/Fnhd/.

CHLG. *Corpus of Historical Low German.* Under preparation by Anne Breitbarth (University of Gent), George Walkden (University of Manchester) & Sheila Watts (University of Cambridge). http://www.chlg.ac.uk/index.html.

GerManC project: A representative historical corpus of German 1650–1800. Maintained by Martin Durrell et al. (University of Manchester). http://www.llc.manchester.ac.uk/research/projects/germanc/.

Kali-Korpus. Maintained by Gabriele Diewald (University of Hannover). http://www.kali.uni-hannover.de/.

Referenzkorpus Frühneuhochdeutsch (1350–1650). Under preparation by Ulrike Demske (University of Potsdam), Stefanie Dipper (University of Bochum), Hans-Joachim Solms (University of Halle) & Klaus-Peter Wegera (University of Bochum). http://www.ruhr-uni-bochum.de/wegera/ref/.

Referenzkorpus Mittelhochdeutsch (1050–1350). Under preparation by Stefanie Dipper (University of Bochum), Thomas Klein (University of Bonn), Klaus-Peter Wegera (University of Bochum) & Claudia Wich-Reif (University of Bonn). http://referenzkorpus-mhd.uni-bonn.de/.

Referenzkorpus Altdeutsch. Under preparation by Karin Donhauser (Humboldt-University Berlin), Jost Gippert (University of Frankfurt am Main) & Rosemarie Lühr (University of Jena). http://www.deutschdiachrondigital.de/korpus/beschreibung/.

Tatian Corpus of Deviating Examples. Maintained by Svetlana Petrova (University of Potsdam and University of Wuppertal). http://www.sfb632.uni-potsdam.de/annis/corpora.html.

French

MCVF. *Corpus MCVF: Modéliser le changement: les voies du français.* Maintained by France Martineau (University of Ottawa). http://www.voies.uottawa.ca/corpus_pg_fr.html.
SRCMF. *Syntactic Reference Corpus of Medieval French.* Maintained by Sophie Prévost (CNRS Lattice, Paris) & Achim Stein (University of Stuttgart). http://srcmf.org.

Portuguese

Tycho Brahe Parsed Corpus of Historical Portuguese. Maintained by Charlotte Galves & Pablo Faria. University of Campinas. http://www.tycho.iel.unicamp.br/~tycho/corpus/en/index.html.

References

Aguilar-Guevara, Ana, Maria Aloni, Angelika Port, Radek Šimík, Machteld de Vos & Hedde Zeijlstra. 2011. Semantics and pragmatics of indefinites: Methodology for a synchronic and diachronic corpus study. In Stefanie Dipper & Heike Zinsmeister (eds.), *Beyond semantics: Corpus-based investigations of pragmatic and discourse phenomena. Proceedings of the DGfS Workshop, Göttingen, February 23–25, 2011* (Bochumer Linguistische Arbeitsberichte 3), 1–16. Bochum: University of Bochum.

van der Auwera, Johan. 2013. Semantic maps, for synchronic and diachronic typology. In Anna Giacalone Ramat, Caterina Mauri & Piera Molinelli (eds.), *Synchrony and diachrony. A dynamic interface*, 153–176. Amsterdam & Philadelphia: John Benjamins.

van der Auwera, Johan & Vladimir A. Plungian. 1998. Modality's semantic map. *Linguistic Typology* 2(1). 79–124.

Baker, Mark C. 2008. The macroparameter in a microparametric world. In Theresa Biberauer (ed.), *The limits of syntactic variation*, 351–373. Amsterdam & Philadelphia: John Benjamins.

Berwick, Robert. 1985. *The acquisition of syntactic knowledge.* Cambridge, MA: MIT Press.

Berwick, Robert & Noam Chomsky. 2011. The biolinguistic program: The current state of its evolution and development. In Anna Maria Di Sciullo & Cedric Boeckx (eds.), *The biolinguistic enterprise: New perspectives on the evolution and nature of the human language faculty*, 19–41. Oxford: Oxford University Press.

Biberauer, Theresa. 2008. Introduction. In Theresa Biberauer (ed.), *The limits of syntactic variation*, 1–72. Amsterdam & Philadelphia: John Benjamins.

Breitbarth, Anne, Chris Lucas, Sheila Watts & David Willis (eds.). 2010. *Continuity and change in grammar.* Amsterdam & Philadelphia: John Benjamins.

Chomsky, Noam. 2000. Minimalist inquiries: The framework. In Roger Martin, David Michaels & Juan Uriagereka (eds.), *Step by step: Essays on minimalist syntax in honor of Howard Lasnik*, 89–156. Cambridge, MA: MIT Press.

Cinque, Guglielmo. 1999. *Adverbs and functional heads. A cross-linguistic perspective.* Oxford: Oxford University Press.

Corbett, Greville G. 2006. *Agreement.* Cambridge: Cambridge University Press.

Coseriu, Eugenio. 1964. Pour une sémantique diachronique structurale. *Travaux de Linguistique et de Littérature* 2. 139–186.

Crisma, Paola & Giuseppe Longobardi. 2009. Change, relatedness, and inertia in historical syntax. In Paola Crisma & Giuseppe Longobardi (eds.), *Historical syntax and linguistic theory*, 1–13. Oxford: Oxford University Press.

Crowley, Terry & Claire Bowern. 2010. *An introduction to historical linguistics*. Fourth edition. Oxford: Oxford University Press.

Eckardt, Regine. 2006. *Meaning change in grammaticalization. An enquiry into semantic reanalysis*. Oxford: Oxford University Press.

von Fintel, Kai. 1995. The formal semantics of grammaticalization. In Jill N. Beckmann (ed.), *Proceedings of the Annual Meeting of the North East Linguistic Society (NELS) 25*. Vol. 2, 175–189. Amherst, MA: GLSA, University of Massachusetts.

Fritz, Gerd. 2012. Theories of meaning change: An overview. In Claudia Maienborn, Klaus von Heusinger & Paul Portner (eds.), *Semantics: An international handbook of natural language meaning*. Volume 3, 2625–2651. Berlin & New York: Mouton de Gruyter.

van Gelderen, Elly. 2004. *Grammaticalization as economy*. Amsterdam & Philadelphia: John Benjamins.

van Gelderen, Elly. 2008. Where did Late Merge go? Grammaticalization as feature economy. *Studia Linguistica* 62(3). 287–300.

van Gelderen, Elly. 2009. Cyclical change, an introduction. In Elly van Gelderen (ed.), *Cyclical change*, 1–12. Amsterdam & Philadelphia: John Benjamins.

van Gelderen, Elly. 2011. *The linguistic cycle: Language change and the language faculty*. Oxford: Oxford University Press.

Gergel, Remus. 2009. 'Rather': On a modal cycle. In Elly van Gelderen (ed.): *Cyclical change*, 243–264. Amsterdam & Philadelphia: John Benjamins.

Gianollo, Chiara, Cristina Guardiano & Giuseppe Longobardi. 2008. Three fundamental issues in parametric linguistics. In Theresa Biberauer (ed.), *The limits of syntactic variation*, 109–142. Amsterdam & Philadelphia: John Benjamins.

Greenberg, Joseph. 1963. Some universals of grammar with particular reference to the order of meaningful elements. In Joseph Greenberg (ed.), *Universals of language*, 73–113. Cambridge, MA: MIT Press.

Greenberg, Joseph. 1966. Synchronic and diachronic universals in phonology. *Language* 42(2). 508–517.

Greenberg, Joseph. 1978. Diachrony, synchrony, and language universals. In Joseph Greenberg, Charles A. Ferguson & Edith A. Moravcsik (eds.), *Universals of human language*. Vol. 1: *Method and theory*, 61–91. Stanford, CA: Stanford University Press.

Haspelmath, Martin. 1997. *Indefinite pronouns*. Oxford: Oxford University Press.

Heine, Bernd & Tania Kuteva. 2002. *World lexicon of grammaticalization*. Cambridge: Cambridge University Press.

Hock, Hans Henrich. 1991. *Principles of historical linguistics*. Second edition. Berlin & New York: Mouton de Gruyter.

Hopper, Paul & Elisabeth C. Traugott. 2003. *Grammaticalization*. Second edition. Cambridge: Cambridge University Press.

Hornstein, Norbert, Jairo Nunes & Kleanthes K. Grohmann. 2005. *Understanding Minimalism*. Cambridge: Cambridge University Press.

Jäger, Agnes. 2010. 'Anything' is 'nothing' is 'something'. On the diachrony of polarity types of indefinites. *Natural Language and Linguistic Theory* 28. 787–822.

Keenan, Edward. 1994. Creating anaphors. An historical study of the English reflexive pronouns. Ms., University of California, Los Angeles.

Keenan, Edward. 2009. Linguistic theory and the historical creation of English reflexives. In Paola Crisma & Giuseppe Longobardi (eds.), *Historical syntax and linguistic theory*, 17–40. Oxford: Oxford University Press.

Kiparsky, Paul. 2012. Grammaticalization as optimization. In Dianne Jonas, John Whitman & Andrew Garrett (eds.), *Grammatical change. Origins, nature, outcomes*, 15–51. Oxford: Oxford University Press.

Kiparsky, Paul & Cleo Condoravdi. 2006. Tracking Jespersen's cycle. In Mark Janse, Brian D. Joseph & Angela Ralli (eds.), *Proceedings of the 2nd International Conference of Modern Greek Dialects and Linguistic Theory*, 172–197. Mytilene: Doukas.

Lahiri, Aditi. 2000. Introduction. In Aditi Lahiri (ed.), *Analogy, levelling, markedness: Principles of change in phonology and morphology*, 1–14. Berlin & New York: Mouton de Gruyter.

Larrivée, Pierre & Richard Ingham (eds.). 2011. *The evolution of negation. Beyond the Jespersen cycle*. Berlin & New York: Mouton de Gruyter.

Ledgeway, Adam. 2012. *From Latin to Romance. Morphosyntactic typology and change*. Oxford: Oxford University Press.

Lehmann, Christian. 1995. *Thoughts on grammaticalization*. Munich: LINCOM Europa.

Lehmann, Winfred P. 1974. *Proto-Indo-European syntax*. Austin, TX: University of Texas Press.

Levinson, Stephen C. 2000. *Presumptive meanings*. Cambridge, MA: MIT Press.

Li, Charles N. (ed.). 1975. *Word order and word order change*. Austin, TX: University of Texas Press.

Lightfoot, David. 1979. *Principles of diachronic syntax*. Cambridge: Cambridge University Press.

Longobardi, Giuseppe. 2001. Formal syntax, diachronic minimalism, and etymology: The history of French 'chez'. *Linguistic Inquiry* 32(2). 275–302.

Nichols, Johanna. 1992. *Linguistic diversity in space and time*. Chicago, IL: University of Chicago Press.

Nichols, Johanna. 2003. Diversity and stability in language. In Brian D. Joseph & Richard D. Janda (eds.), *The handbook of historical linguistics*, 283–310. Oxford: Blackwell.

Paul, Hermann. 1995 [1880]. *Prinzipien der Sprachgeschichte*. 10. unveränd. Aufl. Tübingen: Niemeyer.

Penka, Doris. 2011. *Negative indefinites*. Oxford: Oxford University Press.

Roberts, Ian. 1993. *Verbs and diachronic syntax. A comparative history of English and French*. Dordrecht: Kluwer.

Roberts, Ian. 2007. *Diachronic syntax*. Oxford: Oxford University Press.

Roberts, Ian. 2012a. Macroparameters and Minimalism: A programme for comparative research. In Charlotte Galves, Sonia Cyrino, Ruth Lopes, Filomena Sandalo & Juanito Avelar (eds.), *Parameter theory and linguistic change*, 320–335. Oxford: Oxford University Press.

Roberts, Ian. 2012b. Towards a parameter hierarchy for verb-movement: Diachronic considerations. Paper presented at the *34th Annual Meeting of the Deutsche Gesellschaft für Sprachwissenschaft*, University of Frankfurt/M., 6–9 March 2012.

Roberts, Ian. 2012c. Diachrony and cartography: Paths of grammaticalization and the clausal hierarchy. In Laura Brugé, Anna Cardinaletti, Giuliana Giusti, Nicola Munaro & Cecilia Poletto (eds.), *Functional heads. The cartography of syntactic structures*. Volume 7, 351–367. Oxford: Oxford University Press.

Roberts, Ian & Anna Roussou. 2003. *Syntactic change: A minimalist approach to grammaticalization*. Cambridge: Cambridge University Press.

von Stechow, Arnim. 2009. Tenses in compositional semantics. In Wolfgang Klein & Ping Li (eds.), *The expression of time*, 129–166. Berlin & New York: Mouton de Gruyter.

Sweetser, Eve. 1988. Grammaticalization and semantic bleaching. In Shelley Axmaker, Annie Jaisser & Helen Singmaster (eds.), *Proceedings of the 14th Annual Meeting of the Berkeley Linguistics Society (BLS)*, 389–405. Berkeley, CA: Berkeley Linguistics Society.

Traugott, Elizabeth C. 1988. Pragmatic strengthening and grammaticalization. In Shelley Axmaker, Annie Jaisser & Helen Singmaster (eds.), *Proceedings of the 14th Annual Meeting of the Berkeley Linguistic Society (BLS)*, 406–416. Berkeley, CA: Berkeley Linguistic Society.

Traugott, Elisabeth C. & Richard B. Dasher. 2002. *Regularity in semantic change*. Cambridge: Cambridge University Press.

Traugott, Elizabeth C. & Ekkehard König. 1991. The semantics-pragmatics of grammaticalization revisited. In Elizabeth C. Traugott & Bernd Heine (eds.), *Approaches to grammaticalization*, Vol. 1, 189–218. Amsterdam & Philadelphia: John Benjamins.

Tsimpli, Ianthi M. & Maria Dimitrakopoulou. 2007. The Interpretability Hypothesis: Evidence from wh-interrogatives in second language acquisition. *Second Language Research* 23(2). 215–242.

Willis, David, Christopher Lucas & Anne Breitbarth (eds.), 2013. *The history of negation in the languages of Europe and the Mediterranean*. Volume I: *Case studies*. Oxford: Oxford University Press.

Willis, David, Christopher Lucas & Anne Breitbarth (eds.), forthcoming. *The history of negation in the languages of Europe and the Mediterranean*. Volume II. Oxford: Oxford University Press.

Elly van Gelderen

2 Semantic and formal features: Feature economy in language change

Studying systematic language change provides a unique perspective on the language faculty. We know that internal change is regular, e.g. as in linguistic cycles, and when we formulate this change in terms of semantic and formal features this provides insight into the nature of these features and into the syntax-semantics interface. In this paper, I first look at Minimalist features and then provide examples of systematic linguistic change in semantic and formal features. I finish with an evaluation of the status of features.

1 Introduction

Features have become very prominent in Minimalist work, especially since Chomsky (1995). All parametric variation is now tied to features. Some people would say that their role is too powerful and question how the child would manage to acquire such a rich system of features.

In this paper, I outline some of the current views on features (in Section 2). I then examine what happens to features in language change (in Section 3). I will show that semantic features are reanalyzed as interpretable and then as uninterpretable. Finally, I address (in Section 4) where features "come from". I will argue that the innate component is very rich because some of the features go back to a pre-language stage in the development of our species.

2 Minimalist features

Even as early as Chomsky (1965: 87–88), features have played a role in generative grammar. The lexicon has always been seen as containing information for the phonological, semantic, and syntactic components. Some syntactic features are given in (1).[1]

---

1 Abbrevations in this paper are as follows: ASP is Aspect, CL Classifier, COCA *Corpus of Contemporary American English*, COHA *Corpus of Historical American English*, CVC Cape Verdean Creole, FOC Focus marker, M Modal, N Noun, P Plural, PRT Particle, POSS Possessive, REL Relative, and S Singular.

(1) *Sincerity*   [+N, -Count, +Abstract]
     may   [+M]
     (Chomsky 1965: 85)

Thirty years later, Chomsky (1995: 230, 236, 277) similarly recognizes semantic (e.g. abstract object), phonological (e.g. the sounds), and formal features. The formal ones are relevant to syntax and are divided into intrinsic or optional. The intrinsic ones are "listed explicitly in the lexical entry or strictly determined by properties so listed" (Chomsky 1995: 231) and include categorial features, the Case assigning features of the verb, and the person and gender features of the noun. The person, number, and gender features are usually referred to as phi-features.

Optional features are added arbitrarily and are predictable from linguistic Principles (e.g. nouns need Case or some kind of licensing). They include the tense and agreement features of verbs and the number and Case features of nouns. An example of a noun with its features is provided in Figure 1. Typically, the intrinsic ones are valued and the optional ones get a value assigned to them by checking/matching.

There is, however, a difference between Chomsky (1965) and, for instance, Chomsky (2001: 10). In the latter, semantic and formal features "intersect". This intersection was not there in Chomsky (1965: 142) where semantic features are defined as not involved in the syntax. This difference will become relevant in my account of the diachronic changes.

Apart from optional and intrinsic features, there are interpretable and uninterpretable features. The interpretable ones are relevant for interpretation at LF and include categorial and nominal phi-features. Unlike interpretable features, uninterpretable features are not relevant for LF and are transferred to the

	airplane	*build*	
semantic:	e.g. [artifact]	e.g. [action]	
phonological:	e.g. [begins with a vowel; two syllables]	e.g. [one syllable]	
formal:			
intrinsic	optional	intrinsic	optional
[nominal]	[number]	[verbal]	[phi]
[3 person]	[Case]	[assign accusative]	[tense]

Figure 1: Features of *airplane* and *build* (adapted from Chomsky 1995: 231)

	airplane	*build*
uninterpretable:	[Case]	[phi]
interpretable:	[nominal]	[verbal]
	[3 person]	[assign accusative]
	[non-human]	

Figure 2: Uninterpretable and interpretable features of *airplane* and *build* (adapted from Chomsky 1995: 278)

PF; they mainly involve the Case features of NPs and the phi-features of verbs. There are a number of reasons behind the distinction between interpretable and uninterpretable features. Some features (e.g. phi-features of nouns) remain active after checking. This is the reason nouns (and of course the phrases they head) can move cyclically and provide the phi-features along the way (Chomsky 1995: 282). This is not true of the uninterpretable Case feature. Once Case has been checked by a DP, that DP cannot move to check Case elsewhere. Figure 2 provides the uninterpretable and interpretable features of the noun *airplane* and the verb *build*. Note that many intrinsic features are interpretable (and valued) but that connection isn't absolute.

There is a major change after 1995, in particular in Chomsky (2000; originally proposed in 1998) in that checking through Spec-head agreement is replaced by a probe-goal checking system based on the c-command relationship. Functional categories in need of feature-checking search down the tree for a goal that will value their features. An advantage of this shift is a simplification of the existential construction in English (and other languages that have this). The pre-2000 derivation of (2) involved invisible raising of the post-verbal DP *many buffaloes/a buffalo* to the Spec TP for agreement with the verb in T. The invisibility was achieved by means of LF-raising of the DP or movement of the features of the DP, both very ad-hoc procedures.

(2) a. *There were **many buffaloes** in the house.*

  b. *There was **a buffalo** in the house.*

The now usual AGREE-version of (2a) is given in (3). The agreement features in T find the DP in the Spec of VP (i.e. vP) and the DP values the phi-features of T, plural in the case of *many buffaloes*. (The T also has tense features and assigns nominative to the DP but I leave those out for simplicity).

(3)

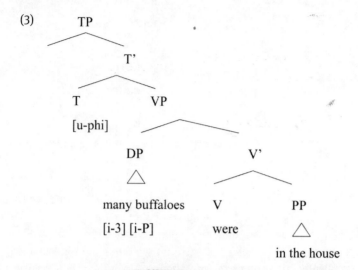

There are various kinds of features: (a) reciprocal features, e.g. the uninter-pretable agreement features and uninterpretable case features value each other, (b) Cinque's (1999) features for e.g. modals, are not involved in checking and are therefore interpretable or semantic, and (c) non-reciprocal features just value one uninterpretable feature, e.g. the negative in Negative Concord languages. A number of checking issues are still debatable: the reciprocity of (a) (see Carstens 2012) and also the direction of the checking (see e.g. Baker 2008). Checking will not be so important in this paper but the features will be.

Especially since 1995, there has been some debate as to the (Universal Grammar) status of features and functional projections that they project (Cinque 1999). I'll be concerned how the learner knows which features are available and with the distinction between semantic and interpretable features. As mentioned, semantic and formal features overlap in Chomsky (1995: 230, 381): "Formal fea-tures have semantic correlates and reflect semantic properties (accusative Case and transitivity, for example)". I understand this to mean that, if a language has nouns with semantic phi-features, the learner will be able to hypothesize uninterpretable features on another F (and will be able to bundle them there).

Why aren't these two types of features (uninterpretable and semantic) enough? There are two reasons that all three kinds of features are relevant: (a) analytic languages may not have uninterpretable features, and (b) in language change, we can see all three at work. I'll focus on (b) and look at how features work in change.

3 Feature Change

Loss of semantic features is well-known in grammaticalization. It occurs when full verbs such as Old English *will* with [volition, expectation, future] features, i.e. purely semantic features, are reanalyzed as having only the grammatical feature [future] in Middle English. The same is true for negatives where semantic features from, for instance, minimizers are reanalyzed as grammatical.

In this section, I look at three well known, frequently occurring changes that can be phrased in terms of feature change, namely the subject pronoun to agreement, the demonstrative to copula, and the demonstrative to article and complementizer change.

3.1 Subject Agreement

The shift from pronoun to clitic to agreement marker is well-known across languages. Here I start with an example from English that is not generally accepted as such a change but it shows the typical stages so will be suitable for my purposes. I then go into the less controversial example of French.

Van Gelderen (2004, 2011) argues that personal pronouns in English are on their way to being reanalyzed as agreement prefixes on the verb. Evidence for such a reanalysis, at least as a weak pronoun, is that we often get doublings, as in (4a, b), by emphatic elements. This change is starting with first and second person singular; for third person, this additional pronoun is rarer and (5) is the only instance I have found in the 200-year period of the *Corpus of Historical American English* (COHA). Compare that to 286 instances of the first person in Figure 3 over the same period with a real increase around 1920.

(4) a. ***Me, I*** *think I'd like a change.*
         (COHA 2001, fiction)

     b. ***You, you****'ve just found, like, the tip of the iceberg.*
         (COCA 2011, spoken)

(5) *The lookout floated free.* ***Him, he*** *got first, with a careful, homing shot.*
     (COHA 1961, fiction).

Other evidence that the pronoun is losing its independence is that you can't really have the subject pronoun on its own, as (6) shows, and that a number of varieties no longer invert the subject and auxiliary, as in (7).

1810	1820	1830	1840	1850	1860	1870	1880	1890	1900
0	0	0	0	1	0	0	4	0	0
	0	0	0	0.06	0	0	0.2	0	0

1910	1920	1930	1940	1950	1960	1970	1980	1990	2000
8	36	28	22	28	18	24	38	33	46
0.35	1.4	1.14	0.9	1.14	0.75	1.01	1.5	1.18	1.56

Figure 3: Raw numbers and frequencies per million words for *Me, I* ... in the COHA

(6) a. *Who did this?*

   b. **I/I did.*
       (Siewierska 2004: 17)

(7) **Which books you can** *loan me?*   Cajun Vernacular English
     'Which books can you loan me?'

This means that the pronouns are being reanalyzed from having interpretable person and number features to being a probe in T with uninterpretable phi-features.

In French, it is less controversial (especially since the work of Lambrecht 1981) that first and second person subjects are agreement markers. In Old French, the subject is completely separable from the verb, as (8) shows, but this is no longer the case in contemporary French. Instead, pronouns have to attach to verbs as (9) shows.

(8) *Se* **je** *meïsme   ne   li   di*   Old French
     If   I   myself   not   him   tell
     'If I don't tell him myself.'
     (Cligès 993, from Franzén 1939: 20)

(9) a. **Je   lis   et   relis*
         I   read   and   reread

   b. *Je   lis   et   je relis*
       I   read   and   I   reread
       'I read and reread.'

In addition, subject-auxiliary inversion is becoming obsolete in colloquial French, showing that pronouns have a fixed position in respect to the verb.

Therefore, (10a) is far more common in spoken French than (10b) and there is also doubling, as in (11), indicating renewal of the erstwhile pronoun.

(10) a. **tu vas** *où*
      2S go where

    b. *Où* **vas-tu?**
       Where go-2s
       'Where are you going?'

(11) **Moi,** *j'écoute tout le temps*
    me, I-listen all the time
    'I listen all the time.'
    (Corpus d'entretiens spontanés)

These changes can be summarized in terms of the feature changes in (12), with a tree, as in (13). There is also an optional *moi* 'me' which can supply the features necessary for valuation of the [u-phi]; otherwise, we have to assume pro-drop.

(12) Standard French > Colloquial French
     je 'I' (SPEC TP)   *je-/j'-* (T)
     [i-1S]   [u-phi]

(13) Standard   Colloquial

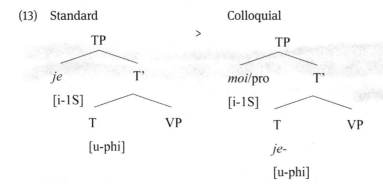

The origin of the renewing pronoun, e.g. *moi* in (11) for first person singular, is an oblique emphatic. In the case of English and French emphatic pronouns, it is not so obvious that they have semantic (rather than interpretable) person features. Southeast Asian languages show this better. Indonesian *saya* 'I' originates from 'servant, slave', but is now the regular first person. Thai is reported to have over twenty first and second person markers, all derived from nouns, with semantic/pragmatic features that make the person clear. The feature cline can therefore be represented as in (14). There is no difference between a head and an affix in this model.

(14) Subject Agreement Cycle

adjunct		specifier		head		affix
emphatic/noun	>	full pronoun	>	head pronoun	>	agreement
[semantic]		[i-1 or 2 or 3]		[u-phi]		[u-phi]

This change from semantic to interpretable to uninterpretable is typical of other change as well, as we'll see.

3.2 Demonstrative, preposition, and verb reanalyzed as copula

Li and Thompson (1977) are among the first to examine the change from demonstrative to copula systematically, and Katz (1996) is one of the first to note its systematic nature and to discuss it as a cycle. Copula cycles occur in many typologically and genetically different languages: Turkish, Uto-Aztecan, Chinese, Hebrew, Palestinian Arabic, Maltese, Kenya Luo, Lango, Logbara, Nuer, Wappo, West Greenlandic, and Creoles. There are other sources for copulas, mainly prepositions and verbs (see Hengeveld 1992; Nicholas 1996; Stassen 1997; and Pustet 2003), that can be accounted for within a framework where the locational and other semantic features are reanalyzed as grammatical.

In the cycle that involves a pronoun, a third person subject pronoun or demonstrative is reanalyzed as a copula verb, initially with its person and number features intact. This change is different from the subject cycle of the previous section, where first and second person are consistently the first to change and where all persons participate. Full verbs are also reanalyzed as copulas as are prepositions, as I briefly discuss. The original semantic features determine the character of the copula.

The way the pronoun to copula cycle has been explained is through the reanalysis of a topic or focus construction (see e.g. Nicholas 1996).

(15) *The elephant* *that* *happy*

TOPIC	SUBJECT	VP
	↓	
SUBJECT	copula	VP

However, if the reanalysis in (15) is correct, the question is why first (or second) person pronouns are never reanalyzed as copulas since they are frequent topics. Van Gelderen (2011) argues that the change is due to the deictic features of the demonstrative that personal pronouns lack. This deictic feature can be reanalyzed as a locational feature on the copula, as in (16).

(16) demonstrative/pronoun   > copula/T   > grammatical marker
    specifier   > head   > affix
    [i-loc]   > [i-loc]   > –
    [i-3S]   > [u-phi]

In the first stage of the change, the phi-features of the T probe are valued by the pronoun or demonstrative in VP and the demonstrative or third person pronoun moves as full phrase to the Spec of TP and the copula moves to T. Modern English represents that stage, as shown in (17). In Modern English, copula *be* is used for possession, location, and existence.

(17) *That*   T
              be
    [i-loc]   [i-loc]
    [i-3S]   [u-phi] > [3S]

In the second stage, the demonstrative is a head and its [loc]-features are very similar to those of the copula and of the T. A reanalysis may therefore take place of the demonstrative as copula, with possible loss of the location features. Old Chinese is representative of this stage. The last stage shows a new demonstrative to provide interpretable phi-features for the T probe; this occurs in Modern Chinese, as I'll now show, based mainly on the discussion in Peyraube and Wiebusch (1994).

In an early period (before 200 BCE), there are no copulas, according to Wang (1958), and *shi* 'this' typically functions as a demonstrative in *shi ri* 'this day'. *Shi* still has this function in very formal contexts, as in (18). In Old Chinese, *shi* also functions as a resumptive pronoun with an empty copula, as in (19).

(18) *jiang* **shi** *xiang jing-fei jibo*   *ben suo*   Mandarin Chinese
    will   D   CL   funding-transfer D   organization
    'He will transfer these funds to our organization.'
    (Hui-Ling Yang, p.c.)

(19) *fu   yu   gui   **shi**   ren   zhi   suo   yu   ye*   Old Chinese
Riches and honor this men PRT PRT desire PRT
'Riches and honor, this is men's desire.'
(Peyraube and Wiebusch 1994: 393)

In (19), it is difficult to determine whether *shi* is a copula or a demonstrative subject. However, examples such as (20) are unambiguous since doubling occurs; in Modern Chinese, this would be rendered as (21) with a demonstrative *zhe*.

(20) **Shi   shi**   *lie   gui*   Old Chinese
this is violent ghost
'This is a violent ghost.'
(Peyraube and Wiebusch 1994: 398)

(21) **Zhe   shi**   *lie   gui*   Mandarin Chinese
this is violent ghost
'This is a violent ghost.'
(Mei Ching Ho, p.c.)

According to Peyraube and Wiebusch (1994: 398), the earliest clear examples like (21) date from 180 BCE.

The demonstrative function of *shi* is (mainly) lost in modern Mandarin Chinese, but the copula function, as in (21), remains. It indicates identity, not location. Location, possession, and existence are expressed in different ways. It is also often used as a cleft or in a presentational construction, as in (22) and (23).

(22) **Shi**   *wo*   *de*   *zuo*   Mandarin Chinese
be 1S POSS fault
'It's is me (who is) at fault.'
(Hui-Ling Yang, p.c.)

(23) **Shi**   *wo*   Mandarin Chinese
be 1s
'It's me.'
(Hui-Ling Yang, p.c.)

Summarizing the situation in Chinese, one can say that this language has seen a reanalysis of the demonstrative *shi* as copula. Which features were relevant for this? In Modern Chinese, *shi* is used for identification whereas *zai* is used for locational meanings, the latter being of prepositional origin. The respective feature bundles I will suggest are given in (24a, b). Because Chinese has no agreement, I leave out the [u-phi] features that the copula might have in other languages (where it grammaticalized from demonstratives).

(24) a.   D   > V
                               shi   *shi*
              semantic   [proximate]   [identity]
              formal   [i-3S]

      b.   P   > V
                               zai   *zai*
              semantic   [place]   [location]

Copulas come in many "flavors". This flavor is due to the semantic features of the source. As a main verb, *remain* and *stay* have [duration] as a semantic feature and *seem* has [visible]. These then become aspectual and modal features respectively.

(25) *be*   *remain*   *seem*   *stay*
      [i-loc]   [i-loc]   [i-loc]   [i-loc]
                 [i-ASP]   [i-M]   [i-ASP]

One of the problems with this system is that it seems rather ad-hoc which features we assign to the lexical items. I return to this issue later. I now turn to another case where copulas within one language derive from different sources in another language and retain some of the original semantic features.

McWhorter (1997) presents examples of demonstrative pronouns that re-analyzed as copula verbs in Saramaccan, as in (26), where *da* derives from the English demonstrative *that*.

(26) a. *Mi **da** i   tatá*   Saramaccan
          I   am   your   father
          'I am your father.'
          (McWhorter 1997: 87)

      b. *Hɛn **dà** dí   Gaamá*
          he   is   the   chief
          'He's the chief.'
          (McWhorter 1997: 98)

He argues that early Saramaccan had a zero copula and the demonstrative subject pronoun *da* 'that' was reanalyzed as an identificational equative copula. This is very similar to the Chinese copula *shi*. McWhorter also argues that earlier *mi* 'I' and *hɛn* 'he' in (26a, b) were in topic position but that they are now in subject position. I am assuming this scenario is correct and therefore a clear case of a demonstrative pronoun reanalyzed as copula followed by a new pronoun appearing in subject position.

Apart from the copula *da*, there is another copula in Saramaccan that is derived from the English locative adverb *there*, namely *dɛ* in (27). It is used for class equatives and locatives.

(27) a. *a* ***dɛ*** *mi* *tatá*   Saramaccan
          he   is   my   father
          'He is my father.'
          (McWhorter 1997: 99)

     b. *Dí* *wómi* ***dɛ*** *a* *wósu*
          the   woman   is   at   house
          'The woman is at home.'
          (McWhorter 1997: 88)

I am not sure how the class equative grammaticalized but the features of the locative adverb *there* are obviously transferred to the copula in (27b).

Baptista (2002) provides sentences from Cape Verdean Creole (hence CVC) showing a similar origin of the copula. In (28), the copula form *e* (used with individual-level predicates) derives from the third person pronoun *el* 'he' and has kept the [3S] interpretable features since this copula can only be used for third person singulars.

(28) a. ***(El)*** *e* *nha* *pai*   CVC
          'He   is   my   father.'

     b. ***(El)*** *e* *spertu*   CVC
          'S/he   is   smart.'
          (Baptista 2002: 255)

The copula *e* in (28) has none of the deictic features since it is purely equational. Because (28) is limited to third person singular, we could also argue that *e* still is the subject and that the optional *el* is a topic. This is what Baptista (2002: 102) suggests: "*e* occupies the syntactic position of a copula but behaves like a pronoun". Later on, she argues that it is also used as a focalizer, as in (29).

(29) **E**   *mi*   *ki*   *ta*   *fika*   *ku*   *kes*   *minizu*   CVC
    FOC   1S   REL   ASP   stay   with   the   kids
    'It is me who stays with the kids.'
    (Baptista 2002: 103)

This means that, as copula, it can also move to the left periphery, and that being a topic or cleft marker is a natural extension of the copula.

CVC also has a stage-level copula *sta* that can be used with any subject, as (30) shows; when used without a pronoun, it can be first, second, or third person.

(30)   *Bu*   **sta**   *livri*   CVC
    'You   are   free.'
    (Baptista 2002: 255)

The origin of *sta* is verbal (I assume *estar* 'be' in Portuguese, which derives from the Latin *stare* 'to stand'). So, CVC shows that a third person pronoun can be used as an individual level copula. It doesn't show evidence of a demonstrative being reanalyzed in a more locational way.

If demonstrative pronouns have deictic features, they can be "confused" with copulas, i.e. are ambiguous, and can be reanalyzed. If ambiguous, a lexical item will be reanalyzed with fewer features. This is due to a Third Factor Principle that I discuss in Section 4.

3.3 Demonstrative to article and complementizer

The history of English demonstratives is very complex. The masculine nominative singular demonstrative *se* evolves into an article around the end of the Old English period. As argued in van Gelderen (2011), the text that really shows this is the *Peterborough Chronicle*, with an early part that abounds in what look like demonstratives, as in (31), and a later part where the demonstratives are articles, as in (32).

(31)   **Ðis** *geares wæs* **se** *mynstre of Cantwarabyri halgod fram* **þone** *ærcebiscop Willelm* **þes** *dæies iiii Nonæ MAI.*
    'This year was that monastery of Canterbury consecrated by that Archbishop William, on that fourth day before the nones of May.'
    (Peterborough Chronicle 1130, Thorpe 1861)

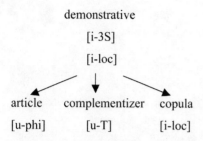

demonstrative

[i-3S]

[i-loc]

article   complementizer   copula

[u-phi]   [u-T]   [i-loc]

Figure 4: Feature Economy and the demonstrative pronoun

(32)   *ðis gære for **þe** king Stephne ofer sæ to Normandi & ther wes underfangen forþi ðæt hi uuenden ðæt he sculde ben alsuic alse **the** eom wes.*
'This year, (the) King Stephen crossed the sea to go to Normandy and was received there because they thought he was like the uncle.'
(Peterborough Chronicle 1137, Thorpe 1861)

In the change, the demonstrative loses overt deictic features and becomes a D head with uninterpretable features. The neuter *þat* 'that' remains a demonstrative.

The complementizer *that* also derives from the demonstrative (the neuter singular demonstrative in this case). See Lockwood (1968: 222) and Hopper and Traugott (2003: 191–192). This means that demonstratives are reanalyzed in two ways: as heads D with loss of interpretable deictic and phi-features and as complementizers with loss of interpretable deictic features. Both developments are shown in Figure 4 together with the one discussed in the previous section.

According to Pesetsky and Torrego (2001), the complementizer *that* is the spell-out of a T with interpretable tense features. Some problems occur with their analysis, in particular regarding the lack of C-deletion in Old English and the absence of "*that*-trace" effects. I will argue that the lack of C-deletion is due to the interpretable features of C in the older period. As they are reanalyzed as uninterpretable, C becomes deletable. I'll provide some more details on this.

Pesetsky and Torrego argue that the finite C has tense features that must be checked by a nominative, or by *that*, or by an auxiliary. Two phenomena that are explained by this checking are the optionality of *that* in English complement clauses (since either the subject DP or *that* can check [u-T]) and the *that*-trace effect in Modern English. This is where a problem appears for their analysis. If *that* is reanalyzed as [i-T] before the Old English period, it should be deletable in Old English as well and there should also be a "*that*-trace" effect. However, van Gelderen (1993: chapter 3) shows that the optionality of the complementizer

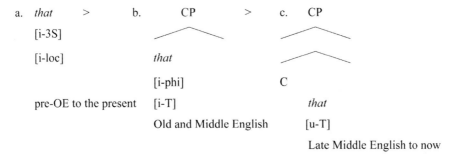

a. *that* >   b.   CP >   c.   CP

[i-3S]

[i-loc]   *that*

            [i-phi]   C

pre-OE to the present   [i-T]

           Old and Middle English   *that*

                               [u-T]

                         Late Middle English to now

Figure 5: Demonstrative to complementizer

appears around 1380 and *that*-trace is not ungrammatical in Old English, as (33) shows, taken from Allen (1977).

(33)   *Ac*   *hwaet*   *saegst*   *ðu*   *ðonne*   **ðaet**   ~~hwaet~~
     But   what   say   you   then   that

     sie   *forcuðre*   *ðonne*   *sio*   *ungesceadwisnes?*
     is   wickeder   than   be   foolishness
     'But what do you say is wickeder than foolishness?'
     (Boethius 36.8, from Allen 1977: 122, Sedgefield 1899)

A solution to this could be that *that* is still a demonstrative in the specifier of the CP and that those are not deletable. Evidence for such a view can in fact be found in van Gelderen (2004), even though there it is not phrased in terms of features. There is in Old and Middle English a complementizer *þe/te* (a bleached descendant of the demonstrative *þa* according to the *Oxford English Dictionary*) that follows *that*, as in (34). That makes it look like *that* is a specifier preceding a head (cf. van Gelderen 2004: 82–87) with interpretable tense features.

(34)   *monig*   *oft*   *gecwæð*   **þæt**   **te**   *suð*
     many   often   said   that   that   south

     ne   *norð*   ...   *oþer*   ...   *selra*   *nære*
     nor   north,   other   better   not-was
     'It was often said that no better one could be found North or South.'
     (Beowulf 858, Klaeber [1922] 1941)

In short, the change from older English to Modern English involves deictic features on *that* being reanalyzed as tense features, as in Figure 5. Demonstratives are first reanalyzed as specifiers of CPs and later as their heads.

In this section, I have shown that many changes can be seen in terms of feature changes. I will now discuss the status of features in the Minimalist Program and suggest that they are part of Universal Grammar. I will also claim that the unidirectional changes in the features observed in the current section find an explanation in a Third Factor Principle, namely Feature Economy.

4 The status of features

In this section, I first discuss some general changes concerning the nature of Universal Grammar in current generative grammar. I then examine some practical issues concerning the number of features. I conclude by arguing that features have to be part of Universal Grammar but that Feature Economy is a Third Factor effect.

4.1 Features: Third Factor or Universal Grammar

The Minimalist Program has shifted the emphasis from Universal Grammar to innate factors that are not specific to the language faculty. One of the reasons to deemphasize Universal Grammar is the evolutionary time it had to develop. If language arose in humans between 1,000,000 and 150,000 years ago, a very specific Universal Grammar would have not had the time to develop. The factors not specific to language are referred to as "third factors", as in (35).

(35) Three Factors (Chomsky 2007: 3):
(1) genetic endowment, which sets limits on the attainable languages, thereby making language acquisition possible; (2) external data, converted to the experience that selects one or another language within a narrow range; (3) principles not specific to FL [the Faculty of Language]. Some of the third factor principles have the flavor of the constraints that enter into all facets of growth and evolution (…). Among these are principles of efficient computation.

Unfortunately, the third factors are not well defined and have been invoked to account for a number of phenomena, e.g. pro-drop (Sigurðsson 2011), phrase structure (Medeiros 2012), language change (van Gelderen 2011).

Generative grammar has also shifted emphasis from syntactic parameters to lexical ones, i.e. features, and these too are not as clear as one would hope and I will turn to that in Section 4.2. The parameters are now, as (36).

Universal Grammar		UG and **Third Factors**
(Principles & Parameters)		(Principles and **lexical** parameters)
+	>>	+
Input (Scottish English, Western Navajo, etc.)		Input
=		=
I-language		I-language

Figure 6: Changes in the model of language acquisition

(36) **Borer-Chomsky-Conjecture** (Baker 2008: 156):
All parameters of variation are attributable to differences in the features of particular items (e.g., the functional heads) in the lexicon.

In Figure 6, I have summarized these two major shifts in the recent framework.

4.2 Practical problems with features

The main problem with features concerns their number and order. If we take the structure, as in (37), proposed in Cinque (1999), the question is how a child acquires this system where features such as past, future, and epistemic occur in a strictly ordered hierarchy.

(37) **The Universal Hierarchy of Clausal Functional Projections**
(Cinque 1999: 106):

[Moodspeech-act	*frankly*	
[Moodevaluative	*fortunately*	CP-adverbs
[Moodevidential	*allegedly*	
[Modepistemic	*probably*	
[Tpast	*once*	
[Tfuture	*then*	
[Moodirrealis	*perhaps*	
[Modnecessity	*necessarily*	
[Modpossibility	*possibly*	
[ASPhabitual	*usually*	
[ASPrepetetive	*again*	
[ASPfrequentative(I)	*often*	TP-adverbs

[Modvolitional	*intentionally*	
[ASPcelerative(I)	*quickly*	
[Tanterior	*already*	
[ASPterminative	*no longer*	
[ASPcontinuative	*still*	
[ASPperfect(?)	*always*	
[ASPretrospective	*just*	
[ASPproximative	*soon*	
[ASPdurative	*briefly*	
[ASPgeneric/progressive	*characteristically*	
[ASPprospective	*almost*	
[ASPsg.completive(I)	*completely*	
[ASPpl.completive	*tutto*	
[Voice	*well*	VP-adverbs
[ASPcelerative(II)	*fast/early*	
[ASPrepetetive(II)	*again*	
[ASPfrequentative(II)	*often*	
[ASPsg.completive(II)	*completely*]]]]]]]]]]]]]]]]]]]]]]]]]]]]]]]]]	

Muysken (2008: 6) says: "I find the generative literature on functional categories rather vague". Cinque and Rizzi (2008) discuss the question of the number of functional categories. There are 30 in (37), 32 in Cinque (1999: 130), and around 40 in Kayne (2005). Cinque and Rizzi, using Heine and Kuteva's (2002) work on grammaticalization, come up with 400 features that are targets in Heine and Kuteva. Benincà and Munaro (2010: 6–7) note that syntax has reached the detail of phonological features. This is the major problem that I will come back to in 4.3.

The second question is how to ensure the valuation of uninterpretable features and also which features are typically checked. The phi-features are relatively easy: [u-phi] gets a person and number value from a third person noun or a pronoun with interpretable features. The set of phi-features can vary across languages, since some have a dual number or gender included. The uninterpretable negation features could of course be checked by a second negation, but also by a minimizer, such as *pas* in French or *butterfly* in English. This shows that semantic features intersect, as also seen in the quote from Chomsky (2001) in Section 2.

4.3 Where do the features come from and how are they ordered?

Chomsky (1965: 142) writes that "semantic features (...) too, are presumably drawn from a universal 'alphabet' but little is known about this today and nothing has been said about it here" and, in Chomsky (1993: 24), there is the very cryptic statement that vocabulary acquisition shows poverty of the stimulus. That means Universal Grammar has to give some concepts and structure. When a child looks at the world, it knows how to categorize things; it is not just abstracting from its environment. This is clear with logical concepts, as the philosopher Geach (1957: 22–23) writes: "[A]bstractionists rarely attempt an abstractionist account of logical concepts, like those of *some, or,* and *not* (...). In the sensible world you will find no specimens of alternativeness and negativeness from which you could form by abstraction the concept of *or* or of *not*". Pinker (1984: 244–245) lists 50 semantic elements that could be universal and they include event, state, thing, count/mass, and substance/aggregate.

The ability to categorize is not unique to humans. Certain animals are excellent at categorization, e.g. prairie dogs have sounds for specific colors, shapes, and sizes (Slobodchikoff 2010). Jackendoff (2002), based on Bickerton (1990), suggests that pre-linguistic primate conceptual structure may already use symbols for basic semantic relations. This may include spatial and causal concepts. "Agent First, Focus Last (...) are 'fossil principles' from protolanguage" (Jackendoff 2002: 249). *Homo erectus* (one million BP) may have had protolanguage. I will therefore assume that semantic features are part of our genotype but probably as a third factor rather than Universal Grammar if the latter is defined very tightly.

Semantic features are, however, not the only ones and I will now look at the acquisition of grammatical features, interpretable and uninterpretable ones, a little more. Here, I will assume a greater role for the third and second factor, as in e.g. Lebeaux (1988: 44) who argues that grammatical categories are centered in cognitive ones. As mentioned above, Chomsky (1995: 230, 381) suggests that "formal features have semantic correlates and reflect semantic properties (accusative Case and transitivity, for example)". This means that, if a language has nouns with semantic phi-features, the learner will be able to hypothesize uninterpretable features on another functional head (and will be able to bundle them there). Initially, a child would use lexical categories (as well as demonstrative pronouns) with interpretable features (see Radford 2000) which then would be experimented with as uninterpretable features. A third factor principle, such as (38), seems to be at work.

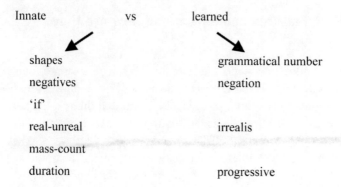

Figure 7: Innate vs learned features

(38) **Feature Economy**

    (a)   Utilize semantic features: use them as functional categories, i.e. as formal features.

    (b)   If a specific feature appears more than once, one of these is interpretable and the others are uninterpretable.

Principle (38a) is adapted from Feature Economy as it appears in e.g. van Gelderen (2011) and (38b) follows from Muysken (2008: 46) who writes that "features which are doubly expressed (...) but receive a single interpretation, must be functional". Thus, innate concepts such as time, cause, agent, etc. together with the data available to the child (modality or past tense) trigger the grammaticalization of the semantic features into interpretable and uninterpretable ones.

In Figure 7, some innate semantic categories are represented, as well as learned ones derived from them.

As we saw in (37), not only is there a substantial set of functional categories and features, there is also a strict order. How is the basic order acquired? There are two answers that are compatible with minimalism. (a) The order is due to a third factor effect, namely the relative scope of these categories. (b) The order and the categories themselves are innate, i.e. provided by Universal Grammar.

A third factor approach might be to think about scope. For instance, Bybee (1985: 15) formulates the notion of semantic relevance: "A category is relevant to the verb to the extent that the meaning of the category directly affects the lexical content of the verb stem". A verb stem describes an action or state so aspect is very relevant to it and will be merged closer to it than mood. Ernst (2002) comes to mind for an account in terms of scope as does Zagona's work (e.g. 2007) that the interpretation of modals depends on what they merge with. Hacquard (2010: 109), similarly, argues in connection with modal auxiliaries that the same modal verb can have a high and low meaning, i.e. epistemic or deontic, depending on how it relates to an event. "[A]n epistemic modal base needs to be bound by a contentful event, which both attitude and speech events are, but regular VP-events aren't". To put it in simpler terms, an epistemic modal expresses the likelihood of an assertion (and need not occur in an actual world) but a deontic modal modifies an actual event (and needs to occur in an actual world). One example of such ordering is that a "[p]erfective takes a predicate of events (VP) and returns a predicate of times, which then combines with tense" (Hacquard 2009: 294) and this determines the order.

The other possibility, namely that the order is given by Universal Grammar, is avoided as much as possible in current minimalism (although I think Chomsky's main worry that there was not enough evolutionary time for Universal Grammar to develop a lot of detail is not warranted if non-humans already have a lot of semantics, as mentioned above). The order could be third factor although Universal Grammar could also be involved, as Chomsky (2001: 12) suggests: "Assume that substantive categories are selected by functional categories. V by a light verb, T by C".

In this section, I have reviewed what is implicit in the Minimalist Program about semantic features, namely that they are innate. Whether this means they are part of the first or the third factor is an open question. Grammatical features can be seen as being abstracted away from these.

5 Conclusion

Semantic and grammatical features are central in the Minimalist Program, with a lot of explanatory power. A child needs to have lexical input for grammatical categories to appear but also needs some sense as to what to look for. In this paper, I have first provided an outline of the status of interpretable and uninterpretable features and have examined how they work in language change. I have also raised some issues on the acquisition of features. My conclusion is that the changes we see in language change are due to the child's use of Feature Economy. As a child learns a language, it will use semantic features in a grammatical way and this fuels the cyclical changes we see.

Sources

Corpus d'entretiens spontanés. Beeching, Kate. 1980–1990. *Un corpus d'entretiens spontanés. Enregistrés et transcrits par Kate Beeching*. Southampton, UK: LLAS Centre for Languages, Linguistics and Area Studies, University of Southampton. https://www.llas.ac.uk//resourcedownloads/80/mb016corpus.pdf.

COCA. Davies, Mark. 2008–. *The Corpus of Contemporary American English: 450 million words, 1990–present*. http://corpus.byu.edu/coca/.

COHA. Davies, Mark. 2010–. *The Corpus of Historical American English: 400 million words, 1810–2009*. http://corpus.byu.edu/coha/.

References

Allen, Cynthia. 1977. *Topics in diachronic English syntax*. Amherst, MA: University of Massachusetts dissertation.

Baker, Mark. 2008. *The syntax of agreement and concord*. Cambridge: Cambridge University Press.

Baptista, Marlyse. 2002. *The syntax of Cape Verdean Creole*. Amsterdam & Philadelphia: John Benjamins.

Benincà, Paola & Nicola Munaro. 2010. Introduction. In Paola Benincà & Nicola Munaro (eds.), *Mapping the left periphery*, 3–15. Oxford: Oxford University Press.

Bickerton, Derek. 1990. *Language and species*. Chicago, IL: University of Chicago Press.

Bybee, Joan 1985. *Morphology*. Amsterdam & Philadelphia: John Benjamins.

Carstens, Vicki. 2012. Delayed valuation: A reanalysis of "upwards" complementizer agreement and the mechanics of Case. http://ling.auf.net/lingBuzz/001432 (accessed 27 December 2013).

Chomsky, Noam. 1965. *Aspects of the theory of syntax*. Cambridge, MA: MIT Press.

Chomsky, Noam. 1993. *Language and thought*. Wakefield, RI: Moyer Bell.

Chomsky, Noam. 1995. *The Minimalist Program*. Cambridge, MA: MIT Press.

Chomsky, Noam. 2000. Minimalist inquiries: The framework. In Roger Martin, David Michaels & Juan Uriagereka (eds.), *Step by step: Essays in minimalist syntax in honor of Howard Lasnik*, 89–156. Cambridge, MA: MIT Press.

Chomsky, Noam. 2001. Derivation by phase. In Kenneth L. Hale & Michael J. Kenstowicz (eds.), *Ken Hale: A life in language*, 1–54. Cambridge, MA: MIT Press.

Chomsky, Noam. 2007. Approaching UG from below. In Uli Sauerland & Hans-Martin Gärtner (eds.), *Interfaces + recursion = language*, 1–29. Berlin & New York: Mouton de Gruyter.

Cinque, Guglielmo. 1999. *Adverbs and functional heads*. Oxford: Oxford University Press.

Cinque, Guglielmo & Luigi Rizzi. 2008. The cartography of syntactic structures. In Vicenzo Moscati (ed.), *CISCL Working Papers on Language and Cognition*, vol. 2, 43–59. Siena: CISCL, Università di Siena.

Ernst, Thomas. 2002. *The syntax of adjuncts*. Cambridge: Cambridge University Press.

Franzén, Torsten. 1939. *Etude sur la syntaxe des pronoms personnels sujets en ancien français*. Uppsala: Almqvist & Wiksells Boktryckeri.

Geach, Peter. 1957 *Mental acts*. London: Routledge & Kegan Paul.

van Gelderen, Elly. 1993. *The rise of functional categories*. Amsterdam & Philadelphia: John Benjamins.

van Gelderen, Elly. 2004. *Grammaticalization as economy*. Amsterdam & Philadelphia: John Benjamins.

van Gelderen, Elly. 2011. *The linguistic cycle*. Oxford: Oxford University Press.

Hacquard, Valentine. 2009. On the interaction of aspect and modal auxiliaries. *Linguistics and Philosophy* 32. 279–315.

Hacquard, Valentine. 2010. On the event-relativity of modal auxiliaries. *Natural Language Semantics* 18(1). 79–114.

Heine, Bernd & Tania Kuteva. 2002. *World lexicon of grammaticalization*. Cambridge: Cambridge University Press.

Hengeveld, Kees. 1992. *Non-verbal predication*. Berlin & New York: Mouton de Gruyter.

Hopper, Paul & Elizabeth Traugott. 2003. *Grammaticalization*. Cambridge: Cambridge University Press.

Jackendoff, Ray. 2002. *Foundations of language*. Oxford: Oxford University Press.

Katz, Aya. 1996. *Cyclical grammaticalization and the cognitive link between pronoun and copula*. Houston, TX: Rice University dissertation.

Kayne, Richard. 2005. Some notes on comparative syntax, with special reference to English and French. In Guglielmo Cinque & Richard Kayne (eds.), *The Oxford handbook of comparative syntax*, 3–69. Oxford: Oxford University Press.

Klaeber, Frederik. 1941 [1922]. *Beowulf*. 3rd edn. Boston: Heath & Co.

Lambrecht, Knud. 1981. *Topic, antitopic, and verb agreement in Non Standard French*. Amsterdam & Philadelphia: John Benjamins.

Lebeaux, David. 1988. Language acquisition and the form of the grammar. Amherst, MA: University of Massachusetts dissertation.

Li, Charles & Sandra Thompson. 1977. A mechanism for the development of copula morphemes. In Charles Li (ed.), *Mechanisms of syntactic change*, 414–444. Austin, TX: University of Texas Press.

Lockwood, William. 1968. *Historical German syntax*. Oxford: Clarendon Press.

McWhorter, John. 1997. *Towards a new model of creole genesis*. New York: Peter Lang.

Medeiros, David. 2012. *Economy of command*. Tucson, AZ: University of Arizona dissertation.

Muysken, Pieter. 2008. *Functional categories*. Cambridge: Cambridge University Press.

Nicholas, Nick. 1996. Copulas from pronouns. http://linguistlist.org/issues/7/7-1776.html (accessed 23 December 2013).

Pesetsky, David & Esther Torrego. 2001. T-to-C movement: Causes and consequences. In Kenneth L. Hale & Michael J. Kenstowicz (eds.), *Ken Hale: A life in language*, 355–426. Cambridge: MIT Press.

Peyraube, Alain & Thekla Wiebusch. 1994. Problems relating to the history of different copulas in Ancient Chinese. In Matthew Y. Chen & Ovid J.L. Tzeng (eds.), *In honor of William S.Y. Wang: Interdisciplinary studies on language and language change*, 383–404. Taipei: Pyramid Press.

Pinker, Steven. 1984. *Language learnability and language development*. Cambridge, MA: Harvard University Press.

Pustet, Regina. 2003. *Copulas: Universals in the categorization of the lexicon*. Oxford: Oxford University Press.

Radford, Andrew. 2000. Children in search of perfection: Towards a minimalist model of acquisition. *Essex Research Reports in Linguistics* 34. 57–74.

Sedgefield, Walter John (ed.) 1899. *King Alfred's Old English version of Boethius*. Oxford: Clarendon.

Sigurðsson, Halldór. 2011. Conditions on argument drop. *Linguistic Inquiry* 42(2). 267–304.

Slobodchikoff, Con. 2010. Alarm calls in birds and mammals. In Michael D. Breed & Janice Moore (eds.), *Encyclopedia of animal behavior*, vol. 1, 40–43. Oxford: Academic Press.

Siewierska, Anna. 2004. *Person*. Cambridge: Cambridge University Press.

Stassen, Leon. 1997. *Intransitive predication*. Oxford: Oxford University Press.

Thorpe, Benjamin. 1861. *Anglo-Saxon Chronicle I and II*. London: Longman.

Wang, Li. 1958. *Hanyu Shi Lunwen Ji* [Collected essays on the history of Chinese]. Beijing: Kexue Chubanshe.

Zagona, Karen. 2007. Some effects of aspect on tense construal. *Lingua* 117. 464–502.

Simon Kasper

3 Linking syntax and semantics of adnominal possession in the history of German

The present article is an attempt towards a unified picture of some central syntactic and semantic changes within complex (possessive) noun phrases in German. First, the expressive adnominal strategies for possessive relations in German are presented and the semantic concept of possession characterized. Then major changes in syntax-semantics linking within German adnominal (possessive) constructions are traced throughout different historical periods, along with changes of a purely structural kind. In what follows, these changes are modeled using the Role and Reference Grammar framework and an attempt is made to unify the observed data using the following principal components: 1) The prenominal position in complex German noun phrases becomes succes- sively reanalyzed as a position for article expressions, i.e., for Role and Reference Grammar operators. 2) This development competes with the tendency to ex- press the more referential/definite/agentive entity in the relation before the less referential/definite/agentive expression in the noun phrase. 3) Changes in the syntax-semantics linking of adnominal possession in the history of German can partially be explained in terms of this competition.

1 Introduction

In the New High German Standard language there are a number of strategies available for the expression of possessive relations by means of (complex) noun phrases.[1] The most important ones are given in (1). In general, the head (or nucleus, adopting Role and Reference Grammar [RRG] terminology)[2] of these constructions is the possessum expression, abbreviated "H". Its case is that of the whole noun phrase in the syntactic context of the clause. In the following examples, this is the nominative case. The dependent, or argument, of the head/nucleus is, if present, abbreviated "D". Its form depends on the construc- tion as a whole.

---

1 The notion of possession is clarified in Section 2.
2 See Van Valin and LaPolla (1997), Van Valin (2005).

(1) a. D-H:
$\qquad$ *Auto-reifen*
$\qquad$ car-tire
$\qquad$ 'car tire'

$\quad$ b. D_{gen} H (prenominal genitive construction):
$\qquad$ *Haralds* $\qquad$ *Hund*
$\qquad$ Harald.GEN $\quad$ dog
$\qquad$ 'Harald's dog'

$\quad$ c. H D_{gen} (postnominal genitive construction):
$\qquad$ *der* $\qquad$ *Hund* $\quad$ *des* $\qquad$ *Mannes*
$\qquad$ Det.NOM $\quad$ dog $\quad$ Det.GEN $\quad$ man
$\qquad$ 'the man's dog'

$\quad$ d. H *von* D_{dat}:
$\qquad$ *der* $\qquad$ *Hund* $\quad$ *von* $\quad$ *dem* $\qquad$ *Mann/von Harald*
$\qquad$ Det.NOM $\quad$ dog $\quad$ of $\quad$ Det.DAT $\quad$ man/of Harald
$\qquad$ lit. 'the dog of the man/Harald' / 'the man's/Harald's dog'

$\quad$ e. H *an/bei* D:
$\qquad$ *der* $\qquad$ *Nachteil* $\qquad$ *an/bei* $\quad$ *Harald*
$\qquad$ Det.NOM $\quad$ disadvantage $\quad$ at $\qquad$ Harald
$\qquad$ lit. 'the disadvantage of Harald'

$\quad$ f. H *zu* D:
$\qquad$ *der* $\qquad$ *Bruder* $\quad$ *zu* $\quad$ *Harald*
$\qquad$ Det.NOM $\quad$ brother $\quad$ to $\quad$ Harald
$\qquad$ lit. 'the brother to Harald' / 'Harald's brother'

$\quad$ g. Poss H:
$\qquad$ *sein* $\qquad$ *Hund*
$\qquad$ his.NOM $\quad$ dog
$\qquad$ 'his dog'

In non-standard varieties, ranging from colloquial German "down" to local dialects (cf. Schmidt and Herrgen 2011), (1c) is not available due to the almost complete absence of the genitive in these varieties (cf. Behaghel 1923: 479; Schirmunski 2010: 496; Mironow 1957: 391–398). There are only residues of constructions like (1b) containing proper names, and such residues are only found in some regional varieties/dialects, e.g., Low German and Valais German (cf. Wipf 1910; Bohnenberger 1913; Henzen 1932; Bart 2006). At the same time there is one construction in non-standard German that is completely absent from the standard but can be found in almost all regional varieties/dialects. It is given in (2).

(2) D_{dat} Poss H (adnominal possessive dative)
    dem   *Mann/*   *(dem)*   *Harald* *sein*   *Hund*
    Det.DAT man   (DET.DAT) Harald his.NOM dog.NOM
    lit. 'the man/Harald his dog' / 'the man's/Harald's dog'

Case is mostly indicated by means of the determiner system in German. Taking the definite masculine singular article as the paradigmatic case, Standard German can be described as a four case system exhibiting nominative, genitive, dative, and accusative. As mentioned above, non-standard varieties display an almost complete loss of the genitive. Most Low German varieties lack the dative as well, which syncretized with the accusative case. Western Central German and Western High German varieties show wide-spread syncretism between the nominative and the accusative with a preserved dative. Some varieties show a complete loss of case distinctions, resulting in a common case (cf. Shrier 1965; Koß 1983). The construction in (2) is usually called an "adnominal possessive dative" but this nomenclature is obviously based on the Standard German case system, where we do not find this construction, a fact which should be kept in mind throughout this article.

In the present article I will demonstrate some changes in the syntax-semantics linking that have come about in the expression of adnominal possession in German since the Old High German period, with a special focus on the adnominal possessive dative and its closest relatives from a semantic perspective – the attributive genitive constructions (1b, c) and the postnominal *von* construction (1d). Earlier research suggests that major, primarily syntactic changes have occurred in the German noun phrase (or the determiner phrase, respectively): the definite article developed in the Old High German period (cf. Oubouzar 1992), possessive pronouns (like those in [1g] and [2]) and genitive attributes (like those in [1b] and [1c]) changed their grammatical status (cf. Demske 2001), and the adnominal possessive dative, the origin of which is still not entirely clear (e.g., Weiß 2012), came into existence (cf. Zifonun 2003; Fleischer and Schallert 2011: 96–99). From a semantic perspective, the loss of the genitive in most German varieties (presumably from the 12th century on; cf. Kiefer 1910) could be expected to trigger a functional pressure to "find" or "invent" some syntactic means of expressing the associated semantics. Furthermore, it could be expected that the Middle High German split between prenominal and postnominal genitive attributes (see [1b] and [1c], cf. Ebert 1986: 89–98) and the grammaticalization of the formerly ablative/locative *von* 'of'/'from' (see [1d]) would have repercussions for the syntax-semantics linking.

In what follows, I first characterize the semantic concept of possession (Section 2), and then trace the changes in the syntax-semantics linking within German adnominal (possessive) constructions through different historical periods (Section 3) along with purely syntactic changes. These changes are modeled using the RRG framework (Section 4). Section 5 presents an attempt at the unification of the observed data. The steps in this unification are as follows. 1) The prenominal position in complex German noun phrases becomes successively reanalyzed as a position for article expressions, i.e., RRG operators. Contemporary German non-standard varieties exhibit different stages within this development. 2) This development competes with the tendency for the more referential/definite/ agentive entity in a relation to be expressed before the less referential/definite/ agentive expression in the noun phrase. 3) Changes in the syntax-semantics linking of adnominal possession in the history of German can partially be explained as a result of this competition.

2 Possession and the range of expressive strategies

Using the term "possession" suggests that there is an easily definable semantic concept of possession. This impression is deceptive because several different conceptual domains contribute to what we think of as possession (cf. Chappell and McGregor 1995; Heine 1997; Lehmann 1998; Seiler 1983, 2009). Rather than giving an exhaustive analysis of the conceptual sources, or ingredients, of possession (for this, see Heine 1997), I confine myself to pointing out its most important conceptual sources on the basis of the lexical or original meaning of the "construction markers" (Koptjevskaja-Tamm 2003) that occur in the constructions in question, i.e., (1b) to (1g) and (2).[3] This procedure yields results that are easily comparable to those of Heine (1997). It is important to note that in contemporary German, the prepositional construction markers found in (1b, d, e, and f) are nearly fully grammaticalized in these constructions with only little spatial meaning remaining. This means that today's grammatical constructions expressing possessive relations make use of markers that once indicated, and in other constructions continue to indicate, spatial relations in German, as shown in Figure 1:

---

3 Construction markers are elements within the NP that indicate a possessive relation between an H and a D.

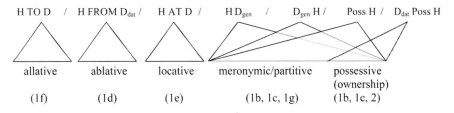

H TO D   /   H FROM D$_{dat}$ /   H AT D /   H D$_{gen}$ /   D$_{gen}$ H /   Poss H /   D$_{dat}$ Poss H

allative	ablative	locative	meronymic/partitive	possessive (ownership)
(1f)	(1d)	(1e)	(1b, 1c, 1g)	(1b, 1c, 2)

Figure 1: Conceptual sources of possession[4]

In the H TO D pattern (which [1f] conforms to), *zu* 'to' is originally, and in other constructions remains, a goal marker. *Von* 'from' in the H FROM D$_{dat}$ construction (cf. [1d]) is originally, and in other constructions in contemporary German remains, a source marker. *An/bei* 'at' in the H AT D construction (cf. [1e]) indicates location in less grammaticalized constructions. The old adnominal genitive (cf. [1b] and [1c]) is usually (and as far as we know) considered to express meronymic and partitive as well as possessive (ownership) relations (besides other relations outside of the realm of adnominal possession, cf. Behaghel 1923: 485–526; Wilmanns 1909: 575).[5] The dative is usually connected to possession (ownership) and participation (as well as other relations that do not belong to the realm of adnominal possession, cf. Behaghel 1923: 609–645). On the far right of the conceptual sources of possession there is "possessive (ownership)". There is a terminological inconvenience here which I do not know how to circumvent: alongside the diverse spatial relations and the part-whole relation presented in Figure 1, the complex conceptual domain of possession has at its core the concept of possession as ownership.

When looking at the conceptual sources of possession as presented in Figure 1, an apparent spatial perceptual basis emerges: allative, ablative, locative, and meronymic/partitive relations can well be characterized as spatial. Only possession as ownership does not immediately conform to this pattern. It seems to have cultural rather than spatial perceptual origins. Conceptually, however, possession as ownership might be reduced to location plus something like

---

4 Shading in the figures throughout this article has no special meaning but is due to the layered structure of the triangles.

5 The genitives named *objectivus*, *qualitatis*, *explicativus*, and *definitivus* belong to the class of non-partitive and non-possessive (ownership) genitives (cf. Eroms 2000: 282/283). The *genitivus subjectivus* is sometimes treated as a type of the *genitivus possessivus* (cf. Wilmanns 1909: 600; extending this argument, one could also treat the *genitivus auctoris* as a possessive genitive.) However, as will become evident in the text, possession (ownership) is reducible to concrete and spatial relationships between objects. The subjective genitive and the genitive of the author (*auctor*) do not express relations of that kind because they involve events or abstract entities that the "subject" or "author" bring about.

control (cf. Stolz et al. 2008: 17–28): the possessum "is at" the (location of the) possessor, who has it "at his/her disposal" (i.e., control). This relation also seems to lie at the heart of the verb *haben* 'have'. Semantically, we actually find that English *have* and German *haben* derive from Germanic **habæ-*, the durative form of Germanic **hafja-* 'lift' (cf. *heben*; cf. Kluge 2011). Thus, *have* has undergone an extension of meaning before which it meant something like 'hold' (German *halten*), which can very well be treated as the durative of 'lift'. Applying these insights to the spatial conceptual structures underlying possession, one can identify it as the combination of H's being located at/with D and at the same time as D's control of H.

Obviously, the relations we are talking about are binary ones, either spatial or possessive. The corresponding predicate-argument structures could look like (3a) and (3b):

(3) a. GO-TO/COME-FROM/BE-AT/BE-PART-OF (x, y)

    b. POSSESS (y, x)

The reversal between the arguments is the result of the fact that if x is at y and if y controls x, then y possesses x.

Another dimension to the domain of possession is that of alienability/inalienability: When looking at (4a) and (4b) we find a potential meaning difference:

(4) a. *Haralds*   *Bein*
        Harald.GEN   leg
        'Harald's leg'

    b. *das*   *Bein* *an* *Harald*
        Det.NOM leg   at   Harald
        lit. 'the leg at Harald' / 'the leg attached to Harald'

(4a) is a quite natural expression of the inalienable relation between Harald and his leg. When hearing (4b), in contrast, we infer that the leg in question need not, or even cannot be Harald's "inherent" leg. The rationale seems to be that the D_{gen} H construction is usually (though not exclusively) used to code inalienable relations, where the leg is initially understood to be inherently relational, while the H *an/bei* D construction is usually used to code alienable relations, where the leg is initially understood to stand in an established spatial relation with Harald (cf. Seiler 1983).

Besides the conceptual sources of possession and the alienability/established vs. inalienability/inherent opposition, animacy also seems to play a role. Note that from the perspective of the conceptual sources of possession depicted in Figure 1, all possessors except the ones standing in an ownership relation to the possessum should be open to any degree of animacy as listed in (5) (cf. Kuno and Kaburaki 1977; Silverstein 1976; Comrie 1989; Bickel 2010):

(5)   human > kin > animate > inanimate > abstract

This is indicated by the examples in (6):

(6)   a. *dem   Haus   sein   Balkon
          DET.DAT   house   its   balcony
          lit. 'the house its roof' / 'the roof of the house'

      b. der   Deckel   zu   dem   Topf
          DET.NOM   lid   to   DET.DAT   pot/pan
          lit. 'the lid to the pan' / 'the lid of the pan'

      c. der   Balkon   des   Hauses/   vom   Haus/
          DET.NOM   balcony   DET.GEN   house.GEN/   from-DET.DAT   house/

          am   Haus
          at-DET.DAT   house
          'the balcony of the house' / 'the balcony at the house'

      d. sein   Balkon
          its   balcony
          'its [= that of the house] balcony'

In other words, possession (ownership) seems to be restricted to at least animate entities, since its possessor must be capable of executing control (6a). The status of (6b) is difficult to assess. On the one hand (6b) seems acceptable, on the other hand *der Balkon zu dem Haus* 'the balcony of the house' and similar constructions seem less acceptable.

Taken together, the expressive adnominal possession strategies found in different periods need to be located within the semantic spectrum just sketched, ranging from the conceptual sources of the possessive relation to the alienability/established vs. inalienability/inherent opposition and to the animacy dimension. The conceptual semantic domains can be expected to remain constant through history and to require expressive strategies, whilst the corresponding syntactic strategies may vary. The next step is therefore to look at the syntactic options for the adnominal expression of possession available at different periods in German. I will focus mainly on the basic strategies represented by the H *von* D construction, the genitive constructions, and the adnominal possessive dative.

3 Syntactic strategies for expressing adnominal possession in the diachrony of German

3.1 Expressive strategies for adnominal possession in Old High German

Starting out from the position that speakers of Old High German needed expressive strategies for communicating ablative, meronymic/partititive and possessive (ownership) relations, we find that the corresponding syntactic options differed from those found in the contemporary standard and the non-standard varieties of German (see [1] and [2]).

The Old High German analogue of the contemporary German H *von* D construction is the NP *fon(n)(e/a)* NP construction. Note that the latter is not a single NP constituent but most probably consists of two adverbal constituents, the relation between which is encoded by a verbal predicate. In contrast, in an adnominal H *von* D construction the exact relation is not overtly coded by a verbal predicate but must be inferred. To my knowledge, there is no H *fon(n)(e/a)* D construction in Old High German that unambiguously expresses adnominal possession (cf. Kiefer 1910). Example (8) illustrates an ambiguous case. The Old High German NP *fon(n)(e/a)* NP construction can thus be assumed to not express meronymic/partitive and possessive (ownership) relations, but mainly adverbal ablative, albeit metaphoric (e.g., temporal) ones (cf. Behaghel 1924: 33–35). Structures like (8) are possible sources for the reanalysis of an adverbal relation as an adnominal one in later periods of German. Another, related observation is that the source role in an ablative relation is often inanimate, often even a location (or point in time), and that the relation is an established and not an inherent one. Additionally, (7) demonstrates that if the noun governed by *fóne* 'from' is in Latin, it appears in the ablative case.

(7)   *Fóne*   *déro*   *questione*   *chúmet*   *si*   *a*   *phisicam*
      From   this.DAT   question   come.3   she.3NOM   to   physiological.ACC
      disputationem
      discussion.ACC
      'From this question she comes to a physiological discussion.'
      (Notker, Consolatio, p. 182, l. 12)

(8)   *gibót*   *iz*   *ouh*   *zi uuáru* \   *ther*   *kéisor*   *fona*   *Rúmu.*
      command.3   it.ACC   and   indeed   DET.NOM   emperor   from   Rome
      'And indeed, the emperor commanded it from Rome.'
      (Otfrid, I, 11, 2)

(9) *Sih   scéident [...] gilíabe [...]   Múater   fona kínde [...].*
each-other separate.3PL loved-ones.NOM mother.NOM from child.DAT
'Loved ones ... separated from each other: ... Mother from child...'
(Otfrid, V, 20, 39–41)

When we look at the analogues of New High German genitive constructions
in Old High German, we find that there are two semantically separate constructions. In partial revision of Behaghel (1932: 181–193), Carr (1933) could show that,
in Old High German, non-partitive genitives almost always appear in prenominal
position. They occur in postnominal position only when a Latin original exhibits
this order. That means all genitive types (see note 5) as well as the one expressing possession (ownership) appear in front of the head/nucleus. An example of
a (probably) *genitivus qualitatis* is given in (10), a *genitivus possessivus* is given
in (11). On the other hand, partitive (and meronymic) genitives usually follow the
nucleus/head (Behaghel 1932: 178).

(10) *uzs   fona   paradises   bliidhnissu*
      away   from   paradise.GEN   joys.DAT
      'away from the joys of paradise'
      (Isidor, 5, 10)

(11) *dhiz   ist   chiquhedan   in   unseres   druhtines   nemin*
      this.NOM   is   said   in   our.GEN   lord.GEN   name.DAT
      'this is said in the name of our lord'
      (Isidor, 3, 3)

Some changes occur with Notker in the late Old High German period. From
this time on there seems to be a tendency to place names and designations
of persons in the prenominal/pre-head position and to place inanimate and
abstract entities in the postnominal/post-head position (cf. Carr 1933). A consequence of this development should be that non-partitive inanimate genitives
should now be placed after the head/nucleus of the complex noun phrase, at
odds with what we find in (10) or before Notker.

(12) *díu   geskáft   téro   dingo*
      DET.NOM   creation.NOM   DET.GEN   things.GEN
      'the creation of things'
      (Notker, Consolatio, p. 81, l. 16)

Turning to the Old High German analogue of the adnominal possessive
dative (D_{dat} Poss H), we can say, with some certainty, that this construction

does not yet exist (cf. Weiß 2012). The only Old High German types of constructions that come close to that construction are exemplified by (13) and (14):

(13) *Sámenont   ímo   sîne   heîligen*
      gather.3PL   him.DAT   his.NOM.PL saints.NOM
      'His saints gathered for him'
      (Notker, Psalter, p. 172, l. 5)

(14) *du   uuart   demo   balderes   uolon   sin-uuoz*
      there was   DET.DAT Balder.GEN   colt.DAT his/its.NOM-foot.NOM
      birenkict
      dislocate.PTCP
      'The foot of Balder's colt was affected by dislocation'
      (2. Merseburger Zauberspruch)

Usually, these constructions should be read as involving an adverbal free *dativus (in)commodi* or a dative of pertinence (*Pertinenzdativ*). These sentences allow an adnominal possessive interpretation, but they also allow a free dative reading in the sense of 'his saints gathered for him' and 'it happened to the disadvantage of Balder's colt that its foot was affected by dislocation'. Therefore, we cannot be sure about the status of these constructions. Other structural reasons why they should probably not be considered D_{dat} Poss H constructions are discussed in later sections (cf. Kiefer 1910; Behaghel 1923; Demske 2001).

The picture that emerges with respect to constant conceptual domains and expressive requirements for Old High German is that the prenominal genitive (D_{gen} H) is the primary, if not only, construction by means of which adnominal possession (ownership) is expressed in Old High German. The postnominal genitive (H D_{gen}) construction is reserved for partitive/meronymic relations in the time before Notker and to relations with inanimate Ds from Notker's time on. There is no adnominal possessive dative in Old High German. These considerations are condensed in Figure 2, which is modeled on Figure 1. The top line lists the conceptual sources of today's possessive constructions. They correspond to semantic domains (spatial ones, like allative, ablative etc., and others that are more than simply spatial, like possessive [ownership]). Old High German requires expressive strategies for these meaning domains and for the specific meanings within them. These are indicated in the bottom line. The triangles relate these expressive strategies not only to the specific meanings they are used to express but also to their own conceptual sources. The NP *fon(n)(e/a)* NP is shown in parentheses because it most probably consists of two adverbal

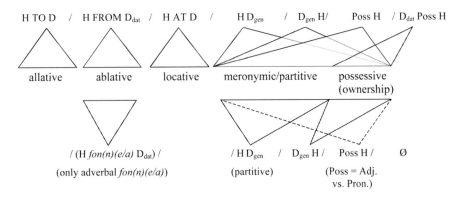

Figure 2: Old High German expressive strategies for adnominal possession

constituents. A consistent syntactic structure corresponding to Poss H does not yet exist in Old High German. It will emerge later from the D_{gen} H construction in Middle High German (see Section 4 for details). But we do find some possessive pronouns "already" behaving like adjectives in Old High German, as in (11), along with pronouns that are "still" personal pronouns in the genitive, as in *ira hûs* 'the house of hers'.

Taking the example of the ablative meaning, we see that there is a one-to-one mapping between the conceptual source H FROM D_{dat} and the expressive strategy NP *fon(n)(e/a)* NP, although this construction appears only adverbally, and with two constituents. We do not expect the ablative meaning to disappear or to change over time, but it is to be expected that syntactic constructions will change with respect to the range of meanings they can express. In Old High German, we do not find that the NP *fon(n)(e/a)* NP construction deviates from its ablative source meaning.

In sum, there appears to be a rather straightforward linking between adnominal syntactic constructions involving a genitival D on the one hand and partitive/meronymic and possessive semantics on the other, even though major syntactic changes already occur at Old High German times, for instance with Notker. Syntax-semantics linking between adnominal constructions involving prepositionally governed Ds and possessive semantics do not exist at this stage.

3.2 Expressive strategies for adnominal possession in Middle High German and Early New High German

Middle High German also requires means to express the meanings depicted in Figure 1, i.e., from allative to possessive (ownership). Turning first to the Middle

High German analogue of the New High German H *von* D construction, we find it in the H *von(e)* D construction. There is often an ambiguity between an ablative and a non-ablative reading in these constructions. Because Middle High German *geschëhen* 'happen' in (16) is not a motion verb, a purely adverbal ablative meaning of *rede von in* (lit. 'speech from him') is unlikely and an overlap of the H *von(e)* D construction with the meaning of the adnominal *genitivus auctoris* seems possible. The use of the latter would have required a genitive form of the personal pronoun of the 3rd Ps. Sg. Masc., i.e., something like *sîner rede* 'the speech of him', a construction that is indistinguishable from one with a possessive pronoun. As Ebert (1986: 92) notes, the *von* periphrasis becomes the primary strategy for expressing functions of the genitive, especially in pronominal contexts where genitives are not marked distinctly. (17) seems to have a partitive meaning, since an adverbal ablative reading of *ein teil von dîner nœte* 'part of your sorrows' seems to be excluded. In (18) the difference between the genealogical origin (ablative) and a possessive reading begins to blur: *dem vogte von den sahsen* could be understood as 'the reeve of the Saxons' and as 'the reeve from the Saxons'.

(15) | *Sus* | *sprach* | *der* | *künec* | *von* | *Brandigân* |
|---|---|---|---|---|---|
| thus | spoke | DET.NOM | king.NOM | of/from | Brandigan |

'Thus spoke the king of/from Brandigan'
(Parzival, 215, 15)

(16) | *dô* | *diu* | *rede* | *von* | *in* | *geschach* |
|---|---|---|---|---|---|
| after | DET.NOM | speech | from/of | him.ACC | happened |

lit. 'After the speech from him happened'
(Parzival, 389, 3)

(17) | «*Obylôt,* | *nu* | *sage mir /* | *ein teil* | *von* | *dîner* | *nœte.*» |
|---|---|---|---|---|---|---|
| Obylot | now | say me.DAT | a part | from/of | your.DAT | sorrows.DAT |

'Obylot, entrust part of your sorrows to me.'
(Parzival, 373, 16/17)

(18) | *Dem* | *vogte* | *von* | *den* | *Sahsen was daz wol geseit* |
|---|---|---|---|---|
| DET.DAT | reeve.DAT | from/of | DET.DAT | saxons was that well known.PTCP |

'This was well known to the reeve from/of the Saxons.'
(Nibelungenlied, A 208, 1; B 207, 1; C 210, 1 [*vogete*])

These observations are backed up by Kiefer (1910) (see also Behaghel 1924: 62; Ebert 1986: 92), who claims that from the 12th century on, the original genitive meanings begin to be expressed by the H *von(e)* D and other constructions discussed below. An important restriction is that a meronymic/partitive or a possessive semantics for a NP *von(e)* NP syntactic construction is possible only where *von(e)* NP is also reanalyzed as an adnominal rather than an adverbal phrase.

With respect to the genitive constructions, the changes found in the Old High German period continue into Middle High German. According to Ebert (1986) and Demske (2001), building on analyses by Carr (1933), expressions designating persons and names occur as prenominal genitives, whereas expressions designating things and abstract entities are placed after the head/nucleus of the complex phrase as postnominal genitives.[6] This development is completed as early as the 15th century (Early New High German period). From the 16th century on, two other developments take place. Firstly, appellative genitive expressions designating persons begin to "move" to postnominal position. This development is completed in the 17th century towards the beginning of the New High German/Modern German period, when these expressions are highly preferred in postnominal position (cf. Prell 2000; Demske 2001: 215–230). Secondly, postnominal partitive/meronymic genitives are reanalyzed as appositional nominatives or accusatives due to the loss of genitival morphology, e.g., *ein fesla guten alten wein* 'a keg of good aged wine' (cf. Behaghel 1923: 532).

The first of these developments seems to have begun in pre-Old High German times. Germanic attributive genitives probably occurred prenominally, independently of their semantics. In early Old High German the partitive ones tend to occur postnominally. The data for Early New High German in the 17th century are thus part of a process of diachronic postposing of attributive genitives that had by then already been going on for maybe a thousand years, and is not yet finished today.

Turning back again to Middle High German and to its analogue of the contemporary adnominal possessive dative (D_{dat} Poss H), we find that this is the period in which we can first identify unambiguous examples of this construction. However, case on the possessor is ambiguous between genitive and dative in (19). Although unambiguously a dative in (20), one should not infer that it is also a dative in (19) because there are also constructions with unambiguous genitives, as in (21).

---

6 This process takes place earlier in Middle High German prose than in Middle High German verse. The latter seems to be more conservative and influenced by the constraints of meter and rhyme (cf. Prell 2000).

(19) *Ich   sach   ir   iren   stolzen   lîp.*
     I   saw   her.GEN/DAT   her.ACC   proud   body
     'I saw her proud body.'
     (Die Beichte, 63)[7]

(20) *dô   sach   man   trüebe   unde   naz /   dem   Bernaer*
     Then   saw   one   hazy   and   wet   DET.DAT   one-from-Berne.DAT
     sîniu   ougen
     his.ACC   eyes.ACC
     'One saw the hazy and wet eyes of the one from Berne there.'
     (Dietrichs Flucht, 7817)

(21) *swaz   ich   von   Parzivâl   gesprach, /   des   sin   âventiur*
     what   I   of   Parzival   told   DET.GEN   his.NOM   adventure.NOM
     mich   wiste,
     me.ACC   know
     'what I told about Parzival whose adventure I came to know'
     (Willehalm 4, 20)

These constructions are only rarely attested in Middle High German and they are not easy to find (cf. Weise 1898; Kiefer 1910; Behaghel 1923: 638–640; Weiß 2012). However, it is remarkable that in the few examples we know of, the dependent possessor expression is mostly one designating a person and mostly a proper name, (19) being an exception. The marginal Middle High German D_{dat} Poss H construction thus shares the tendency with the attributive genitive constructions to place expressions designating persons in the prenominal position. In fact, there is no evidence for postnominal possessive datives in the history of German. Similar to the H *von(e)* D construction, it seems that the syntax-semantics linking between D_{dat} Poss H and possession (ownership) is possible only where NP_{dat} Poss NP has been reanalyzed as one adnominal constituent rather than two adverbal constituents.[8]

---

7 Cf. Schröder (1969) for further information on the editions of this text.
8 When interpreted adverbally, ambiguous constructions like *dass ihm seine Beine schmerzen*, lit. 'that to him his legs ache' are instances of a *dativus incommodi*, where the pain occurs to the disadvantage of the referent of *ihm* 'him'. An adnominal interpretation is no paraphrase of the adverbal one, since there is no *incommodi* meaning. It simply means 'that his legs ache'. Because of their similarity of meaning, however, the adverbal construction is a likely candidate for the source of the reanalysis as an adnominal construction.

Turning to the Poss H construction, it seems to be established in Middle High German with Poss behaving consistently like an adjective, including those cases where Old High German exhibited personal pronouns. This is illustrated in (19) by *iren* 'her.ADJ' (see also Section 4).

The resulting pattern, i.e., the relationship between meanings that need expression and the actual expressive strategies for Middle High German and Early New High German is given in Figure 3 below.

The dotted lines indicate changes in the syntax-semantics linking, where some syntactic structure emerges or extends its semantic range. In the case of Middle High German and Early New High German, the H *von(e)* D construction begins to be used for the expression of meronymic/partitive and possessive (ownership) meanings. Its original ablative meaning lives on. The H D_{gen} construction, restricted to meronymic/partitive meanings in Old High German, begins to be extended to possessive (ownership) relations as well. This happens in those contexts where appellative person expressions "move" into the postnominal position. Possessors (and hence ownership) are necessarily among these expressions. The D_{gen} H construction is thus more and more restricted to relations with human possessors expressed by proper names (and some kin expressions). At the same time we witness the emergence of the first unambiguous adnominal possessive dative constructions. Its characteristic feature in this period is the occurrence of both dative (in Middle and Early New High German) and genitive (possibly in Middle High German, definitely in Early New High German) possessors.

Without attempting to provide a causal explanation, it seems noteworthy that highly relevant processes in the linking of syntax and semantics take place nearly simultaneously in Middle High German and Early New High German: the

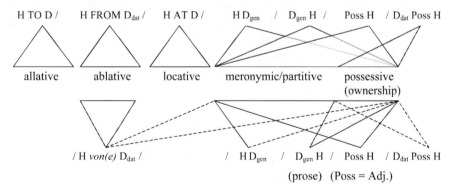

Figure 3: Middle High German/Early New High German expressive strategies for adnominal possession

H *von(e)* D and the D$_{dat}$ Poss H constructions begin to be used for originally genitival functions (see Figure 3) in higher frequency at the same time as the adverbal genitive object begins to come under pressure from other, mostly prepositional and accusative, object types (cf. Fleischer and Schallert 2011: 87–94 for an overview). Importantly, these changes from genitive to accusative and prepositional expressions result in the loss of the original expressive strategy for partitivity. In the adverbal domain, partitivity thus has to be expressed by other means, for instance by using the determiner/quantifier system (*Brot essen* 'eat some bread' vs. *ein Brot essen* 'eat a bread') or prepositional objects with *von* (*vom Brot essen* 'eat some of the bread'; cf. Ebert 1986: 37/38).

Keeping these broader changes in mind, the observable changes in the syntax-semantics linking of adnominal constructions gravitate around two seemingly independent phenomena: firstly, changes that revolve around the prenominal and postnominal positions in the German noun phrase, resulting, for instance, in a broadening of the meanings expressible with the H D$_{gen}$ construction, and secondly, changes that involve the reanalysis of formerly adverbal constituents as a single adnominal constituent, accompanied by the rise of new meanings for the newly developed syntactic constructions.

3.3 Expressive strategies for adnominal possession in contemporary non-standard German varieties

In the introduction I mentioned that non-standard German varieties exhibit different patterns of case syncretism and different degrees of case loss. Very few of them have a preserved, and still productive, genitive, e.g., the highest Alemannic dialects of Valais German (cf. Wipf 1910; Bohnenberger 1913; Henzen 1932, Bart 2006). Three-case systems in Central and High German and two-case systems in Low German varieties predominate. The nearly complete absence of the genitive has important repercussions for the expressive strategies associated with the constant meanings in Figure 1. The H *von* D construction (with its regional characteristics) is omnipresent and has – from the perspective of its areal distribution – become the primary strategy for the expression of meronymic/partitive and possessive (ownership) relations (cf. Mironow 1957: 395; Schirmunski 2010: 495–500). The original ablative meaning of this construction seems to be semantically outweighed by the partitive/meronymic and possessive (ownership) meanings.[9] In the H *von* D construction the case of the

---

9 The ablative meaning can also be expressed using the preposition *aus* 'out of, from', as in *der Schneider aus/von Panama* 'the tailor from Panama'.

possessor is governed by the preposition, depending on the case system of the variety in question. It may thus be a dative where this is a distinct case category (i.e., most West Central German and High German varieties) or an accusative (i.e., East Central German and most Low German varieties) or a common case (i.e., some Low German varieties). The H *von* D construction can also be found in Valais German (cf. Henzen 1932: 100–102) as an expressive strategy for meronymic/partitive and possessive (relations).

Turning to the D_{dat} Poss H construction, we find that it is the other main strategy for expressing meanings formerly associated with the genitive in non-standard German varieties alongside the H *von* D construction. For colloquial German and many regional and dialectal varieties it has been assumed that the adnominal possessive dative is restricted to animate possessors (e.g., Wegener 1985: 49; Behaghel 1923: 540). This would indicate its restriction to "real" possessive (ownership) relations. However, such claims neglect a considerable amount of data. It seems that it is common in Low German varieties to have expressions like (22).

(22)   *mien*   *Huus*   *sien* …
       my   house   his/its
       lit. 'my house its [H]; the [H] of my house';
       (Lindow et al. 1998: 160)

Here, it is perfectly natural to use inanimate possessors. In the context of the research project "Syntax hessischer Dialekte (SyHD)" (cf. www.deutscher-sprachatlas.de/projekte/syhd/index_html and Fleischer, Kasper, and Lenz 2012) we have collected data from Hessian dialects which show that in dialects coming from the Southern Rhine-Franconian parts of Hesse, the construction seems to become increasingly grammaticalized. While the construction with animate possessors like (23) can be found across all of Hesse (and in most High and Central German areas), there are also a number of constructions of the type exemplified by (24).

(23) *de*   *Gertrud ihr*   *Bröll*   East-Hessian, Kerzell
      DET.DAT Gertrud her.NOM glasses.NOM
      lit. 'the Gertrud her glasses' / 'Gertrud's glasses'

(24) *de*   *Bopp*   *ehrn*   *Fuß*   Rhine-Franconian, Ernsthofen
      DET.DAT puppet.DAT her.NOM foot.NOM
      lit. 'the puppet her foot' / 'the foot of the puppet'

These constructions with inanimate but human-like possessors seem to enter Hesse from the South. That similarity to humans probably plays a role is indicated by the fact that just one out of 700 informants produced an adnominal possessive dative for the relation in (25) with an inanimate and non-anthropomorphic possessor (here: a [toy] crane).[10] The *von* construction was almost the exclusive variant here.

(25) *de   Oarm vun deum   Kran*   Rhine-Franconian, Ernsthofen
    DET.NOM arm   of   your.DAT crane.DAT
    lit. 'the arm from your (toy) crane' / 'the arm of your (toy) crane'

The Low German and Hessian data indicate that, if they have a possessor that bears some similarity to human beings, adnominal possessive datives may code partitive/meronymic relations as well, at least in some German varieties.

It is also often purported that the D_{dat} Poss H construction does not appear with first and second person possessors (e.g., Zifonun 2003: 101; Behaghel 1923: 638).[11] However, these can be found in Low German (predicative constructions) and Berlin German:

(26) *dat   is   mien/dien   sien?*
      that   is   my/your   his
      lit. 'that is my/your his; is this mine/yours?'
      (Lindow et al. 1998: 165)

(27) *meiner/deiner   seiner*
      my/your   his
      lit. 'my/you're his'/ 'mine/my / your(s)'
      (Schiepek 1898/1909: 221, cit. in Weiß 2008: 393)

A last observation concerns the status of the possessive element. In some areas it lacks the typical gender agreement with the possessor that for instance

---

10 Methodological wariness prevents me from drawing the conclusion that the D_{dat} Poss H construction is a possible expressive strategy for the partitive/meronymic relation. A single occurrence among 700 is probably an exception.

11 Behaghel even considers a possessor expressed by a third person pronoun impossible, i.e., *ihm sein Hut* (lit. 'him his hat'). This is clearly contradicted by a wealth of data (e.g., Henn-Memmesheimer 1986: 144–146).

occurs in (22) to (24). Instead, a default element is placed between D and H, as exemplified by (28):[12]

(28) *de*   *Gertrud soi*   *Brell*   Central Hessian, Niederweidbach
     DET.DAT.F Gertrud his/its.NOM.M/N glasses.NOM
     lit. 'the Gertrud his/its glasses' / 'Gertrud's glasses'

It was mentioned in the introduction that the designation "adnominal possessive dative" draws on Standard German nomenclature. However, case on the possessor may well differ, depending on the case system of the variety in question. In particular, Weiß (2008: 384) claims that D in this construction bears the genitive in those varieties where this case category is preserved, that it bears the dative where the genitive is lost, that it bears the accusative where both genitive and dative are lost, and that it bears the common case where all case distinctions have been lost. This can be summarized in (29) (cf. Weiß 2008: 384):

(29)   Case of the possessor in the "adnominal possessive dative" construction:
      gen > dat > acc > common

However, Weiß' (2008) generalization does not account for the absence of the whole construction in a variety, as with Valais German, which lacks the adnominal D_{dat} Poss H almost entirely. Revising, we can state that (29) holds true if this construction is available in the given variety. Another possible problem is Henzen's (1932: 101) claim that the dative is an option besides the genitive in predicative constructions, for instance in *dits iš dm luikxas* 'this is the.DAT Lukas' / 'Lukas owns this'. Unless we can exclude that this is change in progress, however, Weiß' generalization need not be dismissed.[13]

In most non-standard varieties, the Poss H construction seems to have a status similar to the Standard German analogue. However, one cannot exclude uses of Poss in conservative varieties, conserving states of Early New High German, Middle High German, or even Old High German. More data are necessary at this

---

12 This observation needs to be distinguished from another: In many West Middle German varieties other than Central Hessian, feminine proper nouns get the neuter gender: *das Gertrud* 'the.NEUT Gertrud'. Poss in these varieties agrees with D_{dat} in gender, e.g., *dem Gertrud seine Brille* ('Gertrud's glasses'). In contrast, Poss in (28) as a default element is independent of the gender of D_{dat}.

13 In fact, Henzen (1932: 101) mentions the optional dative in predicative possessive constructions in the context of his discussion of "changes that alter the traditional status of the genitive" ("[…] daß der gen. auf dem wege ist, in seiner althergebrachten geltung veränderungen zu erfahren.")

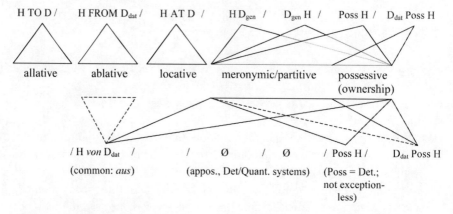

Figure 4: Expressive strategies for adnominal possession in contemporary non-standard German varieties (genitive lost)

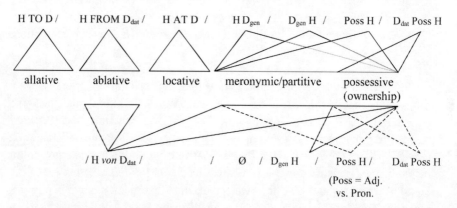

Figure 5: Expressive strategies for adnominal possession in a contemporary non-standard German variety (genitive preserved)

point. One attested exception is Valais German, where we indeed find a pattern similar to the Old High German one with coexisting adjectival and personal pronominal uses (cf. Wipf 1910: 144).

The resulting picture for those varieties lacking the genitive is given in Figure 4. The picture for Valais German as an example of a variety with a preserved genitive is given in Figure 5.

The dotted lines leading from the H *von* D_{dat} construction to the ablative meaning indicate that the primary function of this construction is no longer the expression of ablative relations, but rather to express meronymic/partitive and possessive (ownership) relations. The loss of the genitive constructions for expressing partitivity/meronymy is further compensated for by appositional constructions and the determiner/quantifier systems. The second expressive strategy for possessive (ownership) relations is the D_{dat} Poss H construction. The data from (22) and (24) are reflected in the dotted lines encompassing meronymic/partitive relations.

The pattern in Figure 5 is mainly based on data of Bart (2006), collected in the context of the "Syntaktischer Atlas der deutschen Schweiz (SADS)" (see http://www.ds.uzh.ch/dialektsyntax/ and references there). In the region in question the D_{dat} Poss H is only marginally used. This may be due to the fact that the prenominal genitive is still used for many originally genitival functions.[14] Postnominal genitives are not used at all (Bart, p.c.). However, the observation that the H *von* D_{dat} construction is used very frequently for both meronymic/partitive and possessive relations suggests that there is no simple relationship between the presence or absence of the genitive and the presence or absence of alternative strategies.

Assuming that it is today's non-standard (i.e., regional) varieties which continue the diachronic changes discussed above, and that they – to a certain degree – map diachronic changes onto space,[15] one global tendency in the syntax-semantics linking emerges. An originally few-to-few or even one-to-one mapping between adnominal constructions and meronymic/partitive and possessive (ownership) relations in Old High German (see Figure 2) is developing into many-to-many mappings. The latter are a result of two processes. Firstly, some new adnominal syntactic constructions arise (e.g., D *von* H, D_{dat} Poss H) as means to express meronymic/partitive and possessive (ownership) relations and become established alongside the ones that exist in Middle High German/Early New High German (see Figure 3). Secondly, certain adnominal constructions broaden their semantic range depending on the syntactic options available in the respective varieties (Figures 4 and 5).[16] H D_{gen} in Middle High German extends to possession (ownership); D_{dat} Poss H in contemporary non-standard varieties extends to meronymic/partitive relations (Figure 4). Together with the fact that the D *von* H construction encodes both meronymic/partitive and possessive (ownership) relations from the very beginning, this leads to the existence

---

14 A different explanation would be that D_{dat} Poss H only gradually emerges from the D_{gen} (Poss) H construction, as Weiß (2008, 2012) proposes.

15 The latter aspect is illustrated by the contrast between Valais German and Central German varieties, where the former represents an earlier and the latter represent a later state with respect to the changes discussed here, e.g., the expansion of the D von H and D_{dat} Poss H constructions and the structural changes within the NP.

16 This also concerns the New High German standard variety (see following section).

of several polysemous constructions in Middle High German/Early New High German, the contemporary non-standard varieties, and even contemporary Standard German (see next section). That means, from a syntax-semantics linking perspective, that it is often not initially clear for an interpreter whether some syntactic structure is to be interpreted as a possessive (ownership), meronymic/ partitive, or even an ablative (in the case of D *von* H) relation. I will return to these matters in Section 5.

3.4 Expressive strategies for adnominal possession in contemporary Standard German

Syntax-semantics linking in Standard German can be discussed rather briefly. The H *von* D construction is used for meronymic/partitive and possessive (ownership) relations. Ablative relations are primarily expressed by a construction with *aus* 'out of, from'. The prenominal and postnominal genitives can be connected to earlier developments: Only proper nouns and some kin expressions occur in prenominal position, otherwise this construction seems rather archaic (cf. Demske 2001: 251). Given the necessarily animate status of the possessor, this construction tends to be interpreted as a possessive (ownership) one (see Section 5 below on this point), but partitive/meronymic interpretations are also possible. All other genitives occur in the postnominal position. No restriction to either partitive/meronymic or possessive (ownership) relations can be postulated for this construction. The D_{dat} Poss H construction is absent from Standard German. Note that in both Valais German and Standard German the presence of the genitive correlates with the absence or marginal status of this otherwise highly prominent construction. Poss in the Poss H construction has the status of a determiner and expresses meronymic/partitive and possessive (ownership) relations. These considerations are summarized in Figure 6. The dotted lines from the prenominal genitive construction to the meronymic/partitive meaning indicate a possessive (ownership) relation is dominant for this construction. In addition, the polysemous status of many of the adnominal constructions diagnosed for Middle High German/Early New High German and the non-standard varieties also holds true for Standard German.

After this rather global sketch of the historical states and diachronic processes concerning the linking of syntax and semantics in German adnominal possessive constructions, the next section takes a closer look at rather subtle syntactic changes within the German noun phrase – syntactic changes that must be part of an explanation of the transformations reported on above.

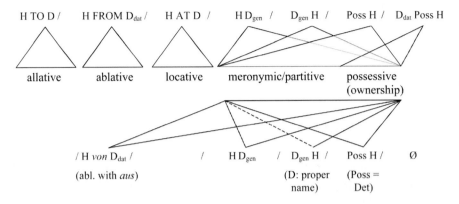

Figure 6: Expressive strategies for adnominal possession in contemporary Standard German

4 Syntactic changes in the German noun phrase: an RRG perspective

The developments sketched in Section 3 seem to follow an inherent "logic": Three developments that extend over several periods in the history of the German language are observable:

i. The genitive as a case category is gradually replaced by other constructions.

ii. Prenominal attributive genitives gradually move into the postnominal position, with only proper nouns and some kin expressions left in the prenominal position.

iii. The almost complete decay of the genitive case category and with it the disappearance of the original expressive strategy for partitivity/meronymy and possession (ownership) is accompanied by the expansion of the H *von* D construction from an original ablative meaning to the original genitive meanings and by the rise of the D_{dat} Poss H construction.

The causes of (i) seem numerous and are not entirely clear. It has been mentioned above that adverbal genitives were gradually replaced by competing constructions featuring accusatives and prepositional objects. This development could be associated with the loss of an aspectual category in German, but fails to provide a sufficient explanation, since it does not cover ditransitive constructions involving a genitive (cf. Fleischer and Schallert 2011: 83–101 for an overview). Another factor seems to be the decay of distinct inflectional genitive forms causing syncretism with other case categories (cf. Behaghel 1923: 479–483). Whether or not, or in which way this is causally connected to the aforementioned considerations is not entirely clear.

The causes of (ii) can probably be connected to syntactic changes in the German noun phrase. The general pattern seems to be as follows: Prenominal elements in German noun phrases are gradually reanalyzed as determiners (for details on this and the following, see Demske 2001). Part of this is a) the development of the definite article out of the demonstrative pronoun in Old High German (cf. Oubouzar 1992), b) the reanalysis of the possessive pronoun as an adjective (Old High German or pre-Old High German) and then as a determiner (New High German), c) the reanalysis of prenominal attributes as determiners (New High German) (cf. Weiß 2008).

a) According to Demske (2001), the demonstrative pronoun in Old High German marks pragmatic definiteness, its absence unmarked definiteness. Whenever it occurs, the demonstrative occurs with adjectival attributes of the weak declension. Strongly inflected attributes occur in the absence of the demonstrative. Unique referents occur without a demonstrative in early Old High German. "In Old High German the definite article word accompanies nominals representing sortal concepts. The noun provides sortal information about the referent which is applicable to precisely one entity in the given context." (Demske 2001: 116, my translation). Thus, the distribution of strong and weak attributive adjectives is semantically motivated in terms of pragmatic definiteness. However, already in late Old High German (with Notker) demonstratives begin to be used with semantically definite expressions (cf. Oubouzar 1992): The referents of these expressions are identifiable independently of the context, e.g., *diu sunna* 'the sun', so the demonstrative is redundant. And in New High German *die Tochter eines armen Bauern* 'the daughter of a poor farmer' "the definite article does not express definite reference, but the definiteness of the connection between the head noun and the article." (Demske 2001: 109, my translation). The association of adjectival declension (strong/weak) and definiteness that worked in Old High German may have become blurred in Early New High German, where the adjectival inflection was partially lost. The relation between article and noun had to be reanalyzed as being morphologically licensed, not semantically: The determiner governs the declension of the attributive adjective morphologically, not semantically.

b) Related to this development is that of the possessive pronoun (cf. Demske 2001: 132–163). In Old High German many possessive pronouns already show the inflection of the strong adjective and agree with the head noun in case, number, and gender. However, some of them behave like personal pronouns in the genitive. In Middle High German the possessive pronoun is established as an adjective. It co-occurs with articles and does not determine the strong or weak forms of attributive adjectives. It may occur prenominally or postnominally, like other adjectives. In New High German adnominal possessive pronouns are not adjectives any more. They show the inflectional pattern of the indefinite article and show complementary distribution with following adjectives as regards strong or weak declension.[17] And in contrast to Old High German and Middle High German, they show complementary distribution with the definite and indefinite articles and cannot occur postnominally. Noun phrases with possessive articles are definite in the sense that their referents are identifiable. As regards the gradual reanalysis of prenominal elements as determiners, the possessive article is hence the product of the same processes as the definite article, and the results are two inflectional paradigms for possessive pronouns in New High German: one for adnominal possessive articles (*sein schönes Buch* 'his nice book'), and one for possessive pronouns (as in: *Seins ist ein schönes Buch* 'His one is a nice book').

c) The changes associated with attributive genitives discussed in Section 3 can also be connected to the reanalysis processes in the German noun phrase discussed above (cf. Demske 2001: 208–230). As a consequence of the rise of morphologically motivated definite articles, prenominal genitives in New High German are reanalyzed as determiners just like possessive pronouns. They show complementary distribution with respect to definite articles (**das Peters Buch* 'the Peter's book'), unlike in earlier times. Postnominal, but not prenominal genitives may be modified to the right (**Peters, der aus Bremen kommt, Buch* 'Peter who is from Bremen's book' vs. *das Buch Peters, der aus Bremen kommt* 'The book of Peter who is from Bremen') and to the left (**des armen Peters Buch* 'poor Peter's book' vs. *das Buch des armen Peters* 'the book of poor Peter'). This was possible up until the Early New High German period. Just like definite and possessive articles, prenominal genitives determine the declension of following adjectives (*Pauls erster Roman* 'Paul's first novel'). The strong declension indicates that *-s* does not bear grammatical information except that indicating possession (ownership) (cf. Weiß 2008).

How can the changes in (iii) be reconciled with this? Prepositional attributes including the H *von* D construction seem not to be affected by the reformation of the prenominal position. Instead, this construction takes over the semantic range of the originally prenominal genitives. When we look at the D_{dat} Poss H construction, we have another prenominal attribute. If the changes reported on above were valid without exception, we would expect diagnoses similar to those for the possessive pronoun and the prenominal genitive. The prenominal cluster

---

17 One of the reviewers provides an alternative characterization of these states of affairs with which I agree, namely that the distribution of the strong or weak adjectival declension is exactly the same as for the indefinite article.

indeed seems to determine the declension of following adjectives (*dem Paul sein erster Roman*, lit. 'the Paul his first novel') and is in complementary distribution with the definite article (**der dem Peter sein erster Roman* 'the.NOM the.DAT Peter his first novel'). However, it may be modified to the left or the right (*dem armen Peter von Gegenüber sein Buch* 'the.DAT poor Peter from across [from here] his book') and it may be multiplied, as in (30), taken from the SyHD data:

(30) *em*   *Peere*   *seiner*   *Freundin*   Rhine-Franconian, Ober-Kinzig
      DET.DAT   Peter   his.DAT   girlfriend

      ihr   *nei*   *Audo*
      her.NOM   new   car
      'the new car of Peter's girlfriend'

The latter observations do not fit the pattern. D_{dat} in the D_{dat} Poss H construction cannot be considered a pure article expression but it seems to have the status of a constituent. Poss alone could be considered an article marking H as definite, in accordance with the reanalysis of possessive pronouns as articles. But the data in (26) to (28) above seem to point in another direction. Poss in these sentences is no longer an anaphor, since it does not agree with D in gender. If it determines the strong declension in following adjectives in these varieties, then it also lacks grammatical features and must be considered an element indicating nothing but a possessive (ownership) relationship. Poss would then no longer be an article in varieties where (28) is possible ([26] and [27] being predicative constructions). I would therefore propose the following: Poss in D_{dat} Poss H constructions is in different states of grammaticalization in contemporary German varieties. Where it develops into a mere marker of a possessive (ownership) relationship (cf. Koptjevskaja-Tamm 2003: 623–626), the construction as a whole including D_{dat} is on its way to being reanalyzed as a definite article expression, just like New High German possessive articles and prenominal genitives. In varieties where it maintains its grammatical features, it may work as a definite article, the D_{dat} component being an argument expression in terms of Role and Reference Grammar (RRG).

In what follows, I propose syntactic representations of Old High German, Middle High German/Early New High German, and Standard New High German possessive noun phrases as well as those from non-standard varieties within the framework of RRG (cf. Van Valin and LaPolla 1997; Van Valin 2005). These representations illustrate the aforementioned syntactic changes within the German (possessive) noun phrase throughout its history.

RRG belongs to the functional tradition of grammar theories and views syntax as standing in the service of semantics and pragmatics. Syntactic units are therefore considered to either have semantic correlates or be pragmatically motivated. The syntactic representation is organized into layers that correspond to pieces of predicate-argument structures, i.e., semantic representation. The idea is that this allows a representation of syntax that is valid for all languages. The syntax-semantics correlations are given below (cf. Van Valin and LaPolla 1997: 27).

Table 1: Correlations between semantic elements and syntactic units in RRG

semantic elements	syntactic units
predicate/reference	nucleus
argument	core argument
non-argument	periphery
predicate + arguments	core
predicate + arguments + non-arguments	clause/NP (= core + periphery)

Inside the clause, but outside the core there is another, non-universal position called the precore slot (PrCS), where *wh*-expressions or topicalized elements can occur, for instance. Left-detached adverbs, noun phrases, or prepositional phrases that are set off from the rest of the clause by an intonational break etc. can stand before precore elements (e.g., *Yesterday, what did you show to Peter?*) in what is called the left-detached position (LDP), considered to lie outside the clause, but inside the sentence. These positions are mainly pragmatically motivated. Categories like definiteness, aspect, negation, modality, tense, evidentiality, illocutionary force and so on are treated as operators, since they are qualitatively different from the semantic notions in predicate-argument structures that underlie syntactic categories. Operators are accorded a representation separate from the syntactic structure, unlike functional categories in the Principles and Parameters or Minimalist frameworks. Different operators in RRG apply to different layers of the clause/NP, where higher layer operators have scope over lower layer ones. RRG acknowledges the considerable parallelism between clauses and noun phrases and grants noun phrases a layered structure, too. One difference is that the analogue of a clausal nucleus dominates a PRED "predicate", while the nominal nucleus dominates a REF "reference". There is nothing in a noun phrase that exactly fits the clausal PrCS, LDP, or the core-internal subject position, since prenominal noun phrases behave like PrCS, LDP, or core internal subject elements in some respects. Therefore, the noun phrase structure includes a unique NP-initial position (NPIP) for these elements. NPIP is outside the core

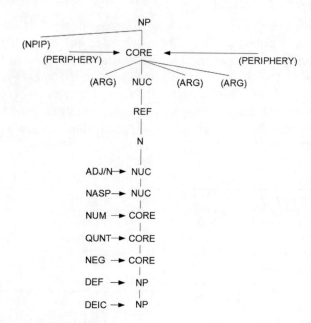

Figure 7: Layered structure of the NP

but inside the noun phrase. The general schema of the layered structure of a noun phrase is given in Figure 7:[18]

The projection below N is the operator projection, above N resides the syntactic representation with its different layers. Note that definiteness appears exclusively in the operator projection of N and has no dedicated role in the syntactic representation (cf. Van Valin 2005: 24).

Applying this to the Old High German D_{gen} H construction expressing a possessive (ownership) relation yields Figures 8 and 9, the latter illustrating the structure of (11) above. What these structures illustrate is the change from an argument personal pronoun (*ira*.GEN.F 'her/of her') to a possessive adjective standing in NPIP (*unseres*.GEN 'of our'), which took place partially in Old High German and in the transition to Middle High German.

Note that in Old High German, genitival attributes can be expanded to the left and to the right by modification (periphery).

As discussed in Section 3, all kinds of D occur prenominally in Old High German, whereas partitive/meronymic genitives occur postnominally. The fact

---

18 Operators: ADJ/N: adjectival/nominal modification; NASP: nominal aspect; NUM: number; QUNT: quantity; NEG: negation; DEF: definiteness; DEIC: deictics. For details see Van Valin and LaPolla (1997: 56).

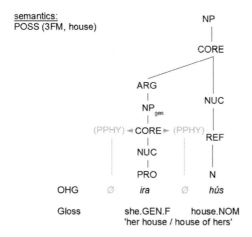

Figure 8: Old High German D$_{gen}$ H construction expressing possessive (ownership) relation

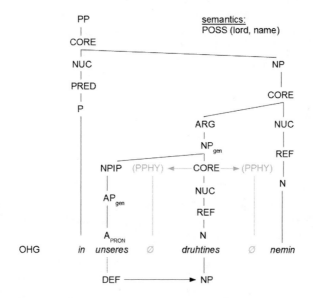

Figure 9: Old High German D$_{gen}$ H construction expressing possessive (ownership) relation

that in late Old High German non-partitive (and, trivially, non-possessive) inanimate and abstract entities tend to be placed post-nominally, is captured in Figure 10, displaying (12). It can therefore be viewed in contrast to the prenominal genitives in Figures 8 and 9.

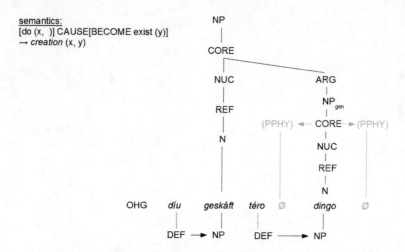

Figure 10: Old High German H D$_{gen}$ construction expressing non-possessive relation

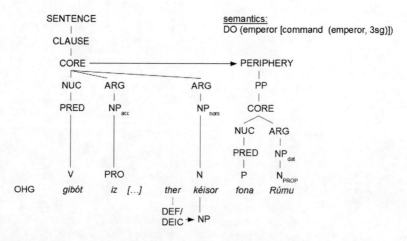

Figure 11: Old High German adverbal PP headed by *fon(n)(e/a)*

In Old High German, possession (ownership) is expressed by genitival attributes. The expansion of other strategies has not yet happened (see Figure 2). Prepositional phrases with *fon(n)(e/a)* 'from' following a noun phrase in adjacent position or an animate NP$_{dat}$ preceding a noun phrase in adjacent position must be interpreted adverbally. The former case is illustrated in Figure 11, illustrating (8). It stands in contrast to Middle High German and younger adnominal prepositional phrases headed by *von* 'from/of' which is shown in Figure 12, illustrating (18). However, the Old High German prepositional phrase headed

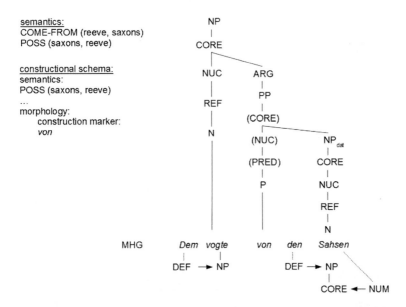

Figure 12: Representation of a Middle High German H *von(e)* D construction expressing a possessive (ownership) relation

by *fon(n)(e/a)* being adjacent to another noun phrase is a probable source of reanalysis towards the H *fon(n)(e/a)* D construction.

Figure 12 illustrates an example from Middle High German where the reanalysis of an adverbal ablative prepositional phrase as an adnominal ablative or possessive prepositional phrase has already taken place. The complex noun phrase seems to be ambiguous between an ablative and a possessive (ownership) interpretation. In the ablative interpretation – COME-FROM (reeve, saxons) –, the preposition *von* 'from' is a predicating element and has a core and a nucleus. In the possessive interpretation, *von* 'of' is not a predicate and lacks a nucleus or a core. It is merely a construction marker, as indicated by its constructional schema. These schemas contain "idiosyncratic, language-specific features of constructions" (Van Valin 2005: 132). Figure 12 only presents the structure corresponding to the possessive interpretation. Accordingly, *von* is specified as a construction marker in the possessive interpretation in the corresponding construction schema.

In Middle High German the D_{dat} Poss H construction also begins to become an expressive strategy for possessive (ownership) relations. This strategy becomes increasingly prominent in Early New High German and is the primary means for expressing possession (ownership) in most contemporary non-standard varieties.

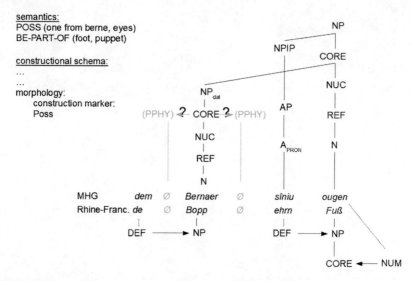

Figure 13: Middle High German and contemporary Rhine-Franconian D_{dat} Poss H construction expressing possessive and partitive/meronymic relations, respectively

In some of these varieties it can already be used for partitive/meronymic relations as well, pointing to a grammaticalization of the construction as a whole. Regularities in this change are discussed in Section 5. Figure 13 illustrates a possessive example from Middle High German – illustrating (20) – and a partitive/meronymic relation from a contemporary Rhine-Franconian dialect, illustrating (24).[19]

In line with my proposal concerning the different grammaticalization states of Poss, *sîniu* and *ehrn* in these constructions each behave like articles and contribute definiteness to their respective Hs (*ougen* 'eyes', *Fuß* 'foot'), making the respective referents identifiable in discourse. At the same time, they function as the construction marker in this construction, as indicated in the constructional schema. The dative noun phrases, coding the semantic possessors, function as arguments to the respective nuclei/Hs. It is expected that NP_{dat} can be expanded to the left and to the right by means of modification. More data are necessary at this point (indicated by the question marks at the periphery branches). At that stage, the D_{dat} Poss part of the construction has not yet been reanalyzed as an article expression, but subsequent changes follow exactly this path. The struc-

---

19 According to the definition of possession in Section 2 (in brief, if *x* is located at *y*, and if *y* controls *x*, then *y* possesses *x*), a puppet cannot be interpreted as a possessor. The reasons why *dem Bernaer sîniu ougen* 'the eyes of the one from Berne' is not interpreted here (in the first instance) as a partitive/meronymic relation are discussed in Section 5.

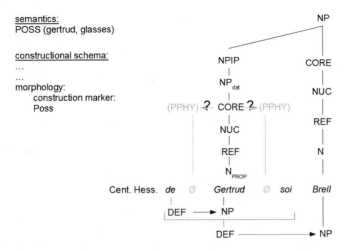

Figure 14: Contemporary Central-Hessian D_{dat} Poss H construction expressing possessive (ownership) relation; Poss grammaticalized

tural reflex of this is the incorporation of D_{dat} into NPIP which was formerly occupied by Poss alone. This process is distinct from the grammaticalization of the whole construction and is restricted to its precore part, i.e., D_{dat} Poss. Figure 14, illustrating the structure of (28), demonstrates this.

Poss no longer behaves like an adjective and it can no longer function as an anaphor to the possessor but it now constitutes the article expression for H/the nucleus together with NP_{dat}. Whether or not NP_{dat} can be expanded to the left and right by modification cannot be decided without additional data (hence the question mark at the periphery branch), but if D_{dat} Poss functions as an article expression, I would predict that it would not work.

Turning to Standard New High German, we find a preserved genitive. As a possessor, only proper nouns and some kin expressions may stand prenominally, i.e., preceding H. An example is given in Figure 15.

In Figure 15, *Paul* and the element *-s* together function as an article expression of H/the nucleus (*Roman* 'novel'), marking it as definite. The categorial status of *-s* is difficult to assess, because it is not clear whether or not it is a genitive marker (cf. Demske 2001; Eisenberg 2006). In any case it is part of NPIP. I consider it a construction marker, analogous to Poss and forms of *von* 'of' in the above cases. Because of the reanalysis of D_{gen} as an article expression, it can no longer be modified (hence the "X" in the branch linking core and periphery in Figure 15). Only if it had maintained its status as an argument, would this be possible. D_{gen} has exactly this status when in postnominal position, as shown in Figure 16.

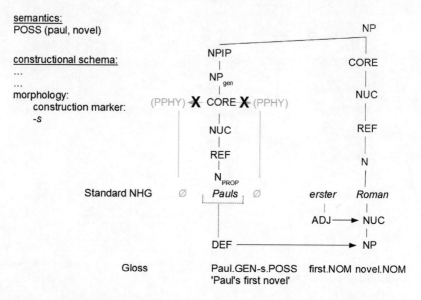

Figure 15: Standard German D$_{gen}$ H construction expressing possessive (ownership) relation

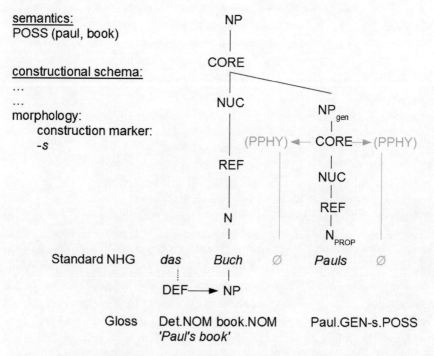

Figure 16: Standard German H D$_{gen}$ construction expressing possessive (ownership) relation

As discussed earlier in this section, D_{gen} can indeed be modified in this position. The similarity between the expressions in Figures 15 and 16 is only superficial. They differ in more than just the positions of the genitive noun phrase. The syntactic status of the prenominal position makes the difference.

5 A tentative unification of syntactic and semantic changes in German adnominal possession

In Sections 3 and 4 I tried to trace changes in German adnominal noun phrases revolving around the concept of possession (in a broad sense). These changes concerned a) the relationship between adnominal expressive strategies in different periods and presumably constant conceptual-semantic differentiations that require expression. The observed changes also concerned b) changes in the structure of the German noun phrase that cannot easily be connected to conceptual-semantic considerations. Is there a unifying pattern in these developments?

Looking first at the changes occurring in the context of the prenominal and postnominal genitive constructions, the following generalization in (31) seems to hold with respect to the major developments:[20]

(31)   Expressions that are "moving" into postnominal position over the history
        of the German complex noun phrase:

partitive	>	non-person non-partitive	>	appellative person
expressions		expressions		expressions
(Germ > OHG)		(OHG > MHG)		(MHG > ENHG)

Switching the perspective to the prenominal position yields the generalization in (32):

(32)   Expressions that are "staying" in prenominal position across the history
        of the German complex noun phrase:

non-partitive	>	person	>	proper names
expressions		expressions		(/kin names)
(Germ > OHG)		(OHG > MHG)		(MHG > ENHG)

At a closer look, the scales in (31) and (32) can be related to a sub-scale of the animacy (or empathy) hierarchy, namely that pertaining to types of referen-

---

20 Abbreviations: Germ = Germanic; OHG = Old High German; MHG = Middle High German; ENHG = Early New High German.

tial expressions. This scale is given in (33) (cf. Lehmann 1998; Yamamoto 1999; Corbett 2000; Langacker 2002; Croft 2003; Stolz et al. 2008):

(33) proper name > kin expression > appellative expression (animate) > appellative expression (inanimate) > abstract/mass noun

The rationale seems to be this: with respect to their inherent definiteness, the concepts shown in (33) decrease from left to right. That means proper names designate referents that are unambiguously identifiable in a given discourse, kin expressions are easily identifiable in relation to someone in a given discourse, animate common nouns designate an indefinite number of animate entities that are similar in a particular respect, etc. The connection to (31) and (32) can be captured in the following way: Expressions moving into the postnominal position in the periods of German (31) "climb up" the referential expressions scale (from right to left). Expressions staying in prenominal position in the periods of German (32) reduce to those at the top (left pole) of the referential expressions scale. That means those referents whose identity is determined easiest in discourse remain in prenominal position. Referents whose identity is less easy determined occur in postnominal position. At the same time the exodus of expression types to the postnominal position constitutes a tendency towards a nucleus > argument or head > dependent order in the complex noun phrase. The exceptions to this order are the highly referential possessor expressions in the D_{gen} H construction in contemporary Standard German and those non-standard varieties that have preserved the genitive.

This cannot be the whole story, however, since there is no plausible reason why appellatives designating inanimate entities should be less identifiable than those designating animate entities. Because of this, a closer look at the relationship between partitive/meronymic relations and possessive (ownership) relations seems necessary. In particular, I propose the following cognitively motivated interpretation principle:

(34) Interpretation principle (implicature):
      Animate D expressions in a complex noun phrase expressing partitivity/meronymy are interpreted as possessors (ownership).

Why should this be the case and how does it contribute to the relationship between (31)/(32) on the one hand and (33) on the other? Concerning the first question, there is a widely acknowledged analogous principle at work in the linking of syntax and semantics. Van Valin and Wilkins (1996), on the basis of Holisky (1987), claim that in clauses, animate causers (or effectors, in their terminology) are interpreted as intentional agents. This leaves many lexical entries of verbs unspecified with respect to agentivity. Agentivity is inferred on the basis of a lexical feature of an argument, namely its animacy. This is the reason why killers, hitters, and the like are interpreted as agents, if animate. Now recall how possession (ownership) was characterized in Section 2: as a spatial relationship plus what I have dubbed "control". Control is an important ingredient of agentivity (cf. Comrie 1989; Primus 1999). I am not aware of any reason why Holisky's observation should hold for animate effectors but not for animate D expressions in the constructions in question. This assumption also explains why the H *von* D_{dat} construction extends not only to partitive/meronymic meanings in the history of German but also to possessive (ownership) ones, namely if D_{dat} is animate, thereby triggering (34) to become active.

With respect to the second question, the relevance of (34) for the relationship between (31)/(32) on the one hand and (33) on the other, we find that (33) is also in part a scale of potential agentivity, and therefore of potential "real" possessors, i.e., those executing control. From a neurolinguistic and cognitive perspective, language users and "the person on the street" strive to identify the causer/controller within a sentence (cf. Bornkessel-Schlesewsky and Schlesewsky 2009) and within a real-life event (Kasper 2013) as fast as possible. A similar process seems to be at work in the complex noun phrases in question. The processes within adnominal genitive phrases have left potential agents in the prenominal position. (Note that in virtually all possessive (ownership) relations the possessor is higher in animacy than the possessum.)

However, language users' cognitive striving to identify the initiator/controller of any event as soon as possible obviously competes with the syntactic tendency to develop an H > D order within the noun phrase, which corresponds to the order possessum > possessor. The only possessor expressions that withstand this tendency are highly referential entities with potential for agentivity, namely the D_{gen} H of Standard German and non-standard varieties with a genitive case and the D_{dat} Poss H constructions found in many non-standard varieties. These constructions involving prenominal possessors are grammatical means for expressing possession (ownership) which obviate the need for the pragmatic implicature in (34). That implicature remains active in postnominal possessor expressions since these – although often animate or human – may in fact be part of "mere" partitive/meronymic relations.

Neither principle – the pragmatic implicature in (34) nor the search for the agent/controller in relations – can explain data in which we find the D_{dat} Poss H construction with an inanimate D_{dat} referent (as in [24] from Rhine-Franconian involving a puppet; [22] from a Low German variety involves a house).[21] In these

---

21 Recall that in Rhine-Franconian, a crane as "possessor" did not work (see [25]). It must at least be human-like.

constructions, inanimate D expressions occur prenominally despite not being possible agents/controllers. They can only be interpreted as expressing meronymic/partitive relations. One could argue that empathy plays a role where D refers to a puppet (cf. Kuno and Kaburaki 1977), causing human-like entities to be treated as humans, but this does not work for the Low German data. At present I have no explanation for these data and can only speculate that they result from an idiosyncratic development of the adnominal possessive dative or the noun phrase as a whole within the history of Low German varieties.[22]

Finally, do the considerations above allow us to offer a causal explanation of changes in the linking of syntax and semantics? The answer is twofold and may also seem disappointing, though I deem it reasonable: Firstly, we cannot say with certainty whether the syntactic changes surrounding the reanalysis of two originally adverbal constituents as a single noun phrase (e.g., D_{dat} Poss H, D *von* H) cause the attested changes in the interpretation of these structures. Allowing for other than purely structural explanations, it is also possible that the reverse is true: If interpreters strive to conceptually establish the relation between two objects as soon as possible (as Kasper 2013 claims), that would provide an impetus for a syntactic reanalysis of two adjacent adverbal constituents as a single one, once this structural adjacency configuration had occurred. Secondly, a clear causal relation between the changes in the prenominal position within the noun phrase and the associated changes in the way they are

---

22 Lübben (1882: 108/109) and Lasch ([1914] 1974) cite Middle Low German data for the origins of the D_{dat} Poss D construction that differ from those that are discussed for Middle and High German. Concerning the latter, the usual explanations allude to the reanalysis of sympathetic adverbal datives (*Er hat [dem Vater] [sein Haus] angezündet* lit. 'He set the father his house on fire' / 'He set the father's house on fire' → *[dem Vater sein Haus] ist abgebrannt* lit. 'The father his house is burned down' / 'Father's house burned down') or the replacement of the prenominal genitive by the dative plus an added emphasizing Poss (*des Vaters Haus* 'Det.GEN father.GEN house' → *des Vaters sein Haus* 'Det.GEN father.GEN his house' → *dem Vater sein Haus* 'Det.DAT father.DAT his house'). The first, probably more prominent, hypothesis was put forward by Behaghel (1923), among others, the latter by Grimm (1837) and recently by Weiß (2012). In contrast, Lübben finds the origins of the Low German variant of D_{dat} Poss D in examples like *dat wîf des he eren sone levendich makede* (the.NOM woman whose.GEN he.NOM its.ACC son alive made; 'the woman whose son he brought/woke to life'). The genitival relative pronoun was then used in the nominative or accusative *deme, de dat pant sîn is* (the-one.DAT who. NOM/ACC the.NOM deposit his is; 'the one whose deposit this is') and later all genitival relations, not only relative constructions, were replaced by constructions like *mîn vader sîn hûs* (my.ACC father.ACC his house; 'my father's house'). Such a course of events differs considerably from those for Central and High German and if it took place in that way, it becomes probable that what we call "adnominal possessive dative" in German is not as uniform as it seems and might have different historical origins and motivations for different areas, at least with respect to Low German vs. High/Central German varieties.

interpreted cannot be provided either. In a similar vein to the above, it might be the case that there is a cognitive (or parsing) routine (cf. Hawkins 2004) applying to a particular structural configuration once it occurs, thus triggering its reanalysis. The solution to questions like these cannot be provided in a large-scale and coarse-grained survey like this article, which covers changes in the syntax-semantics linking over several hundred years. At a minimum, it would require the simultaneous observation across time of some cognizers' language-processing performances and their associated conceptual-semantic activity – a task which lies way beyond what we are actually able to do. For the time being, we must confine ourselves to stating the correlations between syntax and semantics as adequately as possible, leaving matters of causality for the future.

6 Conclusion

This article attempts to unify syntactic and semantics observations pertaining to adnominal noun phrases from the realm of possession across time and in contemporary varieties of German, observations which possibly reflect different developmental states in a continuum of changes within the adnominal expression of possession. It has been demonstrated that different lines of change are at work in the complex German noun phrase, for instance that concerning the prenominal position, that concerning the possessive element, that concerning the D_{dat} Poss H construction as a whole, and that concerning the relationships between the range of expressive strategies German varieties exhibit and the range of conceptual-semantic differentiations that need to be expressed. The inclusion of data from Standard German and very different non-standard German varieties (e.g., Low German vs. Valais German) forces one to conclude that there are no simple causal relationships to be found. In fact, Valais German itself illustrates this. While the preservation of the genitive and its functions could be argued to "block" the frequent use of the adnominal possessive dative, the highly frequent use of the *von* periphrasis in originally genitival functions points to a peaceful coexistence.

Although some important regularities in the change of the mapping between syntax and semantics, and some correlations between syntactic options and possible interpretations could be uncovered, they defy a simple causal explanation at present.

Sources

[2. Merseburger Zauberspruch]: Althochdeutsches Lesebuch. Zusammengestellt und mit Wörterbuch versehen von Wilhelm Braune, fortgeführt von Karl Helm. 17. Auflage, bearbeitet von Ernst A. Ebbinghaus. Tübingen 1994: Niemeyer.

[Die Beichte]: Gesammtabenteuer. Hundert altdeutsche Erzählungen: Ritter- und Pfaffen-Mären, Stadt- und Dorfgeschichten, Schwänke, Wundersagen und Legenden. Hrsg. von Friedrich Heinrich von der Hagen. [3 Bände] Stuttgart/Tübingen 1850: J. G. Cotta'scher Verlag.

[Dietrichs Flucht]: Deutsches Heldenbuch. Zweiter Teil: Alpharts Tod, Dietrichs Flucht, Rabenschlacht. Hrsg. von Ernst Martin. Berlin 1866: Weidmannsche Buchhandlung.

[Isidor]: Der althochdeutsche Isidor. Nach der Pariser Handschrift und den Mondseer Fragmenten. Neu herausgegeben von Hans Eggers. (Altdeutsche Textbibliothek 63.) Tübingen 1964: Niemeyer.

[Nibelungenlied]: Das Nibelungenlied. Paralleldruck der Handschriften A, B und C nebst Lesarten der übrigen Handschriften. Hrsg. von Michael S. Batts. Tübingen 1971: Niemeyer.

[Notker, Consolatio]: Notker der Deutsche: Boethius, „De consolatione Philosophiae". Hrsg. von Petrus W. Tax. [3 Bände] (Die Werke Notkers des Deutschen, Neue Ausgabe 1, 2, 3.) Tübingen 1986, 1988, 1990: Niemeyer.

[Notker, Psalter]: Notker der Deutsche: Der Psalter. Hrsg. von Petrus W. Tax. [3 Bände] (Die Werke Notkers des Deutschen, Neue Ausgabe 8, 9, 10.) Tübingen 1979, 1981, 1983: Niemeyer.

[Otfrid]: Otfrid von Weißenburg: Evangelienbuch. Band I: Edition nach dem Wiener Codex 2687. Hrsg. u. bearb. von Wolfgang Kleiber unter Mitarbeit von Rita Heuser. Teil 1: Text. Tübingen 2004: Niemeyer.

[Parzival]: Wolfram von Eschenbach. Parzival. Hrsg. von Albert Leitzmann. [3 Bände] 6. u. 7. Auflage, revidiert von Wilhelm Deinert. (Altdeutsche Textbibliothek 12, 13, 14.) Tübingen 1961, 1963, 1965: Niemeyer.

[SADS]: Syntaktischer Atlas der Deutschen Schweiz. www.ds.uzh.ch/dialektsyntax/.

[SyHD]: Syntax hessischer Dialekte. www.deutscher-sprachatlas.de/projekte/syhd/index_html.

[Willehalm]: Wolfram von Eschenbach. Fünfte Ausgabe. Hrsg. von Karl Lachmann. Berlin 1891: G. Reimer.

References

Bart, Gabriela. 2006. *Ds Grossvatersch Brilla* oder *di Brilla vam Grossvater.* Zu den Possessivkonstruktionen im Schweizerdeutschen. Lizentiatsarbeit, Deutsches Seminar, Universität Zürich.

Behaghel, Otto. 1923. *Deutsche Syntax. Band 1: Die Wortklassen und Wortformen. A. Nomen. Pronomen.* Heidelberg: Carl Winter's Universitätsbuchhandlung.

Behaghel, Otto. 1924. *Deutsche Syntax. Band 2: Die Wortklassen und Wortformen. B. Adverbium. C. Verbum.* Heidelberg: Carl Winter's Universitätsbuchhandlung.

Behaghel, Otto. 1932. *Deutsche Syntax. Band 4: Wortstellung. Periodenbau.* Heidelberg: Carl Winter's Universitätsbuchhandlung.

Bickel, Balthasar. 2010. Grammatical relations typology. In Jae Jung Song (ed.), *The Oxford handbook of language typology*, 399–444. Oxford: Oxford University Press.

Bohnenberger, Karl. 1913. *Die Mundart der deutschen Walliser im Heimattal und in den Außenorten*. Frauenfeld: Huber & Co.

Bornkessel-Schlesewsky, Ina & Matthias Schlesewsky. 2009. The role of prominence information in the real-time comprehension of transitive constructions: A cross-linguistic approach. *Language and Linguistics Compass* 3(1). 19–58.

Carr, Charles T. 1933. The position of the genitive in German. *The Modern Language Review* 28 (4). 465–479.

Chappell, Hilary & William McGregor (eds.). 1995. *The grammar of inalienability. A typological perspective on body part terms and the part-whole relation*. Berlin & New York: de Gruyter.

Comrie, Bernard. 1989. *Language universals and language typology*. Oxford: Blackwell.

Corbett, Greville G. 2000. *Number*. Cambridge: Cambridge University Press.

Croft, William. 2003. *Typology and universals*. 2nd edn. Cambridge: Cambridge University Press.

Demske, Ulrike. 2001. *Merkmale und Relationen. Diachrone Studien zur Nominalphrase im Deutschen*. Berlin & New York: de Gruyter.

Ebert, Robert Peter. 1986. *Deutsche Syntax 1300–1750*. Bern et al.: Peter Lang.

Eisenberg, Peter. 2006. *Grundriss der deutschen Grammatik. Band 2: Der Satz*. 3. Aufl. Stuttgart & Weimar: Metzler.

Eroms, Werner. 2000. *Syntax der deutschen Sprache*. Berlin & New York: de Gruyter.

Fleischer, Jürg, Simon Kasper & Alexandra N. Lenz. 2012. Die Erhebung syntaktischer Phänomene durch die indirekte Methode: Ergebnisse und Erfahrungen aus dem Forschungsprojekt „Syntax hessischer Dialekte" (SyHD). *Zeitschrift für Dialektologie und Linguistik* 79(1). 1–42.

Fleischer, Jürg & Oliver Schallert. 2011. *Historische Syntax des Deutschen. Eine Einführung*. Tübingen: Narr.

Grimm, Jakob. 1837. *Deutsche Grammatik. Vierter Theil*. Göttingen: Dieterichsche Buchhandlung.

Hawkins, John A. 2004. *Efficiency and Complexity in Grammars*. Oxford: Oxford University Press.

Heine, Bernd. 1997. *Possession. Cognitive sources, forces, and grammaticalization*. Cambridge: Cambridge University Press.

Henn-Memmesheimer, Beate. 1986. *Nonstandardmuster. Ihre Beschreibung in der Syntax und das Problem ihrer Arealität*. Tübingen: Niemeyer.

Henzen, Walter. 1932. Der Genitiv im heutigen Wallis. *Beiträge zur Geschichte der deutschen Sprache und Literatur* 56. 91–138.

Holisky, David A. 1987. The case of the intransitive subject in Tsova-Tush (Batsbi). *Lingua* 71(1–4). 103–132.

Kasper, Simon. 2013. *Grounding the linking competence in culture and nature. How action and perception shape the syntax-semantics relationship*. Marburg: Philipps-Universität Marburg dissertation.

Kiefer, Heinrich. 1910. *Der Ersatz des adnominalen Genitivs im Deutschen*. Leipzig: Hoffmann. [Gießen: Universität Gießen dissertation]

Kluge, Friedrich. 2011. *Etymologisches Wörterbuch der deutschen Sprache*. Bearb. von Elmar Seebold. 25., verb. u. erw. Aufl. Berlin & New York: de Gruyter.

Koptjevskaja-Tamm, Maria. 2003. Possessive noun phrases in the languages of Europe. In Frans Plank (ed.), *Noun phrase structure in the languages of Europe*, 621–722. Berlin & New York: Mouton de Gruyter.

Koß, Gerhard. 1983. Realisierung von Kasusrelationen in den deutschen Dialekten. In Werner Besch, Ulrich Knoop, Wolfgang Putschke & Herbert E. Wiegand (eds.), *Dialektologie: Ein Handbuch zur deutschen und allgemeinen Dialektforschung*. Vol. 2, 1242–1250. Berlin & New York: de Gruyter.

Kuno, Susumu & Etsuko Kaburaki. 1977. Empathy and syntax. *Linguistic Inquiry* 8(4). 627–672.

Langacker, Ronald W. 2002. *Concept, image, and symbol. The cognitive basis of grammar*. 2nd edn. Berlin & New York: Mouton de Gruyter.

Lasch, Agathe. 1974 [1914]. *Mittelniederdeutsche Grammatik*. 2nd edn. Tübingen: Niemeyer.

Lehmann, Christian. 1998. *Possession in Yucatec Maya. Structures – functions – typology*. München: Lincom Europa.

Lindow, Wolfgang, Dieter Möhn, Hermann Niebaum, Dieter Stellmacher, Hans Taubken & Jan Wirrer. 1998. *Niederdeutsche Grammatik*. Leer: Schuster.

Lübben, August. 1882. *Mittelniederdeutsche Grammatik. Nebst Chrestomathie und Glossar*. Leipzig: Weigel.

Mironow, Sergeij A. 1957. Zur vergleichenden Formenlehre der deutschen Mundarten. *Beiträge zur Geschichte der deutschen Sprache und Literatur* 79. 388–414.

Oubouzar, Erika. 1992. Zur Ausbildung des bestimmten Artikels im Ahd. In Yvon Desportes (ed.), *Althochdeutsch: Syntax und Semantik: Akten des Lyonner Kolloquiums zur Syntax und Semantik des Althochdeutschen, March 1–3, 1990*, 69–87. Lyon: Université Lyon III Jean Moulin.

Prell, Heinz-Peter. 2000. Die Stellung des attributiven Genitivs im Mittelhochdeutschen. Zur Notwendigkeit einer Syntax mittelhochdeutscher Prosa. *Beiträge zur Geschichte der deutschen Sprache und Literatur* 122. 23–39.

Primus, Beatrice. 1999. *Cases and thematic roles*. Tübingen: Niemeyer.

Schiepek, Josef. 1899/1908. *Der Satzbau der Egerländer Mundart*. 2 Tle. Prag: Calve.

Schirmunski, Viktor M. 2010. *Deutsche Mundartkunde. Vergleichende Laut- und Formenlehre der deutschen Mundarten*. Edited and commented by Larissa Naiditsch. Frankfurt a. M.: Lang.

Schmidt, Jürgen Erich & Joachim Herrgen. 2011. *Sprachdynamik*. Berlin: Erich Schmidt Verlag.

Schröder, Werner. 1969. Niewöhners Text des *bîhtmaere* und seine überlieferten Fassungen. *Beiträge zur Geschichte der deutschen Sprache und Literatur* 19. 260–301.

Seiler, Hansjakob. 1983. *Possession as an operational dimension in language*. Tübingen: Narr.

Seiler, Hansjakob. 2009. Subjectivity and objectivity in the domain of possession. *Semiotica* 173(1–4). 417–429.

Shrier, Martha. 1965. Case systems in German dialects. *Language* 41(3). 420–438.

Silverstein, Michael. 1976. Hierarchy of features and ergativity. In R. M. W. Dixon (ed.), *Grammatical relations in Australian languages*, 112–171. Canberra: Australian Institute of Aboriginal Studies.

Stolz, Thomas, Sonja Kettler, Cornelia Stroh & Urdze Aina. 2008. *Split possession. An areal-linguistic study of the alienability correlation and related phenomena in the languages of Europe*. Amsterdam & Philadelphia: John Benjamins.

Van Valin, Robert D. 2005. *Exploring the syntax-semantics interface*. Cambridge, MA: MIT Press.

Van Valin, Robert D. & Randy J. LaPolla. 1997. *Syntax. Structure, meaning, and function*. Cambridge: Cambridge University Press.

Van Valin, Robert D. & Wendy Wilkins. 1996. The case for "effector". Case roles, agents and agency revisited. In Masayoshi Shibatani & Sandra Thompson (eds.), *Grammatical constructions*, 289–322. Oxford: Oxford University Press.

Wegener, Heide. 1985. *Der Dativ im heutigen Deutsch*. Tübingen: Narr.

Weise, Otto. 1898. Dem Vater sein Haus. *Zeitschrift für den deutschen Unterricht* 12. 287–291.

Weiß, Helmut. 2008. The possessor that appears twice. Variation, structure and function of possessive doubling in German. In Sjef Barbiers, Olaf Koeneman, Marika Lekakou & Margreet van der Ham (eds.), *Microvariation in Syntactic Doubling*, 381–401. Leiden: Brill.

Weiß, Helmut. 2012. The rise of DP-internal possessors. On the relationship of dialectal synchrony to diachrony. In Gunther De Vogelaer & Guido Seiler (eds.), *The dialect laboratory. Dialects as a testing ground for theories of language change*, 271–293. Amsterdam & Philadelphia: John Benjamins.

Wilmanns, W. 1909. *Deutsche Grammatik. Gotisch, Alt-, Mittel- und Neuhochdeutsch. Dritte Abteilung: Flexion. 2. Hälfte: Nomen und Pronomen*. Strassburg: Karl J. Trübner.

Wipf, Elisa. 1910. *Die Mundart von Visperterminen im Wallis*. Frauenfeld: Huber & Co. [Zurich: Universität Zürich dissertation]

Yamamoto, Mutsumi. 1999. *Animacy and reference. A cognitive approach to corpus linguistics*. Amsterdam & Philadelphia: John Benjamins.

Zifonun, Gisela. 2003. Dem Vater sein Hut. Der Charme des Substandards und wie wir ihm gerecht werden. *Deutsche Sprache* 1/2003. 97–126.

Remus Gergel
4 *Most* historically

This paper investigates the trajectory of the quantificational use of *most* at the syntax-semantics interface. It starts out from the observation that the word originally had a meaning along the lines of 'largest (in degree)' and it discusses how it gained its current semantics of a superlative associated with *many*. It is proposed that the main development consists in a particular type of functionalization of co-occurring lexical material. *Most* in the relevant use incorporated the meaning of a noun meaning 'part'.

1 Introduction

The present paper investigates certain facts in the diachronic trajectory of the quantifier *most* at the syntax-semantics interface.[1] As is well-known, *most* has developed a use as a superlative morpheme attaching to certain gradable expressions, illustrated in (1a) with an adjective, and one that is quantificational, exemplified below in (1b):

(1)   a.   The **most recent** studies supported the criticism.

     b.   **Most studies** didn't seem to support the criticism.

    Most as a quantifying determiner has received a good deal of attention recently in synchronic terms for Present-Day English.[2] Interestingly, Hackl (2009) has argued that at the level of interpretation (i.e. the level of Logical Form, LF), quantificational *most* behaves like a superlative rather than a quantifier in the sense of Generalized Quantifier Theory (cf. Barwise and Cooper 1981). A feature of this type of theory is that it treats quantifiers uniformly, as atomic elements, which, in simplified terms, establish relations between sets. For example,

---

1 I thank the audience of the workshop "Language change at the syntax-semantics interface" at the 2012 Frankfurt *DGfS* for comments, and remain especially grateful to Doris Penka and an anonymous reviewer for spot-on and very helpful observations. Many thanks to the editorial team and Daniel Ferguson for valuable textual suggestions. Solely I am responsible for any shortcomings.

2 I will use terms like quantifier and quantifying determiner rather descriptively to refer to the corresponding use of *most* in Present-Day English. On the analytical side, we will see immediately that a new line of research (cf. Hackl 2009) treats this item as decomposing into further building blocks at the level of Logical Form.

in (1b) above, the respective sets are the salient studies and the entities that did not seem to support the criticism. For such a sentence to be true, more than half of the studies (i.e. the entities of the first set) should have the property of belonging to the second set, too. A body of recent research has, however, questioned the unified character of several quantifiers in the sense of Generalized Quantifier Theory. Treating *most* as a superlative of *many*, as Hackl does (cf. also Bresnan 1973), thus falls into the same line of research. Importantly, in Hackl's (2009: 79) analysis then, *many* is treated "as a gradable modifier that modifies plural NPs ranging over pluralities that can be measured in terms of how many atomic parts they are composed of". Building the superlative on top of such a meaning, e.g. for a phrase such as *most mountains*, will then come down to comparing pluralities of mountains and taking the largest one among them. (We will consider Hackl's technical version of this in Section 4.)

A superlative-quantifier analysis is also attractive in that it offers a parallel of the quantifier to the other function of the same word in English, namely the analytical superlative of gradable expressions, as introduced above and discussed in Section 2. At the same time, it is worth keeping in mind that such a move involves a certain degree of complexity and a decomposition of the word that is not visible at the surfacing structure of the quantifier, but which is required for the purposes of semantic interpretation; cf. also Heim (1985, 1999), Szabolcsi (1986), among many others. Let me make clear that I do not see, at present, a practical way to decide the most intricate questions relative to the contemporary semantic analyses by going diachronic in this case. But the point I should like to make is a different one. If complex approaches such as Hackl's are on the right track, i.e. if some such complexity is required, then the immediate follow-up question enforced upon diachronists interested in modeling syntax and semantics is: how can the complex representations come about over time at all?

In exploring the question of how the quantifier *most* developed over time, I will take into account aspects of structure and meaning from pertinent lines of syntactic and semantic research. I take both to be necessary ingredients towards an explanation. However, the proposal will be that a crucial ingredient towards capturing the trajectory is more concealed than what one might have hoped for (i.e. than something which might have been at the most direct intersection of structure and meaning). Thus, rather than deriving the semantic change solely from structure as tree-geometric properties applied to the realm of meaning (cf., e.g., Gergel 2009), a new (but *prima facie* very old) plot will be pursued here: functionalization of lexical material. This surely takes inspiration from several traditions, including that of grammaticalization. But I will propose to use a notion that feeds directly into the inventory of elements available in semantic interpretation (under relatively tight syntactic configurations). The turn towards what is functional has already been approached under a number of umbrellas, including those available in historical syntax and semantics (e.g., via loss of theta roles or via the tendency towards high types; as, say, in Roberts 1985 and von Fintel 1995, respectively). But theta roles are surely irrelevant here and the types will remain constant.

I will suggest inclusion of a mechanism of development to the known inventories and paths of change, which I will refer to as "ontological semantic functionalization". In a nutshell, *most* will be said to have undergone this type of change because a lexical item that it combined with before the change (namely a noun along the lines of 'part') was incorporated into the meta-language semantically and thus became an integral part of its entry after the change. As a preview illustration, we can imagine that a noun like 'part' can at some point change from its original lexical meaning – in this case as a more or less run-of-the-mill relational noun – to mean partitions in terms of the semantic ontology involved (e.g., pluralities of individuals) when it is combined with *most*:

(2)   MOST [part of [N]] → MOST [N]

N stands for a further noun that is usually combinable with MOST (part of) before and after the reanalysis. I use the notation MOST for the form available before and after the reanalysis. This form carries quite different meanings at the two stages. Crucially, in the reanalyzed structure-meaning mapping, a partition will be taken recourse to via the denotation of *most* itself. But no lexical item along the lines of 'part' needs to be spelled out as such for this to happen. The suggestion in (2) above is rather specific. There are some immediate ways to envision extensions, but given the scope of the paper, I will focus on *most* and only briefly touch upon such extension possibilities (awaiting further case studies) in the final discussion part of the paper.

Overall, the present paper has the following subdivisions. Section 2 outlines the issues with *most* descriptively on the basis of the key points in historical development, after which Sections 3 and 4 will develop the analysis by exploring the pertinent syntactic and semantic aspects, respectively. Given the crucial role of the interface in a compositional enterprise, there will naturally be some interaction between the two areas of grammar, and hence also between the respective sections (i.e. they cannot be "pure" in that sense). Finally, Section 5 contains additional discussion.

2 Approaching the issues of *most* descriptively

The status of *most* is clear from the beginning of the attested historical records in Old English insofar as it has always been a superlative of some sort morphologically. This might represent impressionistic first motivation for a superlative-like analysis coming from the historical camp, but things need to be sorted out. A number of issues become particularly interesting; for example, when we ask which meaning exactly *most* is and was a superlative marker of, i.e. tracing it back during its recorded history.

Two larger issues need to be distinguished in this connection already. The first one has to do with what is currently known as the morphological nature of *most* itself, specifically as a "free" morpheme and alternative exponent to *-est*. This happens in connection with a class of adjectives that are characterized as prosodically long in current English in those cases in which *more* is used in the analytical comparative (see, e.g., Embick 2007 for an account of the morphological facts). However, this distribution was not in place in Old English. (For instance, Ælfric systematically uses synthetic superlatives in his grammar.) Its historical origin as well as its regularization have been, nonetheless, the subject of numerous studies, and they remain outside the scope of this paper (cf. González-Diáz 2008 for recent comprehensive discussion and the references cited there).[3]

The second issue, of immediate relevance to the present study, is the historical trajectory of *most* feeding into its function as a quantifier. In this connection, theoretical explorations are scarce, at least to my knowledge. The historical description of English studies, however, reflected for instance in the *Oxford English Dictionary* (OED) already offers intriguing hints: among the original meanings translations such as 'greatest in size, stature, bulk, or extent' are available. Extensions go on towards 'greatest in intensity, most important, most principal', and others. Some Old English examples from *The York-Toronto-Helsinki Parsed Corpus of Old English Prose* (YCOE) and the epic poem of Beowulf are given in (3) for illustration. Middle English examples from *The Penn-Helsinki Parsed Corpus of Middle English* (PPCME2) are in (4). Notice that both singular and plural nouns could be modified by *most*. (NP word order with regard to Old English is discussed in Section 3.)[4]

---

3 I leave a discussion of adverbial uses aside in this paper for space reasons. One might simplistically assume for the time being that the relevant facts are parallel, but the issue is of interest for further research.

4 Corpus IDs of data from the PPCME2, PPCEME, and YCOE follow the standard conventions of these corpora (cf. the section 'Sources' preceding the references in this paper for URLs with pointers to file names and documentation); reference to other sources is provided in the traditional way, e.g. by page number, joined by the chapter and verse number for Beowulf (vowel length is not marked in the data).

(3) a. *þæt se ðe gyt ne mæg þa* **mæstan beboda** *healdan,*
      that he who yet not may the highest commands observe
      'who may not yet observe the highest commands'
      (coaelhom,+AHom_20:6.2912)

   b. *þætte* **þara wundra mæst** *wæs*
      that the.GEN wonders.GEN biggest was
      'that was the biggest wonder/ (of the wonders)'
      (coorosiu,Or_6:2.135.4.2839)

   c. *Gesloh* *þin* *fæder* **fæhðe mæste**
      caused-by-fighting your father feud greatest
      'Your father caused the greatest feud'
      (Beowulf, 55: VII.459)

(4) a. *her kynred & þei that had ben frendys wer now*
      her kindred & those who had been friends were now

      hyr **most enmys.**
      her biggest enemies
      (CMKEMPE,2.14)

   b. *But this me semeth is the* **moste merueylle**
      but this me seems is the biggest wonder

      þat euere I saugh,
      that ever I saw
      (CMMANDEV,128.3108)

Originally conveyed, then, was a fairly watered-down meaning indicating a high degree on a scale. To keep variation that is momentarily less relevant or even distracting to a minimum, we may observe that we are essentially dealing with 'largest' (cf., e.g., Einenkel 1904 on the relationship of *mæst* and *mycel*, 'great, large, much, etc.'). To strengthen this simple view, we can adduce some direct contemporary evidence from Ælfric's grammar. The Old English grammarian considered *mæst* a superlative adjective, more specifically the counterpart of Latin *maximus* (Ælfric 1880: 16). As a consequence, the issue will be to model syntactically and semantically the reanalysis going from a relatively regular adjective in the superlative, with the meaning along the lines of 'largest', towards a quantifying determiner with the intricate superlative-like denotation which it reveals in Present-Day English.

From the trajectory undergone in English I take one fact to be particularly noteworthy already during the Old English period and continuing during Middle

English; namely, the co-occurrence of the precursors of *most* (i.e. *mæst* and its variants) with nouns meaning 'part'. The typical noun used in Old English and well into the Middle English times is *dæl* (and variants of it), but the French loan *part* (once more with variants) then takes over during Middle English. This is illustrated with early and late Middle English examples, respectively, in (5).

(5) a. | *scheome* | *is* | *þe* | **meste** | **del** | *as* | *seint austin* | *seið* | *of* | *ure* |
         | shame | is | the | largest | part | as | St. Augustin | says | of | our |

       penitence.
       penitence
       (CMANCRIW-1,II.246.3552)

    b. | ... | *killed* | *þe* | **most** | **part** | *of* | *Cristen* | *men* | *in* | *þat* | *cyte.* |
         | | killed | the | most | part | of | Christian | men | in | that | city |

       (CMCAPCHR,72.1201)

Even current *most* still gives some indication of its earlier meaning and this relevant (as we will see: also frequent) early co-occurrence pattern with partitional nouns in the expression *(for) the most part*, meaning clearly '(for) the largest part'. Notably the noun is in the singular in this relic. In general, Present-Day English *most* cannot mean 'largest', 'highest' etc. as it was able to do at earlier stages; and in general, it cannot co-occur with singular (count) nouns any longer either.

A quantificational meaning in conjunction with plurals on the other hand is very clearly visible from the Early Modern English period onwards, as illustrated in (6) with examples from *The Penn-Helsinki Parsed Corpus of Early Modern English* (PPCEME).

(6) a. *Wheras through **most Counties of this Realme** Horstealinge is growen so co~mon,*
      (STAT-1580-E2-H,4,810.6)

    b. *it followeth wel in order to speake of the defect, which is in Publique Lectures: Namely, in the smalnesse and meanesse of the salary or reward which in **most places** is assigned vnto them: whether they be Lectures of Arts, or of Professions.*
      (BACON-E2-H,2,3V.124)

    c. *and it is so made, that a man may walke vpright in **the most places**, both in and out.*
      (JOTAYLOR-E2-H,1,133.C1.159)

What (6b) and (6c) show in addition is that one and the same noun appearing with *most* could be used with, or without, the definite article. (We return to an open issue of the definite article briefly in Section 5.)

Having presented some of the basic linguistic distributions descriptively, we will investigate next the syntax and semantics of the constructions presented over time.

3 Syntactic options for *most* and partitive constructions

This section investigates the change in structural status undergone by *most*. We focus on modeling the minimal structure that is visible or independently required and complement it where necessary.

3.1 Foundations, exploring first possibilities for the quantifier *most*

If *mæst* with its variants was a run-of-the-mill gradable adjective in the superlative, then its surface syntax was without further complications that of a modifier (Bresnan 1973; Bhatt and Pancheva 2004; Embick 2007; Beck et al. 2010, among others).[5] That is, the basic input structure to the syntactic change will be as represented in (7) below.

(7)   Basic function of early English lexical *most* – modification:

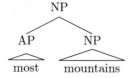

The representation shows the bare scaffolding, with the AP non-projecting in the nominal domain. As far as the linearization is concerned, the word order of modifiers in Old English is predominantly prenominal in general and, according to Fischer et al. (2000: 46), "the most frequent order resembles that of the present-day language". Exceptions with postnominal word order are well known

---

5 Cf., e.g., Gergel (2010) and the references cited there for discussion of and comparison with other approaches.

in general too, especially from poetry. Even though Fischer et al. do not discuss *most* specifically, their observations seem to carry over to its linearization; cf. the examples in (3a) and (3c) above for illustration of pre- and postnominal patterns (the prenominal pattern clearly dominates).[6] The word order in (3b) is quite usual in Old English texts given that the genitive indicating the comparison class of a superlative adjective could precede the adjective itself.

The next relevant question for now is what the original minimal structure turned into syntactically. If the reanalyzed *most* turned into a quantifier, then a simple hypothesis would be to treat it as a head, as in (8) below. (Supplementary dominating determiner-like structure such as the determiner *the* can also be syntactically added, quite independently.)

(8)   Function of re-analyzed *most*: quantificational head?

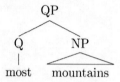

Restricting attention to the basic structures given in (7) and (8), respectively, a first question arises as to whether there is a broader kind of grammatical mechanism that could be responsible for the transition from one to the other. Let us explore this question next.

Structural regularities in syntactic change have been argued for some time now to be relevant in a wide range of case studies (cf., e.g., notably Roberts and Roussou 2003; van Gelderen 2004 for recent studies). Van Gelderen (2004: 11), for example, has explored the structural preference of heads over time and captured this tendency in the following principle, which lends itself to consideration given the structures we have seen for *most*:

(9)   *Van Gelderen's Head Preference or Spec to Head Principle:*
       Be a head, rather than a phrase.

The question is whether a similar line of reasoning can be applied systematically in the present case. The pre-reanalysis structure containing *most* functions as a modifier as discussed (and not as a specifier). Specifically, the constituent

---

6 Genuine postnominal *mæst* appears to be rare even in Old English poetry (e.g. the example in (3c) above is the only one I could find in Beowulf). There are numerous examples of nominal constituents preceding *mæst* in general, but such nominal constituents typically denote the comparison class.

containing *most* is a non-projecting daughter in the nominal that hosts it before the change, i.e. in a configuration like (7). However, van Gelderen already stated that the key difference in the principle is between heads and phrases (not necessarily just specifiers). Given the blurry line between some specifiers and other non-projecting elements (especially in minimalist bare-phrase structure terms), one could thus attempt to extend the principle of change to what it already states; namely to get us towards heads, and hence projecting structures from non-projecting ones (whether specifiers or not). Under such a view, there would be a generalized tendency of producing projecting elements in the process of language change.

Even though this type of thinking geared towards developing syntactic heads may offer interesting generalizations in many cases, there is an issue if we try to apply its fullest extension to the case study at hand. From a semantic point of view, a head-based structure as in (8) above predicts a meaning for *most* in the sense of Generalized Quantifier Theory.[7] At least for Present-Day English *most*, such a prediction is undesirable (this being precisely the point of Hackl 2009 for Present-Day English). The problem of the head-based analysis in the present case is the following. The semantics of a superlative in the major analyses (cf. the introduction and section four for more details) requires several building blocks, i.e. a base and landing site for the quantifier and a position for the predicate in the LF representation. This is not a configuration that is characteristic of head movement in any manner, but it is one that produces the correct truth conditions for a wide range of cases (hence its adoption here). I cannot rule out entirely that a head-based type of structure relying on a quantifying head might have been appropriate at some intermediate stage. (I could, for example, not reproduce/find the kind of more subtle discriminating experimental evidence Hackl uses synchronically for the diachronic stages.[8]) But what emerges is that the head-based structure cannot be the whole story of diachronic development, given its undesired outcome for today's grammars at LF. Given modern conceptions of grammar as interface-bound, we can hence not adopt the possibly more straightforward (and all things being equal, more attractive) narrow-syntactic account and need to search further.

One particularly strong tool in diachronic analysis (when applicable) is the preference of non-movement over movement structures (i.e. some version of *Merge-over-Move*). For example, Roberts and Roussou (2003) and van Gelderen (2004) show how in a broad panorama of relevant cases that involved head,

---

7 Thanks to Doris Penka (p.c.) for pointing this out.

8 Specifically, Hackl (2009) uses a series of three experiments based on verification tasks that can (naturally) only be applied with living speakers.

but also phrasal movement at earlier stages, reduction to non-movement, or the minimalist *First Merge* for that matter, neatly accounts for the respective trajectories. Moreover, in Gergel (2009) a way is shown how this kind of thinking can be transferred, to a large extent, to the level of LF in the sense of compositional semantics – once again: when the premises are met. But let us consider whether the premise is met in the history of *most*. For the case study at hand, there is no convincing movement dependency in the pre-reanalysis surfacing syntax. Hence I cannot see loss of syntactic movement as an explanation for the developments. The quality of LF movement in the case of *most*, on the other hand, which by standard semantic assumptions exists in superlatives (Heim 1985, 1999; Szabolcsi 1986), is slightly more twisted with regard to its applicability for our diachronic case study. (It will be addressed with regard to historical explanatory potential in Section 4 below.)

To summarize so far: One could seek to model the syntactic change as head-based, but one would in this case end up with a largely inadequate LF structure. Given that the current interest lies in finding the closest correlate at the interface, we cannot adopt this modeling (successful in other areas) for the case of *most*. The even more general and hence attractive principle based on Merge-over-Move cannot be applied syntactically in our case either, given that there is no relevant movement dependency to start with.

3.2 Partitive constructions: tightening beyond the functional-lexical line?

Before turning to the necessary semantic aspects of *most* in the next section, there is a syntactic line of thought the basic elements of which I will introduce next.[9] In doing so, I will draw on the syntax of partitive constructions (PCs; cf. van Riemsdijk 1998; Corver and van Riemsdijk 2001). Recall from the description of *most* the co-occurrence of the pre-reanalysis item with nouns meaning 'part' at different stages of the language. Such nouns are, in fact, classical introducers of PCs.

A central piece of motivation for the study of PCs has been the fact that the functional-lexical divide has not in all cases been a satisfactory distinction already within synchronic generative studies. One side of the problem is that certain lexical categories have long been sensed to have functional characteristics (while still not being functional all the way through). We can immediately

---

9 Thanks to Jutta Hartmann (p.c.) for bringing this up.

observe that if this type of blurry border arises synchronically, then it also becomes potentially relevant to language change. Specifically, if semi-functional elements become available, then they could also offer a potential source for creating a pool of functionalized elements over time.

PCs are in simplest terms combinations of two nominal projections. The label has not only been used to describe actual part-denoting nouns (though they also appear under the label) but also for other types of nouns (including container nouns, quantifier nouns, measure nouns, and others). PCs are more specifically classified as direct (DPCs) when they are not mediated by a preposition or genitive case; and as indirect (IPCs), when they are. Van Riemsdijk (1998) gives the following Dutch examples, for illustration of DPCs and IPCs respectively:

(10) a. *een   plak   kaas*
          a   slice cheese

      b. *een   bus   met   toeristen*
          a   bus   with   tourists
          (van Riemsdijk 1998: 12)

A structurally higher noun is not as innocent syntactically as one might have taken it as a lexical noun. In particular, such nouns in DPCs quite naturally induce especially tight structures synchronically. Corver and van Riemsdijk (2001) note, for instance, the inadequacy of the mere functional-lexical distinction when it comes to such nouns. Their key distributional characteristic consists in displaying properties of a single projection even though they take a second projection as a complement. (This is surely reminiscent of the extended-projection type of conception that arose with combinations of a lexical element and a functional projection on top of it.)

What about the combination *most part* + NP_2 in the history of English with regard to PCs? Given that the second NP can only be introduced via a genitive or, after the loss of morphological case, only via a preposition, the input sequence patterns more closely with the IPC rather than the DPC according to the basic definition given above. This categorization can be supported on the basis of two further diagnostics. DPCs are claimed to be able to transmit the same case to the lower noun which they assign to the higher one and they do not allow intermediate determiners. This is different for early English 'part' constructions. Example (11) shows that even though the superordinate NP is assigned the accusative, the lower one displays the genitive (and it moreover has an intervening determiner):

(11) and *þone*   *mæstan*   *dæl*   *þæs*   *folces*   *ofslogon.*
      and   the.ACC   largest.ACC part.ACC the.GEN   people.GEN   killed
      'And (they) killed the biggest part/most of the people.'
      (cocathom2,+ACHom_II,_4:36.213.828)

The major output sequence after the reanalysis, *most* + *NP*, cannot be regarded as a PC according to the definition any longer, but for a trivial reason; namely, that it only has one overt nominal. In narrow syntax, two possibilities in relationship to PCs become available. One would be to assume that the construction still invariably has a noun 'part' in it, but that it is silent. Under this scenario, an IPC will have shifted to a DPC given that the overt nominal does not require introduction via a preposition or case. A second possibility, however, is to assume that the construction has been more radically reduced altogether: there is no invariably projected zero noun in it. On either possibility, we have a clear tightening of syntactic structure, as *most* changes from a lexical gradable adjective towards a quantifier. For the first option to become viable, evidence would be required to support a silent noun invariably projected with *most* in Present-Day English. I am not aware of such evidence. Hence I will adopt the second option (i.e. without a zero noun in the quantifier), given that the semantics after the reanalysis (including the relevant type of partitioning) will be projected by *most* itself at LF. A stipulation of a silent noun in the reanalyzed structure will thereby become superfluous.

4 Semantic options in change and increased functionalization

Our starting issue was how the quantifier *most* could develop into what it is. In order to approach the answer, we will consider more closely the basic semantic properties in current grammars, and we will raise the question of how a transition to such properties can be modeled diachronically.

According to a line of research in theoretical linguistics going back to Bresnan (1973) and revived recently for example in the work of Hackl (2009), the quantifier *most* can be best modeled in Present-Day English grammar intuitively as the superlative of *many*. (It is thus not an atomic element in the sense of Generalized Quantifier Theory.) Slightly more technically, a movement analysis is typically suggested, in which the superlative *-est* moves at the level of LF for type reasons. The constituent containing the superlative (and also containing a covert comparison class C) is an operator of semantic type $<<d,<e,t>>, <e,t>>$.

After movement, the superlative thus binds the degree variable of type <d> available in the degree slot of the base adjective itself.

On the empirical side, the possibility of creating two distinct interpretable structures via movement correlates with the availability of two readings for superlatives in general. The two types of superlative readings for lexical adjectives are available in (12), drawn from Heim (1985).

(12) *John ate the biggest apple.*
    a.   John ate an apple that is bigger than any other apple.

    b.   John ate a bigger apple than anyone else.

The meaning paraphrased in (12a) is referred to as the absolute reading while the one in (12b) is known as the relative reading. An advantage of the movement analysis is that it does not have to assume different lexical entries for the root adjectives or the *-est* operator. By taking recourse to different positionings at LF of what is plausibly one and the same operator in conjunction with the same entry of the adjective, it accounts for the ambiguity of superlatives. According to Hackl and others, this carries over underlyingly to *most*, as indicated in (13) (cf. Hackl 2009: 79, following the movement analysis of Heim 1985, 1999 and Szabolcsi 1986).

(13)   a.   [John climbed [the [-**est** C]$_i$ [d$_i$ -many mountains]]]
     b.   [John [-**est** C]$_i$ [climbed [the d$_i$ -many mountains]]]

On the reading with the LF in (13a), John climbed a set of mountains whose cardinality is higher than that of its Boolean complement, i.e. John climbed more than half of the relevant mountains. Hence, according to Hackl, pluralities of mountains are compared here in terms of how many atomic parts they have.[10] On the relative reading, schematized in (13b), John climbed more mountains than any other salient individual. (The comparison class C includes such individuals here, whereas pluralities were compared in the former case.) The corresponding LF-tree geometry is as follows. In the first LF, the superlative undergoes only short movement and stays within the DP domain, while in the second it moves somewhere to the edge of VP. Superlative *most* distinguishes itself from other adjectives in that it does not have an absolute reading. But note that it does have another interpretation in addition to the relative one, namely the proportional one introduced above and which is equivalent to 'more than half'

---

10 *The* in (13a) cannot be interpreted as a definite on the Heim/Szabolcsi analysis, but it must be interpreted as an indefinite due to the lack of uniqueness.

(cf. Hackl 2009 for some discussion of possibilities as to why the make-up of readings is distinct in superlatives with *most*).

If we tried to approach the development of the quantifier *most* as the loss of an LF-movement dependency over time, we would run into a problem. It is not explanatory. Such a movement account fails (as a diachronic explanation) for a different reason than the syntactic movement account. The reason is that not only adjectives such as 'highest' or 'largest' (close to the meaning of *most* in Old English) are plausibly accounted via movement at LF, but also the quantifier *most* of Present-Day English itself requires LF movement. So, it is reasonable in this case to assume that a movement dependency is available semantically (recall that in terms of surface syntax the problem was we had no obvious movement). However, there is no *loss* of such a LF dependency to predict anything in this case, movement being available quite in parallel both in the old and the new LF of *most*.

Let us turn now to the key element in the semantics of *most* and *many* in the approach of Hackl (2009). Crucially, the quantifier needs to be able to measure pluralities in the denotation of the noun in some way, e.g., via the cardinality function. This is the main point where I take the innovation during the historical process to be located, descriptively and technically. Here is why. In descriptive terms, *most* was closest to a superlative of *mycel*, 'much' in its old sense of 'great in size', as described in Section 2. That is, it meant essentially 'largest' and not yet 'most' in general, as noted by Einenkel (1904: 129). In slightly more technical terms, a relatively normal gradable adjectival predicate was available semantically in Old English (to which the superlative operator could attach in the usual manner). But no reference to pluralities was necessitated before the change. It was not required by any hard-wired grammatical requirement in pre-reanalysis *most*, nor in many cases even possible, e.g., when the adjective modified a singular noun.

The change from the gradable adjective to the quantifier is relatively thorough in the grammar in the sense that the new meaning almost entirely replaces the old one. (As usual in grammar change, the issue of the discrete grammatical option is orthogonal to the spread and regularization of the ultimate new form, the latter being rather gradual in its appearance; cf. Kroch 1989 for discussion). At the same time, a number of propitious key ingredients were in place in the pre-reanalysis form, as we have seen. Analyses that treat the quantifier *most* as a superlative make us in fact understand this even better, given that a relatively watered-down gradable property could specialize on a very exclusive use over time. As for the specific mechanism how this could have happened, the suggestion for the grammatical development of *most* is given in (14) below.

(14) An item undergoes **ontological semantic functionalization** diachronically *iff* it changes from compositionally combining with an originally lexical item *I* at a time t_1 towards incorporating a variant of *I* induced in the meta-language of semantic interpretation at a subsequent time t_2.

Note that the lexical item *I* is one that happens to be in the proximity of the actual item in question and the two combine as separate items, e.g., an adjective like 'largest' and a noun like 'part'. It is only later, when the quantificational 'most' is entrenched in the grammar, that 'part' has shifted into the meta-language, namely in the lexical entry of the quantifier itself. Specifically, I thus suggest that the key to the development of the quantifier *most* in theoretical terms is the semantic-ontological functionalization that arises from the combination with the nouns that originally conveyed the meaning 'part'. This includes all its exponents (*dæl, del, parte, parti*, etc.). The combination then becomes part and parcel of the denotation of the quantifier itself after the change, as summarized in the schema in (15), repeated from above:

(15) MOST [part of [N]] → MOST [N]

In terms of the notation, MOST is used in the schema above only as shorthand for the surfacing form. It conveys the complex quantifier meaning after the reanalysis while it stands in for the superlative of the gradable predicate (essentially 'largest') before the reanalysis.

In view of what we observed, it might strike us as unusual that one noun (what is more: in the singular) should have played a major role historically in producing a relatively complex expression, a key component of which must have now access to quantification and pluralities. But the suggestion is supported on closer inspection by several arguments coming from different areas.

First, the proposal models this change more accurately than alternative suggestions that we explored (and the shortcomings of which we have seen). While it is true that we are dealing with a noun, recall also that it is a partitive one. The pre-reanalysis adjective 'largest' can thus fit in precisely to measure the partition. And the functional notion of partition is exactly what is required after the alteration in meaning is encoded grammatically, i.e. at times at which *most* patterns as the superlative of *many*. As mentioned, the quantifier *most* decomposes into a superlative, i.e. *many* and *-est*, the denotations of which following Hackl (2009) are as follows:

(16) $[[MANY]](d)(A) = \lambda x.[A(x) \& |x| \geq d]$

(17) $[est](C)(D)(x)=1$ *iff*

$\forall y \in C\ [y \neq x \rightarrow \max \{d: D(d)(x)=1\} > \max \{d: D(d)(y)=1\}]$

Recall that Hackl treats *most*, like *many*, as a gradable expression that modifies plural NPs. Pluralities can be measured in terms of how many atomic parts they are composed of, i.e. via the cardinality function (cf. $|x|$ above). In prose, (16) then states that the base quantifier *many* is a property of pluralities, the cardinality of which is larger than a standard d. The form *most* then builds on the superlative as in (17), by requiring the plurality x of which it is true to be more numerous than any other plurality from the contextual restriction C that is distinct from x.

What we have capitalized on, then, is an internal property of the lexical entry (namely of being able to quantize partitioning of pluralities), not anything that relates to the here orthogonal positioning of the building blocks *many* and *-est* via LF movement. That is, this particular development does not rely on the loss of a movement dependency. By using this type of analysis a number of ingredients turn out to be positioned quite advantageously for the transition from the pre-reanalysis to the post-reanalysis meaning, e.g., the semantic types and the movement possibilities. All that it takes, in essence, is a semantic catalyst mechanism, then, to get us from one meaning to the next.[11]

Second, it becomes a good possibility that a noun that was particularly frequently co-occurring with the superlative adjective *most* should have played a major role. Some first relevant figures of co-occurrence based on the Penn-York-Helsinki series of historical corpora are given in (18).

(18) PROPORTIONS OF *DÆL/PART*-NOUNS in tokens with *most* preceding a noun (YCOE, PPCME2 and PPCEME):

Old English:	50/264	= 18.9%
Middle English:	41/159	= 25.7%
EModE-E1 (1500–1569):	41/75	= 54.6%
EModE-E2 (1570–1639):	40/79	= 50.6%
EModE-E3 (1640–1710):	36/88	= 40.9%

---

11 I have focused on the proposed use of partitional nouns within the limits of this contribution. At the same time, just like in well-known cases of syntactic change, it would seem dogmatic to exclude other co-contributing factors (cf., e.g., Denison 1993 for discussion of a series of possibilities in the genesis of *do*-support). For example, while I do not assume null nouns to be available in the Present-Day English representations of *most*, as stated in the main text, I cannot exclude their presence in Old English, where evidence in the grammar might have been available.

E1–E3 are the standard Helsinki sub-periods of the Early Modern English period with the years indicated. Given that a superlative adjective could occur with a variety of nouns, the proportion of one single noun co-occurring with it is strikingly high. The tendency also seems to be in a rough ascending trend up to Early Modern English. A first hint for the full functionalization of the quantifier *most* may then be the point at which the frequency starts declining (the transition between the periods E2 and E3 of Early Modern English).

Third, recall that the syntax already contributes an input structure to the change via the partitive construction that has a particular potential to tightening (hence re-analysis), and which can then be operated on by the semantics. While the specific type of syntactic configuration (PC) has been introduced in Section 3 above, let us consider the issue from a reversed angle here. Specifically, consider a type of change that did not happen. The adjective *most* was clearly not the only one to be able to denote meanings along the lines of a high degree on a scale and build a superlative of it. Superlative adjectives such as 'greatest', 'highest', 'widest' and several others have precursors already in earliest Old English (others like 'biggest' or 'largest' are only attested from early Middle English, for independent historical reasons). However, none of them (or similar ones) gave rise to quantifiers like *most*. Note also that adjectives are in general a potential source for quantifiers (von Fintel 1995; Haspelmath 1995) and adjectives denoting a large degree would also have the relevant lexical input to the change. Such adjectives did not, however, seem to have co-occurrence rates with partitional nouns anywhere as high as *most*. A plausible hypothesis is hence that, in English, the co-occurrence with partitional nouns might have been a relevant factor conducive to the relatively tight syntactic relationship and semantic interpretation.

Finally, let me emphasize that the development suggested has not been thought of as a generalization over how quantifiers develop. This should not be too surprising, given that the starting synchronic observation was that *most* does not comply with Generalized Quantifier Theory following recent semantic approaches. It is beyond present scope to compare *most* with other quantifiers (which might, or might not, have been more well-behaved from the perspective of Generalized Quantifier Theory), but from a historical perspective, we can adduce one more piece of evidence that *most* behaves distinctly from lexical adjectives but also from some (uses of) quantifying determiners such as *every*, *some* and *no*. Specifically, patterns with *one* (anaphora) have not been adopted by *most* at all. The difference is that while the mentioned quantifiers gave rise to forms such as *some-one*, *every-one*, *no-one*, *most* failed to do so (cf. **most-one*).

This may indicate that while *most* has been functionalized, this did not happen on a par with all quantifiers.[12]

5 Summary and discussion

After giving a short summary and listing certain questions for further research, the present section discusses the following issues which are mostly outside the strict scope of the paper: parameters, ontological enrichment, restrictiveness and completeness of theories of semantic change.

In this paper, we have followed a synchronic observation, based principally on Hackl (2009), that the quantifier *most* is on closer inspection decomposable as a superlative of *many* in synchronic terms. Diachronically, we observed that the word originally meant 'largest' in Old English and raised the question of how the change could be modeled in modern conceptions of syntax and semantics. The path ultimately supported was that in this case, on the one hand, relatively little happened. For instance, there was no loss of a movement dependency in either syntax or semantics that would explain the change. On the other hand, the quantificational overall structure did, however, seem to incorporate a partitive structure into its hardwired semantics, which in turn may have been promoted in particular by the co-occurrence with relational nouns meaning 'part'. This may be a relatively moderate case of ontological enrichment (we will mention more radical possibilities below).

There are interesting questions emerging from our brief investigation calling for further research on the topic addressed. First, the proportional reading is the one that most naturally relates to the diachronic connection made via partitivity. A closer inspection of the diachronic trajectory of the relative reading will be required. Second, the claimed role of the definite article in Present-Day English

---

12 Issues remain and one could blame the gap of *most* in the anaphora paradigm on the plurality required by *most*. But adjectives (which are classical licensers of anaphora, Lobeck 1995) can adjust to this apparent obstacle, cf. *(the) red ones* vs. **(the) most ones*. This additional detail may then reinforce the view that *most* has been functionalized historically in a different manner and is not a lexical adjective. However, note that *most* can participate in structure-sharing and ellipsis, similarly to other quantifiers; cf. *most but not all cats* or (i) for an example of nominal ellipsis from the last period (E3) of the Early Modern English corpus:

(i) *Though in many Schooles I observe six a clock in the morning to be the hour for children to be fast at their Book, yet in* **most_**, *seven is the constant time, both in Winter and Summer, against which houre, it is fit every Scholar should be ready at the Schoole.*
    (HOOLE-E3-P2,238.38)

also requires a further look into the past. While it has been observed above that versions of *most* with and without the definite article could alternate historically, there seems to be – from what I have gathered so far – an imbalance at all times in English. Specifically, there is no time at which there was, say, an obligatory presence of the definite article with quantificational *most* as is the case with *(die) meisten*, 'the most' in German (or even a slight majority of examples). On the contrary, examples containing the definite determiner appear to be a minority at all historical major periods up to Early Modern English (and I could not extract a reading correlation for the few examples found[13]). More generally, a comparison with German could reveal further restrictions and/or generalizations.

Given that the suggestions made have been an exploration of the possibilities available in syntax and semantics for *most*, and not about any particularly broad generalizations, it is useful to raise the question: Can larger theoretical constructs such as parameters possibly play a role towards deeper insight? In the spirit of Roberts (2012), we can note that while the notion of a syntactic parameter may appear as harder to construe in minimalist terms than in earlier versions of generative syntax, there are interesting possibilities of raising the issue of a parameter feasibly also from a diachronic perspective (cf. also the lines of syntactic research outlined in Gianollo, Guardiano, and Longobardi 2008). At the same time, choosing and motivating any particular parameters is frequently a difficult issue. In addition, it is conceivable that complexities increase if one tries to integrate parametric possibilities of composition at LF into the accounts (as would be required also for *most*). A desideratum quite generally would be for syntactic work to take interpretation seriously and vice-versa (cf. van Gelderen, this volume, on the possible role of interpretability in language change).

Singular parametric options in semantic terms have been insightfully pioneered by Chierchia (1998), amongst others. It may, nonetheless, seem a particularly daunting task at present to ascertain a particular set of semantic parameters

---

13 For example, (6c) above had *most* with the definite article and, from the context, a clear generic reading. As an anonymous reviewer points out, there is a(n additional) puzzle in current English, in that *most NP* is used only in generic readings and to neutralize the latter *most of the NP* is used. The issue may be related to the old genitive, but also to the nature of partitive constructions more generally, and it is worth to be addressed by future research. Returning to the distribution of the definite, cases of coordination with superlative lexical adjectives may also be of interest in a fuller discussion; cf. (i) where the definite resists insertion despite its availability in the conjunct:

(i) *But it is very vnlike to be true, and yet reported in _ most places, and in **the** best places.*
   (GAWDY-E2-P1,27.66)

as general linguistic properties (rather than singular options), out of which then, say, the full diachronic trajectory of constructions like those involving *most* will follow as such. Nonetheless, there is beginning work conducted on a broader scale pertaining to the possible general options at least in the domain of gradable constructions (cf. Beck et al. 2010; Tiemann, Hohaus, and Beck 2012, as well as references cited there). A hope for future work in terms of the development of motivated parameter theories can therefore only be that the insights of compositional semantics will also find a place in them.

The issue of functionalization that has been suggested here can be viewed against a wider background of variation in combinatorial possibilities at LF, up to fundamental ontological variation. It is conceivable that certain lexical entries or combinations are not available in all languages, and similarly: not at all times in a given language (cf. von Fintel and Matthewson 2008 for a discussion and overview of what should count as universals in semantics, even though the focus is synchronic there). If one agrees with the general idea of semantic variation, then diachronic ontological functionalization can bring in additional combinatorial possibilities and complexities – sometimes wholesale, sometimes only in smaller corners of a language. A note is in order regarding the term "ontological" that I have used. It simply hints at the extreme case in which the ontology of semantic objects is enriched. But of course smaller steps are possible, as we have seen. Furthermore, it is also possible that the import is absorbed more directly into the grammar (and not via a combination with another noun, as was the case with *most*). One particularly extreme case would be that of a new semantic type being imported into the grammar. A point raised for example in Beck et al. (2010) or Bochnak (2013) has to do with the very ontology of degrees. From the comparative angle of such works, it is imaginable that a language lacks degrees at a certain point in time but that it could develop them diachronically.

While semantic parameters in the sense of compositional construction of meaning are a relatively new area of investigation, a number of mechanisms and tendencies have been proposed in recent years for semantic change independently of parameters; cf. especially the conventionalization of side-meanings in a compositional set-up and the solving of "semantic equations" (Eckardt 2006). Work of this type offers not only a useful foundation, but an important specific beginning given that compositionality itself restricts some options in change. We might nonetheless want to make diachronic investigations even more restrictive; for example, by naturally putting the syntax into the compositional panorama and gleaning structural paths, where they are available. But it is likely that not all developments in semantics are fully and solely structure-based (as we have seen above[14]). That is, it may still be worth finding out more about piecemeal developments including different types of functionalization – be it only for the sheer reason of describing as many types of developments as possible before moving towards a more complete understanding of the full range of possibilities of change at the interface.

Sources

[Ælfric]
Ælfric, Abbot of Eynsham. 1880. *Ælfrics Grammatik und Glossar*. Edited by Julius Zupitza. Berlin: Weidmann.
[Beowulf]
Anonymous. 1994. *Beowulf: A Student Edition*. Edited by George Jack. Oxford: Oxford University Press.
[OED]
Oxford English Dictionary. 2002. Oxford: Oxford University Press, 3rd edition.
[PPCEME]
Kroch, Anthony, Beatrice Santorini & Ariel Diertani. 2004. *The Penn-Helsinki Parsed Corpus of Early Modern English*. http://www.ling.upenn.edu/hist-corpora/PPCEME-RELEASE-2/index. html (for a list of the names of the texts available in the corpus, see http://www.ling.upenn. edu/hist-corpora/PPCEME-RELEASE-2/philological_info.html).
[PPCME2]
Kroch, Anthony & Ann Taylor. 2000. *The Penn-Helsinki Parsed Corpus of Middle English, second edition*. http://www.ling.upenn.edu/hist-corpora/PPCME2-RELEASE-3/index.html (for a list of the names of the texts available in the corpus, see http://www.ling.upenn.edu/ hist-corpora/PPCME"_RELEASE-3/info/texts-by-name.html).
[YCOE]
Taylor, Ann, Anthony Warner, Susan Pintzuk & Frank Beths. 2003. *The York-Toronto-Helsinki Parsed Corpus of Old English Prose*. Heslington: University of York. http://www-users. york.ac.uk/~lang22/YcoeHome1.htm (for a list of the names of the texts available in the corpus, see http://www-users.york.ac.uk/~lang22/YCOE/info/YcoeTextFile.htm#list).

References

Barwise, Jon & Robin Cooper. 1981. Generalized quantifiers and natural language. *Linguistics and Philosophy* 4. 159–219.
Beck, Sigrid, Sveta Krasikova, Daniel Fleischer, Remus Gergel, Stefan Hofstetter, Christiane Savelsberg, John Vanderelst & Elisabeth Villalta. 2010. Crosslinguistic variation in comparative constructions. *Linguistic Variation Yearbook* 9. 1–66.

---

14 Cf. Gergel and Beck (2013) for a different diachronic investigation at the syntax-semantics interface based on a combination of structural and non-structural factors.

Bhatt, Rajesh & Roumyana Pancheva. 2004. Late Merger of degree clauses. *Linguistic Inquiry* 35. 1–45.

Bochnak, M. Ryan. 2013. The degree semantics parameter and cross-linguistic variation. Ms. UC Berkeley. http://semanticsarchive.net/Archive/jM5NmFjZ/Bochnak_DegreeSemantics-Variation.pdf (accessed 18 January 2014).

Bresnan, Joan. 1973. The syntax of the comparative clause construction in English. *Linguistic Inquiry* 4. 275–343.

Chierchia, Gennaro. 1998. Reference to kinds across languages. *Natural Language Semantics* 6. 339–405.

Corver, Norbert & Henk van Riemsdijk. 2001. Semi-lexical categories. In Norbert Corver & Henk van Riemsdijk (eds.), *Semi-lexical categories. The function of content words and the content of function words*, 1–22. Berlin & New York: Mouton de Gruyter.

Denison, David. 1993. *English historical syntax*. London: Longman.

Eckardt, Regine. 2006. *Meaning change in grammaticalization*. Oxford: Oxford University Press.

Einenkel, Eugen. 1904. Das englische Indefinitum II. *Anglia: Zeitschrift für englische Philologie* 27. 1–204.

Embick, David. 2007. Blocking effects and analytic/synthetic alternations. *Natural Language and Linguistic Theory* 25. 1–37.

von Fintel, Kai. 1995. The formal semantics of grammaticalization. In Jill N. Beckman (ed.), *Proceedings of the Annual Meeting of the North East Linguistic Society 25*. Vol. 2, 175–189. Amherst, MA: GLSA, University of Massachusetts.

von Fintel, Kai & Lisa Matthewson. 2008. Universals in semantics. *The Linguistic Review* 25. 139–201.

Fischer, Olga, Ans van Kemenade, Willem Koopman & Wim van der Wurff. 2000. *The syntax of Early English*. Cambridge: Cambridge University Press.

van Gelderen, Elly. 2004. *Grammaticalization as economy*. Amsterdam & Philadelphia: John Benjamins.

Gergel, Remus. 2009. Rather – on a modal cycle. In Elly van Gelderen (ed.), *Cyclical change*, 243–264. Amsterdam & Philadelphia: John Benjamins.

Gergel, Remus. 2010. Motivating certain variation patterns in degree constructions: Semantics meets grammaticalization. *Poznań Studies in Contemporary Linguistics* 46. 27–49.

Gergel, Remus & Sigrid Beck. 2013. Early Modern English *again* – a corpus study and semantic analysis. Ms. University of Graz & University of Tübingen (forthcoming *English Language and Linguistics*).

Gianollo, Chiara, Cristina Guardiano & Giuseppe Longobardi. 2008. Three fundamental issues in parametric linguistics. In Theresa Biberauer (ed.), *The limits of syntactic variation*, 109–142. Amsterdam & Philadelphia: John Benjamins.

González-Díaz, Victorina. 2008. *English adjective comparison: A historical perspective*. Amsterdam & Philadelphia: John Benjamins.

Hackl, Martin. 2009. On the grammar and processing of proportional quantifiers: 'most' versus 'more than half'. *Natural Language Semantics* 17. 63–98.

Haspelmath, Martin. 1995. Diachronic sources for 'all' and 'every'. In Emmon Bach, Eloise Jelinek, Angelika Kratzer & Barbara H. Partee, (eds.), *Quantification in natural languages*, 363–382. Dordrecht: Kluwer.

Heim, Irene. 1985. Notes on comparatives and related matters. University of Texas at Austin. http://semanticsarchive.net/Archive/zcOZjYOM/Comparatives%2085.pdf (accessed 22 January 2014).

Heim, Irene. 1999. Notes on superlatives. Ms. MIT.

Kroch, Anthony. 1989. Reflexes of grammar in patterns of language change. *Language variation and change* 1. 199–244.

Lobeck, Anne C. 1995. *Ellipsis. Functional heads, licensing, and identification*. Oxford: Oxford University Press.

van Riemsdijk, Henk. 1998. Categorial feature magnetism: The endocentricity and distribution of projections. *Journal of Comparative Germanic Linguistics* 2. 1–48.

Roberts, Ian. 1985. Agreement parameters and the development of English modal auxiliaries. *Natural Language and Linguistic Theory* 3. 21–58.

Roberts, Ian. 2012. Towards a parameter hierarchy for verb-movement: Diachronic considerations. Paper presented at the *34th Annual Meeting of the Deutsche Gesellschaft für Sprachwissenschaft*, University of Frankfurt/M., 6–9 March 2012.

Roberts, Ian & Anna Roussou. 2003. *Syntactic change: A minimalist approach to grammaticalization*. Cambridge: Cambridge University Press.

Szabolcsi, Anna. 1986. Comparative superlatives. *MIT Working Papers in Linguistics* 8. 245–265.

Tiemann, Sonja, Vera Hohaus & Sigrid Beck. 2012. Crosslinguistic variation in comparison: Evidence from child language acquisition. In Britta Stolterfoht & Sam Featherston (eds.), *Empirical approaches to linguistic theory: Studies in meaning and structure*, 115–146. Berlin & New York: Mouton de Gruyter.

Paola Crisma
5 The "indefinite article" from cardinal to operator to expletive[1]

In this paper, I analyse the diachronic development of *an* in the history of English. I propose that in Old English *an* has the twofold status of a cardinal and an existential operator and has not yet developed into a true indefinite article, whose nature, I argue, is that of an expletive. I show that two distinct stages can be distinguished in Old English, and I propose that the diachronic development of *an* may be analysed as a typical case of grammaticalization.

1 Introduction

All modern Germanic languages, among which Present-Day English (PDE), regularly[2] use the indefinite article before indefinite singular count nouns, with the exception of Icelandic (exemplified in [2]):

(1)　a.　*I found cat in the garden*

　　　b.　*I found a cat in the garden*

(2)　*Ég　fann　kött　í　garðin-um*
　　　I　found　cat　in　garden-the
　　　'I found a cat in the garden'

The indefinite article, however, is a fairly recent development in the Germanic languages, as well as in Indo-European languages in general. Old English (OE) is particularly interesting because it has a somewhat intermediate status, for, in

1 This work was begun while I was a visiting scholar in Cambridge with a contribution from PRIN 2008EHLWYE_005 (Oct–Dec 2010), and benefited from a grant FRA2009 – University of Trieste. It was presented at the *13th Diachronic Generative Syntax* conference in Philadelphia (June 2011) and at the annual meeting of the *Deutsche Gesellschaft für Sprachwissenschaft* in Frankfurt (March 2012): I thank the audiences of both conferences for their helpful comments. I am also grateful to the reviewers of the first version of this paper for pointing out its weaknesses and making useful suggestions.
2 Where not otherwise stated, I will only consider nominals in argument function, typically subjects and objects. I will also abstract away from special cases, such as for example coordinated nominals, exhibiting much inter- and intra-linguistic variation.

prose texts, one finds both PDE-like constructions, where *an* looks identical to the modern indefinite article (compare [3a] to [1b]), and Icelandic-like constructions, where an indefinite singular count noun appears without a determiner (compare [3b] and [2]):

(3) a. & *hiene* *ofslog* **an** **efor**
      and him.ACC kill a boar
      'and a wild boar killed him'
      (ChronA_[Plummer]:885.13.944)

    b. *Her* *sæt* **hæþen** **here** *on* *Tenet*
      here remained heathen army in Thanet
      'In this year a heathen army remained in Thanet'
      (ChronA_[Plummer]:865.1.753)

The problem of this kind of variability is well known to every scholar working on ancient languages, and is traditionally ascribed to the language being at an alleged "transitional stage", somehow instantiating language change in progress. The challenge resides in the fact that in modern languages real optionality is rare, and functional elements do not seem to be freely omitted. So, the first task of the linguist is that of ascertaining whether the observed optionality is in fact only apparent, and rather subject to some subtle grammatical restriction. Should optionality persist, however, the task would become that of modelling variability, as in Kroch (1989) and in much subsequent work.

In this paper I analyse the diachronic development of *an* in the history of English. The paper is organized as follows: I first describe how quantitative data were collected and organized in order to understand the nature of *an* in Old English. I then show that two different grammars for *an* can be detected in Old English, both different from the grammar of the PDE indefinite article. After outlining the properties of *an* at these stages, I show that the development has all the characteristics of a case of grammaticalization.

2 Old English singular indefinites: a database

Examples such as those in (3) may give the impression that the use of *an* in Old English was entirely optional, especially if, as in this case, the examples are from the same manuscript and by the same hand (Ker 1957: 58). However, isolated examples of this kind do not provide any information on the possible existence of restrictions on the distribution of a given element. Such restrictions can only be detected by means of quantitative data, comparing a random sample of nominals introduced by *an* with an analogous sample of singular count nominals occurring "bare",[3] isolating the various possible contexts which may affect the presence vs. absence of *an*.

2.1 Collecting the samples

Quantitative data for syntactic purposes can be collected using extremely powerful tools such as the *York-Toronto-Helsinki Parsed Corpus of Old English Prose* (YCOE), a syntactically annotated corpus of about 1.5 million words.

However, collecting the samples necessary for the present study could not simply be done as an automated procedure, for in the YCOE nouns are not labelled for singular/plural, let alone [± count]. Thus, while it was easy to collect a sample of nominals introduced by *an*, an automated search for "bare" nouns mostly retrieved "bare" plural and mass nouns, irrelevant for the present work. Note that it would have been incorrect to simply make a list of the lexical items that appeared preceded by *an* and then check whether they also occurred "bare", for one must allow for the possibility that a given noun might occur "bare" once or more, but never occur preceded by *an*. Creating the sample of "bare" singular count nouns starting from the sample of nouns introduced by *an* might therefore have resulted in the over-representation of the latter in the set of data.

A lexicon of singular count nouns was therefore built,[4] which was then used to restrict the searches on the YCOE that would generate the relevant samples, one of "bare" nominals headed by a singular count noun, the other of nominals introduced by *an*. The searches were also restricted so that they would only retrieve subjects and objects.

The samples thus collected were then manually tagged according to their interpretive properties, as described in the following section. At that stage, some tokens erroneously retrieved were eliminated. Note at this point that, after the elimination of irrelevant material, the list of "bare" singular nominals amounted to 328 tokens, that of nominals introduced by *an* to 219. These figures might seem disappointingly low, especially considering that, in the texts used as sources, the number of subject and object nominals headed by a common noun totals 53,206. However, when a search was made for subjects and objects introduced by *an*, without restricting it to a pre-established lexicon, the result amounted to

---

3 In the sense of Carlson (1977), though his study actually focuses only on plural nouns.
4 See Appendix for details.

a meagre total of 796. Thus, a sample of 219 nominals introduced by *an* actually represents 27.5 % of the entire population.[5]

2.2 Sorting out the samples

In order to understand the nature of *an* in Old English, it is necessary to individuate the contexts that require or exclude its presence, if any. The obvious point of departure is the grammar of the indefinite article in modern languages, especially the daughter language, Present-Day English.

In Present-Day English, a nominal with the form *a+Noun* can be used in various different ways. It can be a generic, as in (4a); it can be a specific existential, as in (4b); it can be non-specific to the point that its denotation might be hard to pin down, as in (4c); or it can be perfectly ambiguous between a specific and a non-specific reading, as in (4d):

(4) a. *A blue whale eats about 40 million krill a day*

   b. *I want you to meet a student, her name is Sara*

   c. *I would love to have a unicorn, but they don't exist*

   d. *He will invite a minister to open the conference*

In Present-Day English, the presence of *a* in all these cases is obligatory. However, "bare" nouns are perfectly grammatical if plural or mass with a generic or existential interpretation. In the latter case, they easily alternate with nominals introduced by weak *some* or *sm*:

(5) a. *I bought oranges/wine*

   b. *I bought sm oranges/wine*

The presence vs. absence of *sm* is not entirely free, however. In particular, "bare" plurals are not compatible with a specific reading, so (6b) sounds definitely odd, while (6c) does not exhibit the same ambiguity observed in (4d), the only possible readings being the non-specific one:

(6) a. *I want you to meet sm students: Sara, Giovanni and Priscilla*

   b. *?I want you to meet students: Sara, Giovanni and Priscilla*

   c. *He will invite ministers to open the conference*

---

5 It is not possible to determine the size of the population of "bare" singular count nouns in the sources, for a search for "bare" nouns not restricted to a given lexicon also retrieves plural and mass nouns, which turn out to be by far the majority.

These facts can be reduced to the observation that "bare" plurals generally cannot take wide scope,[6] while singular indefinites introduced by *a(n)* and plurals introduced by *sm* can (Carlson 1977: 417–420).

In the light of these alternations, it becomes natural to explore the possibility for the distribution of *an* vs. "bare" singulars in Old English to be governed by similar restrictions. In order to do so, each item in the samples was associated with one of a series of labels describing its denotation properties.

The first distinction was made between nominals receiving an existential interpretation and nominals interpreted as generics (henceforth GNR), the latter exemplified in (7):

(7) GNR

Sua	*sua*	*mid*	*liðre*	*wisðlunga*	*mon*	**hors**	*gestilleð,*	*sua*
so	so	with	soft	whistling	IMPRS	horse	appeases	so

eac	*mid*	*ðære*	*illcan*	*wistlunga*	*mon*	*mæg*	*hund*	*astyrigean*
also	with	the	same	whistling	IMPRS	may	dog	stir.up

'just as with soft whistling one appeases a horse, like-wise with the same whistling one may stir up a dog'
(CP:23.173.21.1178)

Among existentials, various subgroups were distinguished. The first cases to be singled out were those of existentials co-occurring with operators or elements creating intensional contexts and potential scope interactions. These nominals were separated into three groups, those with narrow scope (labelled SCOPE-nrw),[7] those with wide scope (SCOPE-wd) and ambiguous ones (SCOPE-amb):

(8) SCOPE-nrw

a.

forðan	*þe*	*hi*	*furþon*	*noldon*	**ænne**	**fugel**	*acwellan*
because	that	they	even	NEG.want	a	bird	kill

'because they did not want to kill even a bird'
(ÆLS_[Maccabees]:857.5386)

b.

Ne	*scyle*	*nan*	*mon*	**blæcern**	*ælan*	*under*	*mittan*
NEG	shall.SBJV	no	man	lamp	light	under	bushel

'No one ought to light a lamp under a bushel'
(CP:5.43.1.229)

---

6 But see for example Schubert and Pelletier (1987) for some exceptions to this generalization.
7 The notion of "scope" lumps together interactions with items such as quantifiers, negation and *irrealis* modality. However, distinguishing many different sub-sub-groups would have made the labelling extremely cumbersome and unfit to capture some generalizations.

(9) SCOPE-wd

   a. *Ac far þe   to westene, and þu   fintst* **anne wer**
       but go you to desert,   and you find   a   man

     haliges   lifes,   se   hatte   Effrem.
     holy.GEN life.GEN that is.named Effrem
     'but go to the desert, and you will find a holy man, named Effrem.'
     (ÆLS_[Basil]:559.853)

   b. *gað to ðære byrig þe   eow ongean is &   ge   gemetað*
      go to the   town that you opposite is and you find

     þærrihte. **getigedne assan.** *&   his folan samod.*
     thereupon tied   donkey and his foal   together
     'go to the town in front of you, and you will find there a tied donkey
     together with his foal'
     (ÆCHom_I,_14.1:290.6.2561)

(10) SCOPE-amb

   a. *Eft   Isaias   se   witega   awrat   on   his   witegunge   and*
      Again Isaiah the   prophet wrote in   his   prophecies and

     þus   cwæð, Efne **an mæden** *sceal geeacnian...*
     thus said,   Truly a maiden shall conceive
     'Again, the prophet Isaiah wrote in his prophecies and said: Truly a
     maiden shall conceive'
     (ÆCHom_II,_1:7.141.113)

   b. *an   ðæra   witegunga   is, Yssaie, se   awrat*
      one the.GEN.PL prophecy.GEN.PL is, Isaiah, who wrote

     betwux his witegungum þus   cweðende. Efne   sceal
     among his prophecies thus saying: Truly shall

     mæden *geeacnian on hyre innoðe...*
     maiden conceive in her   womb
     'There is one of these prophecies, [by] Isaiah, who wrote among his
     prophecies thus saying: Truly a maiden shall conceive in her womb'
     (ÆCHom_I,_13:282.25.2365)

Of course, most of the nominals in the two samples do not co-occur with any operator or other similar element affecting the presupposition of existence of the referent. Normally, such cases are arguments of a verb in the simple past, therefore the existence of the referent can be inferred. These cases were simply labelled EXS, without further specifications:

(11) EXS

    a. *Him þa   to com **an fiscere***
       him then to came a fisher
       'then a fisher came to him'
       (Or_2:5.48.13.925)

    b. *Hæfde he & wæg   mid hine **twiecge** **handseax geættred***
       had   he and carried with him two.edged dagger   poisoned
       'he had and carried on him a poisoned two-edged dagger'
       (Bede_2:8.122.11.1155)

In some cases, however, such existentials are overtly made specific by the addition of some material that uniquely identifies the designated entity. These nominals, labelled SPC, are similar to those labelled SCOPE-wd in their interpretation:

(12) SPC

    a. *and hæfdon ða   on bendum. **ænne bealdne ðeof.***
       and had.3PL then in bonds   a   bold   thief

       Barraban gecigedne
       Barabba named
       'at that time they had as a prisoner a bold thief named Barabba'
       (ÆCHom_II,_14.1:143.183.3186)

    b. *&   him   **biscop** sendon; Aidan wæs haten*
       and him.DAT bishop sent.3PL Aidan was named
       'and they sent him a bishop named Aidan'
       (Bede_3:2.158.11.1523)

Other cases are those in which *an* is clearly interpreted as a cardinal, meaning "(exactly) one". At the Old English stage, *an* had not yet developed into two distinct morphemes, the indefinite article *a/an* and the cardinal *one*, and the single morpheme *an* was serving both as the cardinal and as the sort of "optional indefinite article" discussed here.[8] So, while in all the examples (8)–(12), *an* was glossed as the indefinite article 'a', glossing it as 'one' would not have been impossible. There are however some cases in which it is clear that the cardinal meaning is intended: these are cases where *an* is contrasted to some other cardinal or to some plurality. Such cases were singled out and labelled ONE:

---

8 See discussion in Section 5.1.

(13) ONE

And	*ealle*	*hi*	*singað*	***ænne***	***lofsang***	*for ðan ðe*	*we*	*&*
and	all	they	sing	one	hymn	because	we	and

hi	*ealle*	*healdað*	***ænne***	***geleafan***
they	all	hold	one	faith

'and they all sing one hymn, because we and they hold one faith'
(ÆCHom_I,_14.1:295.142.2672)

Finally, there was a certain number of items in the samples that did not fall within any of these categories or were simply of unclear interpretation with respect to the above criteria, such as the following, which is in some sense semantically definite for it seems to refer to a uniquely identifiable entity:

(14) | *þa* | *ne* | *wolde* | *se* | *papa* | *þæt* | *þafian (. . .)* | *þætte* | ***swa*** | ***æðele*** | ***wer*** |
|------|------|--------|------|--------|-------|------------------|--------|-----------|------------|-----------|
| then | NEG | wanted | the | pope | that | tolerate | that | so | noble | man |

&	*swa*	*geþungen*	*&*	*swa*	*gelæred*	*swa*	*feor*	*fram*	*him*	*gewite*
and	so	virtuous	and	so	learned	so	far	from	him	go

'and the pope would not tolerate that so noble a man, so virtuous and learned, should go so far away from him'
(Bede_2:1.98.5.912)

Such cases, together with all unclear cases, were excluded from the final survey.[9]

Table 1[10] presents the frequencies of "bare" singular count nominals and those introduced by *an* in each of the sub-groups described in this section.

The texts in Table 1 are tentatively arranged in chronological order, though the result is certainly imperfect: in fact, in most cases the date of composition of a given text is conjectural, while manuscripts can be dated with some certainty, but only with reference to a time span rather than a date. Moreover, there might be a considerable distance between the supposed date of composition of the text and that of the extant manuscript, as e.g. for Bede's *Ecclesiastical History* (Bede) or *Gregory's Dialogues* (C) (GD-C).

The left-to-right arrangement of columns in Table 1 reflects the increasing saliency of the existential presupposition in each group of nominals: it is absent with generics (GNR) and existentials taking narrow scope (SCOPE-nrw), hard to

---

9 For this reason, the totals presented in Table 1 are lower than those of the initial samples discussed at the end of Section 2.1.

10 Some notes on the texts listed in the first column can be found in the Appendix.

Table 1: Designation properties of nominals in the samples

TEXT	GNR Ø	an	SCOPE-nrw Ø	an	SCOPE-amb Ø	an	EXS Ø	an	SCOPE-wd Ø	an	SPC Ø	an	ONE an	TOT Ø	an
ChronA	0	0	1	1	0	1	3	3	0	0	0	2	0	4	7
Bede_head	0	0	1	0	0	0	0	4	0	0	0	0	0	1	4
Bede	5	0	14	0	2	0	12	0	0	0	6	0	0	39	0
CP_head	0	0	0	0	0	0	0	0	0	0	0	0	0	0	0
CP	5	0	10	1	1	1	4	2	0	0	0	0	0	20	4
LawAf 1	0	0	8	0	0	0	0	0	0	0	0	0	3	8	3
LawAfEl	0	0	4	0	0	0	0	0	0	0	0	0	0	4	0
Or_head	0	0	0	0	0	0	0	1	0	0	0	0	0	0	1
Or	0	0	2	0	0	1	4	7	0	2	0	6	2	6	18
Bo_head	0	0	1	0	0	0	0	0	0	0	0	0	0	1	0
Bo	6	0	4	1	0	0	1	0	0	0	1	3	0	12	4
GD-C	1	0	4	3	0	0	8	15	1	0	3	0	2	17	20
verhom	1	0	4	0	0	0	5	2	0	0	1	0	0	11	2
ÆCHom I	6	0	15	4	2	2	9	8	1	0	2	1	13	35	28
ÆCHom II	6	0	9	7	1	3	13	22	1	0	1	6	4	31	42
ÆLS	6	0	8	4	0	4	12	33	0	1	0	9	2	26	53
wsgosp	15	0	10	3	0	0	14	16	0	2	1	0	3	40	24
WHom	11	0	1	0	0	0	3	1	0	0	1	0	2	16	3
TOTAL	62	0	96	24	6	12	88	114	3	5	16	27	31	271	213

determine in the case of ambiguous scope (SCOPE-amb) or in the absence of other logical operators (EXS), obligatory for nominals taking wide scope (SCOPE-wd) or with a designation specified in the environment (SPC). Finally, there are the cases where *an* is clearly interpreted as a cardinal (ONE), where no alternation between presence or absence of *an* is expected, nor is indeed observed.

These top-to-bottom and left-to-right arrangements turn out to roughly reflect a tendency towards increased use of *an+N* rather than "bare" singulars: so, one sees that in Bede *an* is not used at all and in the *Laws of Alfred* (LawAf 1) it is only used as a cardinal; it is used sparingly in other "Alfredian" texts such as *Cura Pastoralis* (CP, 16.6%), and *Boethius* (Bo, 25%), as well as in the *Vercelli Homilies* (verhom, 15.4%); it becomes more common than "bare" singulars in Ælfric's two series of *Catholic Homilies* and his *Lives of Saints* (ÆCHom I, ÆCHom II, ÆLS, 57.2%).[11] Analogously, in the entire sample *an* is not used at

---

11 This is a gross simplification: note for example that *Orosius* (Or) patterns with Ælfric's texts rather than "Alfredian" ones, and, conversely, Wulfstan's *Homilies* (WHom) seem to be more conservative than Ælfric's texts.

all with GNRs, it is preferably avoided with nominals taking narrow scope (19.7%), it is attested at the highest rate (62.8%) with those labelled SPC, while with EXSs it is slightly less frequent (56.6%).

3 The grammar(s) of *an* in Old English

Though, as discussed in Section 2.1, the absolute figures in the samples are low, there is at least one very sharp result, namely that in Old English generics are never introduced by *an*. Also, Table 1 enables one to single out two fairly rigorous grammars as to the use of *an*: one, represented by Bede and Alfred's *Laws*, is essentially an Icelandic-type grammar, with *an* occurring as a cardinal, whenever occurring at all. The other grammar is represented by *Orosius* (Or) and Ælfric's *Lives of Saints*. Here, *an* is obligatory with nominals with an existential specific interpretation, whether or not this results from scope interactions (columns SCOPE-wd and SPC in Table 1); conversely, it is disfavoured, though possible, with existentials taking narrow scope (column SCOPE-nrw), thus "bare" singulars are more common in this case.

This latter grammar is clearly the interesting one for the purposes of the present discussion, because the "intermediate status" of Old English exemplified in (3) turns out here to be a rule-governed one: the distribution of *an* in *Orosius* and *Lives of Saints*, in fact, mirrors[12] that of plural *sm* in Present-Day English. In both cases, an overt morpheme, *an* or *sm*, alternates with a "bare" noun, the former with a singular count noun, the latter with a plural/mass one. And in both cases, the insertion of the overt morpheme is necessary for the noun phrase to be interpreted as specific or take wide scope (though it does not block the narrow one).

Note that this is not the grammar of Icelandic. In Icelandic, in fact, a "bare" singular count noun can also have an indefinite specific reading, i.e. no insertion of an overt morpheme corresponding to *an* is required:

(15) *Íslendingur virðist   hafa   unnið*
      Icelander   seems   have   won
      'A particular Icelander appears to have won'
      'It appears that some Icelander or other has won'
      (Svenonius 2000: 278)[13]

---

12 One major difference is that *sm* does not normally occur in the scope of a negation, where it is replaced by *any*, while OE *an* does (see [8a]). Note however that OE *an* does not have a Negative Polarity Item counterpart analogous to *any*. Note also that OE *an* may also correspond to PDE cardinal *one*, which can occur in the scope of a negation.

13 The word-by-word gloss is my addition to Svenonius' example.

Rather, the grammar of *Orosius* and *Lives of Saints* is similar to that of Hebrew, as described in Givón (1981) and Borer (2005: 150–159). Hebrew *'exád* 'one' has an unstressed and phonologically reduced counterpart, *xit*, about which, in Borer's words, "one could suggest that [its] function (...) is precisely that of an (optional) indefinite article" (Borer 2005: 150). However, as Borer herself shows, this impression is immediately contradicted by its distribution and interpretive properties, which show that it is a specificity marker, forcing wide scope, i.e. a strong reading. Hebrew *xit* seems thus analogous to *an* in *Orosius* and *Lives of Saints*.[14]

In sum, the grammar of *an* in Bede and Alfred's *Laws* on one hand, and that of *Orosius* and *Lives of Saints* on the other, are both coherent grammars, with nothing of the vagueness that is often attributed to so-called "transitional stages". Moreover, both grammars have a modern correspondent, Icelandic for Bede and Alfred's *Laws*, Hebrew for *Orosius* and *Lives of Saints*.

Facts are less clear-cut with other texts, in particular *Gregory's Dialogues* (C), the *Vercelli Homilies* and the first and the second series of Ælfric's *Catholic Homilies*. The evidence from these texts does not allow one to postulate that they are consistent grammars, possibly analogous to some modern language. Rather, they do seem to instantiate a "transitional" stage, where the grammar of *an* is not well established. The key to understanding this "transitional" stage is a comparison of the three works by Ælfric. His *Lives of Saints* were taken as representatives of the grammar using *an* like PDE *sm*, while the two series of *Catholic Homilies*, which are earlier, were taken as examples of inconsistent grammars. Now, it is unlikely that this reflects a change in Ælfric's linguistic competence, for it is not obvious that the I-language of a mature speaker may change so substantially in the course of little more than a decade (the distance that separates the two series of *Catholic Homilies* from *the Lives of Saints*). What is much more plausible is that Ælfric's I-language comprised two grammars for *an*, the conservative one seen in Bede and Alfred and a more innovative one similar to Modern Hebrew: in his earliest composition, Ælfric uses some old-fashioned forms, which he reduces in the second collection of homilies and

---

14 With a notable difference: Hebrew *xit* is incompatible with narrow scope interpretation, while *an* is only disfavored but not excluded in this case (which makes *an* very similar to PDE *sm*). Note however that in Hebrew there are two forms, the stressed cardinal *'exád* (compatible with narrow scope) and the unstressed *xit*. In Old English there is only one written form, and there is no way to tell whether it corresponded only to a stressed form (the scope-ambiguous cardinal), or to an unstressed one (the wide-scope existential), or rather to both, as the successive development might suggest. So, this supposed difference might simply result from the fact that Hebrew is a spoken language while for Old English one has to rely exclusively on written sources.

abandons altogether in the *Lives of Saints*. The grammatical inconsistency of the *Catholic Homilies* is thus reducible to a classical case of grammars in competition (Kroch 1989), and it is reasonable to extend the same treatment to the other "transitional" texts in the samples.

4 A formal characterization of *an*

In the light of the discussion in Section 3, it is clear that one must distinguish at least three morphemes *a(n)* in the history of English: the cardinal of Bede and Alfred's *Laws*, which eventually developed into the modern *one*; the item described as a specificity marker[15] analogous to Hebrew *xit*, which characterizes *Orosius* and *Lives of Saints*; the indefinite article of Present-Day English.

In this section, I will lay out the basic properties of *a(n)* at each stage, in order to better understand its diachronic development in the history of English.[16]

4.1 The syntactic position of *a(n)*

The indefinite article and the cardinal *one*, though normally etymologically related, do not seem to occupy the same syntactic positions. In particular, cardinals and quantity expressions seem to be merged in a position lower than D, possibly the Number projection originally postulated in the early 1990s (see Picallo 1991; Ritter 1991 among others), labelled #P in Borer (2005). Under certain conditions, cardinals can or must rise from that lower position to the D position (or the D field), as suggested by the following pattern observed in Italian:

(16) a. *Tre   miei   amici   sono venuti   a   trovar=mi*
          three   my   friends are   come   to   visit=me
          'Three friends of mine came to visit'

      b. **Miei   tre   amici   sono venuti   a   trovar=mi*
          my   three friends are   come   to   visit=me
          (Crisma 1991: 86)

---

15 For ease of exposition, I will keep using the label "specificity marker" for this use of *an*, even if it will be characterized as something different in Section 5.2.

16 Here I am abstracting away from the fact that while the first two stages are contiguous in time, there is a huge gap separating *Orosius* and the *Lives of Saints* from Present-Day English. This is due to the fact that there is no quantitative study on the use of *an* in Middle English, thus at the moment it is not possible to know when the modern usage established itself, and whether there is any further intermediate stage between the last two.

(17) a. *I   miei   tre   amici ...*
the   my   three   friends
'My three friends ...'

b. *I   tre   miei   amici ...*
the   three   my   friends
same, focused or stylistically marked
(Crisma 1991: 86)

The fact that (17a) is more neutral than (17b) suggests that cardinals are merged in a position that is lower than the one eventually occupied by the possessive adjective, whether the latter is derived or not, both being lower than D. The contrast in (16) can be accounted for postulating that, in the absence of an overt element merged in D, the cardinal crosses over the possessive to reach the D-layer,[17] possibly to satisfy the requirement that arguments have a filled D (Szabolcsi 1987; Stowell 1989).[18]

The indefinite article does not seem to be merged in the same position as cardinals, but rather to be base-generated in D. A first piece of evidence in this sense comes from English, where *one* (and cardinals in general) can co-occur with the definite article or with possessives, while *a(n)* cannot:

(18) a. *The one competent person that can answer these questions is on vacation*

b. **The a competent person ...*

(19) a. *Her one quality is she absolutely speaks her mind*
b. **Her a quality is ...*

Another piece of evidence comes again from Italian. Italian does not have two distinct morphemes, corresponding to *a* and *one* respectively, but a single morpheme *un(-o/-a)*. This morpheme cannot co-occur with the definite article, thus sentences corresponding to (18a) and (19a) can only be obtained with the insertion of adjectives such as *solo/a* or *unico/a*, both meaning 'only':

---

17 But see Borer (2005: 145) for the hypothesis that cardinals may or may not raise to D, thus yielding either a strong or a weak reading of the indefinite.
18 This cannot be the whole story, however: cardinals in fact seem to be attracted to the left-most position even in languages that allow for D-less arguments, such as Polish and Slovenian, as argued in Longobardi (2013).

(20) a. L'   unica   persona   competente   che   può   rispondere   a
     the   only   person   comptetent   that   can   answer   to

     queste   domande   è   in   vacanza
     these   questions   is   in   vacation
     'The one competent person that can answer these questions is
     on vacation'

   b. *La una persona competente ...

Thus, un(-o/-a) seems to correspond to the PDE indefinite article a(n) rather than the cardinal one. Now, we have seen in (16) that cardinals are generated lower than D, but must rise to D when the latter is empty. As is the case with other possible instantiations of D (see Szabolcsi 1987; Stowell 1989), this movement can be expected not to be required for non-arguments: thus, in exclamations cardinals can remain low and appear between a possessive and the head noun, even in the absence of an overt determiner. This position, however, is never available for un(-o/-a), which shows that the indefinite article is not merged in a position lower than the possessive:

(21) a. ?Poveri   miei   tre   amici!
        poor   my   three   friends
        'Poor three friends of mine!'

   b. Povero   mio   (giovane)   amico!
      poor   my   (young)   friend
      'My poor (young) friend!'

   c. *Povero   mio   un   amico!
      poor   my   a   friend
      'My poor friend!'

   d. ?Povero   mio   unico   amico!
      poor   my   a   friend
      'My poor only friend!'

On the basis of these contrasts, one can conclude that the indefinite article and the cardinal one are not merged in the same syntactic position: the former, in fact, always appears high in the structure, which may suggest that it is merged directly in the D-layer. The latter, on the other hand, can appear lower than elements such as the definite article and possessives, though arguably raises from its base position when they are absent. This conclusion is consistent with semantic approaches that argue that cardinals have the semantic properties of adjectives rather than determiners.[19]

Turning to *an* in Old English, at least one thing can be established: *an* can co-occur with the definite article, as *one* in (18a), and in these cases it has a clear cardinal meaning:

(22) a. *Ne   deð   he   ðonne   **ðæt   an**   yfel*   ðæt   he   ne   *lufað*
        NEG   does   he   then   the   one   evil   that   he   NEG   loves

     ða   halgan   ðegnunga
     the   holy   services
     'Then he does not do the only evil of not loving the holy services ...'
     (CP:8.55.3.334)

   b. *&   sohte   **þæt   an   sceap**   þe   him   ætwunden   wæs*
      and   sought   that   one   sheep   that   him.DAT   escaped   was
      'and sought that one sheep that had escaped from him'
      (ÆCHom_I,_24:372.29.4687)

Thus, one can conclude that cardinal *an* in Old English could be merged in a relatively low position, analogous to that of PDE *one* and, more generally, of other cardinals in many languages such as for example Italian. Unfortunately, it is not possible to establish whether the same was true for *an* used as a specificity marker, and one must be content with summarizing the situation along the following lines: cardinal *an* in Old English was merged relatively low, analogous to PDE *one*; the indefinite article in PDE is merged directly in D; there is no way to tell whether the specificity marker was merged in the lower position or in D: the contrast with "bare" nominals with respect to scope-taking properties suggests that the D position is at some point filled by *an*, but there is no way to determine whether *an* is directly merged there or raises from a lower position.

4.2 The interpretive content of *an*

I will set aside the discussion of *an* used as a cardinal, simply assuming that its interpretation was analogous to that of PDE *one*, on which I will return in Section 5.2. In this section, I will discuss the interpretive properties of the indefinite article and the specificity marker, beginning with the former.

---

19 See Landman (2003) for extensive discussion; see also Ionin and Matushansky (2006) for some interesting empirical arguments for this hypothesis.

The label "indefinite article" suggests that such a morpheme should be a mark of indefiniteness. Indeed, in descriptive grammars one finds statements such as: "The indefinite article *a* is the most basic indicator of indefiniteness for singular count nouns" (Payne and Huddleston 2002: 371). However, in languages endowed with definite articles, the indefinite reading "comes for free", for it is the default reading whenever an argument noun phrase is not overtly marked as definite:[20]

(23) a. *I found the/these/John's cats in the garden*

     b. *I found cats in the garden*

(24) a. *I found the/this/John's beer in the fridge*

     b. *I found beer in the fridge*

The "bare" plural and mass nouns in (23b) and (24b) are interpreted as indefinite, with no need of an overt mark for that. Thus, the "indicator of indefiniteness" seems to be required only with singular count nouns, as shown by the examples in (1), repeated here as (25):

(25) a. **I found cat in the garden*

     b. *I found a cat in the garden*

The contrast between (24b) and (25) might suggest an alternative analysis for the indefinite article, most extensively developed in Borer (2005), and, with specific reference to Old English, in Ackles (1997) and Crisma (1997). According to these approaches, nouns are not lexically mass or count, and the indefinite article is responsible for the [+count] interpretation (a "divisor", as well as a "counter", in Borer's terms). A crucial tenet of this analysis is that it is only when the appropriate morpheme is in the appropriate projection that the noun phrase acquires a [+count] reading. This assumption is supported by the so-called flexibility of the mass/count distinction, namely the fact that mass nous can be turned into count (as in *a wine, a love, a thread, a salt, a stone*, Borer 2005: 102) and vice versa (as in *there is dog/stone/chicken on this floor*, Borer 2005: 102). However, there are very good arguments for the opposite view, defended for

---

20 In some languages this possibility does not arise at all. French, for example, normally does not allow "bare" nouns to occur in argument function, whether singular, plural or mass. This is an independent property linked to overt number marking, as convincingly argued in Delfitto and Schroten (1991).

example by Rothstein (2010), rejecting the idea that the mass/count distinction is purely syntactical. I will in fact adopt this more classical approach (e.g., Chomsky 1965) that sees the mass/count distinction as a property of lexical items, represented by a feature [±count] associated with each noun. The immediate consequence is that there is no need for a mark of [+count] or for a "divisor" in Borer's terms, hence the indefinite article is nothing of the sort.

Another possible analysis for the indefinite article might be suggested by the fact that it is cross-linguistically derived from the cardinal for *one*, therefore one might assume that it is a mark for [+singular]. However, languages that have the indefinite article seem to also have independent singular/plural distinctions on nouns; so, it is not clear why a further [+singular] marking would be needed, moreover only for count nouns and anyway with no [+plural] counterpart.[21]

In sum, the indefinite article turns out to be totally redundant from the point of view of interpretation, for, whatever contribution it may add is already made available by some other means:
- the indefinite interpretation is the default reading in the absence of overt definite marking;
- the [+count] feature is a lexical property of the nominal head;
- the singular interpretation is encoded in the Number morphology.

This redundancy, coupled with the observation that the indefinite article is required in some languages but not in others (see the contrast between [1] and [2]), was the starting point in Crisma (2011) to suggest that the indefinite article is actually an expletive. For the present purposes, the only relevant points of this analysis are the fact that the indefinite article is void of any content, and that it is arguably base-generated in D (or in the D-field), as discussed in Section 4.1.

And where does the specificity marker fit? The first obvious difference between the indefinite article in Present-Day English and the specificity marker in Old English is that the former is compatible with a generic reading (see [4a]), while this is excluded for the latter (see column GNR in Table 1). This observation, together with the fact that the rate of presence vs. absence of *an* increases as one moves from left to right in Table 1, suggests that the specificity marker *an* acted as a true existential operator, marking existential presupposition. Thus, it is a sort of singular count counterpart of PDE *sm*.

---

21 According to Borer (2005), plural marking is in fact a classifier, hence it is misnamed and is not interpreted as Number marking. This hypothesis would leave open the possibility for the indefinite article to mark the value [+singular], but is based on the just-rejected assumption, that the count/mass distinction is syntactical.

5 A diachronic scenario

We have seen that the development of *an* in the history of English can be described postulating (at least) three discrete stages:

- *an* is a cardinal merged in a quantity projection lower than D, say NumberP or #P. This is the grammar of Bede's *Ecclesiastical History* and of Alfred's *Laws*, and is similar to that of Icelandic. I will call it "Alfred's grammar". Here OE *an* = PDE *one*.

- *an* acts as an existential operator able to mark specificity, found in D (or in some position in the D-field); it is obligatory when a nominal takes wide scope or is interpreted as specific. This is the grammar of *Orosius* and Ælfric's *Lives of Saints*, and it is similar to Modern Hebrew. I will call it "Ælfric's grammar". Here OE *an* = singular of PDE *sm*.

- *a(n)* is an "indefinite article", i.e. an expletive merged in D. At this stage, "bare" singular count nouns become ungrammatical, and *a(n)* is used also with generics. This stage, which is not attested in Old English, is the grammar of Present-Day English (but it may have arisen much earlier in time).

Two contiguous stages may co-exist in the same community or the same speaker, giving rise to apparent inconsistency.

A diachronic account should analyse how Alfred's grammar develops into Ælfric's grammar, and how the latter develops into a PDE-type grammar, taking into account both syntactic and semantic changes.

The categorial reanalysis that from Alfred's grammar eventually resulted in the grammar of Present-Day English is a case of "upward" reanalysis in the sense of Roberts and Roussou (2003): the morpheme which is originally merged in a quantity phrase lower than D (and then possibly raised to D) is eventually merged directly in D (or the D-field). It is possible that this reanalysis happened already with the first step, but, as discussed in Section 4.1, it is not possible to establish the merging position of the specificity marker. Notwithstanding this gap in the data, the "upward" nature of the reanalysis, together with its being accompanied by loss of movement, makes this change a likely case of grammaticalization. If this is the case, one expects to observe also some form of semantic bleaching and, possibly, of phonological reduction. The latter is more easily dealt with, so I will start from there.

5.1 Phonological reduction

OE *an* is the ancestor of both the PDE indefinite article *a(n)* and the cardinal *one*. The former is a (pro-)clitic, whose vowel is reduced to schwa and whose final -*n* only appears before words beginning with a vowel. The latter is a phonological word and preserves the etymological -*n* in all contexts; its vowel must result from an etymologically long OE *ā*, as confirmed by the addition of final ‹e› and by the fact that the vowel was eventually rounded, a Middle English development characteristic of the Southern and Midland regions which affects OE long *ā* but not short *ă*.[22] The vowel was then[23] reinforced by an initial glide, which is not the normal development of OE /a/ or /o/, whether long or short. Whatever the reason for this development, I will stress that it does not qualify as reduction, quite the opposite.

In Old English, there is no trace of the differentiation of the two forms in their spelling. In particular there is no trace of loss of -*n*, which is always present in all the 2841 occurrences of the relevant morpheme in the YCOE. Also, there is virtually no evidence for the rounding of the vowel, which is spelt ‹o› only once, the other 2840 cases having ‹a› or ‹æ›. As for vowel length, in Old English it is normally not signalled by spelling, so it is not surprising that the relevant morpheme is spelt with ‹aa› only in six cases. This of course does not automatically mean that the two *an*'s, the cardinal and the specificity marker, were not distinguished in actual speech: spelling in Old English was highly standardized, and it is therefore possible that the phonological differentiation pre-dates its being reflected in writing.

Traces of the differentiation appear in the Middle English period, beginning with 1150–1250 texts; from the morpho-phonological point of view, by 1250 the situation is basically that of Present-Day English. This is shown in Table 2 and Table 3, which present data extracted from Crisma (2009: 133).

In Table 2, one sees that after 1250 the article is regularly spelt with the vowel ‹a›, the cardinal *one* with the vowel ‹o›, at least in the South and the Midlands. The relatively high number of ‹a› spellings for the cardinal after 1250 are in fact mostly due to northern texts,[24] 119 instances out of 132, for in the

---

22 See Wyld (1927: 105–107), Brunner (1963: 14).

23 Only two of the texts included in the *Penn-Helsinki Parsed Corpus of Middle English*, second edition (PPCME2, Kroch and Taylor 2000) show traces of this reinforcement, with occasional spellings *won* or *von* for the cardinal *one*. They are *Mirk's Festial* and *The siege of Jerusalem*. The *won/von* spellings are however sporadic: in *The siege of Jerusalem*, there is one case of reinforced spelling against five instances of cardinal *one* that do not show any initial consonant or glide, while in *Mirk's Festial* the rate is 15 to 81. Both texts belong to the latest portion of the PPCME2, being attested in manuscripts from the period 1420–1500, though *Mirk's Festial* was composed at an earlier date, probably in the 1380s. All this data tell is that the glide insertion had taken place by that date, but of course it is well possible that it had taken place at an earlier date and was much more widespread than it appears, but was not reflected in the spelling of the cardinal, as is indeed the case in Present-Day English.

24 In PPCME2, there is no northern text for the period 1250–1350, one for the period 1350–1420, six for the period 1420–1500.

Table 2: Spelling of the vowel of the indefinite article and the cardinal *one* in Middle English

Manuscript date		⟨a⟩	⟨o⟩
1150–1250	indefinite article	607	16
	cardinal 1	401	102
1250–1350	indefinite article	258	5
	cardinal 1	4	90
1350–1420	indefinite article	4452	1
	cardinal 1	20	708
1420–1500	indefinite article	5316	5
	cardinal 1	108	537

Table 3: Indefinite article allomorphy in Middle English

Manuscript date		a	an
1150–1250	/_#V	0	132
	/_#C	162	200
1250–1350	/_#V	0	14
	/_#C	166	0
1350–1420	/_#V	6	295
	/_#C	3764	10
1420–1500	/_#V	67	283
	/_#C	4526	2

North the rounding of $\bar{a}$ did not take place. Though the data before 1250 are nowhere so straightforward, there is evidence that the indefinite article and the cardinal *one* were treated differently even in the period 1150–1250: the rate of ⟨o⟩ spellings for the indefinite article is in fact only 2.6%, while for the cardinal it is 20.3%.

Table 3 shows that by 1250 also the morphology of the indefinite article *a(n)* is basically[25] that of Present-Day English: the final -*n* appears in fact only before words beginning with a vowel, but not before consonants.[26] Again, however, nontrivial signs of the change are detectable in the period 1150–1250: here the reduction of the indefinite article to *a* before consonant is not a regular phenomenon, but it is already attested 44.8% of the times.

---

25 Sporadic inflected forms survive through the first half of the 14th century, but they have not been considered here.

26 In Table 3, word-initial glides are treated like consonants, independently of their spelling. On the other hand, word-initial *n*- and *h*- have been excluded from the count, the former because misplacement of the word boundary is often observed, the latter because of its "weakness" discussed at length in Crisma (2009).

5.2 Semantic bleaching

As convincingly discussed in Eckardt (2006: 30–34), the notion of "bleaching", though widely used in the literature on grammaticalization, is a "slippery" (Eckardt 2006: 30) one, and not all scholars use it in the same way. In this section, I will investigate whether this metaphor may be useful to describe the change in the semantics of *a(n)* in the history of English.

I will begin by discussing the two extremes, the PDE indefinite article and the cardinal, assuming that in Old English cardinal *an* had the same interpretive properties of PDE *one*. As discussed in Sections 4.2 and 4.1 respectively, the indefinite article does not contribute any meaning, while the cardinal has some adjective-like properties. This state of affairs is nicely summarized in Bittner (1994): "Indefinite articles have no translation at all, while other weak determiners are basically interpreted as cardinality predicates". Put this way, the development from one end to the other of the cline does seem to involve some "bleaching", some "fading" of the meaning of the relevant category eventually resulting in total loss.

Things become less obvious when one tries to pinpoint the portion of meaning that "fades away". Intuitively, if a given item is "bleached", its contribution to the truth conditions of its sentence should be different from that of a non-"bleached", adjective-like item; in particular a "bleached" item should contribute *less* than a non-"bleached" one. Thus, the difference between a sentence containing a non-"bleached" item and a sentence containing a "bleached" one should be comparable to the difference between a sentence containing an adjective and a sentence not containing it:

(26) a. *Melita has a black cat*

  b. *Melita has a cat*

The adjective *black* contributes to the truth conditions, so that the circumstances that make (26a) true are in a subset relation with those of the less restricted (26b). Thus, if Melita only has a red cat, (26b) is true and (26a) is false, but there is no conceivable situation in which (26b) could be false while (26a) is true. If the semantic difference between the cardinal *one* and the indefinite article is indeed some loss of meaning, it should be possible to find analogous effects. This seems to be indeed the case:

(27) a. *Melita has one cat*

  b. *Melita has a cat*

(27a) is true in a lower number of circumstances than (27b): so, if Melita has in fact two cats, (27a) is false while (27b) is true, while it is never the case that (27a) may be true while (27b) is false. Thus, *one* contributes to the truth conditions something more than *a*.

A possible account of the contrast between (27a) and (27b) could make use of Horn's (1972: 41)[27] original intuition that the interpretation of cardinals is affected by conversational implicatures; in particular, the lower bound "at least n" is asserted and the upper bound "at most n" is implicated. Thus, the latter but not the former may be cancelled:

(28)   *Three girls came in, in fact, four girls came in*
       (Landman 2003: 215)

Along these lines, one may suggest that the upper bound is part of the *lexical* meaning of *one*, while it is only an implicature in (27b).[28] This hypothesis is supported by the fact that it can be cancelled in the latter case, but not in the former:

(29)   a. *#Melita has one cat, in fact, she has two*

       b. *Melita has a cat, in fact, she has two*

This analysis nicely fits in a framework that tries to treat the case under discussion as a typical case of grammaticalization, for it readily offers a well-delimited portion of meaning that is eventually "bleached": the upper bound.

It is plausible that the upper bound was part of the lexical meaning of OE *an* when it acted as a cardinal, as in (13) and (22), and it is clear that it is absent with the PDE indefinite article, as shown by (29). Given that the diachronic path towards grammaticalization hypothesized here comprises three stages, it is only natural to ask whether the loss of the upper bound from the lexical meaning of *an* took place already with the first step, when *an* began to function (also) as a specificity marker. Examples such as the following show that this is indeed the case:

---

27 But see also Landman (2003).

28 This account makes the crucial assumption that *one* is a special cardinal, for it would be the only one to have the upper bound as part of its lexical meaning rather than an implicature. One may thus wonder what makes *one* special. The simple and plausible answer is that *one* has an alternative for the "at least" reading, namely the indefinite article (or the bare singular in languages that allow them), and ultimately the existence of singular number morphology.

(30) ða   æt sumon gefeohte wearð **an ðegen** Æþelredes
     then at some   battle   was   a   thane   Æthelred.GEN

     cyninges. mid oðrum cempum afylled. se   wæs Ymma gehaten;
     king.GEN with other   soldiers felled who was Ymma named
     'then at a certain battle one of Æthelred's vassals, named Ymma, was
     struck down with other soldiers'
     (ÆCHom_II,_24:204.143.4518)

It is clear that the unfortunate Ymma was not the only vassal of Æthelred's, nor was he the only one among them who got struck down. Hence, the upper bound cannot be part of the lexical meaning of *an*, and we must conclude that it was "bleached" already at this stage. Actually, once one understands the mechanisms of the "specificity marking" in Old English, "bleaching" becomes so obviously expected that it is almost trivial. At the first stage (Bede's *Ecclesiastical History* and Alfred's *Laws*), a "bare" singular count could be interpreted as specific, exactly as in Icelandic (compare [12b] and [15]). If, for whatever reason, at the second stage (*Orosius* and *Lives of Saints*) this is not allowed any more, the most immediate candidate to (eventually) fill the D position is a quantifier that may undergo Quantifier Raising, the cardinal for 'one'. A cardinal asserting only the lower bound, as is the norm for cardinals in general, is perfectly suited to the task, hence the "bleaching". Note that, if this account is correct, the term "specificity marking" must be understood only as an informal metaphor, for there is no feature [+specific], and the specificity only comes as a result of *an* being able to take wide scope as an existential operator.

To conclude, what about the third stage in the development? If the hypothesis in Crisma (2011) that the indefinite article is only an expletive is tenable, the step from the second to the third stage would involve further "bleaching", the loss of any quantificational content, i.e. the lower bound.

6 Conclusions and further issues

In sum, based on the data and the discussion presented in Sections 4 and 5, one reaches the conclusion that the development of *an* in the history of English shares the full cluster of prototypical properties of grammaticalization, in the spirit of Roberts and Roussou (2003):

- it is a case of "upward" movement in the functional hierarchy involving loss of movement: there is in fact good evidence to suppose that *an* is initially merged in some relatively low position from where it can raise to D, but at a later stage is merged directly in D;

- there is clear phonological reduction, for the initial morpheme had a long vowel, which was eventually shortened and reduced to schwa, and was characterized by a final -*n*, which was eventually lost;
- the reanalysis is accompanied by semantic "bleaching", that takes places in two discrete successive steps.

This account of the emergence of the indefinite article in English leaves open a series of issues. The first is the temporal gap between the second and the third stage. It would be desirable to conduct some quantitative study on the use of *an* in Middle English, in order to establish when it was reanalysed as an indefinite article comparable to the PDE one. Then, there are some aspects of the syntax of singular indefinites in Old English that have been entirely left out of the picture, though they certainly bear on the question discussed here. The first is the use and development of *sum*, the ancestor of PDE *some* (and, of course, of *sm*). In Old English, with singular count nouns, it was a competitor of *an* as a marker of specificity (as in *sumon gefeohte* in [30]), it would therefore be interesting to explore how the two competing forms coexisted. The other issue is the distribution of the various types of nominals discussed here with respect to their syntactic position: recent works (Biberauer and van Kemenade 2011; Taylor and Pintzuk 2011) have shown that in early English the placement of subjects and objects in the clause is sensitive to the information structure, therefore it may be interesting to investigate whether the presence or absence of *an* interacts in any meaningful way with the syntactic position of subjects and objects. These topics are left for future research.

Appendix: materials

Since this study could not be based simply on automated data collection but required further tagging, it was restricted to a selection of texts from the YCOE, namely (in parentheses, the labels used in Table 1): *Parker Chronicle* (ChronA), Bede's *Ecclesiastic History of the English People* (Bede), *Cura Pastoralis* (CP), *Laws of Alfred* (LawAf 1), *Alfred's Introduction to Laws* (LawAfEl), *Orosius* (Or), *Boethius* (Bo), *Gregory's Dialogues* (C) (GD(C)), the *Vercelli Homilies* (verhom), Ælfric's *Catholic Homilies I* (ÆCHom I), *Catholic Homilies II* (ÆCHom II) and *Lives of Saints* (ÆLS), the *West-Saxon Gospels* (wsgosp) and Wulfstan's *Homilies* (WHom). Detailed information can be accessed through the YCOE homepage.

Some of these texts (Bede, *Cura Pastoralis*, *Orosius*, *Boethius*) are introduced by a list of chapter headings. Their syntax, in Bede, is remarkably different from that of the main text. I have no explanation for the peculiarity of Bede's heading list, which is unlikely to be a late addition, see Whitelock (1974). Anyway, quantitative results from heading sections are tagged "_head" and kept separate from those of the main texts in Table 1, and, for consistency, this was done not only for Bede but for all the texts presenting a list of headings.

The creation of the database that served as the empirical base for this study required various steps: a first lexicon was initially generated by retrieving from the YCOE a list of all the nouns that occur at least once in the nominative and accusative case with the ending -*as*, the distinctive plural nominative and accusative ending of masculine nouns of the first declension that eventually resulted in PDE plural -*s*. This criterion guaranteed that the nouns in the lexicon all had plural nominative and accusative forms distinct from the singular ones, thus avoiding the retrieval of "bare" plurals. It also guaranteed that the selected nouns could be pluralized, and were therefore very likely to be count nouns. Of course, one could not exclude that this search retrieved also pluralized mass nouns receiving a taxonomic reading. Such cases were subsequently eliminated when the output of the search was manually checked and tagged for interpretive properties.

Since this initial lexicon turned out to be insufficient, for the samples collected using it were too small, it had to be enlarged adding other count nouns to it, which were (not too ingeniously) chosen simply by going through pages of dictionary entries. Different from the initial lexicon, the newly-extended lexicon contains nouns belonging to all noun declensions and to all genders, and is therefore not immune from singular vs. plural ambiguities, thus "bare" plurals where retrieved alongside article-less singular nouns. This problem was however solved during the manual sorting of the different types of nominals, when semantic plurals were excluded from the samples.

The extended lexicon was used to generate two lists of nominals, one introduced by *an* the other "bare", as described in Section 2.1. Each token in the list was subsequently tagged according to its interpretive properties, as described in Section 2.2. This tagging was then used to generate Table 1.

Sources

YCOE

Taylor, Ann, Anthony Warner, Susan Pintzuk & Frank Beths. 2003. *The York-Toronto-Helsinki Parsed Corpus of Old English prose.* Heslington: University of York. http://www-users. york.ac.uk/~lang22/YCOE/YcoeHome.htm (accessed repeatedly since 2003).

All the examples quoted in this paper are retrieved form the YCOE, and identified by a shortened form of their ID label. The relevant printed editions are the following:

ÆCHom I
Clemoes, Peter. 1997. *Ælfric's Catholic Homilies: The First Series*. Early English Text Society s.s. 17. Oxford: Oxford University Press.
ÆCHom II
Godden, Malcom. 1979 [1879]. *Ælfric's Catholic Homilies: The Second Series*. Early English Text Society s.s. 5. London: Oxford University Press.
ÆLS
Skeat, Walter W. 1966 [1881–1900]. *Ælfric's Lives of Saints*. Early English Text Society 76, 82, 94, 114. London: Oxford University Press.
Bede
Miller, Thomas. 1959–1963 [1890–1898]. *The Old English Version of Bede's Ecclesiastical History of the English People*. Early English Text Society 95, 96, 110, 111. London: Oxford University Press.
ChronA
Plummer Charles. 1892–1899. *Two of the Saxon Chronicles Parallel*, Oxford, Clarendon Press.
CP
Sweet, Henry. 1958 [1871]. *King Alfred's West-Saxon Version of Gregory's Pastoral Care*. Early English Text Society 45, 50. London: Oxford University Press.
Or
Bately, Janet. 1980. *The Old English Orosius*. Early English Text Society s.s. 6. London: Oxford University Press.

References

Ackles, Nancy. 1997. *Historical syntax of the English articles in relation to the count/non-count distinction*. Seattle, WA: University of Washington dissertation.
Biberauer, Theresa & Ans van Kemenade. 2011. Subject positions and information-structural diversification in the history of English. *Catalan Journal of Linguistics* 10. 17–69.
Bittner, Maria. 1994. Cross-linguistic semantics. *Linguistics and Philosophy* 17. 53–108.
Borer, Hagit. 2005. *In name only*. Oxford: Oxford University Press.
Brunner, Karl. 1963. *An outline of Middle English grammar*. Oxford: Blackwell.
Carlson, Greg N. 1977. A unified analysis of the English bare plural. *Linguistics and Philosophy* 1. 413–456.
Chomsky, Noam. 1965. *Aspects of the theory of syntax*. Cambridge, MA: MIT Press.
Crisma, Paola. 1991. *Functional categories inside the noun phrase: A study on the distribution of nominal modifiers*. Venezia: Università di Venezia MA thesis.
Crisma, Paola. 1997. *L'articolo nella prosa inglese antica e la teoria degli articoli nulli*. Padova: Università di Padova dissertation.
Crisma, Paola. 2009. Word-initial *h-* in Middle and Early Modern English. In Donka Minkova (ed.), *Phonological weakness in English: From Old to Present-Day English* (Palgrave Studies in Language History and Language Change), 130–167. Basingstoke, UK & New York: Palgrave Macmillan.
Crisma, Paola. 2011. On the so-called 'indefinite article'. Paper presented at the *21st Colloquium on Generative Grammar*, Universidad de Sevilla, 7–9 April.
Delfitto, Denis & Jan Schroten. 1991. Bare plurals and the number affix in DP. *Probus* 3(2). 155–185.

Eckardt, Regine. 2006. *Meaning change in grammaticalization: An enquiry into semantic reanalysis*. Oxford: Oxford University Press.

Givón, Talmy. 1981. On the development of the numeral 'one' as an indefinite marker. *Folia Linguistica Historica* 2(1). 35–53.

Horn, Laurence Robert. 1972. *On the semantic properties of logical operators in English*. Los Angeles, CA: University of California at Los Angles dissertation.

Ionin, Tania & Ora Matushansky. 2006. The composition of complex cardinals. *Journal of Semantics* 23. 315–360.

Ker, Neil Ripley. 1957. *Catalogue of manuscripts containing Anglo-Saxon*. Oxford: Clarendon Press.

Kroch, Anthony. 1989. Reflexes of grammar in patterns of language change. *Language Variation and Change* 1. 199–244.

Kroch, Anthony & Ann Taylor. 2000. *Penn-Helsinki Parsed Corpus of Middle English*, second edition (PPCME2). http://www.ling.upenn.edu/hist-corpora/PPCME2-RELEASE-3/index.html (accessed repeatedly since 2000).

Landman, Fred. 2003. Predicate-argument mismatches and the adjectival theory of indefinites. In Martine Coene & Yves D'hulst (eds.), *From NP to DP. The syntax and semantics of noun phrases* (Linguistics Today 55), 211–237. Amsterdam & Philadelphia: John Benjamins.

Longobardi, Giuseppe. 2013. How universal is DP? Paper presented at the *27th Symposium on Romance Linguistics – Going Romance*, Vrije Universiteit Amsterdam, 28–30 November.

Payne, John & Rodney Huddleston. 2002. Nouns and noun phrases. In Rodney Huddleston & Geoffrey Pullum (eds.), *The Cambridge grammar of the English Language*, 323–523. Cambridge: Cambridge University Press.

Picallo, Carme. 1991. Nominals and nominalization in Catalan. *Probus* 3(3). 279–316.

Ritter, Elizabeth. 1991. Two functional categories in noun phrases: Evidence from Modern Hebrew. In Susan Rothstein (ed.), *Perspectives on phrase structure: Heads and licensing.* [Special issue]. *Syntax and Semantics* 25. 37–62.

Roberts, Ian & Anna Roussou. 2003. *Syntactic change: A minimalist approach to grammaticalization*. Cambridge: Cambridge University Press.

Rothstein, Susan. 2010. Counting and the mass/count distinction. *Journal of Semantics* 27. 343–397.

Schubert, Lenhart K. & Francis J. Pelletier. 1987. Problems in representing the logical form of generics, bare plurals, and mass terms. In Ernest Lepore (ed.), *New directions in semantics*, 387–453. London: Academic Press.

Stowell, Timothy. 1989. Subjects, specifiers, and X-bar theory. In Mark Baltin & Anthony Kroch (eds.), *Alternative conceptions of phrase structure*, 232–262. Chicago, IL: University of Chicago Press.

Svenonius, Peter. 2000. Quantifier movement in Icelandic. In Peter Svenonius (ed.), *The derivation of VO and OV*, 255–292. Amsterdam & Philadelphia: John Benjamins.

Szabolcsi, Anna. 1987. Functional categories in the noun phrase. In István Kenesei (ed.), *Approaches to Hungarian*, volume 2, 167–189. Szeged: Jate.

Taylor, Ann & Susan Pintzuk. 2011. The interaction of syntactic change and information status effects in the change from OV to VO in English. *Catalan Journal of Linguistics* 10. 71–94.

Whitelock, Dorothy. 1974. The list of chapter-headings in the Old English Bede. In Robert B. Burlin & Edward B. Irving jr. (eds.), *Old English studies in honour of John C. Pope*, 263–284. Toronto: University of Toronto Press.

Wyld, Henry C. 1927. *A short history of English*, 3rd edn. London: John Murray.

Nikolaos Lavidas

6 The Greek Septuagint and language change at the syntax-semantics interface: from null to "pleonastic" object pronouns

In this study, I test the hypothesis that the Greek Septuagint reflects an ongoing change at the syntax-semantics interface. The study focuses on "pleonastic" pronouns in contrast to referential null objects. These "pleonastic" object pronouns in the Septuagint have been analyzed in the literature as the result of contact between the Greek language and other languages, primarily Hebrew. The unavailability of referential null objects in later Greek (post-Koine) is also considered to have been affected by Hebrew. The data show an important increase in the frequency of 3rd-person, but not 1st- and 2nd-person, personal pronouns in the Septuagint, as well as in the New Testament. I argue for the lack of a direct relation between the characteristics of transfer from Hebrew in the Greek Septuagint and the relevant change – in contrast to the "traditional" view of the literature – and propose a different form of relation between the change in later Greek and the translation language under examination. I base my discussion of the proposed relation on principles of "typical" change at the syntax-semantics interface (the Feature Economy Principle) and also on processes of language transfer observed in L2 acquisition or L1 attrition according to the Interpretability Hypothesis.

1 Introduction

The aim of the present study is to test the hypothesis that there is a relation between the transfer from Hebrew into Translation Greek in a situation of language contact and a case of language change at the syntax-semantics interface. This hypothesis will be examined using data concerning the presence of object pronouns, as opposed to referential null objects, in the Greek Septuagint (or LXX or Old Testament).[1] "Pleonastic" object pronouns, instead of referential

---

1 In the text, I refer to the following periods, time spans, and chronology of texts: Homeric Greek: 8th cent. BC, Classical Greek: 5th cent. BC–3rd cent. BC, and Koine Greek: 3rd cent. BC–4th cent. AD, encompassing both the Greek Septuagint (mainly 300–200 BC) and the New Testament (50–150 AD).

null objects in the Septuagint and the New Testament, have been analyzed in the relevant literature as the result of contact between Greek and other languages, mainly Hebrew. The unavailability of referential null objects in the post-Koine (post-Septuagint) period is also considered to have been affected by Hebrew, according to histories and grammars of the Greek language (for instance, Jannaris 1897: 347–348 and Moulton and Turner 1963: 37–41). Referential null objects are allowed in Classical Greek (1) but become restricted in Koine Greek (2a).[2] This restriction appears to conform to the Biblical Hebrew characteristic of using pronominal suffixes instead of null objects (2b). Biblical Hebrew does not use enclitics. Instead, it attaches pronominal suffixes to verbs to express the direct object if there is no special emphasis (Janse 2002: 379) or, less often, other case relations such as dative complements (Khan 2013).

(1) *ho dè   empimplàs   hapántōn   tèn gnṓmēn   **apépempe**   Ø*
he PTC satisfied.PTCP every-one.GEN the expectations.ACC dismissed.3SG Ø
'And after having satisfied the expectations of every one of them, he dismissed them.'
(X. An. 1,7,8; Luraghi 2003: 169)

(2) a. *kaì   anéstē   Kain   epì   Abel tòn adelphòn autoû*
   and rose-up.3SG Cain.NOM against Abel the brother his

   *kaì   apékteinen   **autón.***
   and killed.3SG   he.ACC
   'and Cain rose up against Abel, his brother, and killed him.'
   (LXX Ge. 4,8)

   b. *wa-yhî   bi-hyôṯ-ām   baś-śāḏeh   way-yāqom*
   and-it.happened in-being-their in.the-field and-he.rose.up

   qayin 'el-heḇel 'ā-îw   way-yaharḡ-ēhû
   Cain   to-Abel   brother-his and-he.killed-him
   'And it happened in their being in the field and Cain rose up against Abel his brother and killed him.'
   (LXX Ge. 4,8; from George 2010: 269. See below for a discussion of this example.)

---

[2] The generalizations in this study are also based on the following grammars of Greek: Goodwin ([1894] 1978), Kühner and Gerth ([1898/1904] 1963), Stahl (1907), Smyth (1956), Humbert (1945), Schwyzer and Debrunner (1950).

I will examine the transfer affecting overt object pronouns, testing the hypothesis that the influence in the Septuagint is not only the result of a translation strategy but also demonstrates a change in Greek (which is caused by language contact) as observed in the following stages of the language: referential null objects are available in Classical Greek (previous period) but become ungrammatical after Koine Greek. Hence, the main question of this study concerns the presence/absence of a relation between the transfer from Hebrew in the Septuagint as a text of Translation Greek in a situation of contact (does this transfer reflect an ongoing change in pronouns and null objects?) and a new characteristic that will become a rule for Greek in the later stages (overt referential objects). The specific Hebrew interference in the Septuagint – pleonastic instead of null pronouns – will become a characteristic of the grammar of later, post-Koine Greek, representing a significant change in the grammar of Greek, and does not show a transfer from Hebrew that only affects texts of this period; thus, the hypothesis of this study is plausible. Cf. the contrast between the null object in the New Testament (3a) and the obligatory overt object in Modern Greek (3b):

(3) a. *eîpen   autêi [...] kaì ékouon*   Ø *oi   mathētaì   autoû.*
       said.3SG her   and heard.3PL Ø the students.NOM his
       'And he said to her [...] and his students were hearing him.'
       (Ev.Marc. 11,14)

   b. *Ke   tis   ipe*   [...] *ke i   mathites   tu   *(ton) akughan.*
      and her said.3SG   and the students.NOM his he.ACC listen.3PL
      'And he said to her [...] and his students were hearing him.'

The following section (2.1) describes the typology of null objects and their development in Greek. Section 2.2 presents the sociolinguistic status and syntactic characteristics of the text of the Septuagint and its significance for the study of Greek. Section 2.3 discusses the Interpretability Hypothesis, which accounts for transfer in L2 and L1 attrition grammars, and how it can be implemented for the analysis of a translation language in the case of strong contact. Section 3 presents data from the Septuagint, showing the "pleonastic" use of overt pronouns – in contrast to the model of Classical Greek – as well as a large set of characteristics of the pronominal system that may constitute influence from Hebrew. I argue in favor of an analysis of Translation Greek of the period that takes into consideration the principles and characteristics of L2 and L1 attrition grammars (for instance, grammars of heritage speakers). In Section 4, I demonstrate why the characteristics of the Greek Septuagint cannot be described as reflecting the process of an ongoing change, considering relevant principles of language change. Section 5 summarizes the main conclusions.

2 Background on null objects and the Greek Septuagint

2.1 Null objects

Two main types of null objects are distinguished cross-linguistically: referential/ definite/latent null objects (4a) and indefinite/generic (4b). (See Cummins and Roberge 2005, for a detailed presentation of the literature on null objects and relevant examples).

(4) a. A: *Do you like this article?*
         B: **I love Ø.*

     b. *They have the ability to impress and delight Ø.*

According to Cummins and Roberge (2005), who follow Larjavaara (2000) and García Velasco and Portero Muñoz (2002), several structural contexts favor a non-overt object, for instance,
(i) sequences of verbs
     They will steal Ø, rob Ø, and murder Ø.
(ii) imperatives
     Push Ø hard.
(iii) contrastive uses
     She theorizes about language, but they just describe Ø.
(iv) infinitives
     This is a lovely guitar, with an uncanny ability to impress Ø and delight Ø.
(v) generic present tense
     There are those who annihilate Ø with violence, who devour Ø.
     (Cummins and Roberge 2005: 124).

For Modern Greek, Giannakidou and Merchant (1997) and Tsimpli and Papa-dopoulou (2009) have distinguished indefinite or non-referential null objects that are available in Modern Greek from referential null objects that are un-available in Modern Greek (5). Indefinite null objects appear in Modern Greek with NP-ellipsis and the presence or absence of an indefinite antecedent in the discourse.

(5) A: *Efere*   *o*   *Andreas*   *merika* *vivlia?*
         brought.3SG   the   Andreas.NOM   some   books.ACC

     B: *Ne,* *(*ta)*   *efere.*
        yes   (*they.ACC)   brought.3SG
        'A: Has Andreas brought any books? B: Yes, he did.'
        (Tsimpli and Papadopoulou 2009: 1599)

The change from Classical Greek to post-Koine Greek concerns referential null objects and the use of object pronouns, and not indefinite or generic null objects.

Luraghi (2003, 2004) has shown that specific (syntactic and discourse) environments trigger object drop and that there are communicative differences between null objects and clitics in similar contexts in Classical Greek. Null objects that are conditioned by discourse in Classical Greek present highly topical and non-focal information, whereas, according to Luraghi, syntactically conditioned null objects only occur in a set of constructions. Luraghi (2004) argued that these conditions for object drop are similar to the conditions for referential subject drop: coordinated clauses, participles, and yes/no questions. For instance, the object is omitted in the second clause in the case of coordinated verbs that have the same object (6a). Or, the object of a conjunct/ adverbial participle of a transitive verb is omitted if it is the same as the object of the governing verb (6b).

(6) a. *kaí* *min*   *Athēnaîoi*   *dēmosíēi*   *te*   *éthapsan*
        and   he.ACC   Athenians.NOM   public-expense.DAT   and   buried.3PL

        autoû têi   *per*   *épese*   *kaì* Ø *etímēsan*   *megálōs.*
        there where exactly fell.3SG and   Ø honored.3PL   greatly
        'And the Athenians buried him at public expense on the place where he had fallen, and honored [him] greatly.'
        (Hdt. 1,30,4; from Luraghi 2004: 240, ex. 8)

     b. *toùs* *mèn* *paîdas*   *diasṓsas*
        the   PTC   children.ACC   rescue.PTCP.NOM

        toîs goneûsin   *apédōken*   Ø
        the   parents.DAT   restored.3SG   Ø
        'And having rescued the children, he restored [them] to their parents.'
        (Isoc. Hel. 29,1; from Luraghi 2004: 241, ex. 11)

Post-Koine Greek – in contrast to Classical Greek, in which both null objects and overt pronouns are possible in cases of referential objects – does not allow referential null objects, only utilizing object pronouns. By the beginning of the post-classical period, the weak form of a pronoun appears either in the second position within the clause or the phonological phrase (p-phrase) or, with enclitic status, in a post-head (post-V) position (Janse 1993; Taylor 1996, 2002; Pappas 2004; Revithiadou and Spyropoulos 2006). Revithiadou and Spyropoulos (2006) have argued that in some cases (for instance, constructions with a conjunction and a verb), the weak form of the pronoun may appear before the verb (7a) or after the verb (7b) (see also Section 3, for more data).

(7) a. *ean   soi   doksēi*
       if   you.DAT   seems-good
       'if it seems good to you...'
       (Select Papyri 115,8)

    b. *ean   doksēi   soi*
       if   seems-good   you.DAT
       'if it seems to you...'
       (Select Papyri 110,8; from Taylor 1996: 498)

For Revithiadou and Spyropoulos, this variation in post-Classical Greek shows the existence of two grammars in competition: pronominals appear in the second position within the clause or the phonological phrase ("old" grammar); pronominals have an enclitic status and appear after the verb ("new" grammar). In the following section, before analyzing the contrast between pronouns and null objects in the Greek Septuagint, I discuss the status of the Greek Septuagint, which reflects the variety of Koine that is the focus of this study.

2.2 The Greek Septuagint

Because there are obvious sociolinguistic – as well as chronological – differences in the stages of Koine, we refer to the Greek Septuagint in this study, distinguishing the variety represented in this text from the other varieties of this period.[3] Moreover, we must note that the phenomenon we are examining is not

---

3 See below for more details and Janse (2002: 389):

"If the language of the LXX can indeed be qualified as 'good *koiné* Greek' (Thackeray 1909: 13) because of its drawing from the lexical and grammatical resources of the Egyptian *koiné*, especially in the case of the Pentateuch (Swete 1914: 20), this is not tantamount to saying that it can be considered representative of the spoken or even written language of its time in every respect."

just a stylistic feature of the Septuagint because it remained in the language in later stages. The Septuagint is considered significant for the analysis of syntactic changes in Greek because it is the most substantial corpus of post-Classical Greek, extending from the Ptolemaic period to the period of the Roman conquest. The Septuagint constitutes a collection of Greek texts, mainly translations or paraphrases (or with Greek as the original language), from the first half of the third century BC to the first century AD (Thackeray 1909, Drettas 2007). According to the traditional view on the text of the Septuagint – that is, the information included in the letter of Aristeas to Philocrates ("Aristeas' story") – it was Ptolemy II Philadelphus (circa 200 BC) who commissioned a translation of the Hebrew Old Testament. Ptolemy II Philadelphus charged a committee of 70 or 72 Jewish scholars with preparing a Greek translation of the first five books of the Old Testament. The target of this translation was the Greek-speaking Hebrew community who had begun to forget Hebrew (cf., among many others, Janse 2002, Wasserstein and Wasserstein 2006, Karrer and Kraus 2008).[4]

Many characteristics of the language of the Septuagint have been attributed to the process of translation as well as to the bilingual status of the specific translators and their community (see also below regarding the possible scenarios about the translators). Examples of the transfer from Hebrew include, for instance, a preference in the Septuagint for paratactic structures or the tendency for many verbs to take PPs instead of DPs in the accusative (see, among others, George 2010). For Wifstrand (2005) as well, the Septuagint is undeniably full of translation Hebraisms. On the other hand, Wifstrand claims that the similarities between the Septuagint and the New Testament are likely the result of conscious or unconscious imitation of the features of what was, during the entire Koine and early Imperial periods, the authoritative version of the Old Testament. The New Testament has taken these features indirectly via the Septuagint; however, these features may also have been intentionally selected to imitate a certain style (Wifstrand 2005: 29).

There are three possible scenarios with regard to the translators of the Septuagint. First, the translators were L1 speakers of Hebrew who learned Greek

---

4 I refer to Janse's (2002) detailed discussion of the historical and sociolinguistic aspects of the development of post-Classical Greek and of the translation effects in the Septuagint. In fact, the starting point for the use of the Septuagint in the present study as a representative text of a community in strong language contact is Janse's (2002) study:

"[...] since Deissmann's *Bibelstudien* (1895–97) the language of the Greek Scriptures is generally considered to be representative of the *koinē*, i.e. of the Egyptian *koinē* in the case of the LXX, specifically the Pentateuch (Swete 1914: 20), and of the Syro-Palestinian *koinē* in the case of the New Testament." (Janse 2002: 342).

as L2 and transferred Hebrew features into their L2: this is "Aristeas' story"; however, its historical accuracy is disputed. For instance, Janse (2002: 383) argues that the translators may have been native speakers of the Egyptian Koine but not of Hebrew or Aramaic because they were able to follow rules such as Wackernagel's Law. Second, the translators were probably bilingual because a large portion of their community was bilingual. On the other hand, Hebrew interference in the Septuagint is limited to lexical and syntactic extension (Janse 2002: 388–389), also showing a translation technique that is frequent in sacred translations. This remark leads us to the third scenario: that the translators must, of course, have had some level of proficiency in both languages; however, the translators were L1 speakers of Greek who learned Hebrew as L2 – or as heritage speakers – and consciously calqued Hebrew (mainly lexical and stylistic) features into their L1 (translation effect). I believe, however, that the transfer of core grammatical characteristics – overt instead of null objects, for instance – is related to general linguistic mechanisms that are applied in grammars with L1 attrition[5] or L2 grammars (see Section 2.3).

On the other hand, we should note that Bible translations demonstrate faithfulness in translating sacred texts because the status of the model may force the translators to override the features of the target language (Gianollo 2011: 75; see also Taylor 2008, and Drinka 2011). Moreover, the Septuagint is a special case among translations of sacred texts because of two additional characteristics: its various revisions (discussed in Koester 1995 and in Rahlfs' [1935] 1979 introduction to his edition of the text, for example) and the tension between the ideal of literal translation and the wish to write good Greek (either Koine Greek or Atticistic).

The specific phenomenon under examination, however – the extended use of pleonastic pronouns – has a parallel in contemporary and later native (non-Translation Greek) documents, most likely representing an ongoing change from a language that allows referential null objects into a language that uses clitics instead of null objects.

2.3 Transfer in L2 grammars

Changes in the development of a language resulting from internal factors have been considered related to the process of (L1) language acquisition (for instance,

---

5 Cf. Schmid (2013: 119): "The situation of linguistic drift [...], where a migrant achieves a high level of proficiency in the language of his or her new environment, uses this language on a daily basis, and consequently experiences an increase in variability in the manner some lexical, grammatical or phonetic properties of the [first] language are applied, has been termed language attrition."

how features are reanalyzed by the next generation of speakers). Principles of this "typical" change may apply to changes through contact as well. I will claim that changes in cases that involve L2 learners – and perhaps are represented in translation languages – may also follow principles of language transfer in foreign language grammars; hence, I will argue that additional principles should be considered for external change but not for internal change.[6] I will expand the approach followed in the analysis of the grammar of L2 learners and the grammar of speakers with L1 attrition (Interpretability Hypothesis; Tsimpli 2003 and Tsimpli and Mastropavlou 2007) to processes (or techniques) that characterize the grammar of translation languages, especially in cases of contact and L1 attrition (for heritage speakers). Accordingly, I will implement the principles of these areas in the phenomenon under examination: pleonastic pronouns in the Septuagint and their relation to the relevant changes in the history of Greek.

According to the Interpretability Hypothesis, the problems of L2 learners (and L1 attrition, or heritage, speakers) concern the use of uninterpretable features that are absent in the learners' native language or that are present but with a different specification. Tsimpli (2003) and Tsimpli and Mastropavlou (2007) have shown that features that are visible at the LF-interface because of their semantic content – that is, LF-interpretable features – are easier and more accessible to the L2/L1 attrition speakers than uninterpretable features, whose role is restricted to narrow syntax and/or have PF-realization but are not visible at the LF-interface. According to this approach, uninterpretable features are not accessible to L2 learners because they are subject to the critical period constraint – in other words, L1 values associated with these features are difficult to reset. L2 learners have access to LF-interpretable features even if these differ from their L1 (for instance, animacy in Modern Greek and English). L2 learners access interpretable features because these features have a dual status; they are present both in the language system and in the LF-interface. Conversely, LF-uninterpretable features are problematic in L2 acquisition. This is, for example, the reason why L1 Modern Greek learners of L2 English have problems with not using the resumptive strategy; the Interpretability Hypothesis predicts that the developing L2 grammar will utilize interpretable features that are always available independently.

---

6 See Section 4 for details. This approach attempts to connect L2 acquisition processes to language change in cases of language contact. In this manner, it is close to Kroch's analysis (for instance, Kroch 1989) of "internalized diglossia" and "competing grammars" in situations of language contact and change. The emphasis of the present study, however, is on the transfer of features and differences from (internal) change through L1 acquisition.

Tsimpli and Dimitrakopoulou (2007) have investigated the use of subject and object resumptive pronouns in L2 English wh-interrogatives with L1 Greek learners. Modern English (similar to Classical Greek) does not allow resumptive pronouns with subject and object wh-questions, in contrast to Modern Greek. In this respect, Tsimpli and Dimitrakopoulou have examined the role of the interpretable features of animacy and D-linking[7] with resumptive pronouns in L2 wh-questions. Interpretable features such as the animacy feature can constrain the transfer of resumptive pronouns from L1 Modern Greek to L2 English. The animacy feature is a semantic feature grammaticalized on Modern English pronouns but not in Modern Greek, in which grammatical gender distinctions override the animacy specification. Wherever interpretable features such as animacy are involved, improvement of the use of L2 pronouns is observed. On the other hand, uninterpretable features – for instance, resumptive uses of agreement on the pronouns in L1 Modern Greek – cause learnability problems because they are transferred to the L2 grammar.

A similar role has been attributed to interpretable/uninterpretable features with respect to the problems arising in SLI grammars. The incomplete representation of the functional elements causes inaccessibility of uninterpretable features in SLI and problems in the analysis of the input. That is, in SLI, the analysis of the input in terms of identification of formal, uninterpretable features is incomplete. Hence, it appears that the cause may be different in L2/L1 attrition and SLI grammars, but the uninterpretable formal features are the locus of the problem in all cases.

In the next section, I will analyze Translation Greek of the Septuagint with respect to overt referential objects, a significant change for later Greek, from the viewpoint of the Interpretability Hypothesis.

3 The data: "pleonastic" pronouns in the Septuagint

The Septuagint presents clear evidence of influence from Hebrew to Greek in a characteristic that is different in the previous period (Classical Greek) and changes during the Koine period. In accordance with the relevant literature, I will show that influence from Hebrew is clearly evidenced in the case of the

---

7 In D(iscourse)-linking, "a wh-question asks for answers in which the individuals that replace the wh-phrases are drawn from a set that is presumed to be salient both to speaker and hearer" (Pesetsky 2000: 16).

Septuagint. The Interpretability Hypothesis can correctly predict the following for Translation Greek of the Septuagint: constructions that involve uninterpretable features are potentially influenced by Hebrew characteristics, whereas constructions that involve interpretable features constrain the degree of transfer from Hebrew to Greek. The case of the Septuagint is significant from this perspective because the use of "modern" resumptive pronouns is attested for the first time.

The increased use of personal pronouns (direct objects, possessives, and resumptive pronouns) in the Septuagint has been mentioned in many monographs, grammars, and articles as an important example of the Semitic influence on Greek; see (8)–(10). According to Moulton and Turner (1963: 3), for instance, in the Septuagint, "personal pronouns are inserted where they would be unnecessary in classical Greek," whereas in non-Biblical [non-Septuagint and non-New Testament] Koine, "pleonastic" personal pronouns do not occur as often as in the Septuagint. Swete (1914: 307) also describes these "pleonastic" personal pronouns as a Semitic influence: "wearisome iteration of the oblique cases of personal pronouns answering to the Hebrew suffixes." Furthermore, George (2010: 269) observes the presence of the 3rd-person pronoun *autón* three times in a sentence as the subject of an infinitive, a possessive pronoun, and an object pronoun (10a). This example follows the model of Hebrew. In Hebrew, pronominal suffixes are repeated on consecutive verbs or nouns (10b) (Thackeray 1909: 30; Wifstrand 1949–1950: 44–45; Moulton and Turner 1963: 85).

(8) *auxanô*   **se**   *kaì* *plēthunô*   **se**
     increase.1SG you.ACC and   multiply.1SG   you.ACC

     kaì *poiésō*   **se**   *eis*   *sunagōgàs*   *ethnôn.*
     and   make.1SG you.ACC into   multitudes   nations
     'I will increase you, and multiply you and will make of you multitudes of nations.'[8] (LXX Ge. 48,4)

(9) *egéneto* *dè* *en* *tôi* *sklērôs* **autền** *tíktein*
     was   PTC   in   the   hard   she.ACC   give-birth.INF

     eîpen   *autêi*   *hē*   *maîa*
     said.3SG   she.DAT the   midwife.NOM
     'And as she was having great difficulty in childbirth, the midwife said to her.' (LXX Ge. 35,17)

---

8 The majority of the nonliteral translations given are based on *The English Standard Version Bible: Containing the Old and New Testaments with Apocrypha* (2009).

(10) a. *kaì egéneto   en tôi eînai* **autoùs** *en tôi pedíōi kaì anéstē*
and happened in the be.INF they.ACC in the field and rose-up.3SG

Kain   epì   Abel tòn adelphòn **autoû** *kaì apékteinen* **autón**
Cain.NOM against Abel the brother his   and killed.3SG he.ACC

b. *wa-yhî*   *bi-hyôt̲-**ām*** *baś-śā̲d̲eh way-yāqom*
and-it.happened in-being-their in.the-field and-he.rose.up

*qayin 'el-heb̲el 'ā-**îw*** *way-yaharḡ-**ēhû***
Cain to-Abel brother-his and-he.killed-him
'And it happened in their being in the field and Cain rose up against
Abel his brother and killed him.' (LXX Ge. 4,8)

In Figures 1–3, I present the results of a corpus study of the presence of object personal pronouns in Homer, Plato (and Herodotus), the New Testament, and the Septuagint (based on electronic corpora: *BibleWorks*, PROIEL, *Perseus under PhiloLogic*, TLG *online*; see Sources). I conducted a corpus search for the relative frequency of 3rd-person personal pronouns in the accusative (as direct objects) compared with the frequency of overt nouns and other (nonpersonal) pronouns in the accusative (as direct objects). I use relative frequencies to minimize the effect of the different word counts. The decision to search for changes in the frequency of personal pronouns in the accusative (in contrast to other overt DPs) was the result of the fact that there is no coding for null elements in texts from different periods or in the Septuagint in the available corpora of Greek (except for the New Testament). There appears to be a statistically significant increase in the frequency of object pronouns but no difference between their frequency in the Septuagint and the New Testament. A Pearson chi-square test was performed to assess the relation between the periods and the development of the third person personal pronouns (data in Figure 1). The results were statistically significant for the comparison between (a) Classical Greek (Plato) and the Septuagint ($\chi^2 = 3.426$, $p = .044$), with an effect size of $\varphi = .13$, which is a small size effect, and (b) Classical Greek and the New Testament ($\chi^2 = 3.852$ $p = .04$), with an effect size of $\varphi = .14$, which is a small size effect. No statically significant difference was observed between the Septuagint and the New Testament ($\chi^2 = .014$, $p = .905$).

I also conducted a corpus search for differences between the frequency of 3rd-person personal pronouns and the frequency of 1st- and 2nd-person personal pronouns because 3rd-person personal pronouns differ from other forms involving (un)interpretable features. In Tsimpli and Stavrakaki (1999) and Tsimpli and Mastropavlou (2007), 1st- and 2nd-person clitics and 3rd-person object clitics are distinguished in that 3rd-person clitics encode values of uninterpretable features only, whereas 1st- and 2nd-person clitics carry an interpretable feature of

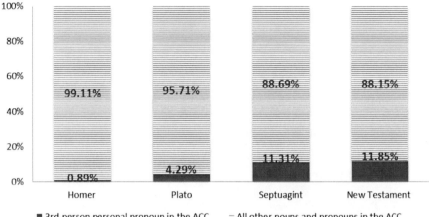

	3rd-person personal pronoun in the ACC	All other nouns and pronouns in the ACC
Homer	0.89% (209 / 23481)	99.11% (23272 / 23481)
Plato[9]	4.29% (3307 / 77053)	95.71% (73746 / 77053)
Septuagint	11.31% (7476 / 66075)	88.69% (58599 / 66075)
New Testament	11.85% (1603 / 13531)	88.15% (11928 / 13531)

Figure 1: Frequency of 3rd-person personal pronouns in the accusative in Homer, Plato, the Septuagint, and the New Testament

person (Manzini and Savoia 1998). Furthermore, 3rd-person clitics in the genitive, which belong to the nominal phrase, also differ from 3rd-person clitics in the accusative, which belong to the verbal phrase (Tsimpli and Stavrakaki 1999). 3rd-person clitics in the genitive bear a person feature and a feature of referentiality because they are theta-marked; this does not hold for 3rd-person clitics in the accusative (cf. Cardinaletti and Starke 1999). According to Tsimpli and Mastropavlou (2007), errors in the use of 3rd-person pronouns in the accusative in advanced adult L2 learners are caused by the assignment of the interpretable feature of referentiality/definiteness on these problematic elements in the grammar of the foreign speaker. I test whether the differences in the features of these pronouns play a role in their frequency and the changes between different periods. Figure 2 shows that no change is manifested for the 1st- and 2nd-person personal pronouns, although there was a change in the frequency of 3rd-person personal pronouns (see Figure 1). A Pearson chi-square test was

---

9 The data from Herodotus are similar both for 1st- and 2nd-person personal pronouns in the accusative and the 3rd-person personal pronouns in the accusative.

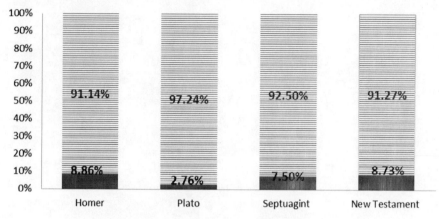

≡ All other nouns and pronouns in the ACC

■ 1st- and 2nd-person personal pronouns in the ACC

	1st- and 2nd-person personal pronouns in the ACC	*All other nouns and pronouns in the ACC*
Homer	8.86% (2081 / 23481)	91.14% (21400 / 23481)
Plato	2.76% (2123 / 77053)	97.24% (74930 / 77053)
Septuagint	7.50% (4954 / 66075)	92.50% (61121 / 66075)
New Testament	8.73% (1182 / 13531)	91.27% (12349 / 13531)

Figure 2: Frequency of 1st- and 2nd-person personal pronouns in the accusative in Homer, Plato, the Septuagint, and the New Testament

performed to assess the relation between the periods and the development of the 1st- and 2nd-person personal pronouns. The results show a difference between Plato and all other texts; however, the differences were not statistically significant (Plato compared with the Septuagint: $\chi^2 = 2.308$, $p = .129$).

Moreover, Figure 3 presents a corpus search in PROIEL that shows no significant change between Herodotus and the New Testament in this respect.[10] A Pearson chi-square test was performed to assess the relation between the periods and the development of overt nouns in the object position. The results were not statistically significant for the comparison between Herodotus and the New Testament ($\chi^2 = .140$, $p = .709$).

Null objects remain available in the New Testament, following the model of the grammar of Classical Greek. 341 examples of null objects were identified in a search of the New Testament in the PROIEL corpus (see 11a–e).

---

10 PROIEL includes syntactic annotation for Herodotus and the New Testament – but not for the Septuagint for overt nouns in the object position – and coding for null objects only for the New Testament but not for Herodotus.

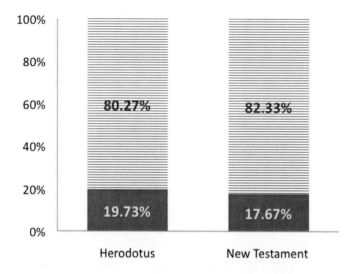

■ Verbs with an overt noun in the object position

≡ Verbs without an overt noun in the object position

	Verbs with an overt noun in the object position	*Verbs without an overt noun in the object position*
Herodotus	19.73% (3373 / 17100)	80.27% (13727 / 17100)
New Testament	17.67% (4502 / 25472)	82.33% (20970 / 25472)

Figure 3: Frequency of overt (common and proper) nouns in the object position in Herodotus and the New Testament

(11) a. *lúsate   autòn   kaì   phérete   Ø*
         unbind.IMP.2PL he.ACC and   bring.IMP.2PL Ø
         'Unbind it (the horse) and bring (it) here.'
         (Ev.Marc. 11,2)

   b. ... *kaì   éthēken   Ø   epì   toû   stauroû*
         and   put.3SG   Ø   on   the   cross
         '[And Pilate wrote a title also] and put (it) on the cross.'
         (Ev.Jo. 19,19)

c. ... *ouk   êlthon   katalûsai   Ø   allà   plērôsai   Ø*
     and   not   came.INF   Ø   but   fulfil.INF   Ø
'[Think not that I came to destroy the law or the prophets.] I came
not to destroy but to fulfill (the law and the prophets).'
(Ev.Matt. 5,17)

d. ... *kaì   éphagon   Ø   pántes   kaì   ekhortásthēsan.*
     and   ate.3PL   Ø   all.NOM   and   were-filled.3PL
'[and the two fishes divided he to all] and they all ate (from them)
and were filled.'
(Ev.Marc. 6,42)

e. ... *kaì   ésthion   Ø   psṓkhontes   Ø   taîs   khersín.*
     and   ate.3PL   Ø   rub.PTCP.NOM   Ø   the   hands.DAT
'[he was going through the grainfields; and his disciples plucked the
ears] and did eat, rubbing (them) in (their) hands'
(Ev.Luc. 6,1)

With respect to the Septuagint, the Psalter is the book in which one can
observe the most frequent uses of personal pronouns (Wifstrand 1949–1950;
Sollamo 2001). For example, Wifstrand identifies 2270 occurrences of personal
pronouns in the Psalter, 850 in Genesis, 840 in Isaiah, and 450 in Sirach.

In addition to the object pronouns, the following cases of overt pronouns in
the Septuagint differ from what is attested in Classical Greek; pronouns or even
nouns with interpretable or semantic features are preferred and transferred from
Hebrew, to be used instead of elements with uninterpretable features (Conybeare
and Stock 1905: 24–25, 52–55):

(i) A "pleonastic" personal pronoun is present after the relative pronoun (resumptive pronoun). This construction is completely new (unattested in Classical
Greek) and remains an important characteristic of the system of pronouns in
later Greek (until Modern Greek). Hebrew relative pronouns are indeclinable,
and a personal pronoun is always added to determine the relative pronoun. The
personal pronoun appears resumptive for Greek because the relative pronoun is
marked for gender, case, and number (12a compared with 12b). Swete (1914: 307)
considers resumptive pronouns with relative clauses to be a result of Semitic
influence: "To the circumstance that the Hebrew relative is indeclinable we owe
the 'pleonastic' use of the pronoun after the Greek relative." Bakker (1974: 9)
names these resumptive pronouns *pronomen abundans*.

(12) a. *hē   gê   ep'   hês   sù   katheúdeis   ep'*
          the   land.NOM.F   on   which.GEN.F   you.NOM   lie.2SG   on

          *autês   soì   dósō   **autền...***
          she.GEN.F you.DAT   give.1SG she.ACC

    b. *hā· 'ā·reṣ 'ă·šer'   at·tāh   šō·ḵēḇ   'ā·le·hā   lə·ḵā   'et·tə·nen·nāh*
        the   land   which   you   lie   above   you   will-give-it
        'The land on which you are lying I will give (it) to you.'
        (LXX Ge. 28,13)

For Bakker, the use of the "pleonastic" pronoun is not a Semitism per se (1974: 33). Bakker argues that the presence of a "pleonastic" pronoun is related to the type of relative clause (restrictive or nonrestrictive): in non-Biblical [non-Septuagint and non-New Testament] Greek, the "pleonastic" pronoun occurs exclusively in nonrestrictive relative clauses (13a and b).

(13) a. *hoîs   eîpen   **autoîs***
          who.DAT.M   said.3SG   they.DAT.M
          'To whom the Lord said.'
          (LXX Ex. 6,26)

    b. *hôn   oukhì   akoúontai   hai   phōnaì   **autôn.***
        which.GEN   not   hear.MID.3PL the   voices.NOM   they.GEN
        'Of which the voices are not heard.'
        (LXX Ps. 19,3)

The pleonastic pronoun can appear as the object of a preposition as well (14).

(14) *gên   ep'   hền   ouk   ekopiásate   **ep'   autês***
      land.ACC.F   on   which.ACC.F   not   labored.2PL   on   she.GEN
      'I gave you a land on which you had not labored.'
      (LXX Jo. 24,13)

In the New Testament, resumptive object pronouns with relative clauses (15) and weak resumptive pronouns with nominative topics are attested. Moulton and Turner (1963: 325) observe that "non-Biblical Greek reveals the same phenomenon" (cf. also Horrocks 2010: 147–152; Maloney 1981; Blass, Debrunner, and Rehkopf 1984: 228–252; Bubenik 1989: 65–67 for a detailed discussion).

(15) eis **hền** d' àn pólin è̱ kố̄mēn eisélthēte,
      in which.F PTC PTC city.NOM.F or village.NOM.F enter.2PL

exetásate tís en **autêi** áxiós estin.
examine.2PL who.NOM in she.DAT worthy be.3SG
'Into whatever city or village you enter, find out who is worthy in it.'
(Ev.Matt. 10,11)

It is obvious that, even though a translation such as the Septuagint presents more frequent instances of influence of the source/foreign language, other texts of the same community – including texts that are not translations and that do not represent Translation Greek of the period – cannot exist without evidence of the influence.

(ii) The 3rd-person pronoun *autós* in the nominative is used in cases in which Classical Greek would use a null subject (*autós éphē* 'he said' instead of the Classical Greek *éphē* 'said'; see also 16).[11] It is less common in the New Testament; however, there are some instances of use of the 3rd-person unemphatic subject (cf. Conybeare and Stock 1905: 52–55). This use of the unemphatic subject pronoun is not observed in later (post-Koine) Greek.

(16) **autós** sou tḗrḗsei kephalḗn...
      he.NOM you.GEN bruise.3SG head.ACC
      'he shall bruise your head...'
      (LXX Ge. 3,15)

(iii) A possessive pronoun in the genitive can be added to express possession (17a and b). This construction is not attested in Classical Greek. The construction remains available in later Greek (but with a clitic); however, the use of multiple possessives in a series of coordinate nouns becomes ungrammatical.

(17) a. kaì taûta tà onómata **autôn** en tais skēnaîs **autôn**
          and these the names.NOM their in the villages their

kaì en taîs epaúlesin **autôn**
and in the encampments their
'And these are their names, by their villages and by their encampments.'
(LXX Ge. 25,16)

---

11 Subject pronouns are attested in Classical Greek only in cases of emphasis or antithesis.

b. *kaì   têide   ên   díduma   en   têi   gastrì   **autês.***
   and   she.DAT   were.3PL   twins.NOM   in   the   womb   her
   'And behold twins were in her womb.'
   (LXX Ge. 38,27)

Similar constructions with possessive pronouns can be observed in the New Testament as well (18).

(18) *autòs   anénenken   en   tôi   sómati   **autoû.***
      he.NOM   bore.3SG   in   the   body   his
      'He himself bore our sins in his body.'
      (1 Ep.Pet. 2,24)

Sollamo (1995) has shown that the repetition of pronominal possessives in a series of coordinate nouns did not correspond to the non-Biblical Koine: in Classical Greek, possessive pronouns are not common, whereas in non-Biblical Koine, their frequency is much lower than in the Septuagint. On the other hand, Hebrew, when possession refers to two or more coordinate nouns, shows a suffix on each noun. Sollamo's results are important: in the Pentateuch, possessive pronouns are repeated in the majority of relevant cases (160/244); possessive pronouns are repeated less frequently in Genesis and Exodus (51% and 40%, respectively) than in Leviticus, Numbers, and Deuteronomy (75%, 86%, and 76%, respectively).

(iv) Furthermore, *idios* can be used as a possessive pronoun in the Septuagint; see (19) (cf. Conybeare and Stock 1905: 24–25). Again, this construction is not attested in later Greek. The Septuagint also shows a duplication of pronouns in the case of the use of the personal pronoun with the reflexive ('me myself'), see (20). This construction is not attested in later Greek either.

(19) *oud'   ou   mê   epistrépsei   éti   eis   tòn   **idion**   oîkon*
      PTC   NEG   NEG   return.3SG   still   to   the   own   house
      'He returns no more to his house.'
      (LXX Jb. 7,10)

(20) *poiésête   **humîn**   **heautoîs**   gluptòn   homoíōma*
      make.2PL   you.DAT   yourselves.DAT   carved   image.ACC
      '[and] make a carved image for yourselves.'
      (LXX De. 4,16)

(v) The noun *adelphós* is used as a reciprocal pronoun, showing an influence from Hebrew (21), and the noun *anḗr* is used as an indefinite pronoun, again purely demonstrating an influence from Hebrew (22). These constructions do not constitute characteristics of the grammar of later (post-Koine) Greek.

(21) kaì ouk eîden oudeìs tòn **adelphòn** autoû
    and NEG saw.3SG nobody.NOM the.ACC brother.ACC his
    'They did not see one another.'
    (LXX Ex. 10,23)

(22) píetai **anḕr** tḕn ámpelon autoû kaì **anḕr**
    drink.3SG each.NOM the vine.ACC his and each.NOM

    tḕn sukḕn autoû phágetai.
    the fig-tree.ACC his eat.3SG
    'Then, each one of you will eat of his own vine, and each one of his own fig tree.'
    (LXX 2 Ki. 18,31)

(vi) A demonstrative adverb (*ekeî*, *ekeîthen*) is used after a relative adverb or a similar phrase to repeat the previously mentioned DP (23a and b). Again, this appears to be a clear example of influence from Hebrew and is not used in texts later than the Septuagint.

(23) a. epì tôn oikiôn en haîs humeîs este **ekeî**
        on the house.GEN.F in which.DAT.F you.2PL are.2PL there
        '[The blood shall be a sign for you] on the houses where you are.'
        (LXX Ex. 12,13)

    b. en toîs éthnesin eis hoùs eisáxei
        in the nations.DAT.N to which.ACC.M[12] drive.3SG

        kúrios humâs **ekeî**
        Lord.NOM you.ACC there
        '... among the nations where the Lord will drive you.'
        (LXX De. 4,27)

In the New Testament, only the Revelation shows some examples of this construction (24).

(24) hópou tréphetai **ekeî**
    where nourish.MID.3SG there
    '... where she is to be nourished.'
    (Apoc. 12,14)

---

12 We should note that the relative pronoun in this example does not agree with the antecedent (*éthnesin* 'nations') with respect to the grammatical gender; it appears in the masculine gender (most likely referring to word *ánthrōpoi* 'humans', which is masculine in Greek) and not in the neuter gender.

To summarize, a tendency toward "pleonastic" pronouns – and a completely different system of pronouns in which elements with interpretable features are transferred from Hebrew and preferred to elements with uninterpretable features – is evident in the data of the Septuagint. In several cases, an influence from Hebrew is obvious. This transfer concerns only the Septuagint in the majority of the examples with pronouns. However, some cases (resumptive pronouns and overt object pronouns instead of referential null objects) appear for the first time in the Septuagint – and in the New Testament, although less frequently – representing also a later change in the history of Greek in the sense that overt object pronouns will remain a basic characteristic of later Greek. Of course, we cannot arrive at the general conclusion that a variety of (Egyptian) Koine (see Section 2.2) influenced by Hebrew affected the development of post-Classical Greek; nevertheless, we must distinguish this specific characteristic of pronouns in Translation Greek as represented in the Septuagint (that remain and consti-tute a significant change in Greek) from all other characteristics and influences of Hebrew or other languages in the Greek Septuagint. However, I do not claim that there is a direct connection between the Septuagint and the relevant change; the characteristics of the Septuagint do not represent an ongoing change. In Section 4, I will show that the differences in the principles applied in each case (Translation Greek of the Septuagint: Interpretability Hypothesis; language change: Feature Economy Principle) can account for the lack of a direct relation between the transfer from Hebrew in Translation Greek of the Septuagint and the relevant language change.

4 Mechanisms of language change vs. mechanisms of L2/L1 attrition grammars as evidenced in the Septuagint

Van Gelderen (2008, 2009, 2011) has shown that language change, in a similar manner to L1 language acquisition, involves reanalysis of semantic features as interpretable and then as uninterpretable features:[13]

---

13 Semantic features are different from interpretable features in van Gelderen's approach (2008: 290, 296):

"From Chomsky (1995) on, features are divided in interpretable (relevant at LF) and un-interpretable (not relevant to the interpretation)" and "assuming a lexicalist hypothesis in which a lexical entry 'contains three collections of features: phonological ... semantic ..., and formal' (Chomsky 1995: 230), a lexical item such as the light verb *go* might have semantic features of [motion, future, location]...".

(25) semantic > [iF] > [uF]

For van Gelderen, a functional element can lose its semantic and interpretable features and become a probe that searches for an element to value its features. Accordingly, for instance, the semantic feature of time of a PP inside a VP (for instance, the English *after*) can be reanalyzed as grammatical time (see 26).

(26) P >   P >   C
      [u-phi] [u-phi] [u-phi]
      [ACC]   [ACC]   [i-time]/[u-time]
      [time]   [i-time]
      (van Gelderen 2008: 299)

This approach is interpreted as a Feature Economy Principle for language change (27). According to van Gelderen, this principle drives children to reanalyze their input while acquiring first language:[14]

(27) *Feature Economy Principle*
      Minimize the semantic and interpretable features in the derivation.
      (van Gelderen 2008: 297).

Hence, as observed, interpretable features help learners acquire the relevant phenomena in situations of foreign language grammars/L1 attrition and contact between languages, whereas, again, interpretable features should be candidates for change, according to the Feature Economy Principle. The clear differences between the Feature Economy Principle of language change and the Interpreta bility Hypothesis for the characteristics of foreign language/L1 attrition speakers and translation languages in cases of intense contact such as the Greek Septuagint can explain the lack of a direct relation between the status of null objects in the Septuagint and the change in the null objects as evidenced in later Greek. On the other hand, the interaction between the principles that determine language change and the principles that determine the grammar of translation languages in the case of contact can explain some aspects of the direction of change in post-Koine Greek. In other words, that we do not observe a change

---

14 Cf. van Gelderen (2008: 287): "Data from language acquisition and language change show that a principle in the internalized grammar of the child (possibly a more general cognitive principle) biases the child toward analyzing certain features as uninterpretable, and also what consequence that has in turn."

from interpretable to uninterpretable features in the phenomenon under examination leads us to the discussion of a potential role played in the development by characteristics that are also evidenced in the translation language.

The important issue here is that later Greek does not follow rules of "typical" change through L1 acquisition in this case (overt pronouns), and Translation Greek of the Septuagint can provide evidence of a mechanism that may function in situations of contact. Of course, I do not claim that the specific text plays a role in the development; in the absence of other direct evidence of contact in antiquity, the grammar of this text – and, more specifically, the mechanisms and strategies involved in the grammar of this text – can help us understand the complex case of ongoing change in situations of contact. Change in cases of language contact is a "special"/complex situation (not a "typical" situation of language change) in that change must follow the principles of "typical" change, whereas the transfer of characteristics of a foreign language, according to the Interpretability Hypothesis, also plays a role in the process of the change. Both mechanisms are in action in cases of language contact because, of course, L1 continues; however, less obviously, intrusion of elements of foreign languages may have played a role in learning L1; the learner is subject to a mixed primary input for L1 in the community because of the speakers of another language or because of intense contact with oral and written texts of another language.

Therefore, speakers may transfer elements related to uninterpretable features – such as resumptive pronouns that appear in the Greek Septuagint – from a foreign language but also try to minimize the semantic features of the derivation when they acquire their language (see Figure 4, below): this can be evidenced in the preference for 3rd-person personal pronouns compared with an avoidance of 1st- and 2nd-person personal pronouns in the Greek Septuagint, for example. According to Tsimpli's (2003) analysis, the referentiality linked to the object pronoun is attributed to a syntactic feature matching the relation with an antecedent. Furthermore, 3rd-person object pronouns are distinguished from 1st- and 2nd-person object pronouns in terms of (un)interpretability: case and phi-features of 3rd-person object pronouns are uninterpretable, whereas the person feature of 1st- and 2nd-person object pronouns is interpretable. Figure 2 in Section 3 has shown that the translators of the Septuagint did not face problems with 1st- and 2nd-person object pronouns that involve interpretable features; it appears there was no influence in the case of 1st- and 2nd-person object pronouns – their frequency remains stable, as in Homeric and Classical Greek. The situation is different with 3rd-person object pronouns that involve uninterpretable features, which are not accessible either to L2/L1 attrition speakers or to

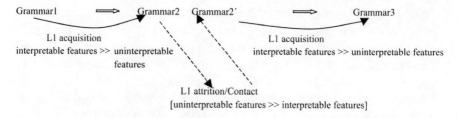

Figure 4: The position of the translation language in the case of change through contact [Grammars 1, 2, 2′, 3 refer to the grammars of the different generations of speakers].

the translators of the Septuagint and which are possible candidates for transfer from the foreign (source of the translation) language.

However, the direction of the change remains similar to the direction attested for the "typical" change. This can mean that the opposite direction (change from uninterpretable to interpretable features) is not attested even in this case and that an actual contrast exists between the influence of foreign language in Translation Greek of the Septuagint and change starting with and after Koine, with respect to features and the relevant mechanisms. Hence, the change described is a change that concerns the uninterpretable case and phi-features of 3rd-person pronouns (referential 3rd-person object pronouns become obligatory) that remain uninterpretable; however, there is a spell-out requirement for them, meaning that null objects are ungrammatical because this cluster of features should be expressed by overt pronouns and not, for example, by characteristics – aspectual or other – of the verb. The uninterpretable features of 3rd-person object pronouns do not acquire a semantic or interpretable content but undergo a different type of change: they must be spelled-out as overt pronouns; i.e., there is a change from uninterpretable features that are not spelled-out to un-interpretable features that are spelled-out by overt pronouns. A violation of the general principles of language change (Feature Economy, for instance) is not evidenced even in this case, in which other principles determine the influence of foreign languages such as those observed in Translation Greek of this period.

For translation languages in situations of contact, the mechanisms described by the Interpretability Hypothesis function; however, the change (if one occurs) cannot be the direct result of the processes in the grammar of the translation language. No direct relation is therefore evident between the change and the transfer from Hebrew as represented in the translation language (or any lan-guage influenced by foreign elements). This is because the change is not the result of the influence of a foreign language but rather emerges through the transfer of grammar from one generation to the next. This intermediate process – the change through L1 acquisition by children – follows the same principles that

L1 acquisition and language change follow in cases without foreign language influence.

Figure 4 shows how complex the situation of change in conditions of language contact should be: change is *not* directly related to the transfer from the foreign language in the grammar of the translation language. The transition from Grammar 1 to Grammar 2 results in reanalysis of some aspects of the grammar of the previous generation (Grammar 1). This reanalysis follows the general principles of "typical" change – that is, semantic and interpretable features are candidates to be reanalyzed as uninterpretable (van Gelderen 2008, 2010, 2011). Grammar 2 is the grammar of the generation of the translators of the Septuagint. The Greek Septuagint represents a translation language that contains characteristics from foreign languages (mainly Hebrew). The influence on Translation Greek follows the principles of typical L2 acquisition/L1 attrition: uninterpretable features are vulnerable and susceptible to transfer from the foreign language to Translation Greek. During the period of language contact, L1 acquisition continues, and the "new" grammar (Grammar 2), which is affected by characteristics of the translation language, is acquired by the next generation of speakers. Any change during this stage will follow the principle of the "typical" changes (interpretable features becoming uninterpretable) again.

5 Conclusions

We have investigated the hypothesis of a relation between characteristics of transfer from Hebrew in Translation Greek of the Septuagint and language change at the syntax-semantics interface using data for the presence of "pleonastic" pronouns (compared with referential null objects) in the Greek Septuagint. These "pleonastic" object pronouns in the Septuagint have been analyzed in the relevant literature as the result of contact between the Greek language and other languages, primarily Hebrew. The unavailability of referential null objects in post-Koine (post-Septuagint period) is also considered in the relevant literature to have been influenced by Hebrew. The data have shown that there is an important increase in the frequency of 3rd-person (but not 1st- and 2nd-person) personal pronouns both in the Septuagint and the New Testament. However, the relevant change appears to follow the principles of "typical" change. Speakers may transfer uninterpretable features such as resumptive pronouns in the Greek Septuagint from the foreign/source language in the case of a translation language but try to minimize the semantic features of the derivation when they acquire their language (preference for 3rd-person personal pronouns compared with avoidance of 1st- and 2nd-person personal pronouns in the Greek Septuagint).

Sources

BibleWorks (Bible software package. Version 9). http://www.bibleworks.com/.
Hunt, Arthur E. & Cowan E. Campbell. 1932. *Select Papyri*. London: William Heinemann.
Perseus under Philologic (Perseus Project Texts Loaded under PhiloLogic).
   http://perseus.uchicago.edu/.
PROIEL (Pragmatic Resources in Old Indo-European Languages). http://foni.uio.no:3000/.
TLG *online* (Thesaurus Linguae Graecae). http://www.tlg.uci.edu/.
For abbreviations of authors and works, see LSJ (Liddell-Scott-Jones Greek-English Lexicon).
   http://stephanus.tlg.uci.edu/lsj/01-authors_and_works.html.

References

Bakker, Willem Frederik. 1974. *Pronomen abundans and pronomen coniunctum: A contribution to the history of the resumptive pronoun within the relative clause in Greek*. Amsterdam: North-Holland.

Blass, Friedrich, Albert Debrunner & Friedrich Rehkopf. 1984. *Grammatik des neutestamentlichen Griechisch*. 16. Aufl. Göttingen: Vandenhoeck & Ruprecht.

Bubenik, Vit. 1989. *Hellenistic and Roman Greece as a sociolinguistic area*. Amsterdam & Philadelphia: John Benjamins.

Cardinaletti, Anna & Michal Starke. 1999. The typology of structural deficiency: A case study of the three classes of pronouns. In Henk van Riemsdijk (ed.), *Clitics in the languages of Europe*, 145–233. Berlin & New York: Mouton de Gruyter.

Chomsky, Noam. 1995. *The Minimalist Program*. Cambridge, MA: MIT Press.

Conybeare, Frederick Cornwallis & St. George Stock. 1905. *Grammar of Septuagint Greek*. Boston, MA: Ginn & Co.

Cummins, Sarah & Yves Roberge. 2005. A modular account of null objects in French. *Syntax* 8(1). 44–64.

Deissmann, Gustav Adolf. 1895. *Bibelstudien*. Marburg: Elwert.

Deissmann, Gustav Adolf. 1897. *Neue Bibelstudien*. Marburg: Elwert.

Drettas, Georges. 2007. The translation (Targum) of the Septuagint. In Anastassios-Fivos Christidis (ed.), *A history of Ancient Greek: from the beginnings to late antiquity*, 887–897. Cambridge: Cambridge University Press.

Drinka, Bridget. 2011. The sacral stamp of Greek: Periphrastic constructions in New Testament translations of Latin, Gothic, and Old Church Slavonic. In Eirik Welo (ed.), *Indo-European syntax and pragmatics: Contrastive approaches*, 41–73. Oslo: Oslo Studies in Language.

García Velasco, Daniel & Carmen Portero Muñoz. 2002. Understood objects in Functional Grammar. *Working Papers in Functional Grammar* 76. Amsterdam: University of Amsterdam.

van Gelderen, Elly. 2008. Where did Late Merge go? Grammaticalization as feature economy. *Studia Linguistica* 62(3). 287–300.

van Gelderen, Elly. 2009. Feature economy in the linguistic cycle. In Paola Crisma & Giuseppe Longobardi (eds.), *Historical syntax and linguistic theory*, 93–109. Oxford: Oxford University Press.

van Gelderen, Elly. 2010. Features in reanalysis and grammaticalization. In Elizabeth Closs Traugott & Graeme Trousdale (eds.), *Gradience, gradualness, and grammaticalization*, 129–147. Amsterdam & New York: John Benjamins.

van Gelderen, Elly. 2011. *The linguistic cycle: Language change and the language faculty.* Oxford: Oxford University Press.

George, Coulter H. 2010. Jewish and Christian Greek. In Egbert J. Bakker (ed.), *A companion to the Ancient Greek language*, 267–280. Oxford: Blackwell.

Giannakidou, Anastasia & Jason Merchant. 1997. On the interpretation of null indefinite objects in Greek. *Studies in Greek Linguistics* 17. 141–155.

Gianollo, Chiara. 2011. Native syntax and translation effects: Adnominal arguments in the Greek and Latin New Testament. In Eirik Welo (ed.), *Indo-European syntax and pragmatics: Contrastive approaches*, 75–101. Oslo: Oslo Studies in Language.

Goodwin, William Watson. 1978 [1894]. *A Greek Grammar*. Reprint. London: St. Martin's Press.

Horrocks, Geoffrey. 2010. *Greek: A history of the language and its speakers*. 2nd edn. Chichester & Malden, MA: Wiley-Blackwell.

Humbert, Jean. 1945. *Syntaxe Grecque*. Paris: Librairie Klincksieck.

Jannaris, Antonius N. 1897. *An Historical Greek Grammar*. London: Macmillan.

Janse, Mark. 1993. La position des pronoms personnels enclitiques en grec néotestamentaire à la lumière des dialects néo-helléniques. In Claude Brixhe (ed.), *La koiné grecque antique I. Une langue introuvable?*, 83–121. Nancy: Presses Universitaires de Nancy.

Janse, Mark. 2002. Aspects of bilingualism in the history of the Greek language. In James N. Adams, Mark Janse & Simon Swain (eds.), *Bilingualism in ancient society: Language contact and the written word*, 332–390. Oxford: Oxford University Press.

Karrer, Martin & Wolfgang Kraus. (eds.) 2008. *Die Septuaginta: Texte, Kontexte, Lebenswelten*. Tübingen: Mohr Siebeck.

Khan, Geoffrey. 2013. Pronominal Suffixes. In Geoffrey Khan (ed.), *Encyclopedia of Hebrew Language and Linguistics*, vol. III, 267–272. Leiden: Brill.

Koester, Helmut. 1995. *Introduction to the New Testament, vol. 1: History, culture, and religion of the Hellenistic Age*. Berlin & New York: de Gruyter.

Kroch, Anthony. 1989. Reflexes of grammar in patterns of language change. *Language Variation and Change*. 1(3). 199–244.

Kühner, Raphael & Bernhard Gerth. 1963 [1898/1904]. *Ausführliche Grammatik der Griechischen Sprache. Zweiter Teil: Satzlehre*. Unveränd. Nachdr. der 3. Aufl., 2 Bdn. Hannover: Hahn.

Larjavaara, Meri. 2000. *Présence ou absence de l'objet. Limites du possible en français contemporain*. Helsinki: Academia Scientiarum Fennica.

Luraghi, Silvia. 2003. Definite referential null objects in Ancient Greek. *Indogermanische Forschungen* 108. 169–196.

Luraghi, Silvia. 2004. Null objects in Latin and Greek and the relevance of linguistic typology for language reconstruction. In Karlene Jones-Bley, Angela della Volpe, Martin Huld & Miriam Robbins Dexter (eds.), *Proceedings of the 15th Annual UCLA Indo-European Conference, Los Angeles, November 7–8, 2003* (JIES Monograph Series 49), 234–256. Washington, DC: Institute for the Study of Man.

Maloney, Elliott C. 1981. *Semitic interference in Marcan Syntax*. Atlanta, GA: Scholars Press.

Manzini, Maria Rita & Leonardo Maria Savoia. 1998. Clitics and auxiliary choice in Italian dialects: Their relevance for the person ergativity split. *Recherches linguistiques de Vincennes* 27. 115–138.

Moulton, James Hope & Nigel Turner. 1963. *A Grammar of New Testament Greek*, vol. III: *Syntax*. Edinburgh: T. & T. Clark.

Pappas, Panayiotis. 2004. Medieval Greek weak object pronouns and analogical change: A response to Condoravdi and Kiparsky (2001). *Journal of Greek Linguistics* 5. 127–158.

Pesetsky, David. 2000. *Phrasal movement and its kin*. Boston, MA: MIT Press.

Rahlfs, Alfred. (ed.). 1979 [1935]. *Septuaginta*. Reprint. Stuttgart: Deutsche Bibelgesellschaft.

Revithiadou, Anthi & Vassilios Spyropoulos. 2006. A typology of Greek clitics with special reference to their diachronic development. Ms., University of the Aegean. http://ling.auf.net/lingbuzz/000496/current.pdf (accessed 13 November 2013).

Schmid, Monika S. 2013. First language attrition. *Wiley Interdisciplinary Reviews: Cognitive Science* 4(2). 117–123.

Schwyzer, Eduard & Albert Debrunner. 1950. *Griechische Grammatik. Zweiter Band: Syntax und syntaktische Stilistik* (Handbuch der Altertumswissenschaft, 2. Abt., 1. Teil, 2. Bd.). München: C.H. Beck.

Smyth, Herbert Weir. 1956. *Greek Grammar*. Cambridge, MA: Harvard University Press.

Sollamo, Raija. 1995. *Repetition of the possessive pronouns in the Septuagint* (SBL Septuagint and Cognate Studies 39). Atlanta, GA: Scholars Press.

Sollamo, Raija. 2001. The Letter of Aristeas and the Origin of the Septuagint. In Bernard A. Taylor (ed.), *X Congress of the International Organization for Septuagint and Cognate Studies*, 329–342. Atlanta GA: Society of Biblical Literature.

Stahl, Johann Matthias. 1907. *Kritisch-historische Syntax des griechischen Verbums der klassischen Zeit*. Heidelberg: Winter.

Swete, Henry Barclay. 1914. *An Introduction to the Old Testament in Greek*. 2nd revision by Richard Rusden Ottley. Cambridge: Cambridge University Press.

Taylor, Ann. 1996. A prosodic account of clitic position in Ancient Greek. In Aaron L. Halpern & Arnold M. Zwicky (eds.), *Approaching second: Second position clitics and related phenomena*, 477–503. Stanford, CA: CSLI Publications.

Taylor, Ann. 2002. The distribution of object clitics in Koine Greek. In Mark R. V. Southern (ed.), *Indo-European perspectives*, 285–316. Washington, DC: Institute for the Study of Man.

Taylor, Ann. 2008. Contact effects of translation: Distinguishing two kinds of influence in Old English. *Language Variation and Change* 20(2). 341–365.

Thackeray, Henry St. John. 1909. *A Grammar of the Old Testament in Greek*, vol. I: *Introduction, orthography and accidence*. Cambridge: Cambridge University Press.

The English Standard Version Bible: Containing the Old and New Testaments with Apocrypha. 2009. Oxford: Oxford University Press.

Tsimpli, Ianthi Maria. 2003. Clitics and determiners in L2 Greek. In Juana M. Liceras, Helmut Zobl & Helen Goodluck (eds.), *Proceedings of the 6th Generative Approaches to Second Language Acquisition Conference* (GASLA 2002), 331–339. Somerville, MA: Cascadilla Press.

Tsimpli, Ianthi Maria & Maria Dimitrakopoulou. 2007. The Interpretability Hypothesis: Evidence from wh-interrogatives in second language acquisition. *Second Language Research* 23(2). 215–242.

Tsimpli, Ianthi Maria & Maria Mastropavlou. 2007. Feature interpretability in L2 acquisition and SLI: Greek clitics and determiners. In Juana M. Liceras, Helmut Zobl & Helen Goodluck (eds.), *The role of formal features in second language acquisition*, 143–183. Mahwah, NJ: Lawrence Erlbaum.

Tsimpli, Ianthi Maria & Despina Papadopoulou. 2009. Aspect and argument realization: A study on antecedentless null objects in Greek. *Lingua* 116(10). 1595–1615.

Tsimpli, Ianthi Maria & Stavroula Stavrakaki. 1999. The effects of a morphosyntactic deficit in the determiner system: The case of a Greek SLI child. *Lingua* 108(1). 31–85.

Wasserstein, Abraham & David J. Wasserstein. 2006. *The legend of the Septuagint: From classical antiquity to today.* Cambridge: Cambridge University Press.

Wifstrand, Albert. 1949–1950. Die Stellung der enklitischen Personalpronomina bei der Septuaginta. *K. Humanistiska Vetenskapssamfundets i Lund Årsberättelse (Bulletin de la Société Royale des Lettres de Lund)* 1949–1950, II. 44–70.

Wifstrand, Albert. 2005. Luke and the Septuagint. In Albert Wifstrand, *Epochs and styles. Selected writings on the New Testament, Greek language and Greek culture in the post-classical era*, ed. by Lars Rydbeck & Stanley E. Porter, transl. by Denis Searby, 28–45. Tübingen: Mohr Siebeck. [English translation of Wifstrand, Albert. 1940. Lukas och Septuaginta. *Svensk Teologisk Kvartalskrift* 16, 243–262].

Magnus Breder Birkenes and Florian Sommer

7 The agreement of collective nouns in the history of Ancient Greek and German

The present paper deals with the agreement of collective nouns within the diachrony of the genetically related languages Ancient Greek and German. Collective nouns are morphologically singular but semantically both singular and plural and may thus trigger plural agreement. By quantitatively analyzing text corpora spanning several centuries, we investigate the role of Corbett's Agreement Hierarchy in diachronic change and the effects of word order and linear distance on non-formal agreement in collective nouns. Special attention is paid to verb agreement, where mismatches are possible both in Ancient Greek and in German. Whereas the Agreement Hierarchy has proven valid at all stages, we raise the question of whether specific verb agreement patterns may have been caused by loan syntax as these are mostly found in religious texts and can be traced back as far as Biblical Hebrew.

1 Introduction

The study of agreement has seen some rapid progress within the last decades. Most of the research has been conducted within either an empirical or theoretical framework. This is not surprising since languages exhibit great diversity in the make-up of their agreement systems. Moreover, the function of agreement is crucial when it comes to establishing theories of language in general, thus making it an apt subject for theoretical and formal consideration. Although diachronic perspectives have not been neglected, this aspect has figured less prominently in current research. The present paper will examine a special case of number agreement at the syntax-semantic interface within the diachrony of the genetically related languages Ancient Greek and German: so-called collective nouns and their agreement.[1]

Such nouns are widely attested in languages belonging to the Indo-European family (but, of course, it is not limited to these languages, see e.g., Corbett 2000:

---

[1] In our understanding, the term collective noun does not apply to Greek neuter plurals (which trigger singular agreement, like in the textbook example $[ta\ z\bar{o}ia]_{PL}\ [trek^hei]_{SG}$ 'the animals run'). These are sometimes misleadingly referred to as "collectives". Whatever their historical background might be, they are simple plurals to neuter singulars from a synchronic point of view.

190–191). "Collective nouns" (cf. Levin 2001 and Depraetere 2003) are often defined as a class of nouns that denote plural entities but show singular morphology. The term collective is in itself rather problematic (cf. Gil 1996). Levin's definition for the term collective noun, which can be adopted for the present purpose, runs as follows: "a noun that refers to two or more entities, and which in the singular can be used with singular and plural verbs and pronouns" (2006: 321 n. 2).[2] The variation within agreement is explicitly used to define "collective noun" on a language-specific basis. But, of course, there is more to it than syntax. One can argue that the unstable syntactic patterns represent the outcome of semantic conflict on a conceptual level. The referents of "collective nouns" are conceptually both singular and plural; pitting syntax against semantics will not do, as was pointed out by Gil (1996). But collective nouns do not represent one single, coherent class, that is, they "differ in the conceptual accessibility of the member level" (Joosten et al. 2007: 86, who rightly emphasize this point).

An extreme case with a high member level accessibility is the noun *committee* in British English. It is reasonable to ask why this behavior has developed in British English, but is rare in other languages (cf. den Dikken 2001: 38). Like den Dikken (2001), we are not able to answer this question in any satisfactory way: Liedtke (1910) shows that plural agreement was still very rare in Old English (similar to our findings on German that will be presented in section 2.2) and first became noticeable in Middle English. As far as the codification of British English is concerned, Dekeyser (1975: 42) shows that most grammarians were never hostile to plural agreement where this was semantically justified, and concludes that "in the late 19th century the sound view prevails that collectives can pattern alike with singular or plural [verbs] and [pronouns] according to the speaker's or writer's frame of reference".

When the targets of collective nouns show plural agreement, this is often referred to as semantic agreement or *constructio ad sensum* in the literature (see e.g., Corbett 2006: 155; Kühner and Gerth 1898: 52–53). However, the term is problematic in this case: Depending on the conceptualization of the entity, the choice of the singular or the plural can both be said to be semantically motivated.[3] Thus, this phenomenon is to be distinguished from the gender agreement of lexical hybrids like German *Weib* 'woman' (cf. Fleischer 2012), where there is, at least from a synchronic perspective, no clear semantic motivation for the

---

2 However, if this definition would be applied *stricto sensu*, it could lead to some strange results: e.g., collectives in Cretan Greek would be excluded, since here plural agreement is rather the norm than the exception (see Wackernagel 1926: 103).

3 We would like to thank the anonymous reviewer for drawing our attention to this important point. Levin (2006: 321 n. 3) avoids the term semantic agreement too, but for different reasons.

neuter form. Instead of formal and semantic agreement, we use the more neutral terms singular agreement or plural agreement. The latter is also referred to as "mismatch" (cf. Corbett 2006: 143–175), since the formal features of controller and target differ. The spread of plural agreement with singular controllers is nonetheless limited as illustrated by the following examples from British English:

(1) *The committee has/have decided.*
　　 *These committee has/have decided.
　　 The committee… It/They…

The examples in (1) show that this kind of variation in simple sentences is restricted to the domain of the predicate. There is no variation within the NP in English. Personal pronouns referring back to these nouns in later sentences may or may not show plural agreement (Corbett 2000: 188–190, 2006: 211–213). It has been shown, however, that the likelihood of mismatches increases with syntactic distance. Observations like these led Corbett (1979: 204) to establish the by now well-known Agreement Hierarchy (see also Corbett 2000: 188–190, 2006: 206–237), which can be applied to non-formal agreement in general, i.e., not only to the relation between collective nouns and their respective targets:[4]

attributive (< copredicative) < predicative < relative pronoun < personal pronoun

The hierarchy is implicational by nature: This means that "[f]or any controller that permits alternative agreements, as we move rightwards along the Agreement Hierarchy, the likelihood of agreement with greater semantic justification will increase monotonically (that is, with no intervening decrease)" (Corbett 2006: 207). The biblical examples in (2)[5] show this (the relevant controllers and targets are marked in bold):

(2) Position　　　　　 Example
　　 attributive　　　　*kai* **pas** **ho** **ok^hlos** *ērkheto* *pros*
　　　　　　　　　　　and　whole.SG　ART.SG　crowd.SG　came　to

　　　　　　　　　　　auton
　　　　　　　　　　　him

　　　　　　　　　　　vnd **alles** **Volck** *kam* *zu* *jm*
　　　　　　　　　　　and　all.SG　people.SG　came　to　him
　　　　　　　　　　　'and all the multitude resorted unto him'
　　　　　　　　　　　(Mk 2,13)

---

4 For an integration of the Agreement Hierarchy into the concept of clause linkage, see Nishina (2006: 53–55).
5 The German text is from Luther's 1545 Bible translation.

(copredicative)

kai	pas	ho	**laos**	**idōn**	edōken
and	whole	ART	people.SG	seeing.SG	gave

ainon	tōi	t^heōi
praise	ART	God

'and all the people, when they saw (it), gave praise unto God.'
(Lk 18,43)

predicative

kai	pas	ho	**ok^{h}los**	**ērk^{h}eto**	pros	auton
and	whole	ART	crowd.SG	came.SG	to	him

vnd	alles	**Volck**	kam	zu	jm
and	all.SG	people.SG	came.SG	to	him

'and all the multitude resorted unto him'
(Mk 2,13)

relative pronoun

meta	tauta	eidon,	kai	idou	**ok^{h}los**	polus,
after	these	saw	and	see	crowd.SG	much

hon	arit^{h}mēsai	auton	oudeis	edunato
which.SG	count	DEM	none	could

'After this I beheld, and, lo, a great multitude, which no man could number'
(Rv 7,9)

Das	**Volck**	**das**	im	finsternis	sass
ART.SG	people.SG	which.SG	in	darkness	sat

'The people which sat in darkness saw great light'
(Mk 2,13)

personal pronoun

kai	pas	ho	**ok^{h}los**	ērk^{h}eto	pros
and	whole.SG	ART.SG	crowd.SG	came	to

auton,	kai	edidasken	**autous**
him	and	taught	them

vnd	alles	**Volck**	kam	zu jm /	Vnd	er
and	all.SG	people.SG	came	to him	and	he

leret	**sie**
taught	them

'and all the multitude resorted unto him, and he taught them'
(Mk 2,13)

The version of the hierarchy adopted here differs from the one presented by Corbett (e.g. Corbett 2000; Corbett 2006) by distinguishing five, not four, positions, the additional position being the "copredicative" in Ancient Greek.[6] For our data this position might be of some importance since it allows us to analyze *participia coniuncta* and adjectives which are neither attributive nor predicative (e.g., a depictive like *drunk* in *He came home drunk*) as a category in their own right.[7] Within a framework of only four positions the agreement behavior of such constructions would go unnoticed. The so-called Predicate Hierarchy first established by Comrie (1975) for honorific plural pronouns will not be applied to the material because our data on predicative adjectives and nouns is not statistically significant.

The Agreement Hierarchy allows us to make predictions as to whether a certain target is likely to show non-formal agreement or not, but other factors play a role, too, as typological research has shown. Word order seems to have an important influence on agreement (Corbett 2006: 181), but its effect does not seem to have been studied systematically for collective nouns. A related problem is that of linear (or "real") distance (see Corbett 2006: 235–236), that is the number of words intervening between controller and target. Research on English has shown that increasing distance between the controller and the target favors plural over singular agreement (Levin 2001: 92–102). Thus the behavior of the collective nouns is perfectly in keeping with the general tendencies of greater liability of agreement mismatches with increasing distance.

Taking these observations as a starting point, the main aim of the present study is to investigate the role of the Agreement Hierarchy in diachronic change and the effects of word order and linear distance on non-formal agreement.[8] We want to achieve this by quantitatively analyzing text corpora spanning several centuries. As is obvious from the title of the present paper, the main objective in conducting our research was to find out if one can observe any diachronic change in the agreement patterns of collective nouns and how such change

---

6 See Haspelmath (1995: 18–20) for the syntactic status of such constructions and especially their relationship to converbal phrases. For a recent overview on secondary predication see Himmelmann and Schultze-Berndt (2005).

7 Although the agreement behaviour exhibited by the copredicate seems to be very similar to verbal agreement when it comes to number mismatches (compare Tables 3 and 6 below), one nonetheless feels inclined to keep these two positions apart, since copredicates are external to the VP. Predicate verbs and copredicates should not be lumped together under the same heading. To clarify this issue, further research on the agreement of Ancient Greek (and preferably on other languages, too) is needed. For instance, an interesting question would be whether copredicates are more liable to show gender mismatches as well.

8 Other contextual factors like verbal semantics might have an influence on agreement. However, they were not studied systematically since it is rather difficult to measure their effects in large corpora.

could be explained. But since there are no previous studies available that could provide the necessary data, this will include synchronic work as well. By choosing German and Greek, we aimed at a "small-scale typology" of collective nouns within the Indo-European family, which can serve as the starting point for further investigation on other languages. Furthermore, the two languages provide us with an important parallel text, the Holy Bible, and thus, at least to some extent, make a direct comparison possible. This allows for investigating the translation effects on agreement phenomena.

2 Corpus Study

2.1 The Greek Data

Almost all reference grammars of Ancient Greek devote several pages to agreement phenomena. Of course, the problem of "aberrant" agreement forms with collective nouns is not left unmentioned, given the relative frequency of plural agreement here.[9] But for all their worth, these works suffer from one major drawback: the presentation of the material. Examples of various types are grouped together under the same heading, and grammatical descriptions are often rather vague. At times the data found in these handbooks can even be misleading (see Section 2.1.4).

2.1.1 Controllers

The controllers investigated in our Greek corpus are *ok^hlos* 'crowd, throng', *dēmos* 'people, inhabitants of a district, the common people' and *laos* 'people', the latter included to compensate for the fact that *dēmos* is virtually absent from the New Testament, a text of high importance to the present study.[10] Included are only instances of these nouns in the nominative case, since only in such

---

9 See Kühner and Gerth (1898: 53–55), Schwyzer (1950: 603–604, 608), Humbert (1960: 81), Cooper (1998: 938–941, 1013) (for Attic Prose), Blass and Debrunner (1979: 111) (for the Koine of the New Testament). Ancient Greek does not seem to figure very prominently (if at all) in most current comparative research on agreement, despite the rich variety of its agreement system documented by these grammatical descriptions.

10 The polysemy of *dēmos* to some extent poses a problem. For the broad semantic range of this lexeme see Liddell and Scott (1940: 386–387). But since in our corpus it mostly means some sort of people, be it the inhabitants of a country or the popular assembly at Athens and not places, it can generally be classified as a collective noun.

cases can the Agreement Hierarchy be applied in its full range. This goes for the German data (see Section 2.2.1) as well.

Since we aimed at a set of controllers as homogenous as possible, other lexemes like *plēthos* 'great number, multitude' have been excluded from our systematic survey. Although *plēthos* often designates a group of people, the semantic scope of this word is much broader and includes notions such as 'magnitude, size, extent'. Furthermore, it differs from the three lexemes chosen here by not being a masculine *o*-stem but rather a neuter *s*-stem.[11] Nouns like *plēthos* will nonetheless be cited to illustrate points of general importance when there are no examples available from our triadic set.

2.1.2 The Greek corpus

In the Greek corpus, the agreement patterns of the three collective nouns *okʰlos*, *dēmos* and *laos* have been investigated in the following authors/texts (taken from the *Thesaurus Linguae Graecae*), as listed in Table 1. Note that the numbers given therein indicate the agreement relations with these nouns and do not represent the attestations of the nouns themselves.

Table 1: The Greek corpus

Text(s)	Date	Targets
Thucydides	5th century B.C.	133
Xenophon	5th/4th century B.C.	168
Orators (Isocrates, Demosthenes, Aeschines)[12]	5th/4th century B.C.	350
Aristoteles	4th century B.C.	190
Diodorus Siculus	1st century B.C.	430
Plutarch	1st century A.D.	599
Novum Testamentum	1st century A.D.	175
Ioannes Malalas	6th century A.D.	60
Total		2105

The texts have been chosen mainly for practical reasons. They show a relatively high frequency of the controllers in question. From a diachronic point of view, only such texts can be drawn on for valid data. This means that well-

---

11 It remains a subject for further research to investigate the impact of morphological features on the agreement patterns of collectives in Ancient Greek. To exclude possible interference, we decided not to work with morphologically incoherent material.

12 The orators Isocrates, Demosthenes and Aeschines are grouped together, since they do not seem to differ in their treatment of agreement (at least with respect to our three collective nouns) and apart from Demosthenes would form too small a corpus.

known texts like Homer and Hesiod have not been included. As can be seen from Table 1, there are no metrical texts in our corpus for the same simple reason that this text type lacks relevant data. In Sophocles, for instance, ok^hlos only occurs once (Tr. 424).[13] The results on the agreement of collective nouns presented in this survey can therefore only claim to hold true for Attic and Koine prose.[14] However, by limiting ourselves to these texts, we have additionally avoided a phenomenon which might otherwise have harmed the validity of our data, namely authors' selection of certain grammatical forms on metrical grounds.

2.1.3 The Agreement Hierarchy

The distribution of the mismatches among the relevant positions of the Agreement Hierarchy is as follows:

Table 2: Mismatches along the Agreement Hierarchy in Ancient Greek

	Attributive	Copredicative	Predicative	Pronouns
Thucydides	0% (0)	23% (7)	29% (16)	90% (9)
Xenophon	0% (0)	38% (6)	27% (17)	58% (7)
Orators	0% (0)	8% (3)	5% (8)	8% (1)
Aristoteles	0% (0)	–	4% (3)	–
Diodorus Siculus	0% (0)	6% (6)	10% (17)	75% (3)
Plutarch	0% (0)	11% (12)	7% (17)	33% (2)
NT	0% (0)	45% (5)	30% (21)	87% (13)
Ioannes Malalas	0% (0)	45% (5)	38% (6)	–

As Table 2 shows, the results of the quantitative analysis are more or less in keeping with the hierarchy established by Corbett (1979), although not as clear-cut as one would expect. Within the domain "attribute" there are no mismatches attested in our corpus. Generally speaking, Ancient Greek does indeed show cases of non-formal agreement with lexical hybrids within this domain, but they seem to be restricted to poetic diction, see Kühner and Gerth (1898: 53). Furthermore, these mismatches seem to be restricted to the feature gender. The

---

13 Although such data has been collected, too, it has not been included in the present analysis, for the reasons just stated.
14 Data from the dialects as attested in inscriptions could not be included either, although this would be of great importance for the bigger picture of agreement in Ancient Greek. For instance, Wackernagel (1926: 103) notes that in the Greek dialect of Crete collective nouns "gewohnheits-mässig" (habitually) trigger plural verb agreement.

majority of the examples cited is of the type [p^hile]$_{VOC.SG.M}$ [$teknon$]$_{VOC.SG.N}$ 'dear child'. In vocative expressions of this kind, we have a masculine form of an adjective together with a term that is either of neuter or feminine gender. So here we are dealing with instances in which the referent of such a term is situated on the higher end of the Animacy Hierarchy (cf. Corbett 2000: 55–56). It would therefore be highly unusual if one would come across attributive mismatches with collective nouns outside the sphere of the nominative.[15] In the following discussions we focus on the copredicative and the verb, since agreement with pronominal elements is rather poorly attested, rendering any diachronic evaluation of such data implausible.

2.1.4 The verb

It is a well-known fact that singular nouns can take plural verbal agreement in Ancient Greek when they refer to a multitude of human beings, as in the following sentence from the New Testament:

(3) *kai   pas   ho   **ok^hlos   ezētoun   haptest^hai   auton***
    and   whole.SG   ART.SG   crowd.SG   sought.PL   touch   him
    'And the whole multitude sought to touch him'
    (Lk 6,19)

An overall quantitative survey of verbal agreement in our corpus yields the results listed in Table 3:

Table 3: Verbal agreement in Ancient Greek

Text(s)	Singular	Plural	% Pl.
Thucydides	40	16	28.6%
Xenophon	47	18	26.7%
Orators	151	8	5.0%
Aristoteles	71	2	2.7%
Diodorus Siculus	156	17	9.8%
Plutarch	242	17	6.6%
Novum Testamentum	51	21	29.2%
Ioannes Malalas	13	7	35.0%
Total:	771	106	12.1%

---

15 There are only very few attestations of such collective nouns in the vocative singular. We found no occurrences with attributive adjectives.

As Table 3 shows, Greek collective nouns can trigger plural agreement in all examined texts and authors. This behavior is especially common in the earliest literary Attic prose, and again in the later texts of our sample, namely in the New Testament and in Malalas. However, one has to keep in mind that in the corpus of Xenophon the spurious *Atheniensium respublica* is included, too, and the 17 mismatches in Xenophon are found in this single text. Thus, all the mismatches of early Attic prose stem from Thucydides and the *Atheniensium respublica*. The orators Isocrates, Aeschines, and Demosthenes tend to avoid plural verbs with collective nouns. The numbers are slightly higher for Diodorus Siculus and Plutarch.

The data in Table 3 suggest a fairly high degree of plural agreement in most authors. The picture changes, however, when one takes the analysis of the relevant data one step further. In Table 4, the mismatches are differentiated in terms of the syntactic environment in which they occur. The specification [+same clause] signifies that controller and target appear in the same clause, [-same clause] that they are set apart by a clause boundary. The columns [+attraction] show how many of the mismatches of the types [+same clause] and [-same clause] could be caused by attraction due to their controllers being modified by a plural noun (for example an attribute in the genitive or a PP) respectively. All in all, one can see that mismatches of the kind *The committee have decided*, i.e., a collective noun controlling a same clause verb with a plural value without being at the same time modified by a plural noun, are not very common. Henceforth we will call this special kind of agreement "the committee type".

Table 4: Mismatches of verbal forms in Ancient Greek

Text(s)	[+same clause]	[+attraction]	[−same clause]	[+attraction]	"committee type"
Thucydides	5	5	11	3	0
Xenophon	0	0	17	1	0
Orators	0	0	8	2	0
Aristoteles	0	0	2	0	0
Diodorus Siculus	3	1	14	5	2
Plutarch	2	0	15	0	2
Novum Testamentum	8	0	13	0	8
Ioannes Malalas	0	0	7	2	0
Total	18	6	87	13	= 12

This naturally leads us to the next point. Since it is well known that "real" distance (see the introduction) is a crucial factor when it comes to plural agreement with collective nouns, the first step in accounting for the differences between the authors and the texts of the corpus would be to see whether plural agreement correlates with increasing distance between the controlling noun and the following verb. The numbers are shown in Table 5:

Table 5: Average distance: verb[16]

Text(s)	Singular	Plural
Thucydides	8.9	27.8
Xenophon	2.5	40.0
Orators	4.3	26.3
Aristoteles	3.5	13.7
Diodorus Siculus	7.6	21.5
Plutarch	3.7	18.4
Novum Testamentum	1.3	7.7
Ioannes Malalas	2.3	20.0
Average	4.3	22.0

Thucydides shows an extraordinarily high number of words between controller and the following targets. This not only has to do with the long and complex sentences we find in this author's texts, but also with the high number of cases (n = 23) in which the target does not appear in the same clause as the collective noun. Overall, such agreement configurations are not uncommon since Ancient Greek is pro-drop.[17] At the same time 28.6% of the cases in Thucydides show plural agreement, which would square well with increasing average distance. Interestingly, the data of the orators, Aristoteles, Diodorus Siculus, and Plutarch, seems to support such a hypothesis: they show a comparatively modest distance between controller and target and a low percentage of plural agreement. But the New Testament, on the other hand, has a low average distance of intervening words and the same high degree (29.2%) of mismatches. So distance in and of itself cannot account for the degree of plural agreement. One gets the impression that agreement in Ancient Greek is affected by the genre and style of the text in question.

---

16 Note, however, that these statistics are based not only on agreement relations in single clauses or sentences, but also those crossing sentence boundaries in cases of pro-drop and other constructions with non-overt subjects.

17 In using the common term pro-drop, we do not wish to imply that we are assuming any kind of null elements in our analysis. We have opted for a word class based classification of agreement relations. Within other frameworks, such phenomena would not be classified as verbal agreement but as pronominal coreference. However, it seems doubtful whether the distinction between agreement and pronominal coreference should be upheld at all; see discussion in Section 3.1 and Croft (2013).

But real distance of course has its effect on the choice of agreement forms:[18] the greater the distance, the more likely plural agreement, as is shown by the fact that the average distance for plural agreement is 22 words, while for targets with singular agreement it is only 4.3.

Another condition on agreement is word order (see Corbett 2006: 180). Here the picture is clear: The order of target – controller precludes plural agreement in our diachronic corpus of eight texts. One example in Revelation is still worth citing, even though here *ho laos* 'people' functions as vocative singular (see Blass and Debrunner 1979: 122):

(4) **Exelt^hate**,   *ho*   **laos**   *mou,*   *ex*   *autēs,*   *hina*   *mē*
     exit.PL   ART.SG   people.SG   my   from   her   that   not

     sugkoinōnēsēte   *tais*   *hamartiais*   *autēs,*   *kai*   *ek*   *tōn*   *plēgōn*
     impart.PL   art   faults   her   and   from   art   strokes

     autēs   *hina*   *mē*   *labēte*
     her   that   not   take.PL

     'Come out of her, my people, that ye be not partakers of her sins, and that ye receive not of her plagues.'
     (Rv 18,4)

It seems likely that we are again dealing with a situation in which the referent of the noun *laós* as a speech-act participant is individualized to the extent that plural agreement becomes possible. In an author not included in our main sample, Dio Chrysostom, we find another interesting example of a preposed target in the plural. Dio has a discussion with someone about Hesiod in the presence of a large company. The interlocutor asks Dio, referring to the crowd:

(5) *Kai*   *pōs*   *humas*   **anexontai**   *tosoutos*   **ok^hlos**   *peri*
     and   how   us   bear.PL   so large.SG   crowd.SG   about

     toioutōn   *dialegomenous?*
     such things   talking

     'How will so large a crowd bear with us if we discuss such matters?'
     (Dio Chrysostom Or 77/78, 2)

One gets the impression that here again the presence of the people referred to results in a high degree of individuation and thus favors mismatches.

---

18 For the importance of "real distance" for agreement see the literature cited in Section 1.

In Pseudo-Xenophon we find a committee-like agreement pattern showing verb before subject, this time with the controller *polis* (feminine singular) 'city':

(6) **t^huousin**   oun   dēmosiai   men   hē   **polis**   hiereia   polla
    sacrifice.PL   then   publicly   PTCL   ART.SG   city.SG   victims   many
    'The city now sacrifices many victims at the public expense.'
    (X.Ath. 2.9)

Such cases have often been translated along the lines of Schwyzer (1950: 608),[19] who seems to have interpreted preposed plural verbs as not being controlled by the following collective noun. He translates our example (7) from the Iliad (Iliad B 279) by *so sprachen sie, die Menge* 'thus they spoke, the multitude', thereby assuming a null element. But such an interpretation is of course an unnecessary assumption in view of the general tendency of collective nouns to trigger plural agreement. Furthermore, it would not account for mismatches with preposed copredicative targets, see Section 2.1.5 below.

But nonetheless, the fact that we have almost no real instances of preposed verbal mismatches with *ok^hlos*, *dēmos* or *laos* in our systematic analysis of these lexemes and only meager evidence from other collective nouns is significant because it makes the *locus classicus* of verbal plural agreement with collective nouns rather problematic:

(7) hōs   **p^hasan**   hē   **plēt^hus**
    thus   spoke.PL   ART.SG   multitude.SG
    'thus spoke the multitude'
    (Iliad B 279)

This example represents the exception rather than the rule because we have verb before subject, not subject before verb. It is obvious that the word order is due to the restrictions of the hexameter: *hōs hē plēt^hus p^hasan* is impossible.[20] To sum up, the evidence from our texts shows that precedence is a very powerful relative condition on agreement with strong leanings to being absolute (for these terms cf. Corbett 2006: 180), precluding verbal mismatches. Other factors, however, like metrical convenience, can override this constraint.

---

19 See Kalinka (1913: 75) for a translation of this kind, but cf. Lapini (1997: 189–190).
20 In Kühner and Gerth (1898: 53) this is the only instance of verb before subject. Cooper (1998: 1013) cites Aeschylus Ag. 188f. which is, however, choric song and therefore subject to similar metric restrictions.

2.1.5 The copredicate

Since there is no plural agreement in attributive position, the next position will be that of the copredicate,[21] comprising mainly participial constructions (*participia coniuncta*). The copredicative construction is of great interest for studies on agreement in Ancient Greek since it formally partakes of inflectional nominal agreement (gender, same morphological plural markers as nouns) while at the same time being functionally close to the predicate. It is common knowledge that, like the verb, such forms can show plural agreement as in (8):

(8)   *kai*   *eutʰus*   *pas*   *ho*   **okʰlos**   **idontes**   *auton*
     and   right   whole.SG   ART.SG   crowd.SG   seeing.PL   him
     exetʰambētʰēsan
     were amazed.PL
     'And straightway all the people, when they beheld him, were greatly amazed.'
     (Mk 9,15)

The attestations of copredicative constructions as targets in our corpus are as follows:

Table 6: Copredicative agreement in Ancient Greek

Text(s)	Singular	Plural	% Pl.
Thucydides	24	7	22.6%
Xenophon	10	6	37.5%
Orators	35	3	7.9%
Aristoteles	21	0	0.0%
Diodorus Siculus	91	6	6.2%
Plutarch	98	12	10.9%
Novum Testamentum	6	5	45.5%
Ioannes Malalas	6	5	45.5%
Total	291	44	13.1%

As Table 6 clearly shows, the actual number of attested copredicative constructions with collective nouns is not very impressive, especially for our last two texts, which we take into account only for the sake of completeness. The percentage of plural agreement is slightly at variance with the one for the verb

---

[21] For the term see the literature cited in note 6. In traditional grammars one finds designations like "semi-predicative adjectives or participles" (Cooper 1998: 939).

and the picture is not coherent. Compare, for example, Plutarch and Diodorus: The ratio of verb : copredicate is 6.6% : 10.9% for the former and 9.8% : 6.2% for the latter. The orators are a bit more licentious with the copredicate than with the verb, but this might be the result of chance.

The distance of controller and following copredicate is more or less the same as that of controller and following verb:

Table 7: Average distance: copredicate

Text(s)	Singular	Plural
Thucydides	6.1	25.3
Xenophon	3.7	20.7
Orators	5.2	22.3
Aristoteles	2.5	N.A.
Diodorus Siculus	5.9	30.2
Plutarch	5.7	23.2
Novum Testamentum	0.6	8.3
Ioannes Malalas	0.8	16
Average	3.8	20.9

Since it could be shown that word order acts as a very strong condition on verbal agreement, one expects the same for copredicative constructions. And indeed we found only one example of a plural target preceding its controller in our whole corpus.

(9) *tas de allas oute mikras oute peri mikrōn genomenas*
ART PCTL other neither small nor about trifles being

antʰupeikontes allēlois, pʰobōi men hoi dunatoi tōn pollōn,
yielding RECP fear PTCL ART.PL noble.PL ART many

aidoumenoi *de tēn boulēn ho* **dēmos,** *epauon.*
respecting.PL PTCL ART senate ART.SG people.SG end.PL
'the other (seditions), which were neither trivial nor broke out for trivial matters, they ended by mutually yielding to each other, the nobles from fear of the multitude, and the commons out of respect for the senate.' (Plut.TG 20,1)

Here one is inclined to think that the plural of the participle *aidoumenoi* – if not a scribal mistake – was chosen due to the juxtaposition of the plural *hoi dunatoi* 'the nobles' and the singular *ho dēmos* to stress the plurality of the latter. The participle, followed by *de*, however, has to occupy the clause initial position to contrast with *pʰobōi men*. But it is important to note that this is the only instance of a plural target preceding its controller out of 340 copredicative agreement relations. Therefore one can safely conclude that word order is again a crucial factor for plural agreement.

2.2 The German data

For this study we have only examined High German texts, leaving Low German aside.[22]

2.2.1 Controllers

We investigated several lexemes within the semantic field 'people': For Old High German, we looked at *folc, liût, thíot* 'people', *cunni* 'family' and *menigi* 'crowd', for Middle High German *liut, volc* 'people', *gesinde* 'servants', *her* 'army, crowd', *menige* 'crowd' and *schar* 'flock, troop', and for Early New High German and New High German only *Volk* 'people' and *Menge* 'crowd'. This choice was necessary for two reasons: First and foremost, not all lexemes have been used continuously from the oldest sources to the present day (cf. Herold 1941; Ehrismann 1970). *folc* is relatively rare in Old High German, *liût* being preferred, especially by Otfrid and Notker.[23] Other collective nouns, such as *thiot* and *gesinde* have either completely died out or they have at least been marginalized. The second reason for considering more than one collective noun was that we wanted to investigate whether some controllers trigger more plural agreement than others: Levin (2001, 2006) has shown this for English collective nouns, although the range of meanings there is considerably larger than in our study. Our collective nouns, on the other hand, solely refer to human beings, mostly in large groups. That may also be the reason we did not find any noteworthy differences between the number of mismatches and a particular controller. Thus, for reasons of space, we will treat all collective nouns as one.

---

22 Firstly, Low German is not an integral part of our agreement project. Secondly, the Low German corpus is problematic: For Old Saxon, only two longer texts exist (cf. Behaghel 1897 on agreement in Old Saxon) and there is a big gap in written transmission between Old Saxon and Middle Low German. Modern Low German texts, on the other hand, are sparse because of the decreasing use of the language since the decline of the Hanseatic League.

23 Interestingly, *liut* in its singular form died out during the Middle High German period, leaving only the plurale tantum *liute* (NHG *Leute*).

2.2.2 The corpus

Our German corpus consists of 12 texts or text collections (cf. Table 8). All texts were available electronically, but only the texts from the *Bonner Frühneuhoch-deutschkorpus* were also annotated. In all other cases, we found the relevant agreement controllers and targets by using regular expressions.

Table 8: The German corpus

Text(s)	Date	Targets
Tatian	first half 9th century	140
Otfrid's Evangelienbuch	863–871	208
Notker (all texts)	before 1022	128
Kaiserchronik	first half 12th cenutry / end-12th century	179
Parzival	beg-13th century / mid-13th century	224
Prosalancelot I–IV	13th/15th century	213
Bonner Frühneuhochdeutschkorpus	1350–1700	239
Luther Bible: Old Testament (Genesis / Exodus) / New Testament (the four Gospels)	1545	443
Abraham a Sancta Clara (all works)	1686	181
Goethe (all prose texts)	1772–1828	444
Karl May (all texts)	1892/1913	206
IDS: Mannheimer Korpora 1+2	1949–1974	417
Total		3022

We needed to use texts that were long enough to allow us to cover all of the positions of the Agreement Hierarchy. Whereas attributive articles occur very frequently, relative pronouns are much rarer. According to a quantitative survey on German conducted by us, the former targets occur by an average of 72 times per 1.000 words in German, the latter occur only 11 times per 1.000 words. Longer texts were also needed in order to capture the variation between plural and singular agreement and to isolate the factors which favor each agreement type.[24]

The three selected Old High German texts/authors represent the classic, larger texts of their period. Tatian and Notker are translations of biblical and philosophical works written in Latin, only Otfrid is an independent German

---

24 The only exception here is the *Bonner Frühneuhochdeutschkorpus* which consists of smaller text portions of up to 30 so-called normalized pages, due to computational limits in its day (cf. Wegera 2000: 1310). It was included because of the diversity of text genres and regions represented in the corpus, including prose texts such as chronicles that have otherwise not been digitalized.

text, albeit a metrical one. As it is, all longer texts in Old High German are either translations or metrically bound texts (cf. Fleischer 2006: 30). The rare independent texts in prose (for example the *Pariser Gespräche*) are too short for a study of agreement. In the case of Middle High German, two of the selected works represent the classical poetry of the High Middle Ages. They are problematic not only because of their form but also because of their history: The original manuscripts no longer exist, we only have later copies. But frankly, this is typical for Middle High German texts in general (cf. Wegera 2000: 1310) and the selected texts have the advantage that they are relatively long. We are aware that current research on Middle High German syntax has dispensed with classical medieval poetry and now deals only with prose texts (cf. Wegera 2000; Prell 2001: 5–6) that were neglected by scholars of German for decades. Unfortunately, these texts have yet to be made available electronically.[25]

Although we have based our work on digitalized, normalized editions, interesting agreement forms showing plural agreement were later compared with the manuscript(s). From Wapnewski (1972: 155; cited in Fleischer 2012: 180) we know that normalization may also effect agreement: in Old and Middle High German, we find certain, rather spectacular examples of plural agreement within the nominal phrase together with the lexical hybrid *wîp* 'woman' (morphologically a neuter). In one *Minnesang* of the famous Wolfram von Eschenbach, for example, *offenú suezú* (feminine) in the NP *ein offenú suezú wirtes wîp* 'a lawful sweet wife' has been corrected to *offen süeze* (neuter), seemingly because the editors looked upon them as mere agreement errors. On the other hand, normalization has the positive effect that it constrains graphematic variation and hence searching for particular forms in a non-annotated normalized text is still quite comfortable.

The number of occurrences of specific controllers in different texts turned out to be a problem. The use of 'people' of course depends on the subject and genre of a text: especially in biblical texts, they are highly frequent, whereas they are hardly used at all in more abstract, philosophical works. Thus, in order to get a significant number of targets, we had to take more texts of certain authors into consideration. That especially applies to Notker, for whom we found relatively few relevant collective nouns, despite searching through all of his works. Only in one text, Martin Luther's Bible translation, did we have to restrict the survey to specific parts, in this case the first two Books of Moses and the four Gospels.

---

25 The *Korpus zur Mittelhochdeutschen Grammatik*, located at the University of Bochum, has not yet been made available for public use.

2.2.3 The Agreement Hierarchy

We now turn to our findings and begin by looking at how the mismatches are distributed across the different positions of the Agreement Hierarchy, as illustrated in Table 9.

Table 9: Mismatches along the Agreement Hierarchy in German

Text(s)	Attributive	Predicative	Pronouns
Tatian	0% (0)	23% (10)	61% (17)
Otfrid	0% (0)	7% (5)	81% (46)
Notker	0% (0)	0% (0)	54% (25)
Kaiserchronik	0% (0)	0% (0)	90% (43)
Parzival	0% (0)	3% (2)	74% (29)
Prosalancelot I–IV	0% (0)	12% (10)	59% (20)
Bonner Corpus	0% (0)	5% (3)	65% (35)
Luther	0% (0)	8% (11)	78% (93)
Abraham a Sancta Clara	0% (0)	0% (0)	72% (18)
Goethe	0% (0)	4% (5)	15% (12)
Karl May	0% (0)	0% (0)	21% (8)
IDS	0% (0)	0% (0)	7% (4)

Table 9 shows that our mismatches confirm to the Agreement Hierarchy. The numbers for pronominal mismatches[26] are generally high, but at no stage of German do we find plural agreement in attributive relations such as determiners or adjectives. This fits in well with the findings in Fleischer (2012: 177–181) where only highly marginal cases of semantic agreement are attested in the attributive position together with *Weib* 'woman'. The predicate also mostly shows singular agreement: in seven texts, however, we find a small number of verbal targets showing plural agreement, where the highest numbers can be found in translations of biblical texts, in Luther's Bible, and in the Old High German Tatian, a translation text that closely follows the Latin original. Only in pronoun agreement are mismatches common throughout German language history, although singular agreement slowly seems to be prevailing here as well. It is interesting to note that New High German is highly different from Early New High German in that we almost never find verbal plural agreement and that plural agreement in personal and relative pronouns has been reduced to a minimum. In the following, we shall concentrate on verbal and pronominal agreement forms, since the attributive ones do not show any variation between singular and plural agreement and thus no diachronic development.

---

26 "Pronouns" in Table 9 refers to all anaphorically used pronominal targets found. In Section 2.2.5, we shall consider only the personal pronoun because the numbers for the other pronouns are too low.

2.2.4 The verb

Table 10 shows how the agreement forms of the collective nouns distribute in our corpus:

Table 10: Mismatches of verbal forms

Text(s)	Singular	Plural	% Pl.
Tatian	34	10	22.7%
Otfrid	65	5	7.1%
Notker	29	0	0.0%
Kaiserchronik	49	0	0.0%
Parzival	67	2	2.9%
Prosalancelot I–IV	74	10	11.9%
Bonner Corpus	57	3	5.0%
Luther	132	11	7.7%
Abraham a Sancta Clara	42	0	0.0%
Goethe	135	5	3.6%
Karl May	58	0	0.0%
IDS	110	0	0.0%
Total	852	46	5.1%

Mismatches of verbal forms can thus be found at all stages of German, with peaks at the very beginning of the Old High German period and in Early New High German, but at the same time they are relatively rare compared to the singular forms, especially in New High German.[27] We shall start by looking at an example of a typical verbal mismatch in New High German:

(10) *wenn   die   große   **Menge   geputzter   Bauersleute**,*
    When   ART.SG   large.SG   crowd.SG   dressed-up.PL   peasants.PL

    oft   noch   mit   Gebetbuch   und   Rosenkranz,   aus
    often   still   with   prayer-book   and   rosary,   out (of)

    *der   Kirche   kommend,   die   Schanze   **füllten**,*
    ART   church   coming.SG/PL   ART   entrenchment   filled.PL

    *sich   **umsahen,   schwatzten**   und   **schäkerten***
    REFL   looked.PL   chatted.PL   and   joked.PL
    'when the large crowd of dressed-up peasants coming out of the church, often with prayer book and rosary still in hand, filled up the entrenchment, looked around, chatted, and joked'
    (Goethe, Belagerung von Mainz, 10, 378)

---

27 Compare this to earlier observations in the literature that the verb often appears in the plural even within the same sentence (cf. Behaghel 1928: 7–8 and Dal 1966: 157). Paul (1920: 189), on the other hand, is more careful.

In New High German, as illustrated by (10), verbal mismatches are only licensed when the controller is followed by a plural modifier, most typically a genitive plural or a PP with an NP in plural (cf. Duden Grammatik 2009: 1014 and Grimm 1898: 194). Syntactic distance may equally favor plural agreement, as seen in the example above (there is a participial clause between controller and target). In these cases, attraction (cf. Acuña-Fariña 2012) can be made responsible for the choice of the agreement form. Mismatches of the "committee type", on the other hand, where controller and target appear in the same clause, are not tolerated in New High German, as Findreng (1976: 258–260) and the present study show.

We want to make the claim that verbal mismatches triggered by collective nouns without any attributive modifiers or appositions actually at no point have been grammatical in High German. Instead, we interpret the rare cases in which they actually occur as a result of either loan or rhyme syntax (cf. Section 3.2). Table 11 shows this: "Committee type" agreement forms, occurring in the same clause as the unmodified controller, are highly marginal in German. In Old High German, we find no single instance of this; verbal mismatches occur only in sentences in which the subject for various reasons has been omitted (see also Grimm 1898: 223–224), and in Middle and Early New High German there are only a few, problematic examples of mismatches in the same clause as an overt subject, to which we will soon return.

Table 11: Mismatches of verbal forms: differentiated

Text(s)	[+same clause]	[+attraction]	[−same clause]	[+attraction]	"committee type"
Tatian	0	0	10	1	0
Otfrid	0	0	5	1	0
Notker	0	0	0	0	0
Kaiserchronik	0	0	0	0	0
Parzival	2	0	0	0	2
Prosalancelot I-IV	2	0	8	0	2
Bonner Corpus	1	0	2	0	1
Luther	0	0	11	0	0
Abraham a Sancta Clara	0	0	0	0	0
Goethe	1	1	4	4	0
Karl May	0	0	0	0	0
IDS	0	0	0	0	0
Total	6	1	40	6	5

Old High German seems to be a good test field for grammaticality judgments on the agreement of collective nouns. The Old High German text with the most verbal agreement mismatches in our corpus is Tatian (Cod. Sangallensis 56), a Gospel harmony translated from Latin into German at the beginning of the 9th century. Its language follows the original in nearly every respect, the translation method most resembles that of interlinear glossing (cf. Lippert 1974). In recent times, however, Dittmer and Dittmer (1998) have shown that Tatian is perhaps one of the most valuable Old High German texts for syntactic investigation (cf. Fleischer et al. 2008). Although on the whole the translation is very faithful to the original,[28] it does deviate from it in certain cases. These deviations can often be interpreted as exponents of genuine German syntax as the Latin structure was deemed too ungrammatical to be translated directly. The value of this text is demonstrated by the following examples:

(11) *Et* **erat** **plebs** *expectans* *Zachariam,*
and be.SG people.SG awaiting.SG Zacharias

et **mirabantur** *quod* *tardaret* *ipse* *in* *templo.*
and wondered.PL that hinder he in temple

Inti **uuas** *thaz* **folc** *beitonti* *Zachariam,*
and was.SG ART.SG people.SG awaiting.SG/PL Zacharias

inti **vvuntorotun** *thaz* *her* *lazzeta* *in* *templo.*
and wondered.PL that he tarried in temple
'And the people waited for Zacharias, and marvelled that he tarried so long in the temple.'
(Tatian 2, 10; Lk 1,21)

In (11), we find two agreement forms in the singular in the first main clause (the German *beitonti* 'awaiting' is actually not marked for number, but the Latin participle clearly is singular) and one agreement form in the plural in the coordinated clause. The interesting thing here is that the mismatch occurs in a sentence with subject ellipsis. In fact, all 11 verbal mismatches in the German Tatian appear in a (coordinated) clause with a non-overt subject, be it as a result of coordinative ellipsis or pro-drop. We never find them in the same clause as the controller itself, and all mismatches are accounted for by a parallel in the Latin original. We do, however, find structures which are deviant with respect to the Latin model in which the Old High German text uses singular although the original uses the plural, as in (12):

---

28 For example, Tatian is the only text in which we find mismatches in copredicative participles similar to the Greek ones. All mismatches follow the Latin original.

(12)   *Et*   *omnis*   **populus**   *libenter*   **audiebant**   *eum*
      and   all.SG   people.SG   gladly   heard.PL   him

      Al   *thaz*   **folc**   *lustlicho*   **hórta**   *inan*
      all   ART.SG   people.SG   gladly   heard.SG   him
      'And the common people heard him gladly'
      (Tatian 141, 5; Mk 12,37)

This example is particularly interesting because a verbal mismatch in the same sentence as the full subject NP is scarcely attested in the history of German. This deviant structure shows that this may in fact not be a coincidence: We interpret it as sign of this type of mismatch being ungrammatical in German even at the time of the Tatian translation. The lacking mismatch is all the more striking because the Gothic Bible actually allows a similar mismatch where the reconstructed Greek text shows singular (cf. Mk 3,32),[29] supporting the thesis that mismatches of the "committee type" were grammatical in Proto-Germanic. The Old High German example, on the other hand, poses a serious threat to the old theory that the development of rigid syntactic agreement in German is mostly due to Latin influence (cf. Behaghel 1928: 2; Dal 1966: 157). Another explanation could be that the translator wanted to "correct" the Latin. Agreement forms of the "committee type" are seldom in Classical Latin, but are frequently found in Old and Late Latin, cf. Kühner and Stegmann 1912: 22–23).

In Otfrid's *Evangelienbuch*, an example of Old High German biblical poetry, we find the same correlation between mismatches and non-overt subject as in Tatian, but at the same time we find a notable decrease in occurrences of plural agreement; only five out of 65 verbal forms (7%) are mismatches. This may be due to the fact that Otfrid's *Evangelienbuch* is a unique original German text and that cases of non-overt subject realization, especially pro-drop, are rarer: while in Tatian the subject pronouns are dropped in 40% of the verbs, Otfrid does so in only 11% according to Eggenberger (1961: 84–85 and 34–35).[30] Importantly, Otfrid's use of pro-drop can often be accounted for by the demands of the meter, as in (13):

---

29 Behaghel (1928: 8) lists three further Gothic examples of a verb in plural in the same clause as a full subject NP: Mt 8,32; Jn 12,18 and Lk 6,19, all of which deviate from the Greek text.
30 Lack of pro-drop may be the reason why Notker does not show any verbal mismatches at all.

(13)   *Ther*   **liut**   *thia sprácha*   *al*   **firdrúag**   *unz*   *sin*
      ART.SG people.SG the   language   all   accepted.SG   before   his

      wórt   *tho*   *thés giwuag*;   *tho*   **íltun**   *sar*   *bi nótin,*
      word   then   this   mentioned;   then   hurried.PL   quickly   in   passion

      thaz sie   *nan*   *stéinotin.*
      that they   him   stoned

      'The people accepted what was said, before he mentioned this,
      they hurried quickly in passion, so that they could stone him.'
      (Otfrid III, 22, 33)

A subject pronoun would introduce a new unstressed syllable and thus break the metric structure of the long verse. We also see that pro-drop does not appear in the subordinated clause (this is an interesting asymmetry in Old High German syntax, cf. Axel and Weiß 2011: 22), but that the plural form, once introduced, is used further on.

In Middle and Early New High German, the same pattern of the first verb in singular, the second in plural can be found, but in our material only in translations such as the *Prosalancelot* or Luther's Bible.[31] In Middle High German, however, we find four examples of a verbal mismatch in the same clause as the controller (the "committee type"), which, as we have seen, was not possible in Old High German:

(14)   *Hin*   *von*   *den*   *zinnen*   **vielen**
      down   from   ART   merlons   hurried.PL

      und   **gâhten**   *zuo*   *den*   *kielen*
      and   rushed.PL   to   ART   ships

      daz   *hungerc*   **her**   *durch*   *den*   *stoup*
      ART.SG   hungry.SG   crowd.SG   through   ART   dust

      'the hungry crowd rushed down from the merlons through the dust to
      the ships'
      (Parzival 5947–5949; 200, 17–19)

In (14), an example often cited in the older literature (cf. Grimm 1898: 224; Behaghel 1928: 8; Dal 1966: 157), we mainly hold the verse form responsible for the mismatch, as one of the plural forms is standing in rhyme position (*vielen*

---

31 This genre effect is at least partly confirmed by Reiten (1964: 22–23) who finds this agreement pattern in the religious texts of Berthold von Regensburg, as well as in an independent German text, namely *Heinrich von Kempten* by Konrad von Würzburg.

'rushed'– *kielen* 'ships'). A semantic motivation for the plural could be that *her* in this case does not mean 'army' in terms of a military unit, but rather a crowd of individuals and that the action thus requires a distributive reading (cf. Gärtner 1970: 35). It is important, however, to note that a mismatch of this type does not occur anywhere else in our *Parzival* material, and that similar examples in other texts are rare and often problematic (cf. Reiten 1964: 17–25 and Gärtner 1970: 31–41).[32] Interestingly, a similar context can be found in (15), although a cataphoric personal pronoun is realized next to the agreement target, so that this is better seen as an instance of pronominal agreement:

(15) *dô* **fuoren** *si* *ûf* *des* *küneges* *sal,*
    then went.PL they to ART king's hall

    daz *inre* **her** *von* *der* *stat*
    ART.SG inner.SG army.SG of ART city
    'then they went to the king's hall, the defenders of the city'
    (Parzival 11732–11733; 393, 14)

It is possible that a subject pronoun is intended in (14) as well, but that it cannot be realized phonologically for poetic reasons. The word order in both examples is highly unusual: in German, and even more so in Greek, mismatches generally occur after and not before its controller (in 95% of all our German mismatches, the controller precedes the target). Whereas metrics seems to be the factor conditioning the mismatch in (14), this certainly cannot be valid for the prose example in (16):

(16) *Sie* *begunde* *fragen* *warumb* *das* **volck** *so* *sere*
    she began ask why ART.SG people.SG so much

    zu *dem* *thurn* **wurffen** *und* **schúßsen**
    to det tower threw.PL and shot.PL
    'She began to ask why the people were throwing and shooting at the tower'
    (Prosalancelot I, 242, 27)

Here, semantics may be the real motivation for the mismatch: It is clear from the context that 'people' here requires a distributive reading. It is possible, however, that the mismatch is caused by loan syntax, as the *Prosalancelot* was

---

32 Reiten (1964: 25) finds seven examples of plural verbs versus 40 in the singular (=15% plural agreement), mostly in religious texts. Gärtner (1970: 41) finds 14 verbal mismatches in Wolfram von Eschenbach versus 170 singular (=7,6% plural agreement). However, cases where attraction can be held responsible for the mismatch are included in these numbers.

translated from Old French into German (cf. Hennings 2001). It is worth noting that the pattern first verb in singular, second in plural, which seems to be tied to translations, occurs in the *Prosalancelot* as well.

In Early New High German, we find several examples of verbal mismatches, but none of the true "committee type".[33] The closest would be (17) and (18):

(17) *vnnd   alles   **Volck**   das   an   dem   Vfer   vnder   den*
     and   all.SG   people.SG   that.SG   on   ART   bank   under   ART

     *Bǎumen   stundt/   **blieben**   stehen*
     trees   stood.PL   were.PL   stand
     'and all the people that stood on the bank under the trees stood still'
     (Bonner Frühneuhochdeutschkorpus, 245 (1599))

(18) *das   ain   **volck**   Coseri   genant/   von   den*
     that   ART.SG   people.SG   Coseri.PL   called.SG/PL   from   ART

     *Reissen   Tribut   genumen   **haben***
     journeys   tribute   taken   have.PL
     'that a people called Coseri have taken tribute from the journeys'
     (Bonner Frühneuhochdeutschkorpus, 115 (1557))

In both examples, however, we are dealing with constructional mismatches. In (17), the plural verb is in the same clause as the NP controller, but there is a relative clause between them. In (18), a participial clause and attraction (*Coseri* is most probably plural here) can be made responsible for the choice of the agreement form. The other verbal mismatches from the Early New High German period are ones of the pattern "singular + plural", which is especially frequent in Luther's Bible. In total, we find (nearly) no evidence for this construction in genuine German texts. Of the two occurrences of this construction in the *Bonner Frühneuhochdeutschkorpus*, one is in a translated chronicle text written by the Spaniard Augustinus Cassiodorus Reinius. In Section 3.2 we shall argue that this is most likely a case of loan syntax, that, at as far as biblical texts are concerned, can be traced back to the Hebrew Bible.

---

33 We are aware of very few exceptions to this outside our corpus (cf. Ebert et al. 1993: 442), of which at least one is problematic: *Vnd das gantze Jsrael steinigeten jn* 'And all Israel stoned him with stones' (Luther 1545; Jos 7,25). Interestingly, the plural is used together with 'Israel' in the Hebrew Bible and the Septuagint as well, but not in the Vulgate (cf. Section 3.2 for further discussion of such examples).

2.2.5 Pronominal agreement

We consider here only the personal pronoun, since the numbers for the other pronouns are too low to say anything about their agreement patterns. Treating all pronouns alike would be problematic, especially considering the fact that relative pronouns, due to their nature as noun modifiers on the one hand and referring pronouns on the other, behave differently than other pronouns (cf. Corbett's Agreement Hierarchy and Fleischer 2012: 181–184). Data on the personal pronoun can be found in Table 12:

Table 12: Mismatches in personal pronouns[34]

Text(s)	Singular	Plural	% Pl.
Tatian	4	14	77.8%
Otfrid	3	34	91.9%
Notker	6	13	68.4%
Kaiserchronik	0	37	100.0%
Parzival	2	15	88.2%
Prosalancelot I–IV	8	17	68.0%
Bonner Corpus	4	23	85.2%
Luther	8	81	91.0%
Abraham a Sancta Clara	4	12	75.0%
Goethe	31	9	22.5%
Karl May	14	8	36.4%
IDS	14	4	22.2%
Total	98	267	73.2%

The personal pronouns show a much clearer diachronic development than do the verbs. Semantic agreement in personal pronouns seems to have been grammatical at all stages of German and even the rule up until Early New High German.[35] In accordance with Levin (2006: 337) for English and the Agreement Hierarchy, pronouns show more plural agreement than do verbs with singular collectives; however, the numbers are lower because verb agreement is generally more frequent than pronominal agreement (cf. 147 verbal targets per 1.000 words versus 70 personal pronoun targets in our quantitative survey).

In the few (partly) deviant structures in Tatian, where the scribe needed to use a subject pronoun (namely in the subordinate clauses), we always find a

---

34 We chose to exclude the ambiguous forms that occur with the lexeme *Menge* 'crowd', where a target like *sie* or *die* 'they' could be both plural and singular when surfacing as a direct object.
35 Reiten (1964: 25) finds that 35 out of 46 pronouns (76%) with a collective noun as controller show plural agreement.

plural pronoun where the Latin text has a plural verb and the same goes for the singular. Compare this to the verbal forms, where we find true deviant structures (plural verb in Latin, singular in Old High German). Otfrid confirms this tendency with an even higher number of plural pronouns. His numbers are only surpassed by the Middle High German *Kaiserchronik*, another text of true German origin, in which there is in fact no single instance of singular agreement. Thus, plural agreement in pronouns seems to be typical for genuinely German texts, while for verbs it is not.

Then, within the century that lies between the writings of Abraham a Sancta Clara and Goethe, the number of mismatches decreases from three quarters to below a quarter of all forms. We think we are dealing with a massive standardization effect here: this is the period during which a homogeneous standard language in the German-speaking area emerged, which brought about the stigmatization of certain constructions (cf. Davies and Langer 2006: 73). Thus, in the spoken varieties of German, we expect the numbers for plural agreement to be higher than in the written language.[36]

Syntactic distance plays an important role in determining agreement. Pronouns generally show more of a tendency for semantic agreement than do verbs due to their more loose connection to their antecedents. Whereas there are generally more than 10 words between a controller and a personal pronoun, there are usually about two words between a controller and its verbal target, according to our quantitative data on German. In our study on collective nouns, the distance between controller and target averages 11.3 (N = 100) words in syntactic agreement and 23.8 (N = 267) words in semantic agreement.[37] Semantic factors play a role as well, although we did not study this systematically. From studies on other languages we know that the plural is more frequent when the referents are thought of as persons acting individually, the singular when an aggregate reading should be evoked (cf. Levin 2006: 321–322).

3 Comparison

In this section, we compare the Greek and German data introduced above. We will focus on the predicate, since this is the only position where our data are

---

36 Corbett (2006: 213) points at a similar difference between written spoken varieties of British and American English.

37 We only provide the general numbers here, because the per-text numbers are generally too low.

comparable. The attributive position is not relevant for the present study due to the lack of mismatches. The copredicative and pronominal positions differ: Greek on the one hand makes extensive use of copredicative participles, whereas German has various subordinate clauses or coordinated main clauses. On the other hand, pronouns are much more frequent in German due to the "pro-drop parameter" in Greek. As far as the predicate is concerned, we want to discuss a special phenomenon shared by both Ancient Greek and German, which has not received much attention in the literature: verbal mismatches in sentences that lack an overt subject, be it in the form of pro-drop and topic-drop or ellipsis. We want to approach this phenomenon both theoretically and philologically.

3.1 Verbal mismatches and affixal status

To recapitulate, our general finding in the previous part was that verbal mismatches with an unmodified adjacent same-clause NP controller (like in the textbook example *The committee have decided*) are extremely rare in both Greek and German: they only account for 12 out of 876 verbal targets in Greek (cf. Table 4), of which as many as seven are attested in the New Testament. In German, they represent five out of 898 targets (cf. Table 11), and there are as we have seen, good reasons for questioning their grammaticality. Mismatches in sentences lacking an overt controller, on the other hand, where the subject pronoun (for various reasons) has been left out, occur quite often in both corpora. Thus, an interesting pattern emerges: verbal targets in clauses lacking an overt controller behave differently in terms of agreement than do verbs surfacing with full NPs as their subject arguments, cf. Table 13 for Ancient Greek and Table 14 for German:

Table 13: Mismatches vs. controller in Ancient Greek

Ancient Greek	Full NP controller	No overt controller	Total
matches	641 (83%)	129 (17%)	770
mismatches	18 (17%)	88 (83%)	106
total	659	217	876

Table 14: Mismatches vs. controller in German

German	Full NP controller	No overt controller	Total
matches	754 (88%)	98 (12%)	852
mismatches	6 (13%)	40 (87%)	46
total	760	138	898

The differences in agreement behavior of targets surfacing with and without a full NP controller are striking. Thus in both languages, there seems to be a clear correlation between mismatches and non-overt subject arguments.

Here, however, we face a general problem that has received quite a lot of attention in recent literature (Siewierska 2004; Siewierska and Bakker 2005; Corbett 2006; Hengeveld 2012; Croft 2013; Haspelmath 2013): Do the affixes of verbs in clauses lacking a noun phrase controller represent pure agreement markers, agreeing with a full NP controller in another clause, or are these affixes referential, behaving more like free pronouns? Hengeveld (2012: 472) recounts three different approaches to this problem that have been defended within various frameworks: First, one could consider the affixes to be agreement markers regardless of the presence of a corresponding noun phrase. In cases where no NP is present, one would suppose that the affix agrees with a pronominal argument that has been left out for reasons of redundancy (cf. the pro-drop parameter in generative linguistics). Second, one could take the affixes to be referential in either case: When a NP is present, an appositional relation between the affix and the noun phrase is postulated (as assumed in Functional Grammar). A third, hybrid approach would be to consider the affixes as agreement markers when a corresponding noun phrase is present and referential in all other cases, as argued for by Siewierska (2004) among others, referring to these as "ambiguous agreement markers".

Hengeveld (2012: 472–473) combines the first and second approach claiming that reference and agreement cannot be present in parallel as postulated by Siewierska (2004). In accordance with Functional Discourse Grammar, he argues "that grammatical phenomena should be considered on a language-specific basis" (Hengeveld 2012: 472). Siewierska's ambiguous agreement markers should in his opinion be differentiated into either appositional referential markers or contextual agreement markers depending on the language, see Table 15. Common within the Indo-European family is the latter type: here these markers generally occur with pivotal arguments, in this case with the subject. If these markers were to be analyzed as appositional referential markers one would expect them to occur not only with contextually given and activated arguments,[38] but with a wide range of verbal arguments.

---

[38] This ties in well with the general tendency of agreement to correlate with topicality (cf. Givón 1976).

Table 15: Referential markers and agreement markers[39]

	Never with NP	Optionally with NP	Always with NP
Reference	Unique referential marker	Appositional Referential Markers	–
Agreement	–	Contextual Agreement Markers	Syntactic Agreement Markers

In a pro-drop language like Ancient Greek, then, contextual agreement markers are a fairly common phenomenon. On the other hand, one could argue that German agreement markers are purely syntactic. Hengeveld (2012: 475) does this for Dutch, a structurally similar language, but such an analysis would miss the well-known cases of topic-drop in (Modern) German and the more controversial cases of pro-drop in Old High German (cf. Huang 1984; Axel 2007). The morphology of Greek and German verbs lends some support to the existence of contextual agreement markers in these languages as well. As Hengeveld (2012: 474) and earlier studies (cf. Givón 1976; Bybee 1985; Siewierska 2004) demonstrate, agreement markers tend to occupy a position that is external to that of other verbal elements (like tense-aspect-mood or TAM markers). Since Greek and German roughly show the morphological pattern verbal stem + tense/aspect/ modality + person/number (cf. Duhoux 2000: 34 and Dammel and Nübling 2004), one can reasonably analyze the morpheme encoding person/number as an agreement marker. The typology of Hengeveld (2012) precludes the structure *V-TAM-REF (where REF refers to person/number agreement). Thus, there is some evidence that pro-drop and topic-drop phenomena could be analyzed as instances of (contextual) agreement.

Now the question arises why verbs lacking an overt subject are more likely to take plural agreement than those not separated from their controller by a clause boundary. Here, the factor linear distance comes into play:

Table 16: Mismatches and linear distance

	Average linear distance: matches	Average linear distance: mismatches
Ancient Greek	4.3 words	22 words
German	2.2 words	7.6 words

---

39 Table adapted from Hengeveld (2012: 474).

As Table 16 shows, there is a clear correlation between linear distance and the mismatches: In Ancient Greek, the pro-drop parameter allows for greater distance between controller and verbal target, whereas German uses pronouns in similar cases which serve as controllers for the verbs in their respective sentences (cf. Corbett 2006: 235–236; Croft 2013: 112–13; as already pointed out by Behaghel 1928: 2–3 and others).[40]

3.2 Perspectives on Bible syntax

In the previous section, we looked at mismatches from a theoretical perspective and the question why verbs lacking an overt controller are more susceptible to mismatches than those co-occurring with a full NP. There, we took this to be something close to a typological universal that first and foremost results from syntactic distance. In this section, we want to investigate the same phenomenon from a more philological point of view: We noticed that this pattern is most frequent in biblical texts in both languages (the Old Testament). For that reason, we looked at parallel structures in the Latin Vulgate and the Hebrew Bible.[41] We were astounded to see that many of the alternations used by Luther in 1545, could actually be traced all the way back to the Hebrew Bible, as (19) reveals.

(19)　Hebrew Bible:　**wa-y-yēšɛḇ　hā̊-ʿā̊m**　　lɛ-ʾɛ̄ḵōl　wə-šā̊ṯōʷ
　　　　　　　　　　　　and=sat.SG　the=people.SG　to=eat　and=drink

　　　　　　　　　　　wa-y-yā̊qumūʷ　lə-ṣaḥēq
　　　　　　　　　　　and=rose.PL　　to=play

　　　Septuagint:　　*kai*　**ekatʰisen**　　*ho*　　**laos**　　*pʰagein*　*kai*
　　　　　　　　　　　and　sat down.SG　ART.SG　people.SG　eat　　and

　　　　　　　　　　　piein　*kai*　**anestēsan**　*paizein*
　　　　　　　　　　　drink　and　stood up.PL　play

---

40 Other theoretical analyses of the agreement behavior of collective nouns are sparse. Baker (2008) does not consider mismatches at all in his work on agreement and den Dikken (2001) only deals with plural agreement with controllers of the "committee type", which, as we have seen, is marginal in Ancient Greek and German and therefore of less relevance for this paper. For an analysis of collective nouns in Serbo-Croat within the framework of Head-driven Phrase Structure Grammar, see Wechsler and Zlatić (2000).
41 We thank Jürg Fleischer and Lea Schäfer for helping us with the Hebrew.

Vulgate:	*et*	***sedit***	***populus***	*comedere*	*ac*	*bibere*	*et*
	and	sat.SG	people.SG	eat	and	drink	and

	surrexerunt	*ludere*
	rose.PL	play

Luther 1545:	*Darnach*	***satzt***	*sich*	*das*	***Volck***	*zu*	*essen*
	Thereafter	sat.SG	REFL	ART.SG	people.SG	to	eat

	vnd	*zu*	*trincken /*	*vnd*	***stunden***	*auff*	*spielen*
	and	to	drink	and	stood.PL	up	play

'and the people sat down to eat and to drink, and rose up to play'
(Ex 32,6)

In this case, all listed biblical translations reflect the Hebrew construction with the first verb in the singular and the second in the plural. According to Gesenius and Kautzsch (1909: 485) and Levi (1987: 52), this is a common pattern in Biblical Hebrew. Biblical Hebrew is classified as verb-first and the verb in this position often remains in the singular even when the subject is in the plural. This is especially frequent when the subject consists of two coordinated NPs (cf. Doron 2005: 241). The latter phenomenon is often referred to as "partial agreement" because the target only agrees with its subject in certain features (cf. Corbett 2006: 154–155). Although (19) is obviously not a typical case of partial agreement – the first verb actually agrees with its controller in number, gender and person – restrictions on the agreement of the sentence-initial verbs might have led to the asymmetries found in the Hebrew Bible. More examples of this construction are listed in Table 17:

Table 17: Old Testament parallel structures[42]

Old Testament	Luther 1545	Vulgate	Septuagint	Hebrew Bible
Ex 14, 31	sg + pl	=	=	X (both pl.)
Ex 19, 8	sg + pl	X (verb left out)	=	X (both pl.)
Ex 24, 3	sg + pl	X (verb left out)	X (part. pl.)	=
Ex 32, 3	sg + pl	X (both sg.)	X (both pl.)	X (both pl.)
Ex 32, 6	sg + pl	=	=	=
Ex 32, 31	sg + pl	=	=	=
Ex 33, 10	sg + pl	=	X (two controllers)	X (both sg.,)

---

42 "=" stands for full correspondence with Luther, "X" for non-correspondence.

Table 17 shows that, out of seven mismatches in Luther's Bible (Exodus), three can be traced back to the Hebrew Bible, with the Septuagint and the Vulgate showing the same agreement behavior in two of these mismatches. One further example can be found both in the Septuagint and the Vulgate, and the two last ones in either the Septuagint or the Vulgate. These seem to be clear instances of loan syntax, the actual source, however, remains unclear. Perhaps Luther even used this pattern by analogy in Exodus 32, 3 where the other texts show either singular or plural in both verbs. A plural verb with a singular NP controller, as is the case in the Hebrew Bible and the Septuagint, is only very rarely attested in Greek and German as we have seen. However, further research on the question of loan syntax in Martin Luther's Bible translation is needed to provide satisfactory answers on the nature of these constructions.

4 Conclusion

In this paper, we dealt with the agreement of collective nouns in Ancient Greek and German, that is, nouns that are morphologically singular but semantically both singular and plural and thus may trigger plural agreement. We have seen that the Agreement Hierarchy can account for the distribution of such agreement forms – the mismatches increase as we move towards the right of the hierarchy – and that if there is any diachronic change, it is in accordance with the Agreement Hierarchy. Further, we have seen that verbal mismatches are relatively rare in both Greek and German and that when they occur, they are rarely realized in the same clause as the full NP, but rather in coordinate or subordinate clauses lacking an overt subject. Particular attention was paid to coordinate structures in which the first verb stands in the singular, the second in the plural. These agreement patterns are found in both languages, particularly in religious texts and in Old Testament Greek and German, some of which can be traced all the way back to Biblical Hebrew.

Acknowledgements

The research for this paper was conducted within a project on the contrastive study of the agreement systems in the Indo-European languages Ancient Greek, German, Hittite, and Welsh ("Diachrone Entwicklung von Kongruenzsystemen in vier flektierenden indogermanischen Sprachen") at the University of Marburg funded by the Deutsche Forschungsgemeinschaft (1.4.2011–31.3.2014, RI 1730/4).

The project was supervised by Jürg Fleischer, Elisabeth Rieken, and Paul Widmer. We would like to thank Greville G. Corbett, Antje Dammel, Jürg Fleischer, Oliver Schallert, Lea Schäfer, Per Erik Solberg and Paul Widmer for discussion and Sara Hayden and Jeffrey Pheiff for correcting our English. Special thanks go to Chiara Gianollo and an anonymous reviewer of this paper.

Sources

Abraham a Sancta Clara (all works), Goethe (all works):
Deutsche Literatur von Luther bis Tucholsky: Großbibliothek (Digitale Bibliothek 125). Berlin 2005: Directmedia.

Aristoteles, Diodorus Siculus, Ioannes Malalas, Novum Testamentum, Isocrates, Demosthenes, Aeschines, Plutarch, Thucydides, Xenophon:
Thesaurus Linguae Graecae. http://www.tlg.uci.edu.

Bonner Frühneuhochdeutschkorpus:
Das Bonner Frühneuhochdeutschkorpus. Maintained by Werner Besch, Winfried Lenders, Hugo Moser & Hugo Stopp (University of Bonn). http://www.korpora.org/Fnhd/.

Hebrew Bible, Septuagint, Vulgate:
Bibleworks 8. http://www.bibleworks.com.

IDS: Mannheimer Korpora 1+2:
Deutsches Referenzkorpus. Institut für Deutsche Sprache, Mannheim. http://www.ids-mannheim. de/cosmas2/.

Kaiserchronik:
Die Kaiserchronik eines Regensburger Geistlichen. Edited by Edward Schröder (Deutsche Chroniken und andere Geschichtsbücher des Mittelalters 1,1). Hannover 1892: Hahn.

Karl May:
Karl Mays Werke (Digitale Bibliothek 77). Berlin 2003: Directmedia.

Luther Bible:
Die Luther-Bibel. Originalfassung 1545 und revidierte Fassung 1912. (Digitale Bibliothek 29). Berlin 2002: Directmedia.

Notker, Otfrid, Tatian:
Thesaurus Indogermanischer Text- und Sprachmaterialien (TITUS). University of Frankfurt. http://titus.fkidg1.uni-frankfurt.de/indexe.htm.

Parzival:
Bibliotheca Augustana. Fachhochschule Augsburg. http://www.hs-augsburg.de/~harsch/augustana. html.

Prosalancelot:
Prosalancelot I–IV. Nach der Heidelberger Handschrift Cod. Pal. germ. 147, herausgegeben von Reinhold Kluge, ergänzt durch die Handschrift Ms. allem. 8017–8020 der Bibliothèque de l'Arsenal Paris. Übersetzt, kommentiert und herausgegeben von Hans-Hugo Steinhoff (Bibliothek des Mittelalters 14). Frankfurt am Main 1995: Deutscher Klassiker Verlag.

References

Acuña-Fariña, Juan Carlos. 2012. Agreement, attraction and architectural opportunism. *Journal of Linguistics* 48(2). 257–295.

Axel, Katrin. 2007. *Studies on Old High German syntax. Left sentence periphery, verb placement and verb-second* (Linguistics Today/Linguistik Aktuell 112). Amsterdam & Philadelphia: John Benjamins.

Axel, Katrin & Helmut Weiß. 2011. Pro-drop in the history of German. From Old High German to the modern dialects. In Melani Wratil & Peter Gallmann (eds.), *Null pronouns*, 21–51. Berlin & New York: de Gruyter.

Baker, Mark C. 2008. *The syntax of agreement and concord.* Cambridge: Cambridge University Press.

Behaghel, Otto. 1897. *Die Syntax des Heliand.* Praha: Tempsky.

Behaghel, Otto. 1928. *Deutsche Syntax: eine geschichtliche Darstellung*, Band III: *Die Satzgebilde.* Heidelberg: Winter.

Blass, Friedrich & Albert Debrunner. 1979. *Grammatik des neutestamentlichen Griechisch.* Bearb. von Friedrich Rehkopf. 15., durchges. Aufl. Göttingen: Vandenhoeck & Ruprecht.

Bybee, Joan L. 1985. *Morphology.* Amsterdam & Philadelphia: John Benjamins.

Comrie, Bernard. 1975. Polite plurals and predicate agreement. *Language* 51(2). 406–418.

Cooper, Guy L. III. 1998. *Attic Greek prose syntax. After K. W. Krüger.* Vol. 2. Ann Arbor; MI: The University of Michigan Press.

Corbett, Greville G. 1979. The agreement hierarchy. *Journal of Linguistics* 15. 203–224.

Corbett, Greville G. 2000. *Number.* Cambridge: Cambridge University Press.

Corbett, Greville G. 2006. *Agreement.* Cambridge: Cambridge University Press.

Croft, William. 2013. Agreement as anaphora, anaphora as coreference. In Dik Bakker & Martin Haspelmath (eds.), *Languages across boundaries: Studies in memory of Anna Siewierska*, 95–118. Berlin & New York: de Gruyter.

Dal, Ingerid. 1966. *Kurze deutsche Syntax auf historischer Grundlage.* 3., verb. Aufl. Tübingen: Niemeyer.

Dammel, Antje & Damaris Nübling. 2004. Relevanzgesteuerter morphologischer Umbau im Frühneuhochdeutschen. *Beiträge zur Geschichte der deutschen Sprache und Literatur* 126(2). 177–207.

Davies, Winifred V. & Nils Langer. 2006. *The making of bad language: Lay linguistic stigmatisations in German: past and present* (VarioLingua 28.) Frankfurt a. M.: Lang.

Dekeyser, Xaiver. 1975. *Number and case relations in 19th century British English: A comparative study of grammar and usage.* Antwerpen: Uitg. de Nederlandsche Boekhandel.

Depraetere, Ilse. 2003. On verbal concord with collective nouns in British English. *English Language and Linguistics* 7. 85–127.

den Dikken, Marcel. 2001. Pluringulars, pronouns and quirky agreement. *The Linguistic Review* 18. 19–41.

Dittmer, Arne & Ernst Dittmer. 1998. *Studien zur Wortstellung – Satzgliedstellung in der althochdeutschen Tatianübersetzung* (Studien zum Althochdeutschen 31). Göttingen: Vandenhoeck & Ruprecht.

Doron, Edit. 2005. VSO and left-conjunct agreement: Bibilical Hebrew vs. Modern Hebrew. In Katalin É. Kiss (ed.), *Universal grammar in the reconstruction of dead languages*, 239–264. Berlin & New York: Mouton de Gruyter.

Duden Grammatik. 2009. *Duden Band 4: Die Grammatik*. Hg. v. d. Dudenredaktion. 8., überarb. Aufl. Mannheim, Leizig, Wien & Zürich: Dudenverlag.

Duhoux, Yves. 2000. *Le verbe grec ancien. Éléments de morphologie et de syntaxe historiques*. 2e éd., rev. et augm. Louvain-la-Neuve: Peeters.

Ebert, Robert Peter, Oskar Reichmann, Hans-Joachim Solms & Klaus-Peter Wegera. 1993. *Frühneuhochdeutsche Grammatik*. Tübingen: Niemeyer.

Eggenberger, Jakob. 1961. *Das Subjektspronomen im Althochdeutschen: ein syntaktischer Beitrag zur Frühgeschichte des deutschen Schrifttums*. Chur: Sulser.

Ehrismann, Otfrid-Reinald. 1970. *Volk: eine Wortgeschichte (Vom Ende des 8. Jahrhunderts bis zum Barock)*. Gießen: Universität Giessen dissertation.

Findreng, Ådne. 1976. *Zur Kongruenz in Person und Numerus zwischen Subjekt und finitem Verb im modernen Deutsch*. Oslo: Universitetsforlaget.

Fleischer, Jürg. 2006. Zur Methodologie althochdeutscher Syntaxforschung. *Beiträge zur Geschichte der deutschen Sprache und Literatur* 128(1). 25–69.

Fleischer, Jürg. 2012. Grammatische und semantische Kongruenz in der Geschichte des Deutschen: eine diachrone Studie zu den Kongruenz von ahd. *wīb*, nhd. *Weib*. *Beiträge zur Geschichte der deutschen Sprache und Literatur* 134. 163–203.

Fleischer, Jürg, Roland Hinterhölzl & Michael Solf. 2008. Zum Quellenwert des althochdeutschen Tatian für die Syntaxforschung: Überlegungen auf der Basis von Wortstellungsphänomenen. *Zeitschrift für germanistische Linguistik* 36. 210–239.

Gärtner, Kurt. 1970. Numeruskongruenz bei Wolfram von Eschenbach: zur constructio ad sensum. *Wolfram-Studien* 1. 28–61.

Gesenius, Wilhelm & Emil Kautzsch. 1909. *Wilhelm Gesenius' hebräische Grammatik*. 28. Aufl. Leipzig: Vogel.

Gil, David. 1996. Maltese 'collective nouns': A typological perspective. *Italian Journal of Linguistics/Rivista di Linguistica* 8(1). 53–87.

Givón, Talmy. 1976. Topic, pronoun, and grammatical agreement. In Charles N. Li (ed.), *Subject and topic*, 151–188. New York, San Francisco & London: Academic Press.

Grimm, Jacob. 1898. *Deutsche Grammatik. Band 4. 1. Teil*. Besorgt durch Gustav Roethe und Edward Schröder. Göttingen: Dietrich.

Haspelmath, Martin. 1995. The converb as a cross-linguistically valid category. In Martin Haspelmath & Ekkehard König (eds.), *Converbs in cross-linguistic perspective. Structure and meaning of adverbial verb forms – adverbial participles, gerunds*, 1–55. Berlin & New York: Mouton de Gruyter.

Haspelmath, Martin. 2013. Argument indexing: A conceptual framework for the syntax of bound person forms. In Dik Bakker & Martin Haspelmath (eds.), *Languages across boundaries: Studies in memory of Anna Siewierska*, 197–226. Berlin & New York: de Gruyter.

Hennings, Thordis. 2001. *Altfranzösischer und mittelhochdeutscher Prosa-Lancelot: Übersetzungs- und quellenkritische Studien*. Heidelberg: Winter.

Hengeveld, Kees. 2012. Referential markers and agreement markers in Functional Discourse Grammar. *Language Sciences* 34. 468–479.

Herold, Günter. 1941. *Der Volksbegriff im Sprachschatz des Althochdeutschen und Altniederdeutschen*. Halle: Akademischer Verlag.

Himmelmann, Nikolaus P. & Eva F. Schultze-Berndt. 2005. Issues in the syntax and semantics of participant-oriented adjuncts: An introduction. In Nikolaus P. Himmelmann & Eva F. Schultze-Berndt (eds.), *Secondary predication and adverbial modification*, 1–68. Oxford: Oxford University Press.

Huang, C. T. James. 1984. On the distribution and reference of empty pronouns. *Linguistic Inquiry* 15(4). 531–574.

Humbert, Jean. 1960. *Syntaxe Grecque*. 3ᵉ éd., rev. et augm. Paris: Klincksieck.

Joosten, Frank, Gert de Sutter, Denis Drieghe, Stef Grondelaers, Robert Hartsuiker & Dirk Speelman. 2007. Dutch collective nouns and conceptual profiling. *Linguistics* 45(1). 85–132.

Kalinka, Ernst. 1913. *Die pseudoxenophontische ΑΘΗΝΑΙΩΝ ΠΟΛΙΤΕΙΑ. Einleitung. Übersetzung. Erklärung*. Leipzig & Berlin: B.G. Teubner.

Kühner, Raphael & Bernhard Gerth. 1898. *Ausführliche Grammatik der griechischen Sprache. Zweiter Teil: Satzlehre*. 3. Aufl. in zwei Bänden. In neuer Bearb. besorgt von Bernhard Gerth. Erster Band. Hannover: Hahnsche Buchhandlung.

Kühner, Raphael & Carl Stegmann. 1912. *Ausführliche Grammatik der lateinischen Sprache. Zweiter Band: Satzlehre*. 2. Aufl. in zwei Teilen, neubearb. von Dr. Carl Stegmann. Erster Teil. Hannover: Hahnsche Buchhandlung.

Lapini, Walter. 1997. *Commento all'* Athenaion politeia *dello Pseudo-Senofonte*. Firenze: Università degli Studi di Firenze.

Levi, Jaakov. 1987. *Die Inkongruenz im biblischen Hebräisch*. Wiesbaden: Harrassowitz.

Levin, Magnus. 2001. *Agreement with collective nouns in English* (Lund Studies in English 103). Stockholm: Almqvist & Wiksell.

Levin, Magnus. 2006. Collective nouns and language change. *English Language and Linguistics* 10(2). 321–343.

Liddell, Henry Georg & Robert Scott. 1940. *A Greek-English Lexicon*. A new edition, revised and augmented throughout by Sir Henry Stuart Jones. 9th edn. Oxford: Oxford University Press.

Liedtke, Ernst. 1910. *Die numerale Auffassung der Kollektiva im Verlaufe der englischen Sprachgeschichte*. Königsberg: Karg & Manneck.

Lippert, Jörg. 1974. *Beiträge zu Technik und Syntax althochdeutscher Übersetzungen*. München: Fink.

Nishina, Yoko. 2006. *Satzverbindung und Satzreduktion. Untergeordnete Konstruktionen des Japanischen in sprachtypologischer Perspektive*. Bochum: Universitätsverlag Dr. N. Brockmeyer.

Paul, Hermann. 1920. *Deutsche Grammatik*. Band 4: Syntax (2. Hälfte). Halle/S.: Niemeyer.

Prell, Heinz-Peter. 2001. *Der mittelhochdeutsche Elementarsatz. Eine syntaktische Untersuchung an Prosatexten des 11. bis 14. Jahrhunderts*. Oslo: Unipub forlag.

Reiten, Håvard. 1964. *Über die Kongruenz im Numerus im Mittelhochdeutschen*. Oslo: Universität Oslo.

Schwyzer, Eduard. 1950. *Griechische Grammatik. Zweiter Band. Syntax und syntaktische Stilistik*. Vervollst. und hrsg. von Albert Debrunner. München: C.H. Beck'sche Verlagsbuchhandlung.

Siewierska, Anna. 2004. *Person*. Cambridge: Cambridge University Press.

Siewierska, Anna & Dik Bakker. 2005. The agreement cross-reference continuum: Person marking in FG. In Caspar de Groot & Kees Hengeveld (eds.), *Morphosyntactic expression in functional grammar*. Berlin & New York: Mouton de Gruyter.

Wackernagel, Jacob. 1926. *Vorlesungen über Syntax: mit besonderer Berücksichtigung von Griechisch, Lateinisch und Deutsch*. Erste Reihe. 2. Aufl. Basel: Birkhäuser.

Wapnewski, Peter. 1972. *Die Lyrik Wolframs von Eschenbach: Edition, Kommentar, Interpretation*. München: Beck.

Wechsler, Stephen & Larisa Zlatić. 2000. A theory of agreement and its application to Serbo-Croatian. *Language* 76(4). 799–832.

Wegera, Klaus-Peter. 2000. Grundlagenprobleme einer mittelhochdeutschen Grammatik. In Werner Besch, Anne Betten, Oskar Reichmann & Stefan Sonderegger (eds.), *Sprachgeschichte. Ein Handbuch zur Geschichte der deutschen Sprache und ihrer Erforschung* (Handbücher zur Sprach- und Kommunikationswissenschaft 2.2), 1304–1320. 2., vollst. neu bearb. Aufl. Berlin & New York: de Gruyter.

Antje Casaretto and Carolin Schneider

8 Vedic local particles at the syntax-semantics interface[1]

In this paper we discuss the status of Vedic local particles regarding their syntactic function. As in other early attested IE languages such as Hittite and Homeric Greek, these forms may be used as adverbs, adpositions, or preverbs. The adverbial use is the oldest; other uses developed out of it over time. Our analysis shows that Vedic represents a very early stage in the development of these new functions: the majority of the instances points to the Vedic local particles acting as adverbs (e.g., with a modified noun). Adpositional use is still in its pre-stages, with the case of the noun being governed by the verb and not by the particle. Development towards preverbial use, on the other hand, is more frequent, including semantic change and/or altered syntactic behavior of the verb. Still, most particle-verb combinations remain on the border between metaphorical use and lexicalization, i.e. the process is still in its early stages. Both types of development display a constant interaction of syntax and semantics within grammaticalization and lexicalization processes.

1 Introduction

Many Indo-European (in the following: IE) languages use the same set of morphemes in two functions, either as preverbs or as adpositions (e.g., Germ. *auf* 'on'). But if one looks at some early attested IE languages (2nd and 1st millennium BC), these forms appear to be only loosely connected with verbs or nouns, i.e. they are not necessarily adjacent to the modified word, and they may also function as independent adverbs. This is the situation in Hittite, Homeric Greek, and Vedic. In the later stages of these languages, the relatively autonomous status of these words has been replaced by a new system of functionally discernible adverbs, adpositions, and preverbs. Among most linguists the communis opinio is that the origin of these forms lies mostly in local adverbs, which

---

1 The research leading to this paper has been conducted in the framework of a research project at the University of Würzburg funded by the DFG ("Die Funktion und Entwicklung von Lokalpartikeln im Vedischen").
Abbreviations: LP = local particle, ab_{sep} = ablative of separation, ab_{dis} = ablative of distance, acc_{goal} = accusative of goal, acc_{path} = accusative of path, i_{sep} = instrumental of separation.

evolved over time to new syntactic functions. Regarding adpositions, one of the earliest proponents of this view is Behaghel (1924: 33–34), who argues that adpositions evolved from adverbial modifications of nominal case forms. The choice of the case form was not determined by the adverb, but by the valency of the verb. It was only later that out of these adverbs adpositions which govern the case form of their dependent noun developed.[2] This process has to be understood as part of a typological shift in which free word order and complex inflectional systems were gradually replaced by fixed word order and massively reduced morphological systems, where adpositional phrases express local and other relations formerly expressed by case forms.[3] By forming a syntactic and semantic unit with a verb, adverbs are also able to develop into preverbs. This two-fold tendency, the ability to modify nouns and verbs, is typical of local adverbs in ancient IE languages (more on this below).

The aim of our paper is to analyze the processes by which adpositions and preverbs (or their pre-stages) emerged from adverbs in Vedic Sanskrit (in the following: Vedic).[4] Although the directionality of this grammaticalization[5] process is mostly unchallenged, the individual stages of this development in Vedic have never been closely studied. Our analysis of the syntactic and semantic relations between Vedic local particles and their modified nouns or verbs demonstrates the continuous interlocking of syntax and semantics in the development of new syntactic functions. In this paper we present a survey of typical tendencies of grammaticalization and lexicalization processes in the development of adpositions and preverbs that we have found in our corpus.

---

2 A different view is expressed by Delbrück (1893: 665), who argues that adverbs have evolved from preverbs, cf. also Hackstein (1997: 35) supporting this view.

3 Cf. on the process also Hewson and Bubenik (2006: 47): "(…) how a set of common and frequent adverbial particles was used originally to complement and clarify the adverbial reference of nouns in oblique cases, and then began to form a phrasal adverb with the NP, by establishing a configurational syntax."

4 The term "Vedic" is derived from the earliest attestations of the Indo-Aryan (as opposed to non-IE languages of India like Tamil etc.) languages, the Vedas (from *véda-* 'knowledge'), the oldest being the so-called Ṛgveda (or Rig-Veda; in the following: RV), a collection of 1028 religious hymns. Since these hymns have been transmitted orally over many centuries, the precise dating of the text is impossible; the communis opinio gives the end of the 2nd millennium BC as approximate time for its completion (Fortson 2010: 207–208). Due to its early and rich attestation, this language has been of paramount importance for IE studies. For further information on Vedic and its tradition see Witzel (1997).

5 Our concept of grammaticalization is based on Lehmann (2002), cf. especially p. 146 on the correlation of grammaticalization parameters (integrity, paradigmaticity, paradigmatic variability, structural scope, bondedness, syntagmatic variability).

Before we turn to the Vedic data in more detail, we briefly define how we use the terms "adverb", "adposition", and "preverb" in our analysis (cf. also Hettrich 1991: 29–30):

a) Adverb: uninflected morpheme that is either part of a phrase, or that is used independently in the sentence. Its function is to modify (locally, temporally, modally, etc.) verbs, adjectives, other adverbs, or whole sentences. In ancient IE languages it may also modify nouns, cf. Class. Gk. *hoi nȳn ánthrōpoi* 'the people (living) now' with the temporal adverb *nȳn* 'now', a construction that because of the lack of agreement would be unusual or prohibited in most modern IE languages.

b) Adposition:[6] like the adverb, the adposition is uninflected, but it can never appear on its own and is always part of a phrase containing a noun which is governed by the adposition (more on this in Section 2). The whole adpositional phrase may then, like an adverb, modify the verb, the whole sentence, or another noun.

c) Preverb: morpheme that forms a semantic unit with a verb, usually in proclitic position. In contrast to a verbal prefix, which is a bound morpheme, a preverb may also appear as an independent word, mostly at the beginning of the sentence with the verb appearing somewhere later in the sentence (tmesis), a situation found in Vedic and Homeric Greek, among others.[7] Its function is to modify the verb semantically. Both constituents may retain their original meanings (cf. Lat. *ex-ire* 'go out'), or they may be subject to lexicalization, i.e. the meaning of preverb and verb combined does not equal the meaning of both constituents alone (cf. Germ. *auf-hören* 'stop', literally 'listen up').

In order to express local relations, Vedic uses either case forms with a local meaning or local adverbs. Vedic adverbs can be divided into two groups: adverbs in the usual sense (in the following: local adverbs) and another group for which we use the more neutral term "local particles" (in the following: LPs) and which are the topic of our current research.[8] A division between these two

---

6 We use the term "adposition", since in Vedic the particle may precede or follow the noun. In the later stages of Indo-Aryan, though, a system of postpositions has been established (cf. the overview in Hewson and Bubenik 2006: 111–130).

7 The positional types are defined in Watkins (1963) and applied to different IE languages (e.g., Old Irish, Hittite, Indo-Iranian). Hale (1987) specifically sheds light on the situation in Vedic and Iranian.

8 On the methodological background see Hettrich, Casaretto, and Schneider (2004[2010]). A list of the already published papers on individual LPs can be found under www.vergl-sprachwissen-schaft.phil1.uni-wuerzburg.de/forschung/.

groups can be drawn on morphological, syntactic and semantic levels. Morphologically, local adverbs are of diverse origin, cf. the local adverbs Ved. *tátra* 'there', *ihá* 'here' based on the pronominal stems IE **to-* and **ei-/i-* (both demonstrative pronouns), or *arvā́k* 'hither' based on the accusative singular neuter of the adjective *arvā́ñc-* 'facing hither'. LPs, on the other hand, are at least synchronically opaque with regard to their derivational basis, cf. Ved. *abhí* 'towards', *úd* 'upwards', *ā́* 'hither'.[9] More important, though, is the different syntactic and semantic behavior of both groups: LPs may function as independent adverbs, but more frequently they are used in order to modify local relations already existing between the verb and a noun in an oblique case. In other words: They interact with the semantics of the verbs as well as of the nouns, thus explaining their two-fold tendency to develop characteristics of adpositions and preverbs respectively. Regarding word order, three basic types are possible: (a) adjacency of LP and noun, (b) adjacency of LP and verb, (c) none of the above. Type (a) has the potential of developing into an adpositional phrase, while type (b) could lead to reanalysis of the LP as preverb.

Let us start with type (a): Both LP and modified noun are part of an adverbial phrase (with either the LP or the noun as the head). This kind of behavior is not possible for local adverbs like the ones above, which never form a syntactic unit with a noun. The semantic relationship between LP and noun is either attributive or appositive (terminology according to Seiler 1960; Lehmann 1984): If the LP functions as attributive adverb, it selects a certain semantic feature of the case form acting as modifying satellite, while the modified noun is the nucleus of the phrase, cf. example (1) with *ádhi* 'on':

(1) RV 5,33,3

tíṣṭhā	*rátham*	*ádhi*	*tám*
go:PRS.IMP.ACT.2SG	chariot:ACC.SG.M	on:LP	this:ACC.SG.M

'Climb **on this chariot**!'

Without LP, the meaning of the sentence would be less explicit: 'Go to this chariot!'. The LP *ádhi* restricts the goal of the action to the surface of the chariot, while specifying the movement of the verb as being upwards. Note that in this construction the LP has to be analyzed as modifying adverb, since in Vedic the semantic role GOAL can also be expressed by a simple accusative without an accompanying LP. The case form of the noun is therefore determined by the verb and not by the LP. The main function of the LP *ádhi* is to clear the ambiguity

---

9 The phonological shape of Vedic LPs contains mostly only one or two syllables (e.g., CV, VC, VCV) and is therefore similar to other (non-local) particles like *nú* 'now'.

of the noun in the accusative; syntactically it functions as an adverb (Hettrich, Casaretto, and Schneider 2004[2010]: 24).

If, on the other hand, the LP is used as appositive adverb, LP and noun relate semantically to the same term so that both might be analyzed as nucleus or satellite, cf. example (2) with Ved. *úpa* 'towards', where the LP simply emphasizes the directionality of the movement without specifying the goal in any way (Hettrich, Casaretto, and Schneider 2004[2010]: 49):

(2) RV 3,51,2

gíro	*ma*	***índram***	***úpa***	*yanti*
praise:NOM.PL.F	my	Indra:ACC.SG.M	towards:LP	go:PRS.IND.ACT.3PL

'My praises go **towards Indra**.'

Since LPs may also be used as independent adverbs, their functional range is broader than that of local adverbs. Without the noun in the accusative, (2) would translate as 'My praises come hither' with the position of the speaker as point of reference. In this construction, *úpa* is exchangeable with a local adverb of similar meaning, e.g., *arvā́k* 'hither', cf. (3) and (4):

(3) RV 2,39,8

tā́ni	*narā*	*jujuṣāṇā*	***úpa***
these:NOM.PL.N	hero:VOC.PL.M	enjoy:PTC.PERF.MED.VOC.PL.M	hither:LP

yātam
go:PRS.IMP.ACT.2PL

'Having enjoyed these [praises], o heroes, **come hither**!'

(4) RV 1,118,2

trivandhuréṇa [...]	*ráthena [...]*	***yātam***
having.three.seats:INSTR.SG.M	chariot:INSTR.SG.M	go:PRS.IMP.ACT.2PL

arvā́k
hither:ADVERB

'**Come hither** with the chariot having three seats!'

Constructions like (2) have sometimes been confused with adpositional phrases, mostly because the LP often appears adjacent to the noun modified by it (see on this also Hagège 2010: 52–53). A more thorough analysis shows, however, that these constructions lack characteristics ascribed to adpositional phrases, such as governing of the case by the adposition and obligatory adjacency of adposition and noun (in Vedic, adjacency appears to be optional, also, the LP may be pre- or postposed). Vedic seems to represent an early stage regarding the development of adpositions. In most cases the constructions in question contain a combination of an adverb with a modified noun. Nonetheless, there are some transitional structures, which point to a more fully-fledged adposition-like form (more on this in Section 2). The fact that adverbs tend to be the source of adpositions may be seen in connection with their lack of inflectional morphology, which facilitates the process of decategorization necessary to evolve new functions (Di Meola 2001: 70).[10]

In parallel to the modifying of nouns, we also find transitions from adverb towards preverb, even more often than the transition from adverb towards adposition. The distinction between adverbial and preverbial use is often obscured by the free word order, though, and therefore cannot be defined only by adjacency of LP and verb. Thus, the prime criterion for the development from adverb to preverb is lexicalization due to the LP. The term "lexicalization", however, includes a wide spectrum of possible semantic developments ranging from simple metaphors to directional (or other) antonyms, or – on a syntactic level – from an increase of valency to restructuring the arguments of the predicate.

With regard to the Vedic LPs, our understanding of lexicalization is based on Hettrich, Casaretto, and Schneider (2004[2010]: 34), according to which lexicalization requires at least one of the following conditions: a) The LP reduces semantically contradictory characteristics of the basic verb, i.e. the LP evokes an antonym of the verb, b) semantic bleaching of the LP, c) syntactic change in the basic verb due to the LP, or d) the meaning of both, verb and LP, is restricted. In a corpus like ours, the existence of antonyms, although by no means the only or most typical condition, has proven itself a very useful tool for distinguishing lexicalized from non-lexicalized meanings. In other words: This type of semantic change gives clear evidence for the process of lexicalization. It is further of

---

10 On other sources for adpositions, e.g., verbs and nouns, cf. Bortone (2010: 89–106). On p. 103 he suggests a chain "noun > adverb > preposition" illustrated by Class. Gk. *thýra* 'door'. In our corpus there are some LPs believed to be derived from nouns, although the etymology is sometimes controversial, especially when form and function differ: while the hypothesis of nominal origin works well with Ved. *ánti* 'before' < IE *$h_2$ént-i*, locative singular of a root noun preserved in Hitt. *ḫant-* 'front', there are problematic forms like Ved. *sácā* '(in)to, at; also', whose ending *-ā* points to the instrumental singular of a (not attested) root noun *sac-* 'fellowship; follower' (cf. the verb Ved. *sac* 'follow'). If it were indeed an instrumental, one would expect the accompanying noun to be a genitive. What we find, however, is a locative, as in RV 7,32,2 *suté sácā* 'at the Soma' (*suté*: LOC.SG of *sutá-* 'Soma'), see on this in more detail Schneider (2011[2012]). Cf. on this problem, with examples from other IE languages, also Dunkel (1992: 159). A somewhat too optimistic view, at least in our opinion, is given in Hewson and Bubenik (2006: 350–356), where adverbial endings are assigned to case forms based on formal equations, regardless of syntactic functions.

interest to note that often only a certain number of all instances shows lexicalization of the LP and the verb, whereas the meaning remains unchanged in the rest. Also, the line between metaphoric and / or metonymic use and a newly emerged, lexicalized meaning of a word cannot always be drawn unequivocally, cf. Mumm (1996: 29–31). We try to handle this by grouping similar instances into one meaning and only assume separate meanings if a distinct "semantic gap" opens up between the original and the other "potential" meaning in the object language.[11]

To begin with, the verses below illustrate the difference between adverbial and preverbial use of LPs in the RV: The LPs *áva* 'down' and *úd* 'up' in RV 1,164,51 are adjacent to the verb, but do not have a lexicalizing effect on the verb *éti* 'goes'; each component sticks with its original meaning. Herein, the LPs function as adverbs (like *úpa* in (2) and *arvā́k* in (4) given above). As such, they could easily be substituted by other local, temporal, or modal adverbs like 'home', 'tomorrow', or 'hastily' without changing the sentence structurally, cf. example (5):

Local particles (*áva*, *úd*) as adverb:
(5) RV 1,164,51

samānám	*etád*	*udakám*	***úc***
same:NOM.SG.N	this:NOM.SG.N	water:NOM.SG.N	up:LP

caíty [=ca éti][12]		*áva*	*cā́habhiḥ [=ca áhabhiḥ]*
and.goes:PRS.IND.ACT.3SG		down:LP	and.day:INSTR.PL.N

'This same water **goes up and down** in the course of days.'

In opposition, in the next two passages the same LPs *áva* and *úd* are adjacent to their respective verbs, but also modify them semantically: *úd vap* 'dig out, excavate' versus *vap* 'sow, scatter, strew' and, by creating an antonym, *áva tan* 'undraw, loosen' versus *tan* 'tighten, stretch, become taut'. Further, *áva tan* is part of an idiomatic expression: *sthirā́* or *sthirám* + *áva tan* 'undraw the taut [bowstring(s)]':[13]

---

11 Apart from that, there are several ways to cover the phenomenon "lexicalization"; an overview of the different approaches is given in Brinton and Traugott (2005: 18–22 and 32–61).

12 The euphonic merging in *caíty* and *cā́habhiḥ* is called "Sandhi", a term from Classical Sanskrit grammar (Sanskrit *saṃ-dhi-* 'connection, junction; univerbation'). Sandhi is a common phenomenon in Vedic.

13 The phrase is rather well attested throughout the RV (also in 4,4,5; 8,19,20; 10,116,5 and 10,134,2).

(6) RV 1,117,12

híraṇyasyeva [= híraṇyasya iva]   *kalā́śaṃ*   *níkhātam*   **úd**
gold.like:GEN.SG.M   jar:ACC.SG.M buried:ACC.SG.M up:LP

ū́pathur   *daśamé*   *aśvínāhan [=aśvínā áhan]*
SOW:PERF.ACT.3DU tenth:LOC.SG.N Aśvin.day:VOC.DU.M.AND:LOC.SG.N
'**Have you two dug up** [the one (~ Vandana)] on the tenth day, [who] was buried like a jar of gold, o you two Aśvins?'

(7) RV 2,33,14

áva   *sthirā́*   *maghávadbhyas*   **tanuṣva**
down:LP taut:ACC.SG.N generous:D.PL.M stretch:PRS.IMP.MED.2SG
'Undraw the taut [bowstrings] for the generous ones!'

Another, even clearer example is the combination of the LP *ápa* 'off, away (from)' and *var^i* 'split open; open (up)' against the simplex *var^i* 'close, enclose':

(8) RV 1,11,5

tvā́ṃ   *valásya*   *gómató*
you:NOM.SG Vala:GEN.SG.M provided.with.cows:GEN.SG.M

'pā́var   *adrivo*   *bílam*
off:LP.open:AOR.ACT.2SG provided.with.a.rock:NOM.SG.M cave:ACC.SG.N
'**You**, provided with a rock, **have split open** the Vala (~ a mythical mountain) containing cows (~ dawn).'

Given the difficulties of Vedic as a dead language as well as the small part of the Vedic society represented in the RV, we prefer to define the term "lexicalization" in a rather close-meshed way ("antonymicization" of the basic verb; semantic bleaching of the LP; syntactic change; restriction). By this, we gain a rather multiple-layered picture of non-lexicalized beside lexicalized forms of one and the same LP-verb combination, which provides us with a philologically very useful set of lexical shades for each LP.[14]

It is also worth noting that the semantic merging of the two elements – LP and verb – normally leads to syntactic merging or univerbation as well. Though,

---

14 A particular feature of Classical Sanskrit is that certain LP-verb combinations – but also the vocabulary in general – develop into technical terms with partly very specific meanings depending on the genre, cf. *adhi* 'up to, to(wards); above' + *gam* 'go' has a literal meaning 'go up to, get up onto, climb' in the RV, but diversifies in the later language – the literal meaning survives as well – into 'cope, manage'; 'marry'; 'enter, copulate'; 'find out, understand' > 'study, read'; etc. This and more examples can be looked up in the common dictionaries; yet, there is no exhaustive research on the topic.

as already mentioned, univerbation as such can never be the only criterion to define the status of LPs as preverbs in Vedic. The distinction between a "true" lexical compound and a mere "syntactic" or non-lexicalized compound cannot be drawn solely on account of the univerbation of LP and verb both. "Syntactic compound" means that the LP and the verb coalesce only superficially, i.e. syntactically as well as phonologically;[15] the semantic level of both terms – verb and LP –, however, is not affected by their univerbation: thus, syntactic and phonological coalescence does not necessarily mean semantic coalescence, too. In return, even in lexical compounds constant univerbation is not decisive, cf. Germ. *aufhören* 'stop' in the question *Wann **hört** der Regen **auf**?* 'When does it stop raining?' in which the verb and the preverb are phonologically separated, yet remain one lexical unit.[16]

As already mentioned, word order in Vedic is free for most components of the sentence. Moreover, a finite verb is subject to different accent rules depending on the type of clause. In subordinate clauses the verb is accented, whereas the LP is not. Both elements usually appear as accentual and syntactic unity, i.e. as a syntactic compound. In main clauses, however, the LP is accented, whereas the verb is not – a syntactic unity in terms of adjacency is not necessarily given but possible.[17] Conditions like these require a careful philological investigation of the data.[18] The following passages exemplify the above mentioned possibilities:

Main clause
1) Syntactic and phonological univerbation; lexical independence of LP and verb

(9) RV 3,33,6
ápāhan [=ápa ahan]   *vr̥trám*   *paridhím*   *nadínām*
off:LP.strike:AOR.ACT.3SG Vr̥tra:ACC.SG.M encloser:ACC.SG.M river:GEN.PL.F
'**He repelled** Vr̥tra, the encloser of the rivers.'

---

15 The term "syntactic" grasps the situation of the Vedic language better than "phonological", because the accentual or phonological unity of an LP and a verb strongly depends on the specific type of sentence, i.e. on syntactic conditions. On the difference between a phonological and a lexical word, phonological univerbation yet lexical independence is not an unusual process, cf. Lyons (1968: 196–202) and Lehmann (2002: 135). The evidence in Vedic is abundant; for further examples cf. Hettrich (2002: 224–225), also Pinault (1995: 47).
16 Cf. Hettrich, Casaretto, and Schneider (2004[2010]: 22).
17 On the word order properties of Vedic see for instance Delbrück (1888: 15–25) or Speijer (1886: 9–10) on the classical language etc. On the matter of superficial syntactic contact, tmesis and univerbation against lexical univerbation see also Hettrich (2007: B.b.IV.2), further Pinault (1995: 42–43) and certainly Watkins (1963).
18 We also have to keep in mind that the word breaks as seen here are just editorial convention; most of them do not occur in the manuscripts.

2) No syntactic and phonological univerbation; lexical independence of LP and verb

(10)   RV 1,94,9
    vadháir   duḥśáṁsāṁ   **ápa**   dūḍhyò
    weapon:INSTR.PL.M   wicked:ACC.PL.M   off:LP   malevolent:ACC.PL.M
    jahi
    strike:PRS.IMP.ACT.2SG
    'With your weapons **repel** the wicked, the malevolent (people)!'

Subordinate clause
1) Syntactic and phonological univerbation, yet lexical independence of LP and verb

(11)   RV 5,40,6
    svàrbhānor   ádha   yád   indra   máyáḥ [...]
    Svarbhānu:GEN.SG.M   once   when   Indra:VOC.SG.M   sorcery:ACC.PL.F
    avā́han [ava áhan]
    off:LP.strike:AOR.ACT.2SG
    'Once, when **you**, o Indra, **repelled** the sorceries of Svarbhānu.'

2) No syntactic and phonological univerbation, yet lexical independence of LP and verb[19]

(12)   RV 1,80,2
    yénā   vr̥trám   **nír**   adbhyó
    which:INSTR.SG.M   Vr̥tra:ACC.SG.M   off:LP   water:ABL.PL.F
    jaghántha   vajrinn   ójasā [...]
    strike:PERF.ACT.2SG   provided.with.a.Vajra:VOC.SG.M   power:INSTR.SG.N
    '(The Soma) with which **you repelled** Vr̥tra from the waters with your strength, o Vajrin!'

Thus, if the combination of an LP and a verb is only syntactic and both terms retain their original meaning, they are "syntactic compounds" only. As such, the LP holds syntactic functions other than "preverb". If, on the other hand, the combination of an LP and a verb results in a new lexical entry, the LP semantically functions as preverb. This development is usually, yet not

---

19 This type is somewhat rarer than the rest.

always, bound to syntactic univerbation as well. With all these implications in mind, we try to give some conclusive examples of the many ways of semantic change caused by local particles in the Vedic language.

Our presentation is organized as follows: In Section 2 we discuss transitions from adverb to adposition, Section 3 is about transitions from adverb to preverb. In Section 4 we deal with the question of whether Vedic LPs may develop simultaneously in both directions, i.e. adposition and preverb, a process well known from Classical Greek and Latin. Finally, Section 5 presents our conclusions and compares the Vedic evidence with that from other closely related IE languages, attested at the same time depth, in order to classify the Vedic system within the IE language family.

2 From adverb towards adposition

As already mentioned, the Vedic language lacks adpositions as we know them from Classical Greek and Latin. In other words, none of the Vedic LPs functions as a proper adposition, although some constructions show similarities to adpositional phrases. We have used the following criteria to establish adpositional function:

- Adpositions govern their dependent term, normally a noun. The case form of the noun is determined by the adposition, not by the valency of the verb.[20] Both constituents are related to a head, in most cases a verb, a noun, or an adjective (Hagège 2010: 8–9, on government cf. Lehmann 1983a).
- The adposition is obligatory (more on this below).
- The case form of the governed noun is often desemanticized, cf. Germ. *mit dem Buch* (dative) vs. *ohne das Buch* (accusative).[21]
- Adposition and noun are adjacent.[22]

---

20 Some adpositions govern several case forms, cf. Hom. Gk. *pará* + genitive 'from the side of', + dative 'at the side of', + accusative 'to the side of' (Bortone 2010: 143–150) or Germ. *in*, which expresses location, when combined with the dative (*in dem Haus* 'in the house'), and direction, when combined with the accusative (*in das Haus* 'into the house'). There are no examples like this in Vedic.

21 On the general role of desemanticization in grammaticalization processes cf. Lehmann (2002: 114), Heine and Kuteva (2002: 2–5). Cf. also the examples with Germ. *in* above for retained meaning of the case in local expressions.

22 Cf. Di Meola (2001: 68) on German prepositions, also p. 68–72 for other preconditions for the development of adpositions by reanalysis (e.g., word and phrasal autonomy).

These criteria are only partially met by the Vedic LPs. Nonetheless, there are some intermediate stages between a modifying adverb and an adposition showing a clear direction from adverb to adposition even at this early stage. We examine these cases in the following sections. Section 2.1. is devoted to constructions with (mostly) obligatory status of the LP without desemanticization of the case. Section 2.2. deals with constructions where the case has additionally been desemanticized.

2.1 No desemanticization, but the LP is (mostly) obligatory: accusative of path (acc$_{path}$)

Since Vedic is a language with a rich nominal and verbal inflection, case forms are able to express many local relations autonomously, i.e. without accompanying LPs (or adpositions).[23] The use of the accusative for the semantic role GOAL (acc$_{goal}$) has already been mentioned in connection with example (1). Closely connected to this, but on the fringe of the normal accusative function, is the accusative denoting the path of movement (acc$_{path}$, on this and other accusative functions see Hettrich 2007: B.a.VI.). An accusative combined with a verb of motion is normally interpreted as acc$_{goal}$, as shown by (13):

(13)   RV 1,162,21
  devā́m   íd   eṣi   pathíbhiḥ
  god:ACC.PL.M particle go:PRS.IND.ACT.2SG path:INSTR.PL.M
  sugébhiḥ
  well.passable:INSTR.PL.M
  'Even **to the gods** you go along well-passable paths.'

Still, there are a few examples with the accusative referring to the path rather than the goal of the movement. In these instances the verb is a verb of movement or transfer and the modified noun has a meaning consistent with PATH, cf. (14):

(14)   RV 2,16,3
  yád   āśúbhiḥ   pátasi   **yójanā**   **purú**
  when fast:INSTR.PL.M fly:PRS.IND.ACT.2SG league:ACC.PL.N many:ACC.PL.N
  'when you fly **many leagues** with the fast ones'

---

23 On the autonomous meaning of the Vedic case forms and on the relation between desemanticization and the rise of adpositions see Hettrich (2007: B.a.I.).

In this sentence the meaning of the verb and especially of the noun make the analysis of the accusative as acc_{path} more plausible than the one as acc_{goal}. But there is only a handful of constructions like this attested in our corpus (also RV 5,37,4; 7,70,2; 7,90,6, cf. Casaretto 2011: 39–40 following Hettrich 2007). In the overwhelming majority of the cases, where the accusative is an acc_{path} rather than an acc_{goal}, we find additionally a directional LP determining the precise function of the accusative. For these constructions, LPs with different meanings related to the concept of PATH may be used, e.g., *ánu* 'along', *tirás* or *ví* 'through', *áti* or *abhí* 'over'. Although the case is not desemanticized – as shown by (14) –, the statistics show that the construction of an acc_{path} without accompanying LP can be considered by far the exception to the rule, i.e. the choice of the appropriate LP is almost, if not quite, obligatory. This construction is illustrated by (15) with *ánu* 'along':

(15) RV 5,51,15

svastí	**pánthām**	**ánu**	*carema*
happily	path:ACC.SG.M	along:LP	walk:PRS.OPT.ACT.1PL

sūryācandramásāv	*iva*
sun.and.moon:NOM.DU.M	like

'Happily we may walk **along (our) path** like the sun and the moon.'

Due to the semantics of the verb and the modified noun, one might still argue that *ánu* is not obligatory for the meaning of the sentence (as in (15) above). But consider (16):

(16) RV 9,109,7

pávasva	*soma [...]*	**mahā́m**	**ávīnām**
purify:PRS.IMP.MED.2SG	Soma:VOC.SG.M	large:ACC.SG.M	sheep:GEN.PL.M

ánu	*pūrvyáḥ*
along:LP	first

'Purify yourself, oh Soma, **along the large (back) of the sheep**, as the first one!'[24]

Without the LP *ánu* the accusative would be analyzed as denoting the goal of the movement, i.e. 'purify yourself towards X'. We can conclude that the LP is obligatory if the verb of the sentence is not a verb of movement or transfer. Still,

---

24 The back of sheep is here (and elsewhere) used as a metaphor for the sieve (made of wool) through which the Soma is poured during the ritual.

even in this construction *ánu* cannot be considered as an adposition, since the case form of the modified noun is not desemanticized but remains within the normal range of functions of the Vedic accusative. To complicate matters further, *ánu* can also be combined with other cases or case functions, cf. (17) and (18) with *ánu* + acc$_{goal}$[25]:

(17)   RV 3,55,7

dvimātā́		*hótā*	*vidátheṣu*
born.of.two.mothers:NOM.SG.M		hotar:NOM.SG.M	worship:LOC.PL.N

samrā́ḷ	*ánv*	*ágraṃ*	*cárati*
sovereign.king:NOM.SG.M	along:LP	top:ACC.SG.N	go:PRS.IND.ACT.3SG

budhnáḥ
bottom:NOM.SG.M

'The hotar (priest, here: the sacrificial flame), born of two mothers, is the sovereign king during the worships; he goes **to the top**, the bottom remains (still).'

(18)   RV 3,1,17

ánu	*devā́n*	*rathiró*	*yāsi*
along:LP	god:ACC.PL.M	charioteer:NOM.SG.M	go:PRS.IND.ACT.2SG

sā́dhan
determinedly

'You, as the charioteer, go determinedly **to the gods**.'

These examples show that the choice of the LP and the meaning of the modified noun are not the only factors that establish the precise case function: the context and the general knowledge of the addressee are also highly relevant. In (18), the normal function of the acc$_{path}$ would also be consistent with the meaning 'go among the gods'. The subject of the sentence, however, is the god Agni, who is, among other things, famous for driving his steeds to the gods in order to call them to the sacrifice. Knowing this, it is clear that the accusative in this sentence denotes the goal and not the path. Admittedly, this usage of *ánu* is less often attested; in the majority of cases *ánu* is combined with the acc$_{path}$.

To sum up: In combination with the acc$_{path}$ the accompanying LPs are still to be considered as adverbs, although they share some characteristics with

---

25 *Ánu* may also – rarely – be combined with a noun in the dative denoting the recipient of the action (Casaretto 2011: 17–18).

adpositions: They are mostly obligatory and – in many, but not all cases – adjacent to the noun they modify (more on adjacency at the end of Section 2.2.2). The modified noun is not governed by the LP but by the verb, as shown by the very few examples of this construction without LP. The case form is not desemanticized, but functions within the normal range of the Vedic accusative.

2.2 Desemanticization

While the accusative still retains its meaning, there are some instances of desemanticization with other case forms: partially with the ablative and completely with the instrumental. Let us first have a look at the ablative constructions.

2.2.1 Ablative of separation/distance

In Vedic the ablative may be used for denoting separation or distance ($ab_{sep/dis}$) depending on the semantics of the verb (dynamic or stative, cf. Hettrich 2007: C. a.IV., 2.). In order to express additional semantic features, the noun in the ablative has to be combined with a LP. In (19) and (20) with *purás* 'in front of', the context indicates that one draft animal is yoked in front of another:

(19) RV 3,53,23
    *ná gardabhám   **puró**   áśvān   nayanti*
    NEG donkey:ACC.SG.M in.front.of:LP horse:ABL.SG.M lead:PRS.IND.ACT.3PL
    'They do not lead the donkey (as being yoked) **in front of the horse**.'

(20) RV 1,54,3
    ***puró**   háribhyāṃ   vr̥ṣabháḥ*
    in.front.of:LP dun:ABL.DU.M bull:NOM.SG.M
    'The bull (is yoked) **in front of the two dun-colored (horses)**.'

In these constructions the phrase LP + ablative has a special function: The verbal action is looked at from a certain point of origin, which is expressed by the ablative. The LP *purás* renders the space of the action more precisely, i.e. 'in front of X' (X = ablative). If *purás* were omitted, this would change the meaning of the sentence. (19) would translate as 'They do not lead the donkey away from the horse', which, of course, would be a whole different affair.

To sum up: The ablative in constructions like (19) and (20) is used outside its normal local function, which would give a meaning 'away from'; the special meaning 'in front of' can only be expressed in combination with the LP *purás*.[26] Still, the desemanticization of the case form is not complete, since the notion of distance, which is part of the ablative function, is clearly retained. On the other hand, contiguity of LP and noun as well as obligatoriness of the LP, are factors consistent with adpositional usage. Strictly speaking, *purás* shows characteristics of both adverb and adposition.

A similar situation can be found with the etymologically related LP *purā́* 'before, formerly' (always temporal), also in combination with the ab$_{sep/dis}$. In (21), the verbal action takes place before the event expressed by the noun in the ablative happens:

(21) RV 3,32,14

stávai	***purā́***	***pā́ryād***	*índram*
praise:PRS.SUBJ.MED.1SG	before:LP	crucial:ABL.SG.N	Indra:ACC.SG.M

áhnaḥ
day:ABL.SG.N
'I want to praise Indra **before the crucial day**.'

Note that in this sentence the starting point of the described event lies in the future – the crucial day has not yet come. Normally, the ablative, if used temporally, denotes a starting point in the past, from which on the action happens, as in *From this day on I started to X*. So the same sentence without LP would mean 'I want to praise Indra from the crucial day on', which would be an entirely different meaning. For this reason the ablative in constructions like (21) may be called 'inverse ablative' (Hettrich 2007: C.a.IV., 5.2.; Bichlmeier 2011: 368), because in contrast to the ab$_{sep/dis}$ the order of the triggering event and the expected result is inversed: the triggering event takes place in the future (i.e. the crucial day), while the expected result takes place in the present (i.e. the praising).

Since the Vedic ablative is unable to autonomously express an action that takes place before the starting point denoted by this case, it is clear that the LP *purā́* is obligatory in this construction. As in (19) and (20) with *purás*, it has to be noted that the desemanticization of the case form is not complete: the ablative is still denoting a distance, even if the order of events is reversed. Another fact that differentiates this construction from adpositional phrases is the adjacency

---

26 There are parallels for this kind of opposition, cf. Hagège (2010: 291): "[I]n languages with both case affixes and Adps [i.e. adpositions], spatial directions, such as 'into', 'out of', 'across', etc., will often be expressed by bound morphemes, while spatial dimensions, such as 'inside', 'above', 'in front of', 'beside', will tend to be expressed by independent morphemes like Adps."

argument: while Ved. *purā́* + ablative in the meaning 'before X' is attested 19 times, adjacency is found only in 14 instances.

The grammaticalization of a word denoting FRONT to BEFORE has typological parallels, as in Bulgarian *pred* 'in front' > *predi* 'before' (Heine and Kuteva 2002: 141–142).[27] Similarly, the expression of temporal concepts via spatial concepts is a general process often occurring in languages throughout the world, i.e. it is typologically unremarkable (Haspelmath 1997: 61, 140; Bortone 2010: 57–62). There is also a Vedic example showing exactly this transition: The LP *purás* 'in front of' (see (19) and (20) above) is once attested with a temporal meaning:

(22) RV 2,28,5

mā́	*mā́trā*	*śáry*	*apásaḥ*	***purā́***
NEG	measure:NOM.SG.F.	break:AOR.PASS.2SG	skilful:GEN.SG.M	before:LP

r̥tóḥ
right:GEN.SG.M
'Nor shall the measure of the skilful one break **before the right (time).**'

Here, the abstract meaning of the modified noun prohibits the normally local meaning of *purás*.

2.2.2 Instrumental of separation

In Vedic, desemanticization of case forms is a very rare phenomenon; the inherited case forms mostly retain their local meanings. An interesting example can be found, however, in some combinations of the LP *ví* 'asunder, apart' with the instrumental meaning 'separate, keep away from X'. This meaning is contrary to the prototypical meaning of the Vedic instrumental which would be 'with' (expressing means, cf. Hettrich 2007: B.a.II.). The construction with *ví* is only attested in Vedic, and it is assumed that its origin lies in the analogical transfer from antonymic constructions with *sám* 'together' + instrumental in sociative function[28], cf. (22):

---

27 The other direction, i.e. FRONT > LATER, is also possible, cf. Heine and Kuteva (2002: 142) with the example Moré *béoghé* 'go ahead', 'be in front' > *béogho* 'tomorrow', 'the following day'. On the development of abstract spatial meanings cf. also Svorou (1994: 86–89), specifically on temporal uses see p. 140–143.

28 Cf. on this Bichlmeier (2011: 263).

(22) RV 2,18,8

ná	ma	índreṇa	sakhyáṃ	ví
NEG	my	Indra:INSTR.SG.M	friendship:NOM.SG.N	asunder:LP

yoṣat
keep.away:AOR.SUBJ.ACT.3SG
'Not shall my friendship keep itself away **from Indra**.'

In this sentence an underlying instrumental is still conceivable, since the phrase *índreṇa sakhyám* literally means 'friendship with Indra' (the sociative function is another well attested feature of the Vedic instrumental). In (23), though, the case form is fully desemanticized, and the meaning of the phrase is consistent with the meaning of the LP, not with the meaning of the case form:

(23) RV 10,18,3

imé	jīvā́	ví	mṛtáir
this:NOM.PL.M	living:NOM.PL.M	asunder:LP	dead:INSTR.PL.M

ā́vavṛtran
hither:LP.TURN:IMPF.IND.MED.3PL
'These living ones have separated themselves **from the dead ones**.'

A translation trying to acknowledge the instrumental in its usual function would be something like 'These living ones have rolled themselves asunder **with the dead ones**'. It is further of interest to note that if the LP were omitted, the meaning of the sentence would then require the ab$_{sep}$ instead of the instrumental, cf. (24):

(24) RV 2,33,1

mā́	naḥ	sū́ryasya	**saṃdṛ́śo**	yuyothāḥ
NEG	us	sun:GEN.SG.M	sight:ABL.SG.F	keep.away:PRS.SUBJ.MED.2SG

'Don't keep us **from the sight of the sun!**'

Since the instrumental is clearly unable to convey a separative meaning without *ví*, one might tend to assume that *ví* + i$_{sep}$ is indeed an adpositional phrase. But again not all criteria are met: The only example with adjacent position of LP and noun is RV 10,18,3 (see (23) above); in the other attestations *ví* is positioned closely to the verb (see (22) above) or in ambiguous position (i.e. between noun and verb). The closeness to the verb is peculiar and normally consistent with the behavior of preverbs or adverbs. It demonstrates clearly that despite the obligatoriness of *ví* in this construction and the fact that no other

LP can express this special meaning, *ví* is still not an adposition, but remains a modifying adverb. Still, if one would arrange the Vedic LPs on a scale ranging from modification to government, *ví* would come very close to the government ending of that scale.

What have we learned about the syntactic functions of the Vedic LPs in relation to the modified noun so far? The criteria establishing adpositional function are only partly met. In combination with the acc_{path}, the LP is not completely obligatory and the case is not desemanticized. With the ablative the LP is obligatory, but the case is only partly desemanticized. Only in the construction of *ví* with the instrumental are desemanticization of the case and obligatoriness of the LP present. But because of the lack of adjacency in most instances, one should refrain from analyzing *ví* as an adposition. So the hypothesis discussed at the beginning of this paper, namely that the language of the RV has not yet developed full adpositions, has so far been corroborated by our data.

At this point a short discussion of the word order of the LP in relation to the noun and the verb is necessary. Due to the relatively free word order in Vedic, the LP may stand in virtually any position in the sentence. As already mentioned, an adposition should be adjacent to its governed term. The LPs analyzed in this section show the following word order, cf. Table 1:

Table 1: Word order of Vedic LPs with respect to the noun or the verb

LP	preposed	postposed	adverbal[29]	ambiguous[30]	other
ánu (+ acc_{path})	18	20	20	27	1
purás (+ $ab_{sep/dis}$)	3	–	–	–	–
purā́ (+ $ab_{sep/dis}$)	13	1	–	–	6
ví (+ i_{sep})	1	–	5	4	–

We find that preposed and postposed position are equally possible with different preferences for the individual LPs.[31] While *ánu* frequently occurs in both positions, *purā́* strongly favors the preposed position (*purás* and *ví* are too rarely attested to be relevant here). Thus, Vedic LPs may be pre- or postposed. This situation is also found in some languages which have adpositions; these forms are called ambipositions, bipositions or alterpositions, and the respective

---

29 I.e. preceding the verb.

30 I.e. either adnominal or adverbal, e.g., following the noun (postposed) but preceding the verb (adverbal), cf. example (2).

31 This is also the case with LPs that do not show any tendencies towards turning into an adposition like *ácchā* 'towards', which is always used as an adverb, but mostly occurs in the position after the modified noun or the verb, cf. Casaretto (2012: 15).

pre- and postposed variants are sometimes distinguished by stress or meaning, cf. the examples given by Hagège (2010: 116–124) from IE and Non-IE languages. On p. 113 he argues for functional differences of pre- and postpositions in Finnic languages. Such a difference based on word order is not evident for the Vedic material. This is also true for the later attested Classical Sanskrit, where both positions are possible, although the postposed position is favored (MacDonell [1927] 1989: 144; Ziegler 2012: 110).

3 From adverb towards preverb

In this section, some of the lexical and syntactic changes LPs evoke in verbs are to be illustrated. As mentioned above, LPs may have an effect on verbs in both ways: semantically in changing the lexical value as well as structurally in modifying the arguments or the valency of the verb. If these conditions are met, the LP functions as preverb. However, both lines of development – the semantic and the structural / syntactic one – usually go hand in hand and represent different levels of lexicalization.[32]

Thus, generally speaking, most R̥gvedic LPs cause at least some sort of semantic change in verbs, but may vary considerably in the degree of that change, which includes a wide range of different processes like metaphoric use, generalization, semantic bleaching, narrowing down or restricting the meaning of the verb in technical terms, etc.[33] Structural modifications like the increase of valency or changes in the argument structure of a verb normally go along with semantic modifications, too, but are on the whole considerably less well attested; examples of these phenomena are given in the following sections.

3.1 Metaphors and figurative use

Metaphors and figurative use imply that a lexeme displays a meaning it does not possess inherently.[34] A common example is the replacement of a concrete with

---

32 Typologically, three different basic functions of preverbs can be carved out: first, the qualification of the predicate in terms of actionality; second, determining the locality of the verbal action, and third, establishing the participants of the predicate cf. Rousseau (1995: 171–173) According to the present state of research, this corresponds to the LPs in Vedic, when they function as preverbs.

33 A general overview on the different processes is given by Traugott and Dasher (2002: 27–34), Fritz (2006: 42–69), and also Lakoff and Johnson (1980).

34 See Mumm's (1996: 29–31) careful overview on the matter of distinction.

an abstract term.[35] According to Mumm (1996: 3), the formal feature of metaphoric use is:

> wenn ein Bedeutungselement eines Verbums in einem Kontext nicht getilgt wird, obwohl der VHT [Verbalhandlungsträger] dieses Bedeutungselement nicht besitzt, wie in *Rust eats iron*.
>
> [If one element of the lexical meaning of the verb is not erased in a specific context, although the subject/agent itself does not [intrinsically] possess this element as in *Rust eats iron*.]

Nonetheless, this definition is not easily put to practice in a text like the RV, which lives on deliberately chosen metaphors, metonymies, and allusions.[36] Two examples of this process are given here. One of them is the combination of the LP *párā* '(far) away from; off' and the verb *dā* 'give, bestow', which, apart from the literal and expected meaning 'to give something (ACC) away to someone (DAT)', also shows semantic bleaching of the local meaning of the LP while the accusative object gains a wider semantic scale. The accusative object of *dā* normally comprises inanimate terms, but in *párā dā* its semantic range is widened to animates as well. The LP-verb combination then receives a specified meaning 'to turn / hand someone (ACC) over to (DAT), turn someone in, betray', cf. (25):

(25) RV 5,3,12
 náha ayám   *agnír*   **abhíśastaye** *no*   *ná*
 NEG   this:NOM.SG.M   fire:NOM.SG.M   libel:DAT.SG.F   we:ACC.PL   NEG
 ríṣate   *vāvṛdhānáḥ*   **párā**   **dāt**
 damage:DAT.SG.N   grown:PTC.PRS.NOM.SG.M   away:LP   give:AOR.INJ.ACT.3SG
 'This Agni (fire) here, the grown one, shall **hand** us **over** neither **to libel** nor **to harm**!'

The second passage contains the combination of the LP *ní* 'down, downwards' and the verb *yā* 'go, move, drive', which is also attested both, in the literal sense as 'to move / go downwards to (ACC)' and figuratively as 'to haunt someone (ACC), strike someone down'. First, here too, the particular local meaning of *ní* starts to fade; and second, in a way, the combination *ní yā* gets transitivized, as the accusative in 'go down' represents the GOAL, whereas the

---

35 In Vedic, this could be for instance *sá samudrám gacchati* 'He goes to the sea' in contrast to *sá mahimā́nam gacchati* 'He becomes great', literally 'He goes to greatness'.
36 Some of the Ṛgvedic stylistic features and peculiarities are discussed in Elizarenkova (1995: 29–34) or Renou (1965).

accusative in 'haunt' may, at least in some cases, be judged as direct object, cf. (26):

(26) RV 6,16,28

agnís	tigména	śocíṣā	yā́sad
fire:NOM.SG.M	sharp:INSTR.SG.N	flame:INSTR.SG.N	go:AOR.INJ.ACT.3SG

víśvaṃ	ny	átriṇam
every:ACC.SG.M	down:LP	Atrin:ACC.SG.M

'Agni (fire) **shall strike every Atrin** (class of demonic beings) **down** with his sharp flame!'[37]

Thus, although the local meaning of *párā* and *ní* both, starts to fade, it still can be derived easily from imaging the very movement of a) the sacrificer, who is subject to 'extradition' (*párā*) or b) Agni, who burns down (*ní*) the enemies.

3.2 Increase of valency and telicity

The increase of valency is very often a dynamicization of mono- or bivalent verbs by providing them with a directional specification. Further, originally intransitive verbs can be transitivized, for which we already may see an example in (26) above. Both processes are well-known and well-attested throughout the RV and therein both terms, LP and the verb, usually keep their original meaning, and are – as well as metaphoric use – not judged as lexicalization proper.[38]

Thus, the transitive, bivalent verb *as* 'throw, cast something (ACC)' gains a semantic specification of directionality when an LP is attached and becomes trivalent. As a rule, verbs can be combined with different (often more than one) LPs, depending on the type of directionality and the intrinsic semantics of the verb itself.[39] The passage given here includes once again the LP *párā* '(far) away from', cf. (27):

---

37 Here, we cannot just say that the semantic range of the accusative was widened like in *párā dā* above, because there is one instance in the RV showing the literal meaning with an 'animate goal', cf. RV 5,75,5 víbhiś **cyávānam** aśvinā **ní yātho** 'You two (Aśvin) are to go down (i.e. from heaven to earth) to Cyavāna (an old man rejuvenated by the Aśvin) with your birdlike (horses)!'. On *ní* see Schneider (2010).

38 In German – especially with verba dicendi and verba videndi – a similar process can be caused by the addition of the syllable *an-* as in *schreien* 'cry, shout' vs. *an-schreien* 'shout at', *sehen* 'look' vs. *an-sehen* 'look at'. It is also possible with usually monovalent verbs such as *schleichen* 'creep' vs. bivalent *an-schleichen* 'creep up on', see Stiebels (1996: 162–165).

39 Yet in the Ṛgveda, we seldom find more than two LPs at once. In the later language, though, there is a tendency to amass LPs, cf. Delbrück (1888: 434–437).

(27) RV 10,72,8

> **párā**   *mārtāṇḍám*   **āsyat**
> away:LP   Mārtāṇḍa:ACC.SG.M   cast:IMPF.ACT.3SG
> 'Mārtāṇḍa she (Aditi) **cast away** (from herself).'

In contrast to this, the verb *as* is also attested without LP, as such usually lacking a specific directionality, cf. (28):[40]

(28) RV 10,61,8

> *sá*   *īm*   *vŕṣā*   *ná*   *phénam*
> he:NOM.SG.M   particle   bull:NOM.SG.M   like   foam:ACC.SG.M
>
> **asyad**   *ājáu*
> emit:IMPF.ACT.3SG   fight:LOC.SG.M
> 'Just like a bull in a fight he **emitted** foam (i.e. frothed at the mouth).'

The verb *svar* 'make a sound; be loud' can be adduced as an example for the dynamicization of a monovalent verb. Combined with the LP *sám* 'together', *svar* not only gets a local specification, but syntactically also shows the trivalent structure of verbs like *dā* 'give, bestow' or *bhar* 'bring, bear, carry' and is used as metaphorical transfer verb, cf. (29):

(29) RV 9,101,11

> **íṣam**   **asmábhyam**   *abhítaḥ*   **sám**
> refreshment:ACC.SG.F   we:DAT.PL   from.all.sides:ADVERB   together:LP
>
> **asvaran**   *vasuvídaḥ*
> be.loud:IMPF.ACT.3PL   finding.goods:NOM.PL.M
> 'From all sides **they roared together refreshment for our benefit**, finding goods.'

That an LP serves as transitivizer, and thus introduces telicity to a verb, is a specialty within this group. Herein, we may see a "perspectivization" of the verbal action.[41] Generally, this process is quite rare throughout the RV; however,

---

40 In the Ṛgveda the verb *as* 'throw, cast' is also attested beside the LPs *ápa* 'off, away from', *áva* 'down(wards)', *ví* 'asunder', and others, cf. Grassmann (1996: s.v. *as*) or Krisch (2006: s.v. *as*) for further references and the instances showing the simple verb.

41 This is based on the fact that the inherent semantics of some verbs do not require a particular set of participants at all times; they can be added if necessary and put the verbal action into a structural perspective. Mumm (1996: 31–32) labels this as "quantitative valency". An example of the phenomenon can be seen in the verb 'shoot' (monovalent, intransitive) vs. 'shoot a lion' (bivalent, transitive) vs. 'shoot at the tree' (bivalent, intransitive).

another example is presented in the next passage including the verb *meh* 'piss, urinate' and the LP *áva* 'down, downwards':

(30) RV 9,74,4

táṃ	*náro*	**hitám**	**áva**
he:ACC.SG.M	man:NOM.PL.M	driven:ACC.SG.M	down:LP

mehanti
urinate:PRS.IND.ACT.3PL
'The men **piss down** (Soma), **the one set in motion**.'[42]

On a purely structural or syntactical level, a directional interpretation would be possible, too, i.e. 'The men **piss down on** the one set in motion.' This, however, is ruled out by the context and our knowledge of the Vedic ritual: Soma is a plant as well as the product of that plant (the juice or the essence). The whole process is a common metaphor for fertility in the Ṛgveda.[43]

3.3 Changes in the event structure or actionality

To a certain extent, changes in the event structure could be connected to the process of transitivization illustrated in Section 3.2 above, because in some instances LPs can bring about a change in the actionality or event structure of the verb, including a "perspectivization" of the verbal action as well.[44] Yet, just like metaphoric use, this change of perspective usually surfaces on the semantic, not on the syntactic level.

---

42 On a cosmogonic and mythological level, Soma shows a close relationship with other fluids playing a role in Vedic cosmogony and mythology. These are especially milk, water, rain, and seed. The 'men' mentioned here are the priests as mediators between earthly and divine beings, and further the Marut (a certain class of gods), as pointed out by Geldner ([1951] 2003: s.v.).

43 Cf. Oberlies (1999: 32).

44 Actionality describes the course of any verbal action independent from the speaker's point of reference. Thus, it is a lexical category directly referring to the intrinsic meaning of the verb. According to Hoffmann (1976: 523–540) different actionalities like durative, selective (~ Germ. *punktuell*), present / current, terminative / resultative can be established in Vedic. The actionalities as defined by Vendler (1957) are somewhat rougher (state, activity, achievement, accomplishment). A short overview based on Vendler's work is given by Van Valin and LaPolla (1997).

In contrast to the lexical category "actionality", the category "aspect" is the grammatical definition of an action with regard to a point of reference set by the speaker. Actionality could also be described as "lexically inherent aspect" of the verb, cf. Fortson (2010: 91). Whether aspect as a grammatical category existed in Vedic is under ongoing scrutiny that has no direct impact on the present paper. However, some of the relevant data are presented and assessed in Tichy (1997) and Dahl (2010).

A prominent development is that a LP evokes a resultative or telic notion in the predicate to which it is attached. This happens in particular with the LPs *sám* 'together', *áva* and *ní* both 'down, downwards' and *ví* 'asunder'. This process is usually an interaction of both, LP and verb, because it not only depends on the semantics of the LP but also on that of the verb. Compare for instance the following passage containing the LP *ní*, which adds telicity to the monovalent, static verb *cay* 'be aware of, perceive'. The two terms combined then result in *ní cay* 'investigate, find out, experience', cf. (31):

(31) RV 10,124,9d

índraṃ	*ní*	*cikyuḥ*	*kaváyo*
Indra:ACC.SG.M	down:LP	experience:PERF.IND.ACT.3PL	seer:NOM.PL.M

maṇīṣā́
Insight:INSTR.SG.F

'The seers **experience** (the god) Indra by (their) insight.'[45]

The LP *sám* also often adds telicity, mostly in a way that can be interpreted as a process of 'wrapping up' and has a resultative meaning.[46] The following passage has the verb *sám jūrv* 'singe, burn':[47]

(32) RV 8,60,7

yáthā	*cid*	*vṛddhám*	*atasám*	*ágne*
like	just	grown:ACC.SG.N	shrub:ACC.SG.N	Agni:VOC.SG.M

saṃjū́rvasi	*kṣámi*
consume:PRS.IND.ACT.2SG	ground:LOC.SG.F

'Just like **you consume** the grown shrub on the ground (wholly), o Agni!'

In contrast to the resultative function of *sám*, the LP *prá* 'forward' can indicate the instigation of an event. In these cases it has an ingressive meaning and can often be translated as 'now' or interjective as 'Up!' or 'Come on!' cf. (33):[48]

---

45 The passage means that the seers are able to recognize and fully experience Indra in other things and beings by their special and somehow "esoteric" visions, see also Geldner (2003: s.v.).
46 In German, this can be expressed by the prefixes *ver-* in *verbrennen* ~ 'burn to ashes' versus *brennen* 'burn' or *zer-* in *zerbrechen* 'break to pieces' versus *brechen* 'break', cf. Fleischer and Barz (2012: 389–391).
47 On *sám* see Schneider (*forthcoming*: 8.2.2).
48 However, the matter is not entirely sure; an exhaustive presentation is given by Casaretto (2013).

(33) RV 1,62,1
prá   **manmahe**   *śavasānā́ya*   *śūṣám*
forwards:LP think.of:PRS.IND.MED.1PL strong:DAT.SG.M praise:ACC.SG.M
'We are about to concoct a praise for the strong one (now).'

3.4 Change of syntactic structure

In some cases, though only seldom, LPs induce the restructuring of the arguments of a predicate while their number remains the same. Usually, a change
in the argument structure also results in a change in meaning.

A transparent example of this development is the combination of *áva* 'downwards' and *dā* 'give, bestow': in Vedic – and in many other Indo-European languages such as Greek and Latin – the basic verb (Latin *dō*, *dare*, Greek *dídōmi*)
is constructed with an accusative as direct and a dative as indirect object. However, the connection of *dā* with *áva* is attested only with an accusative and an
instrumental meaning 'to bestow someone (ACC) with something (INSTR)', in
contrast to 'to give someone (DAT) something (ACC)' of the basic verb. Herein,
the LP evokes a syntactic change, cf. (34):[49]

(34) RV 2,33,5
áva   *stómebhī*   *rudrám*   *diṣīya*
down:LP   praise:INSTR.PL.M Rudra:ACC.SG.M give:AOR.OPT.MED.1SG
'I want to bestow Rudra with praise!'

Another syntactic change is shown in the combination of the LP *práti*
'towards, against' and the verb *ay* 'go, move'. If the verb governs the accusative,
the meaning of *práti* and *ay* remains literal 'to go, move towards (ACC)'. If a
genitive is included in the construction, *práti ay* means 'be aware of something'
and as such shows the typical feature of a verb of perception, cf. (35):

---

49 It has long been noted that some transitive Vedic verbs are capable of adapting two different
argument patterns, consisting in two kinds of accusative objects, whereas the second object is
either a dative or an instrumental, cf. *arc* 'to sing something (a song/praise; ACC) for someone
(DAT)' (RV 5,16,1) versus *'to besing someone (ACC) with a song (INSTR)' (RV 3,51,4). Similarly,
añj 'to anoint something (ACC) on' (RV 5,54,1), 'to anoint someone (ACC) with something
(INSTR)' (RV 3,14,3). In the literature, the argument patterns are labeled differently, e.g., "trans-
lative" and "ornative" in Hettrich (2007: B.b.I); "two pattern" transitive verbs in Kulikov (2012:
26–27 and 701–703); "théorie des deux modèles" in Haudry (1977: 175–177). In German, the
same phenomenon appears in pairs like 'etwas (ACC) werfen' in contrast to 'etwas / jemanden
(ACC) mit etwas bewerfen', cf. Ickler (1990: 2–5) and Zifonun, Hoffmann, and Strecker (1997:
1315–1318 and 1347–1348).

(35) RV 8,67,17

pratiyántaṃ   cid **énasaḥ**   dévāḥ
against:LP.go:PTC.PRS.ACT.ACC.SG.M just fault:GEN.SG.N god:NOM.PL.M

kṛṇuthá   jīváse
do:PRS.IND.ACT.2PL live:INF

'**He who is aware of his own fault** – him you gods let live.'

3.5 Antonyms

As mentioned before, one of the clearest types of semantic change is the one in which the LP reduces semantically contradictory characteristics of the basic verb, i.e. the LP "antonymicizes" the basic verb, which does not necessarily surface on the structural or syntactic level (on the different types of antonyms see, for example, Blank 2001: 32). One example of this development has already been given in Section 1, ex. (7). This specific type of semantic change only works if LP and verb show opposite or contradictory lexical features, and is therefore restricted to certain groups of verbs and LPs.[50] Another clear example of this type is the verb sā 'bind, fasten', which, together with the LP áva 'down, down-wards', means 'release', cf. (36):

(36) RV 6,74,3

áva   **syataṃ**   muñcátaṃ ...
down:LP bind:PRS.IMP.ACT.2DU release:PRS.IMP.ACT.2DU

kṛtám   éno   asmát
done:NOM.SG.N sin:NOM.SG.N we:ABL.PL

'**Relieve**, release from us the sin committed.'

3.6 Results

To sum up, complete lexicalization of LPs and verbs is still an extremely rare phenomenon in the RV. Apart from the above mentioned instances, there is a significant number of LPs that do not cause any kind of semantic change in connection with a verb.

Between complete lexicalization and no lexicalization at all, though, there is a huge range of possible semantic changes: on the semantic level, we find an abundant amount of metaphors, metonymies, and figurative uses as well as

---

50 We hope to do further research on this point in the future.

changes in the actionality of the verb, yet (still) mostly in a telic or ingressive way.[51] Structurally, a significant change in meaning can be induced by the increase of valency or reorganization of the verbal arguments. And in some cases, depending on the inherent meaning of LP and verb, the LP triggers the antonym of the basic verb.

For the time being, we can say that the above depicted semantic changes strongly seem to depend on the LP being part of the verbal argument structure. In further research it will be crucial to investigate the factors that are responsible for the quite different tendencies the LPs show in lexicalization processes.

4 LPs functioning as preverbs and adpositions simultaneously

Since adverbs may turn into adpositions and preverbs, it is to be expected that we find both usages frequently with the same LP in Vedic.[52] Furthermore, in related languages, such as Greek and Latin, we find evidence for a grammaticalization path where an adverb first changes into an adposition, which then in turn changes into a preverb (Hagège 2010: 63–64).

However, neither of these observations is in agreement with the Vedic data: If a Vedic LP shows a tendency towards changing its basic adverbial function, it will in most cases be either that of an adposition or that of a preverb. Changes in both directions simultaneously are very rare. Also, the grammaticalization path that results in preverbs is found much more frequently than that resulting in adpositions, the latter never being completed in our corpus. These processes do not seem to be related to one another, i.e. there is no unidirectionality leading from adverb to adposition to preverb. The reason why the development of adpositional phrases occurs so rarely in Vedic is of course connected with the fact that morphological cases in this language still retain their diverse semantic values, i.e. most concepts can be expressed by case alone without accompanying LP (see Section 2.1 on the accusative). Only for some few spatial – and temporal – concepts is the combination with a certain adverb obligatory. However, the case form is still dependent on the valency of the verb, not on the LP.

---

51 Our research into this complex is still ongoing. We hope to present the matter in an exhaustive and more detailed way in the future.

52 Cf. Lat. *ad, cum, de, sub*, etc. which may function as prepositions or preverbs, also Germ. *an, auf, um*, etc. Still, we also find cases where only one function is possible, cf. Germ. *be-, er-, zer-* etc., all of which may only function as preverbs, not as prepositions, cf. for more on this topic Hagège (2010: 64–66).

The tendency to develop new syntactic functions differs greatly from LP to LP, at least partly depending on its semantics. In our corpus we find four types of LPs:

I. Tendency towards adpositional function:

ánu 'along, after', tirás 'over; through', parás 'off, in a distance (from)', purás 'forward, in front of', purā́ 'before' (temp.)

II. Tendency towards preverbal function:

ápa 'away from', áva 'downwards', úd 'up(wards)', úpa 'towards', ní 'down (wards)', níṣ 'out of, away from', párā 'off, away (from)', práti 'against', sám 'together, with'

III. Tendency in both directions:

ví 'asunder', áti 'over (and beyond)'

IV. Preservation of adverbial function:

ácchā 'towards', abhí 'towards, against', ā́ 'towards', prá 'forward', purástāt 'forward, in front of'

The impression given here that a relatively large number of LPs tends towards adpositional function is deceiving. As we have seen in Section 2, these cases share only a part of the characteristics of proper adpositional phrases. None of them can be considered as a fully-fledged adposition. Still, all of them add semantic specifications that cannot be expressed by the case form alone. The second group, on the other hand, contains LPs which share the most relevant characteristic of a preverb, i.e. lexicalization (see Section 3 above). The third group is very small, and the clearest example is ví 'asunder', whose adpositional function was discussed in Section 2.2.2. As a preverb it occurs mostly in constructions where the meaning of the simple verb is reversed, cf. the list in (37):

(37) oh 'praise' : ví oh 'scorn'
      kar 'make' : ví kar 'destroy'
      cart 'knot' : ví cart 'loosen'
      tan 'span, stretch' : ví tan 'loosen'
      dāś 'worship' : ví dāś 'despise, disown'
      (Casaretto 2011[2012]b: 172–173)

The only other LP in this group, áti 'over (and beyond)', shares some adposition-like properties in combination with the acc_{path}, comparable to ánu in Section 2.1, cf. (38):

(38) RV 1,42,7

áti	*naḥ*	*saścáto*	*naya*
over:LP	us:ACC.PL	pursuer:ACC.PL.M	lead:PRS.IMP.ACT.2SG

'Lead us **over (and beyond)** the pursuers!'

Without *áti* the sentence would translate as 'Lead us to the pursuers', which would be a completely different meaning. As a preverb *áti* is only very rarely attested, e.g., in combination with the verbal roots *oh* 'praise' and *man* 'think', both combinations meaning 'scorn' (Casaretto 2011[2012]a: 212–213). Since these are clear cases of lexicalization, *áti* has been classified into group III.

The LPs of the fourth group show only adverbial function. Four of them have a very general directional meaning, while *purástāt* 'forward, in front of' is a special case (Casaretto 2012): it is synchronically transparent as a derivation from *purás* with the suffix *-tāt* that is used to derive adverbs from other adverbs, adjectives, or nouns. Although it has been stated in the beginning of our paper that Vedic LPs are synchronically opaque, we have decided to include formations like *purástāt* into our study, since it is of interest to compare them with the "LPs proper". They are relatively recent formations unknown outside Indic. Compared to *purás*, *purástāt* shows, despite the similar meaning, quite a few significant differences: it is never used for modifying nouns, and there is no close relation to the verb and no lexicalization. Its syntactic function is that of an independent adverb, and a typical example would be:

(39) RV 3,27,7

devó	*ámartyaḥ*	*purástād*	*eti*
god:NOM.SG.M	immortal:NOM.SG.M	forward:LP	go:PRS.IND.ACT.3SG

māyáyā
sorcery:INSTR.SG.F

'The immortal god goes **forward** with mysterious power.'

5 Conclusions

In this paper we have discussed the status of Vedic local particles regarding their syntactic function as adverbs, adpositions, or preverbs. The following results seem to emerge for the time being: Regarding the modification of nouns, the majority of the instances points to the Vedic LPs acting as adverbs – either with a modified noun or as independent adverbs. Adpositional use in connection with governing a dependent term is not attested in the Ṛgvedic language, only different pre-stages thereof, including different stages of obligatoriness of the LP, desemanticization of the modified noun, and adjacency of both constituents (Section 2). The lack of adpositions must be understood within the system of Vedic morphology: Since the nominal cases retain their semantic values, concepts like GOAL and SOURCE can be expressed by case alone. Case syncretism and the accompanying loss of semantic distinctions, on the other hand, are much more advanced in Greek and Latin, which therefore had a greater necessity for developing adpositions in order to express certain semantic concepts (more on this below). Accordingly, our analysis shows that LPs with a general directional meaning like 'towards' do not develop an adpositional function in Vedic, because the Vedic accusative is perfectly capable of carrying this semantic load on its own. Only when a LP adds a semantic specification not expressible by the respective case do we find the beginning of a grammaticalization path that leads to new syntactic functions. Still, the choice of the individual case is dependent on the verb, and the case function remains at least partly within its normal local range, as with the ablative (Section 2.2.1). Complete desemanticization of the modified noun, as with the instrumental (Section 2.2.2), is very rare.

On the other hand, development towards preverbial use, again with different pre-stages, is relatively frequent – along with semantic change and sometimes with an altered syntactic behavior of the verb, as in the increase of valency (Section 3). The frequency itself, though, is very much dependent on the LPs in use. Complete lexicalization, including reversal of meaning, is only comparatively rarely attested, i.e. there is only a limited number of LPs which can be analyzed as preverbs with some certainty. Most cases remain on the border between metaphorical usage and lexicalization. What is striking, though, is that, while real adpositions are not attested, the transition from adverb to preverb is completed as early as the RV. While the nominal morphology is mostly sufficient in order to express spatial and other semantic concepts, the range of semantic concepts expressed by verbal constructions is so vast that a more flexible system of simple verbs, verbs with modifying adverbs, also in metaphorical usage, and lexicalized combinations of preverbs and verbs seems to be necessary. At the beginning of Section 3.1 it has been mentioned that due to the nature of our text metaphorical usages are abundant in the RV making it a rich hunting ground for semantic modifications of verbal meanings.

In order to understand the relative position of the Vedic system within the IE languages concerning local expressions, we now have a short look at some other early attested IE languages: Most closely related genetically to Vedic are the Old Iranian languages (the Indo-Iranian languages form a subgroup of IE), so one would expect the earliest representative of this language family, Old or Gathic

Avestan, to present a similar picture regarding the expression of local relations. Instead, we find that the system of adpositions seems much more advanced in Avestan than in Vedic, with prepositional position clearly favored in Avestan, while the slightly younger Old Persian is mostly postpositional (cf. the overview in Hewson and Bubenik 2006: 131–137, on Avestan LPs also Bichlmeier 2011). Adjacency of particle and noun or verb is more frequently attested than in Vedic, so that Iranian is more reminiscent of Classical Greek and Latin.

The closest match to the Vedic state of affairs can be found in Homeric Greek where adverbial particles may be connected either with a noun in an oblique case or with a verb (Horrocks 1981; Fritz 2005; Luraghi 2003; Haug 2009; Bortone 2010; cf. also the overview in Hewson and Bubenik 2006: 54–80). As in Vedic, particle and noun or verb are not always adjacent to each other – the particle may precede or follow the modified word or it may appear in tmesis –, and it is not always easy to decide which is the modified word. There are some rare instances where the particle occurring beside a noun may be analyzed as the head of the phrase, thereby displaying preposition-like characteristics (Hewson and Bubenik 2006: 60f–61 on examples taken from Luraghi 2003: 168, 170, 175). In Classical Greek, as in Latin, on the other hand, adpositions are always preposed and form the head of a PP, while preverbs directly precede their verb having undergone univerbation (on Latin Baldi 1979; Lehmann 1983b; Luraghi 1989; Untermann 1996). It is of interest to note that in Vedic there is no continuous process with adverbs becoming over time more like adpositions or preverbs. Although there is, admittedly, strictly speaking no linguistic successor of Vedic – the later attested Classical Sanskrit as well as the Middle and Modern Indo-Aryan languages evolved from more or less closely related dialects –, the system that emerged in later times shows a complete remodeling of form and function (Hewson and Bubenik 2006: 111–130): The Vedic LPs showing beginnings of adpositional and preverbal function are mostly not continued in the younger languages, which use different forms altogether, cf. the Hindi postposition *mẽ* 'in' from the Ved. noun *mádhye* loc.sg. 'in the middle'. In this respect there is a close parallel to be found in Hittite, which seems – on first sight – to resemble the picture presented by Vedic and Homeric Greek: the same forms could function as adverbs, adpositions (postpositions), and preverbs. However, the Old Hittite evidence points to nominal origin of some of these forms, e.g., Old Hitt. *andan* 'in' may take – among other case forms – an adnominal genitive. These originally nominal forms in the later stages of the language evolved into adverbs, postpositions, and preverbs (Starke 1977; also Tjerkstra 1999; Luraghi 2000; Brosch 2014).

We can conclude that Vedic, together with Homeric Greek and Hittite, represents a very early stage in the development of adpositions and preverbs, which is probably close to what is to be assumed for Proto-IE. The different processes are also completely independent from one another, as was shown in Section 4. There is still some work to be done on the precise relation between the semantics of the LP and its tendency towards changing its syntactic function. As a preliminary result we can state that LPs with a simple directional or separative meaning do not develop into an adposition in Vedic, since the accusative and ablative may express the goal or source of an action on their own, so that there was simply no need for adpositions. Adposition-like use is only found in LPs whose semantics are more specific than merely denoting source or goal. With the preverbs the situation is much less clear-cut, although there seems to be a tendency especially for LPs denoting vertical movements to complete the transition from adverb to preverb.

Let us conclude with some more general remarks: what is to be gained by studying Vedic local particles regarding their semantic and syntactic properties? On the one hand, the relevance of our research for IE studies lies in getting new insight in the situation of Proto-IE by comparing the results with those of other early attested IE languages, showing Vedic to be a very conservative language with a limited set of word classes. For linguistic typology, on the other hand, our work is relevant by providing a detailed and extensive study showing how language change may lead to the evolving of new word classes beyond the boundaries of already existing categories. During this language change there is a constant interaction of syntax and semantics within grammaticalization and lexicalization processes. Concerning the development of adpositions, we find that only adverbs of a specialized local (or temporal) meaning have an – at least initial – impact on the syntactic construction of LP and noun. We are also able to provide further examples for the established role of desemanticization in grammaticalization processes. Concerning the development of preverbs, on the other hand, the interaction of syntax and semantics is clearly visible within the lexicalization process, especially in cases including valency increase, where both levels are affected in equal measure.

References

Baldi, Philip. 1979. Typology and the Indo-European prepositions. *Indogermanische Forschungen* 84. 49–61.

Behaghel, Otto. 1924. *Deutsche Syntax. Eine geschichtliche Darstellung*. Band II. Die Wortklassen und Wortformen. B. Adverbium. C. Verbum. Heidelberg: Winter.

Bichlmeier, Harald. 2011. *Ablativ, Lokativ und Instrumental im Jungavestischen. Ein Beitrag zur altiranischen Kasussyntax*. Hamburg: Baar-Verlag.

Blank, Andreas. 2001. *Einführung in die lexikalische Semantik für Romanisten*. Tübingen: Max Niemeyer Verlag.

Bortone, Pietro. 2010. *Greek prepositions from antiquity to the present.* Oxford: Oxford University Press.

Brinton, Laurel J. & Elizabeth C. Traugott. 2005. *Lexicalization and language change.* Cambridge: Cambridge University Press.

Brosch, Cyril. 2014. *Untersuchungen zur hethitischen Raumgrammatik* (Topoi Berlin Studies of the Ancient World 20). Berlin & New York: Mouton de Gruyter.

Casaretto, Antje. 2011. Syntax und Wortarten der Lokalpartikeln des R̥gveda. IX: *ánu. Münchener Studien zur Sprachwissenschaft* 65. 7–64.

Casaretto, Antje. 2011[2012]a. Syntax und Wortarten der Lokalpartikeln des R̥gveda. XVI: *áti* und *tirás. International Journal of Diachronic Linguistics and Linguistic Reconstruction* 8. 173–216.

Casaretto, Antje. 2011[2012]b. Syntax und Wortarten der Lokalpartikeln des R̥gveda. XII: *ví. Historische Sprachforschung* 124. 134–177.

Casaretto, Antje. 2012. Syntax und Wortarten der Lokalpartikeln im R̥gveda. XXI: *purás, purástāt und purắ. Münchener Studien zur Sprachwissenschaft* 66. 11–53.

Casaretto, Antje. 2013. Syntax und Wortarten der Lokalpartikeln des R̥gveda. XIX: *prá. Indogermanische Forschungen* 117. 15–74.

Dahl, Eystein. 2010. *Time, tense and aspect in Early Vedic grammar. Exploring inflectional semantics in the Rigveda* (Brill's Studies in the Indo-European Languages & Linguistics 5). Leiden & Boston: Brill.

Delbrück, Berthold. 1888. *Altindische Syntax* (Syntaktische Forschungen V). Halle: Verlag der Buchhandlung des Waisenhauses.

Delbrück, Berthold. 1893. *Vergleichende Syntax der Indogermanischen Sprachen. Erster Theil.* Strassburg: Karl J. Trübner.

Di Meola, Claudio. 2001. Vom Inhalts- zum Funktionswort. Grammatikalisierungspfade deutscher Adpositionen. *Sprachwissenschaft* 26. 59–83.

Dunkel, George E. 1992. Die Grammatik der Partikeln. Rekonstruktion und relative Chronologie. In Robert S. P. Beekes, Alexander Lubotsky & Joseph J. S. Weitenberg (eds.), *Rekonstruktion und relative Chronologie. Akten der VIII. Fachtagung der Indogermanischen Gesellschaft, Leiden, 31. August – 4. September 1987* (Innsbrucker Beiträge zur Sprachwissenschaft 65), 153–177. Innsbruck: Institut für Sprachwissenschaft der Universität Innsbruck.

Elizarenkova, Tatjana. 1995. *Language and style of the Vedic r̥ṣis.* Edited with an introduction by Wendy Doniger. New York: State University of New York Press.

Fleischer, Wolfgang & Irmhild Barz. 2012. *Wortbildung der deutschen Gegenwartssprache.* 4., völlig neu bearb. Aufl. Berlin: De Gruyter.

Fortson, Benjamin W. IV. 2010. *Indo-European language and culture. An introduction.* 2nd edn. Malden, MA: Blackwell.

Fritz, Gerd. 2006. *Historische Semantik.* 2., aktual. Aufl. Stuttgart & Weimar: J.B. Metzler.

Fritz, Matthias A. 2005. *Die trikasuellen Lokalpartikeln bei Homer: Syntax und Semantik.* Göttingen: Vandenhoeck & Ruprecht.

Geldner, Karl F. 2003 [1951]. *Der Rig-Veda. Aus dem Sanskrit ins Deutsche übersetzt und mit einem laufenden Kommentar versehen* (Harvard Oriental Series 63). Reprint. Cambridge, MA & London: Harvard University Press.

Grassmann, Hermann. 1996. *Wörterbuch zum Rig-Veda.* 6., überarb. und erg. Aufl. / bearb. von Maria Kozianka. Wiesbaden: Harrassowitz.

Hackstein, Olav. 1997. Präverb, Post- und Präposition im Tocharischen. Ein Beitrag zur Rekonstruktion urindogermanischer Syntax. *Tocharian and Indo-European Studies* 7. 35–60.

Hagège, Claude. 2010. *Adpositions. Function-marking in human languages.* Oxford: Oxford University Press.

Hale, Mark Robert. 1987. *Studies in the comparative syntax of the oldest Indo-Iranian languages.* Cambridge, MA: Harvard University dissertation.

Haspelmath, Martin. 1997. *From space to time: Temporal adverbs in the world's languages* (Lincom Studies in Theoretical Linguistics 3). München & Newcastle: Lincom Europa.

Haudry, Jean. 1977. *L'emploi des cas en vedique. Introduction á l'étude des cas en Indo-Européen.* Lyon: Éditions L'Hermès.

Haug, Dag. 2009. Does Homeric Greek have prepositions? Or local adverbs? (And what's the difference anyway?). In Vit Bubenik, John Hewson & Sarah Rose (eds.), *Grammatical change in Indo-European languages. Papers presented at the workshop on Indo-European Linguistics at the XVIIIth International Conference on Historical Linguistics, Montreal, 2007,* 103–120. Amsterdam & Philadelphia: John Benjamins.

Heine, Bernd & Tania Kuteva. 2002. *World lexicon of grammaticalization.* Cambridge: Cambridge University Press.

Hettrich, Heinrich. 1991. Syntax und Wortarten der Lokalpartikeln des Ṛgveda. I: *ádhi. Münchner Studien zur Sprachwissenschaft* 52. 27–76.

Hettrich, Heinrich. 2002. Syntax und Wortarten der Lokalpartikeln des Ṛgveda. III: *pári.* In Matthias Fritz & Susanne Zeilfelder (eds.), *Novalis Indogermanica: Festschrift für Günter Neumann zum 80. Geburtstag,* 215–242. Graz: Leykam.

Hettrich, Heinrich. 2007. *Materialien zu einer Kasussyntax des Ṛgveda.* Würzburg: Universität Würzburg, Institut für Altertumswissenschaften / Lehrstuhl für Vergleichende Sprachwissenschaft. http://www.vergl-sprachwissenschaft.phil1.uni-wuerzburg.de/fileadmin/04080400/Materialien.pdf (accessed 30 November 2013).

Hettrich, Heinrich, Antje Casaretto & Carolin Schneider. 2004[2010]. Syntax und Wortarten der Lokalpartikeln im Ṛgveda IV. I. Allgemeines, II. *úpa,* III. *áva. Münchener Studien zur Sprachwissenschaft* 64. 17–130.

Hewson, John & Vit Bubenik. 2006. *From case to adposition. The development of configurational syntax in Indo-European languages.* Amsterdam & Philadelphia: John Benjamins.

Hoffmann, Karl. 1976. *Aufsätze zur Indoiranistik.* Band II. Hrsg. von Johanna Narten. Wiesbaden: Reichert.

Horrocks, Geoffrey C. 1981. *Space and time in Homer. Prepositional and adverbial particles in the Greek epic.* New York: Arno Press.

Ickler, Irene. 1990. Kasusrahmen und Perspektive. *Deutsche Sprache* 18. 1–37.

Krisch, Thomas. 2006. *Rivelex. Rigveda-Lexikon Band 1. Wörter beginnend mit a.* Unter Mitarbeit von Christina Katsikadeli, Stefan Niederreiter & Thomas Kaltenbacher. Graz: Leykam.

Kulikov, Leonid. 2012. *The Vedic -ya-presents. Passives and intransitivity in Old Indo-Aryan.* Amsterdam & New York: Rodopi.

Lakoff, George & Mark Johnson. 1980. *Metaphors we live by.* Chicago, IL: The University of Chicago Press.

Lehmann, Christian. 1983a. Rektion und syntaktische Relationen. *Folia Linguistica* 17. 339–378.

Lehmann, Christian. 1983b. Latin preverbs and cases. In Harm Pinkster (ed.), *Latin linguistics and linguistic theory. Proceedings of the 1st International Colloquium on Latin Linguistics, Amsterdam, April 1981* (Studies in Language Companion Series 12), 145–161. Amsterdam & Philadelphia: John Benjamins.

Lehmann, Christian. 1984. *Der Relativsatz. Typologie seiner Strukturen, Theorie seiner Funktionen, Kompendium seiner Grammatik.* Tübingen: Narr.

Lehmann, Christian. 2002. *Thoughts on grammaticalization – second revised edition* (ASSidUE Arbeitspapiere des Seminars für Sprachwissenschaft der Universität Erfurt 9). Erfurt: Seminar für Sprachwissenschaft, Universität Erfurt. http://www.db-thueringen.de/servlets/ DerivateServlet/Derivate-2058/ASSidUE09.pdf (accessed 30 November 2013).

Luraghi, Silvia. 1989. The relationship between prepositions and cases within Latin prepositional cases. In Gualtiero Calboli (ed.), *Subordination and other topics in Latin: Proceedings of the Third Colloquium on Latin Linguistics, Bologna, 1–5 April 1985* (Studies in Language Companion Series 17), 253–271. Amsterdam & Philadelphia: John Benjamins.

Luraghi, Silvia. 2000. The development of local particles and adverbs in Anatolian as a grammaticalization process. *Diachronica* 28. 31–58.

Luraghi, Silvia. 2003. *On the meaning of prepositions and cases. The expression of semantic roles in Ancient Greek* (Studies in Language Companion Series 67). Amsterdam & Philadelphia: John Benjamins.

Lyons, John. 1968. *Introduction to theoretical linguistics*. Cambridge: Cambridge University Press.

MacDonell, Arthur A. 1989 [1927]. *A Sanskrit grammar for students*. 3rd edn. Oxford: Clarendon Press.

Mumm, Peter-Arnold. 1996. *Parameter des einfachen Satzes aus funktionaler Sicht. Abriß einer onomasiologischen Semantik. Teil I: Relationierung der Lexeme in der Prädikation: Valenz, Numeralität und Aspektualität des Verbs*. München: Lincom Europa.

Oberlies, Thomas. 1999. *Die Religion des R̥gveda. Zweiter Teil. Kompositionsanalyse der Soma-Hymnen des R̥gveda*. Wien: Gerold; Delhi: Motilal Banarsidass.

Pinault, Jean-Georges. 1995. Le problème du préverbe en Indo-Européen. In André Rousseau (ed.), *Les préverbes dans les langues d'Europe: Introduction à l'étude de la préverbation*, 35–59. Lille: Presses Universitaires du Septentrion.

Renou, Louis. 1965. Remarques générales sur la phrase védique. In Adam Heinz, Mieczysław Karaś, Tadeuz Milewski, Jan Safarewicz & Witold Taszycki (eds.), *Symbolae Linguisticae in honorem Georgii Kuryłowicz*, 230–234. Wrocław, Warszawa & Kraków: Zakład Narodowy Imienia Ossolińskich Wydawnictwo Polskiej Akademii Nauk.

Rousseau, André. 1995. Fonctions et fonctionnement des préverbes en allemand. Une conception syntaxique des préverbes. In André Rousseau (ed.), *Les préverbes dans les langues d'Europe: Introduction à l'étude de la préverbation*, 127–188. Lille: Presses Universitaires du Septentrion.

Schneider, Carolin. 2010. Syntax und Wortarten der Lokalpartikeln des R̥gveda. VII: *níṣ*. *International Journal of Diachronic Linguistics and Linguistic Reconstruction* 7. 149–193.

Schneider, Carolin. 2011[2012]. Syntax und Wortarten der Lokalpartikeln des R̥gveda. Teil XV.1: *sácā, sahá*. *International Journal of Diachronic Linguistics and Linguistic Reconstruction* 8. 117–160.

Schneider, Carolin. forthcoming. Syntax und Wortarten der Lokalpartikeln des R̥gveda. Folge XI: *sám*. *Historische Sprachforschung*.

Seiler, Hansjakob. 1960. *Relativsatz, Attribut und Apposition*. Wiesbaden: Harrassowitz.

Speijer, Jakob S. 1886. *Sanskrit Syntax*. Leiden: Brill.

Starke, Ferdinand. 1977. *Die Funktionen der dimensionalen Kasus und Adverbien im Althethitischen*. Wiesbaden: Harrassowitz.

Stiebels, Barbara. 1996. *Lexikalische Argumente und Adjunkte. Zum semantischen Beitrag von verbalen Präfixen und Partikeln*. Berlin: Akademie Verlag.

Svorou, Soteria. 1994. *The grammar of space*. Amsterdam & Philadelphia: John Benjamins.

Tichy, Eva. 1997. Vom idg. Tempus/Aspekt-System zum vedischen Zeitstufensystem. In Emilio Crespo & José Luis García-Ramón (eds.), *Berthold Delbrück y la sintaxis indoeuropea hoy. Actas del Coloquio de la Indogermanische Gesellschaft Madrid, 21–24 de septiembre de 1994*, 589–609. Madrid & Wiesbaden: Reichert.

Tjerkstra, Françoise A. 1999. *Principles of the relation between local adverb, verb and sentence particle in Hittite*. Groningen: STYX Publications.

Traugott, Elizabeth C. & Richard B. Dasher. 2002. *Regularity in semantic change*. Cambridge: Cambridge University Press.

Untermann, Jürgen. 1996. Sprachwandel, beobachtet an lateinischen Präverbien. In Hanna B. Rosén (ed.), *Aspects of Latin. Papers from the Seventh International Colloquium on Latin Linguistics, Jerusalem, April 1993*, 153–168. Innsbruck: Institut für Sprachwissenschaft der Universität Innsbruck.

Van Valin, Robert D. & Randy LaPolla. 1997. *Syntax. Structure, meaning and function*. Cambridge: Cambridge University Press.

Vendler, Zeno. 1957. Verbs and times. *The Philosophical Review* 66. 143–160.

Watkins, Calvert. 1963. Preliminaries to a historical and comparative analysis of the syntax of the Old Irish verb. *Celtica* 6. 3–51.

Witzel, Michael. 1997. The development of the Vedic canon and its schools: The social and political milieu. In Michael Witzel (ed.), *Inside the texts – beyond the texts. New approaches to the study of the Vedas. Proceedings of the International Vedic Workshop, Harvard University, June 1989* (Harvard Oriental Series, Opera Minora 2), 257–345. Cambridge, MA: Department of Sanskrit and Indian Studies, Harvard University.

Ziegler, Sabine. 2012. *Klassisches Sanskrit*. Wiesbaden: Reichert.

Zifonun, Gisela, Ludger Hoffmann & Bruno Strecker. 1997. *Grammatik der deutschen Sprache*. Band 2 (Schriften des Instituts für Deutsche Sprache 7). Berlin & New York: Walter de Gruyter.

Cleo Condoravdi and Ashwini Deo

9 Aspect shifts in Indo-Aryan and trajectories of semantic change[1]

The grammaticalization literature notes the cross-linguistic robustness of a diachronic pattern involving the aspectual categories resultative, perfect, and perfective. Resultative aspect markers often develop into perfect markers, which then end up as perfect plus perfective markers. We introduce supporting data from the history of Old and Middle Indo-Aryan languages, whose instantiation of this pattern has not been previously noted. We provide a semantic analysis of the resultative, the perfect, and the aspectual category that combines perfect and perfective. Our analysis reveals the change to be a two-step generalization (semantic weakening) from the original resultative meaning.

1 Introduction

The emergence of new functional expressions and the changes in their distribution and interpretation over time have been shown to be systematic across languages, as well as across a variety of semantic domains. These observations have led scholars to construe such changes in terms of "clines", or predetermined trajectories, along which expressions move in time. Specifically, the typological literature, based on large-scale grammaticalization studies, has discovered several such trajectorial shifts in the domain of tense, aspect, and modality. Three properties characterize such shifts: (a) the categories involved are stable across cross-linguistic instantiations; (b) the paths of change are unidirectional; (c) the shifts are uniformly generalizing (Heine, Claudi, and Hünnemeyer 1991; Bybee, Perkins, and Pagliuca 1994; Haspelmath 1999; Dahl 2000; Traugott and Dasher 2002; Hopper and Traugott 2003; Kiparsky 2012).

A well-known trajectory is the one in (1). In this shift, morphological markers denoting resultative aspect diachronically generalize to denote the perfect, including the resultative perfect, and later to encompass the perfective as well (Dahl 1985, 2000; Bybee, Perkins, and Pagliuca 1994).

1 We would like to thank the editors, Chiara Gianollo, Agnes Jäger and Doris Penka, for inviting us to contribute to this volume. The paper, which builds on Condoravdi and Deo (2009), has benefited from the comments of Andrew Garrett, Itamar Francez, Andrew Koontz-Garboden, an anonymous reviewer, and the editors Chiara Gianollo and Doris Penka, all of whom we gratefully acknowledge. Deo gratefully acknowledges NSF support (CAREER 1255547, INSPIRE 1248100).

(1) RESULTATIVE ≫ PERFECT ≫ PERFECTIVE

Romance languages and Chinese are familiar instantiations of the successive changes in (1). Our own comparative study of distinct diachronic stages in Indo-Aryan, which we document here, reveals that Indo-Aryan also exhibits these two aspect shifts. This is an empirical claim about Indo-Aryan diachrony which has not been previously made in the literature.

The trajectory in (1) naturally gives rise to the four questions in (2).

(2) a. What is the semantic content of the resultative, the perfect, and the perfective categories?

 b. What logical relation between the meanings of these categories allows the construal of these trajectories as generalizations?

 c. What are the mechanisms that effect trajectorial linguistic changes?

 d. What motivates the change in any particular case?

In this paper we answer the first two of these questions through a close examination of the Indo-Aryan diachronic facts. We propose an analysis that explicates the logical relation between the resultative, the perfect, and the perfective aspects, thus enabling an account of the diachronic pattern as a two-step generalization (semantic weakening) from the original resultative meaning.

The first step towards understanding a particular semantic change is synchronic, empirically adequate analyses of the relevant categories. The second step is an appropriate characterization of the relation between them. Although notions like "generalization", "bleaching", and "extension" have been invoked in descriptions of the resultative to perfect to perfective shift (Bybee, Perkins, and Pagliuca 1994; Dahl and Hedin 2000; Schwenter 1994; Schwenter and Cacoullos 2008, among others), there has been no formally explicit reconstruction of these notions, much less one that embeds them within a semantic analysis of aspectual categories. Moreover, a persistent problem in the grammaticalization literature has been the employment of these notions to answer both questions (2b) and (2c), which are, in fact, completely separate from one another. As Deo (2014: 3) puts it, "neither bleaching nor generalization are construable as the mechanisms that effect language change. These terms can be understood as static descriptions of the relation between the meanings of an expression before and after the change."

The focus of this paper is to provide such a static description of the logical relation between the input and output categories of a particular grammaticalization path. From a semantic point of view, to say that the meaning of an expression gets generalized across two stages of a language is to say that the expression at Stage I entails the expression at Stage II.[2] We show how this is indeed the case for the path in question.

In Section 2 we describe the three distinct stages of Indo-Aryan with reference to the changing meaning of an originally (result) stative morphology, -ta, and establish that it systematically undergoes the resultative to perfect to perfective shift, a fact gone largely unnoticed in the vast literature on Indo-Aryan. In Section 3 we characterize the meanings of the aspectual operators that are involved in the analysis of -ta across the delineated stages. The first diachronic generalization effects a change such that an entailment of the resultative, namely that of the prior occurrence of an event of the type denoted by the lexical predicate, becomes conventionalized as part of the meaning of the operator at a later stage (the perfect stage). The second diachronic generalization associates with the aspectual operator a more general relation for instantiating eventuality descriptions within temporal intervals. In Section 4 we discuss the implications of our analysis for theories of language change. In particular, we touch upon (2d) in the context of Indo-Aryan as well as upon the contrast between the conventionalization of semantic entailments and the conventionalization of invited inferences.

2 Indo-Aryan Stages

2.1 The -*ta* form

The Indo-Aryan branch of Indo-European inherited the deverbal result stative form with the affix -*ta* (allomorph -*na*) (reconstructed for Indo-European as *-*to/-no*). -*ta*, attested at all stages of Old and Middle Indo-Aryan, attaches directly to the root, and the resulting stem is adjectival, inflecting for number and gender like any other adjectival forms. Cognates to the Indo-Aryan -*ta*/-*na* forms include deverbal adjectives in Greek and past participles in Latin (inherited in the Romance languages), Gothic (inherited in Modern Germanic languages), and Slavic. Just like in Romance, Germanic, and Slavic, the -*ta*/-*na* form is non-finite and gets recruited to express aspectual and voice categories of the language's verbal system. It is well-known that, at least in Romance and Germanic,

---

2 Roughly speaking, an expression α_1 entails an expression α_2 of the same type iff α_2 describes a wider set of entities, or times, or circumstances, etc. (depending on their type) than α_1. It follows that if α_1 entails α_2, then the set of entailments of α_1 is a superset of the set of entailments of α_2. Weakening of meaning or generalization is thus reduction in the set of entailments associated with an expression.

paradigms based on this form become central to the expression of past time reference in the language, often replacing older inflectional past tense forms.

For Old Indo-Aryan, the traditional view has it that predicative -ta forms express past time reference and are tightly integrated into the verbal paradigm (similar to Modern French, Italian, and German). This view is based on its uses in Epic and Classical Sanskrit, where it is one of the most common exponents of past tense. However, Jamison (1990) showed that this is not true in Vedic, where predicative -ta predominantly has present time reference and is uniformly stative.

In this paper, we show that the distribution and interpretation of predicative -ta changes between Vedic and the later stages of Indo-Aryan in a particular way. Specifically, we claim that it undergoes systematic expansion, instantiating at three historical stages the three points in the trajectory in (1). We establish this by providing original data for the distinct readings available to the -ta form at each of these stages, and distributional diagnostics, such as the presence of overt agent phrases, compatibility with particular temporal adverbials, use in narrative discourse, etc. The three stages of Indo-Aryan are given in Table 1. The rightmost column gives the texts representative of the delineated periods, from which we extracted the data. Approximate dates are from Witzel (1999), Jamison and Witzel (2002), Alsdorf (1936).[3]

Table 1: Chronology

TIMELINE	STAGE	LANGUAGE	SOURCE
1900BCE–1100BCE	I	**Early Vedic**	Ṛgveda (RV)
1000BCE–200BCE	II	**Later Vedic**	Baudhāyana Dharma Sūtra (BS) Bṛhaddevatā (BD) Bṛhadāraṇyaka Upaniṣad (BAU)
300 BCE–700CE	III	**Middle Indo-Aryan**	Vasudevahiṁḍi (VH)

In the earliest stages of Indo-Aryan (Early Vedic), we find that -ta generally attaches to the root of a change of state verb whose meaning makes reference to a result state. The -ta form has two distinct but related readings. On the first, **purely stative** reading, observed in both attributive and predicative positions, it predicates a stative property corresponding to the verb's result state of the verb's direct object argument, just like the English past participles (e.g., *hide x*

---

3 These are approximate periods and the first of these, especially, only gives the broad window within which Northern and Northwest India were settled (Jamison and Witzel 2002: 6). The composition of the texts that have been used for our research, for the most part, took place in the later parts of each of the three delineated chronological stages.

→ *x is hidden, hidden x*). Despite the restriction to change of state verbal roots with an associated result state, the *-ta* form need not entail the existence of a prior event of the type denoted by the corresponding verb. This is like the contrast between *The town is hidden behind the mountains*, which does not imply a prior hiding event, and *The treasure is hidden behind the mountains*, which commonly implies a prior hiding event. On the second, **resultative** reading, the *-ta* form is in a predicative position and the sentence entails the existence of a prior event of the type denoted by the corresponding verb, just like *The treasure has been hidden behind the mountains*, on the resultative construal of the perfect, implies both a prior hiding event and that the treasure remains hidden at reference time. It is the second reading that is of primary concern to this paper because, as we view it, it is with respect to that reading that *-ta* undergoes semantic change. The distribution of *-ta* forms on the first reading remains constant throughout.

Before we discuss the structure of the semantic change from Stage I to Stage II and beyond, let us introduce the relevant readings by relating them to the readings of the English Perfect and Past perfective clauses.[4] The resultative perfect applies to predicates of events with associated result states and asserts that the relevant state holds at the reference time as a result of an event of the type denoted by the verb having occurred. For instance, (3a) implies that the cake is now in the oven as a result of John's putting it there. The existential perfect applies to predicates of any type and has a backshifting effect: it asserts that the predicate holds at some time before the reference time. (3b) implies the past occurrence of many separate visits to Korea by John. On the universal perfect reading, the predicate is understood to have continuously held throughout an interval stretching from some time in the past up to the reference time, as in (3c). With perfective aspect a predicate is asserted to hold within the reference time. Contrasting with the perfect aspect, a typical use of perfective aspect is in narrative discourse to advance the reference time, compare (4a) with (4b). The English perfect morphology, unlike the German or French perfect, does not express perfective aspect and cannot be used in narratives (de Swart and Molendijk 2001; Pancheva and von Stechow 2004).

(3) a. *John has put the cake in the oven.*

   b. *John has visited Korea many times.*

   c. *John has lived in Korea for the last three years.*

---

4 For discussion of the descriptive issues and analytical choices pertaining to the syntax and semantics of the perfect see Alexiadou, Rathert, and von Stechow (2003).

(4) a. *John iced the cake. He (then) went shopping.*

    b. *#John has iced the cake. He (then) went/has gone shopping.*

At Stage II, *-ta* exhibits the resultative, the existential, and the universal perfect readings, patterning like a familiar perfect marker. In Stage III, while retaining its resultative, existential, and universal readings, *-ta* is also regularly used in narrative discourse and is compatible with past referring definite frame adverbials giving rise to the implication that the described eventuality occurred within the time specified by the frame adverbial. Table 2 summarizes the expansion of readings across the three stages.

Table 2: The readings of *-ta* over time

READINGS	Resultative Stage I	Perfect Stage II	Perfective Stage III
Resultative perfect	√	√	√
Existential perfect	∅	√	√
Universal perfect	∅	√	√
Eventive/Past	∅	∅	√

2.2 *-ta* and the broader tense-aspect system

The Old Indo-Aryan verbal system consists of several paradigms covering distinct combinations of temporal, aspectual, and modal categories (see overviews in Delbrück [1888] 1968; Whitney 1889, 1892; Kiparsky 1998; Dahl 2008; Deo 2012). In particular, the finite verbal system has three forms that convey past temporal reference – the Imperfect, the Aorist, and the reduplicated Perfect. On Kiparsky's (1998) analysis, the system works as follows. The Aorist expresses the resultative perfect and recent past meanings, while the reduplicated Perfect forms "stative presents" for a class of achievement predicates and conveys past reference with other predicates. The reduplicated Perfect, despite its name, encompasses the varieties of the English Perfect that we discussed above, but does not strictly correspond to it because of its frequent use for past time reference. The Imperfect, unlike its Greek and Latin counterparts, is aspectually neutral and allows for both imperfective and perfective interpretations.

The *-ta* form, at this stage, appears much less frequently than in the later stages, and is clearly not part of the finite verbal system of the language. This is different from its status in Middle Indo-Aryan (and throughout New Indo-Aryan), where, following the loss of the older finite forms, it is fully integrated into the tense-aspect system. Modeling this set of changes is beyond the scope of this paper, but see our speculative discussion in Section 4.

Finally, we note that Indo-Aryan, at all stages, is an optional copula language, which means that all non-verbal predicates (including *-ta* forms, which are adjectival) may appear without an overt finite copula inflecting for person and tense. Thus, in the absence of an overt copula, *-ta* predicates appear with only gender and number inflection – distinguishing them from overtly finite verbs. Nonetheless, copula-less clauses are finite and get their temporal reference from context. We treat *-ta* clauses with and without overt copulas as being semantically equivalent. Their increasing integration into the finite verbal system over the history of the language fully supports this view.

2.3 Early Vedic: Stage I

2.3.1 Plain stative and result-stative readings of *-ta*

Much of the literature on Sanskrit treats *-ta* as used to refer to events occurring in an indefinite or proximate past time (e.g., Whitney 1889: 340, 362; Speijer [1886] 1973: 4), or as expressing exclusively the result state of an action (Jamison 1990), or a completed action whose results persist in the present (e.g., Keith 1909: 247). We agree with the latter authors that *-ta* does not have a past perfective reading at Stage I (Vedic), but we distinguish between two *stative* readings available to *-ta* – a distinction in use that has already been noticed by Vedic scholars focusing on the temporal and aspectual semantics of the Sanskrit verbal system (Wackernagel 1954: 583; Delbrück 1968: 385).[5]

These two readings – the plain stative and the result stative reading – are illustrated below in examples (5)–(8).[6] (5) illustrates the predicative uses of the *-ta* form with purely stative readings.[7] In (5a), the *-ta* form predicates of the tree

---

5 The Modern Greek cognate of *-ta*, the participle in *-tos/ti/to*, exhibits only the plain stative reading and contrasts with *-menos/meni/meno* participles which exhibit the result stative reading. For discussion and other references see Anagnostopoulou (2003).

6 We gloss *-ta* as PERF regardless of its distribution and readings at distinct stages of Indo-Aryan. The other glosses are as follows: PRES = present; PST = past; IMPF = Old Indo-Aryan Imperfect; PFCT = Old Indo-Aryan Perfect; IMP = imperative mood; OPT = optative mood; PASS = passive voice; NEG = negation marker; NOM = nominative; ACC = accusative; DAT = dative; INS = instrumental; ABL = ablative; GEN = genitive; LOC = locative; VOC = vocative; M = masculine; F = feminine; N = neuter; SG = singular; DU = dual; PL = plural; PRT = particle; FOC = focus particle.

7 As is often the case in Vedic clauses with non-verbal predicates, including predicative *-ta* clauses, (5a) and (5b) do not include an overt copula, which would explicitly provide tense information. The temporal reference of such tenseless clauses must therefore be established in the context of the text in which they appear. Here we follow the choices made in Geldner's (1951) translation or in Jamison (1990). For the later periods, temporal reference is based on our interpretation of the context.

the state of being fixed/established in a certain location, and it certainly does not imply the existence of any event that resulted in the coming about of this state. (5b) is part of a characterizing description of Maruts (minor storm deities), which enumerates stable attributes of these deities rather than describing a result state obtaining from a prior event. The visors are understood as being in a spread-out position without there being a prior event by which they come to be in such a position.

(5) a. *káḥ   svid   vṛkṣó   **níṣṭh-ito**   mádhy-e   árṇas-o*
   Which   indeed   tree.NOM.SG   fix-PERF.M.SG   middle-LOC.SG   sea-GEN.SG

   yá-ṃ   taugryó   nādhi-táḥ   paryáṣasvaj-at
   which-ACC   Taugrya.NOM.SG   supplicate-PERF.M.SG   cling-IMPF.3.SG
   'Which tree (was it) that *was fixed* in the middle of the sea, to which Taugrya (the son of Tugra), in a state of supplication, was clinging to?' (RV 1.182.7)

   b. *agníbhrājas-o   vidyút-o   gábhastiy-oḥ   śípr-āḥ*
   fire.glowing-NOM.PL   lightening-NOM.PL   hand-LOC.DU   visor-NOM.PL

   *śīrṣá-su   **víta-tā**   hiraṇyáy-īḥ*
   head-LOC.PL   spread-PERF.M.PL   golden-NOM.PL
   'Lightenings glowing with fire are on your hands; visors wrought of gold *are spread* on your heads.'
   (RV 5.54.11)

(6) is an example of a prenominal attributive *-ta* form, derived from the root *su* 'press', that agrees in case and number with the head noun it modifies, *soma*.

(6) *índrāvaruṇā   sutapāv   imá-ṃ   **su-tá-ṃ***
   Indra.Varuṇa.VOC.DU   soma.drinker.VOC.DU   this-ACC   press-PERF.ACC.M.SG

   sóma-ṃ   piba-tam
   soma-ACC.M.SG   drink-IMP.2.DU
   'O Indra and Varuṇa, the pressed-juice (Soma) drinkers, drink this *pressed* Soma.' (RV 6.68.10a)

The plain stative reading of *-ta* forms contrasts with their result stative reading. The latter asserts the existence of a prior event and the result state it brings about. This is the familiar resultative reading of the perfect aspect, where the result state of the event is understood to hold at the contextually salient reference time. This reading of *-ta* becomes salient in the presence of agentive and instrumental phrases, as well as adverbial modifiers of the underlying eventive predication. In (7a) the three short clauses with *-ta* describe three events essential to the preparation of the Soma drink and undertaken in order to offer the drink to Indra. In (7b) the result stative reading becomes salient because of the presence of the agentive phrase. In (7c) and (7d) the result stative reading is again made prominent by the presence of the benefactive dative-marked arguments.

(7) a. *nṛ-bhir*   ***dhū-táḥ***   ***su-tó***   *áśna-iḥ*
         man-INS.PL wash-PERF.M.SG press-PERF.M.SG stone-INS.PL

         áv-yo   *vā́ra-iḥ*   ***páripū-taḥ***
         wool-GEN.SG filter-INS.PL strain-PERF.M.SG
         'It (the Soma) *has been washed* by men, *pressed* with the help of stones, *strained* with wool-filters.' (RV 8.2.2)

    b. *johū́tro*   *agní-ḥ*   *prathamá-ḥ* *pit=éva*
         neighing.NOM.M.SG agni-NOM.M.SG first-NOM.M.SG father.NOM.M.SG=FOC

         iḷáspad-e   *mánuṣ-ā* *yát* ***sámid-dhaḥ***
         worship.seat-LOC.SG man-INS.SG PRT kindle-PERF.M.SG
         'Agni, neighing, the first one, as a father, *has been kindled* by man upon the seat of worship.'
         (RV 2.10.1)

    c. *ayáṃ* *hí* *te*   *śunáhotre-ṣu* *sóma*
         this   FOC you.GEN.SG S-LOC.PL soma.NOM.M.SG

         índra   *tvā-yā́*   ***páriṣik-to*** *mád-āya*
         indra.VOC.SG you-DAT.SG sprinkle-PERF.M.SG delight-DAT.SG
         'This Soma juice *has been sprinkled* among the Sunahotras, in love, for your delight, Indra.'
         (RV 2.18.6c)

    d. *tú-bhyaṃ* ***su-tó***   *maghavan*   *tú-bhyam*
         you-DAT.SG press-PERF.M.SG maghavan.VOC.SG you-DAT.SG

         ā́bhṛ-tas
         offer-PERF.M.SG
         'For you, Maghavan, it (the Soma) *has been pressed*, for you, it *has been offered*.' (RV 2.36.5)

(8) illustrates the two readings of a *-ta* form with the same verbal root *yuj* 'yoke'. In (8a) the state of being yoked is predicated of the bull and the dolphin.

A prior yoking event is inferrable, but arguably not part of the meaning of the sentence. In (8b) the state of being yoked is understood to be brought about by a prior event of yoking, which is clearly what the adverbial modifier *by means of prayer* is associated with.

(8) a. *yád   áyā-taṃ   dívodās-āya   vartí-ḥ ...   revád*
       when   come-IMPF.2.DU   D-DAT.SG   abode-ACC.SG   riches.ACC.SG

   uvāh-a   sacan-ó   rátho   vā́ṃ
   carry-PFCT.3.SG   good-M.PL   chariot.NOM.SG   you.GEN.DU

   *vr̥ṣabhá-ś   ca   śiṃśumā́ra-ś   ca   **yuk-tā́***
   bull-NOM.M.SG   and   dolphin-NOM.M.SG   and   yoke-PERF.M.PL
   'When you (Aśvins) *came to* Divodāsa, (to his) abode, your chariot *carried* rich goods. A bull and a river dolphin *were yoked* to it.'
   (RV 1:116:18, cited in Jamison 1990: ex. [23])

   b. *ā́tiṣṭha   vr̥trahan   rátha-ṃ*
      mount.IMP.2.SG   Vr̥tra.slayer.VOC.SG   chariot-ACC.SG

   yuk-tā́   te   bráhmaṇ-ā   hárī*
   yoke-PERF.M.DU   your   prayer-INS.SG   steed.NOM.M.DU
   'Mount the chariot, O Slayer of Vr̥tra (Indra), your steeds *have been yoked* by means of prayer.'
   (RV 1:84:3)

2.3.2 -*ta* as the resultative operator

We have established that -*ta* has a result stative reading distinct from the plain stative reading, characteristic of its Indo-European origin as a deverbal adjective. Now we proceed to show that, in Early Vedic, as an aspectual operator, it has only the resultative reading and not the larger range of readings associated with the perfect (specifically, the existential and the universal perfect readings). As mentioned in Section 2.2, this larger range of readings is available to the reduplicated perfect at this stage (Renou 1925; Dahl 2008, among others). Moreover, -*ta*, contra most standard grammars, also does not have a perfective reading, with past eventive reference at this stage (contrast with the Aorist, whose perfective status is under no doubt, cf. Delbrück 1968; Hoffman 1967; Kiparsky 1998; Dahl 2008).

A close survey of Vedic data by Jamison (1990) shows that predicative -*ta* forms are uniformly stative at this stage and overwhelmingly make reference to result states (see also Keith 1909: 247). Jamison claims that the vast majority of instances of -*ta* forms without the copula at this stage refer to a present result state. We offer three empirical arguments to corroborate her finding that -*ta* forms do not have existential perfect or eventive readings at this stage.

First, we conducted a small study of Sanskrit verbs (n = 92) for which the -*ta* form is first attested at Stage I.[8] The hypothesis was that the availability (as inferred from attestation) of the -*ta* form at this stage should vary with lexical subclasses, if -*ta* denotes result states. Result states are expected to be more easily accessible with change of state verbs. The study revealed a striking asymmetry between predicates which encode a change of state and those which do not with respect to the attestation of -*ta* forms at Stage I. As Table 3 shows, the -*ta* participial form is attested for 80% of verb roots encoding change of state but only for 10.5% of simple verb roots. This distribution of -*ta* strengthens the case for its being associated with the resultative aspect at this stage.

Table 3: Distribution of a sample of -*ta* forms attested in the Ṛgveda (Stage I)

VERBS	CHANGE OF STATE			OTHERS
	BARE	PREVERBED	TOTAL	
Number of roots	44	10	54	38
-*ta* attested	33	10	43	4
% -*ta* forming roots	75%	100%	**80%**	**10.5%**

Second, we examined all instances of -*ta* forms for some very frequent change of state verbs in the Ṛgveda in order to determine the readings they exhibited in context. This set of verbs is given in Table 4. None of the predicative instances of verbs in this set exhibited the existential perfect or past perfective reading. Although the set of verbs investigated is small, the consistent absence of an existential or past eventive reading for the -*ta* forms in context supports the case for its resultative status.

Table 4: Attested (non-)resultative readings for -*ta* forms of high-frequency change of state verbs in the Ṛgveda (Stage I)

verb	-*ta* form	Count	Existential/ Past reading
su 'press out'	*suta*	58	0
yuj 'yoke'	*yukta*	46	0
idh 'kindle'	*iddha*	30	0
badh 'bind'	*baddha*	15	0
gṛbh 'grasp'	*gṛbhīta*	15	0
vi + tan 'spread'	*vitata*	15	0

---

8 The information for the first attested -*ta* forms for lexical roots and the roots themselves has been gleaned from Grassmann ([1872] 1964) and Whitney (1885).

Third, we investigated the co-occurrence of *-ta* forms with indefinite past referring and frequency adverbials. The reasoning is that if the *-ta* form can trigger eventive reference for the sentence it occurs in, then it should be possible for the predicate to be modified by indefinite past and frequency adverbs. However, this expectation is not met in the textual data. As shown in Table 5, of all occurrences of three representative adverbials, namely *purā* 'of old, earlier', *pūrvam* 'before', and *purudhā* 'often', only one each appear with the *-ta* form, and two of these three instances occur in the part of the text known to be authored much later than the original text (the 10th Book).

Table 5: Past referring adverbials with *-ta* forms

Adverbial		Occurrence	modification of *-ta*
purā	'of old, earlier'	45	1 (RV 6.60.4)
pūrvam	'before, in the past'	8	1 (RV 10.97.1)
purudhā	'often'	9	1 (RV 10.27.21)

We take these facts, together with Jamison's (1990) quantitative study, to show that *-ta* realizes only the resultative aspect at Stage I. The next section discusses the generalization of *-ta* to the perfect category in Stage II, which is the language of Late Vedic (Vedic prose).

2.4 Late Vedic: Stage II

Two changes characterize Late Vedic: (a) the availability of the existential and the universal perfect readings for *-ta* forms; and (b) the extension of *-ta* to lexical predicates which do not encode change of state.[9] The original resultative perfect reading (ongoing result state) is still available to *-ta*, indicating an expansion in the set of readings from Stage I to Stage II rather than a non-generalizing change.

---

9 It is difficult to precisely draw a line of clean separation between Stage I and Stage II corresponding to Vedic verse and Vedic prose. Specifically, there is no exhaustive study of Vedic verbs that establishes that *-ta* appears only with change of state predicates in Early Vedic (Stage I). Nevertheless, *-ta* is overwhelmingly used to describe result states. Early Vedic texts (the Mantras) were composed over a long period and represent multiple linguistic layers. What we are able to clearly show in this section is that Stage III (the period characterized by Middle Indo-Aryan and possibly Epic and Classical Sanskrit) is preceded by a period during which *-ta* functions as the perfect with existential, universal, and resultative readings. At this stage, covering the bulk of the Vedic prose, "the tendency is to assimilate the part.[iciple] to the present" (Keith 1909: 248). This tendency is most clearly visible in the *Dharmasūtras*, the youngest texts within Vedic prose.

The following examples illustrate the existential reading of *-ta*. In (9a), the verb *dṛś* 'see' does not imply a change of state. The sentence with *dṛṣ-ṭa* simply makes reference to a prior seeing of the formulae (the formulae are considered divine, incapable of being written by human effort), not to any result state associated with such a seeing. This is a case where an existential reading is associated with a lexical predicate that does not encode change of state. The existential reading may also be available with lexical verbs that do encode a result state. In (9b) *smṛ* 'teach' can be associated with the result state of successful knowledge transfer. The context provides a description of barley (grains), which are being praised. (9b), in this context, only refers to the pronouncement on the part of the sages regarding the sin-banishing abilities of barley. There need be no implication that any state has resulted from this event; the existential reading is salient. (9c) is another illustration of a sentence with the existential reading, where the *-ta* form is based on the non-change-of-state verb *vac* 'speak'.

(9) a. *mantrā*   *nānāprakār-āḥ*   *sy-ur*   **dṛṣ-ṭā**
      formula.NOM.M.PL various.sort-NOM.M.PL be-OPT.3.PL see-PERF.M.PL

      ye   *mantridarśi-bhiḥ*
      which.NOM.PL seer-INS.PL
      'The formulas, which have been seen by the sages (or seers), may be of various sorts.' (BD 1.34)

   b. *nirṇoda-ḥ*   *sarvapāpā-nāṁ* *pavitra-m*   *ṛṣi-bhiḥ*
      banishment-NOM.SG all.sin-GEN.PL filter-NOM.N.SG sage-INS.PL

      smṛ-tam
      taught-PERF.N.SG
      '(You) have been taught by the sages as the filter (for) banishment of all sins.' (BS 3.6.5.1)

   c. *iti*   *trayā-ṇām*   *ete-ṣām*   **uk-taḥ**   *sāmāsik-o*
      thus   three-GEN.PL these-GEN.PL state-PERF.M.SG general-NOM.SG

      vidhi-ḥ
      rule-NOM.SG
      'Thus, the general rule about these three (Gods) has been stated.' (BD 1.79)

(10) illustrates the use of *-ta* with stative predicates, where the relevant inference is that the state denoted by the lexical verb continues to hold throughout some interval from a time in the past until the reference time. This is the universal perfect reading. The context before (10a) describes how the original father

produced (*ajanayat* Imperfect) seven kinds of foods and how he apportioned (*abhājayat* Imperfect) them. One of these foods (viz. milk) he gave (*prāyacchat* Imperfect) to the animals. Since this apportioning, milk has been the basis for living and non-living beings. The *-ta* modified predicate *prati+sthā* 'rest' denotes the state which has held since the completion of the apportioning event.[10] (10b) is a similar example from a later text with the verb *man* 'think'. In this case too, the belief or thought is considered to have held throughout an interval stretching from a past time up until the present.

(10) a. *ta-smin*   *sarva-ṃ*   **pratiṣṭh-itaṃ**   *yat*   *ca*   *prāṇi-ti*
           it-LOC   all-NOM.SG   rest-PERF.N.SG   which   and   live-PRES.3.SG

           yat   *ca*   *na*
           which   and   NEG
           'On it (milk) everything has rested; that which lives and that which does not.' (BAU 1.5.1)

     b. *loka.saṃgrahaṇa.artha-ṃ*   *hi*   *tad*   *amantr-āḥ*
         world.adultery.purpose-ACC.SG   PRT   then   non.mantra-NOM.F.PL

         striy-o   **ma-tāḥ**
         women-NOM.F.PL   think-PERF.F.PL
         'It is due to their adulterous nature that women have been thought un-entitled to knowledge of the Vedas.'
         (BS 1.5.11.7)

The final example in this section serves to illustrate the continuation of the original resultative reading available to the *-ta* form.

(11) *saṃjñā*   *tu*   *viśva-m*   *iti*   *eṣā*
      term.NOM.F.SG   PRT   collective-NOM.SG   thus   this.F.SG

      sarvāvāpt-au   **nipāt-itā**
      all.comprehensiveness-LOC.SG   lay.down-PERF.F.SG
      'The term *viśvam* (collective) has thus been laid down in (the sense of) all comprehensiveness.'
      (BD 2.134)

---

10 Note that the universal reading of the perfect is absent in several languages, such as Greek and Russian. In these languages, the universal reading is expressed by the present tense forms. *-ta* forms with stative predicates occurring in Vedic prose may often be translated in the English present tense (e.g., Keith 1909). However, the fact that this translation is possible with a form expressing resultative or perfect meaning provides evidence that the form allows universal perfect readings.

2.5 Middle Indo-Aryan: Stage III

The Middle Indo-Aryan languages (illustrated here by their most literarily developed dialect Mahārāṣṭṛī Prākrit) are characterized by a simpler past marking system, having lost most of the inflectional past tense morphology of Old Indo-Aryan. The inflectional system of verbal contrasts in Old Indo-Aryan changed to a relatively morphologically impoverished inflectional system in Middle Indo-Aryan, with loss of most of the past referring categories. Pischel ([1900] 1981), on the basis of careful textual study, reports that the Imperfect, the Aorist, and the Perfect occur in Middle Indo-Aryan texts only as a few scattered forms for a few verbs.[11] Bloch ([1934] 1965: 228–233) reaches the same conclusion. The result of this morphological loss is that -*ta* becomes the default morphology for past time reference. This change is, in fact, also evident from the period of at least the Epic Sanskrit texts from the Old Indo-Aryan stage. So, in addition to its perfect readings retained from Late Vedic, -*ta* exhibits a past perfective reading.

Every study of Middle Indo-Aryan grammar recognizes the perfective use of the -*ta* form as central to its distribution (Pischel 1981; Bloch 1965; Bubenik 1996, among others). In addition to relying on this observation from the literature, we use two distributional diagnostics to argue that -*ta* sentences can be used to describe culminated past events. First, in contrast to earlier periods, -*ta* is the only form available for narrating sequences of past events. In simple narrative discourse, where consecutive sentences typically move reference time forward, verbs in these sentences inflect with -*ta*. Second, in contrast to the earlier period, -*ta* appears with definite past referring adverbials.

The narrative fragment in (12) illustrates the perfective readings available to -*ta*. The main predicate in each of the sentences in (12) is a -*ta* form. The story describes the events before the sacrifice of a goat, beginning with the departure of the family (with their friends and relatives) to the sacrificial stake. Every successive sentence after the first one is understood to describe an eventuality that is temporally ordered after the eventuality described in the previous sentence.[12] Thus, the going (12a) is understood to occur prior to the goat-taking (12b), which is before the worshipping (12c), which is followed by the elders' announcement (12d) and the leaving of the son (12e).

---

11 The single instance of the Imperfect retained in Middle Indo-Aryan is the Imperfect form of the verb *as* 'be' (Pischel 1981: 421–22). The Aorist occurs relatively more frequently (Pischel 1981: 422–24), while the Perfect is preserved only as an archaism for a few verbs.

12 Also see VH:KH 3.10–17, VH:KH 7.7–11, VH:KH 23.8–12, VH:D 29.19–23, VH:D 31.1–8, VH:D 34.18–25 as examples in support of the claim that -*ta* forms allow eventive reference and in narrative discourse are understood to advance reference time.

(12) a. *tato te*   *mittabāndhava-sahi-ā ...*   **ga-yā**
then they.NOM.M.PL friends.relatives-with-NOM.M.PL go-PERF.M.PL
'Then they went there with their friends and relatives.'

b. *chagalo*   *vi*   *ya*   *maṇḍe-uṃ*   *tatth=eva*   **ni-o**
goat.NOM.M.SING also and decorate-INF there=FOC take-PERF.M.SG
'And the goat also was taken there to be decorated.'

c. *gandhapupphamallapuyāvises-eṇa*   *ya*
sandal.flower.garlands.worship.ingredients-INS.SG and

acchi-yā   *devayā*
worship-PERF.M.PL god.NOM.M.PL
'The Gods were worshipped with sandalwood paste, flower garlands,
the ingredients of worship.'

d. *gharamahattara-ehi ya* **bhaṇi-yam** *chagalao*
house-elders-INS.PL and say-PERF.N.SG goat-NOM.SG

āṇ-ijja-u
bring-PASS-IMP.3.SG
'And the house elders said: Let the goat be brought.'

e. *tato ta-ssa*   *putto...*   *chagalay-am āṇe-uṃ* **ga-to**
then he-GEN.SG son.NOM.M.SG goat-ACC.SG bring-INF go-PERF.M.SG
'At that, his son... went to bring the goat.' (VH:D 29.25-28)

The other piece of evidence that the *-ta* form has past eventive reference is
that it may be modified by definite past adverbials. Definite time adverbials
specify particular intervals within which eventualities are realized. The *-ta*
form, when modified in this way, indicates that a completed event obtains
within the time denoted by the definite time adverbial. The impossibility of
modification by definite temporal adverbials is one of the defining features of
the English present perfect. The *-ta* form (which may have present reference
in the absence of tense auxiliaries), on the other hand, can be freely modified
in this way. In this respect, it patterns like the German or French perfect, which
are also observed to have undergone a perfect-to-perfective shift.

(13) a. **tato** *kaiva-esu*   *divas-esu*   *aikkan-t-esu...*
then many-LOC.PL day-LOC.PL pass-PERF-LOC.PL

diṭ-ṭhā   *me*   *taruṇajuvati*
see-PERF.F.SG I-INS young.woman.NOM.F.SG
'Then, upon the passing of many days, I saw the young woman.'

b. ***tamm-i***   ***ya***   ***sama-e...***   *so*   *mahiso*
that-LOC.SG   and   time-LOC.SG   that   buffalo.NOM.M.SG

n̩-eṇa   *kiṇe-uṇa*   ***mār-io***
he-INS.SG   buy-GER   kill-PERF.M.SG
'And, at that time, having bought that buffalo, he *killed it*.'
(VH:KH 14:21)

The following examples show that the earlier perfect readings of the *-ta* form continue to be available at this stage. (14a) illustrates the resultative reading; (14b) illustrates the existential reading, while (14c) illustrates the universal reading for *-ta*. This means that the change involves an expansion in the set of readings available to the *-ta* form.

(14)   a.   *amhe-him̩*   *maṇussajamma-ssa*   *phala-m̩*
         we-INS.PL   human.life-GEN.SG   consequence-NOM.N.SG

         sayala-m̩   ***gihi-yam̩***
         all-NOM.N.SG   grasp-PERF.N.SG
         'We have grasped all the consequence of human existence.'
         (VH:KH 5.8)

     b.   *tubbhe-him̩*   *mamā-o*   *vi*   *airitta-m̩*   *dukkha-m̩*
         you-INS.SG   I-ABL.SG   even   more-NOM.N.SG   sorrow-NOM.N.SG
         pa-ttam
         receive-PERF.N.SG
         'Have you received (experienced) even more sorrow than me
         (at any point in time)?'
         (VH:DH 35.25)

     c.   *kim*   *mann-e*   *devī*   *passamāṇī*
         why   think-PRES.1.SG   lady.NOM.F.SG   watching.NOM.SG

         nicchalcchī   ***ṭhi-yā***
         unmoving.eyes.NOM.SG   stand-PERF.F.SG
         'Why, I wonder, has the watching lady, stood (been standing) with
         an unmoving gaze?'
         (VH:KH 9.7)

3 Analysis

3.1 Preliminaries

In the previous section, we provided evidence for the instantiation of the resultative to perfect to perfective shifts in Indo-Aryan, through the changes in the interpretation of the -*ta* form from Vedic to Late Vedic to Middle Indo-Aryan. In this section we characterize the meaning of the aspectual operators implicated in the analysis of predicative -*ta* forms across the three distinct stages and show how each shift involves a generalization of the meaning of the relevant aspectual operators. We are assuming that saturated clausal predications, sentence radicals, denote properties of eventualities which get instantiated by aspectual operators. Most of our assumptions are standard, but we make a new proposal about the lexical denotation of change of state predicates with associated result states and introduce an aspectual operator, dubbed PERV, whose meaning encompasses that of perfect and of perfective.

Let $\mathcal{E}$ be a domain of eventualities, sorted into a set of events $\mathcal{E}^E$ and a set of states $\mathcal{E}^S$, and $\mathcal{T}$ a domain of non-null temporal intervals (with points as a special case) partially ordered by the relation of temporal precedence $\prec$ and by the subinterval relation $\sqsubseteq$. A function τ from $\mathcal{E}$ to $\mathcal{T}$ gives the time span of an eventuality. Basic eventive predicates have an eventuality argument of the sort E (event); basic stative predicates have an eventuality argument of the sort S (state). Sentence radicals arising out of such predicates then are either eventive or stative predicates. Aspectual operators, such as the perfect and the perfective that we discuss below, apply to such sentence radicals to yield predicates of times within which the properties denoted by sentence radicals are instantiated. Instantiation of properties of eventualities involves the familiar existential quantification over the Davidsonian event variable. In (15) we define how properties are instantiated for both predicates of eventualities and predicates of times.

(15) **Property Instantiation**

$$\text{INST}(P, i) = \begin{cases} \exists e \in \mathcal{E}\,[P(e) \wedge \tau(e) \sqsubseteq i] & \text{if } P \subseteq \mathcal{E} \\ P(i) & \text{if } P \subseteq \mathcal{T} \end{cases}$$

The relation of instantiation (INST) between a predicate of events P and a time interval i holds iff there is at least one event e of type P occurring anywhere within i. The relation INST between a predicate of times P and a time interval i holds iff P holds of i.

We assume that a semantic tense operator, dependent on a contextually determined reference time, instantiates a property of eventualities/times within/at that time. As we discussed in Section 2.2, Indo-Aryan, at all stages, is an optional-copula language, which means that not all predicative -*ta* clauses will have overt morphosyntactic tense. Still, all of them will have semantic tense. There is agreement between the semantic tense and the morphosyntactic manifestation of tense when present. We use the operator TNS indexed to a time variable i whose content is given in (16). The time of utterance Now is always available as a potential reference time, i.e., as a value for i.

(16) Relative to context c and contextual variable assignment g_c,
$$\text{TNS}_i = \lambda P \; \text{INST}(P, g_c(i))$$

We additionally define two notions that we will use in the discussion to follow. The first one is the notion of the temporal correlate $P[i]$ of a predicate of eventualities P, given in (17). $P[i]$ is the set of time intervals that correspond to the time span of any event of type P.

(17) For any $P \subseteq \mathcal{E}$, $P[i] = \lambda i \exists e[P(e) \wedge i = \tau(e)]$

The second one is the notion of non-final instantiation, given in (18). The idea is that $\text{NFINST}(P, j, i)$ holds as long as there is some e of type P within j but before i (a final subinterval of j).

(18) $\text{NFINST}(P, j, i)$ is defined only if i is a final subinterval of j
$\text{NFINST}(P, j, i) = \exists k[\text{INST}(P, k) \wedge k \sqsubseteq j \wedge k \prec i)]$ if defined

To illustrate, suppose that e is an event of type P. Then, in the situation depicted by the picture below, where i is a final subinterval of j, and k precedes i, it holds that $\text{NFINST}(P, j, i)$ since e is within k.[13]

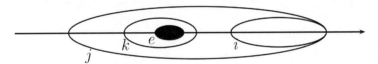

Figure 1: Non-final instantiation: Case 1

By contrast, suppose that we have the situation depicted in the picture below, where i and i' are both final subintervals of j, and that e is the only event of type P occurring within j. Then, because e occurs within i, it does not hold that $\text{NFINST}(P, j, i)$ but it does hold that $\text{NFINST}(P, j, i')$.

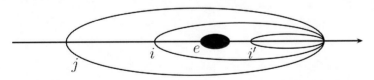

Figure 2: Non-final instantiation: Case 2

---

13 According to (18), $\text{NFINST}(P, j, i)$ would still hold in this situation if there is also an event of type P within i.

3.2 *-ta:* Lexical stativizer and resultative perfect

The ambiguity of predicative *-ta* forms between the **purely stative** and the **result stative** readings that we motivated in Section 2 shows two distinct functions of *-ta*: one as a lexical, derivational operator operating on change of state verbs, the other as a phrasal aspectual operator over sentence radicals. The historical changes under discussion involve the latter function. Below we briefly outline our view of *-ta* as a lexical operator and then go on to analyze its meaning as an aspectual operator. Let us note at this point that our focus in this paper is on characterizing the semantics of the relevant aspectual operators, so as to be able to construe the historical changes as meaning generalization. In our discussion below we identify *-ta* with aspectual operators but this is not essential. In principle, one could also view *-ta* as a morphosyntactic element that agrees with an abstract aspectual operator, rather than directly denoting the operator.

First, let us consider the contribution of the verbs that *-ta* combines with. Based on various kinds of empirical evidence, Kratzer (2000), Piñón (1999) and von Stechow (2003) have made a convincing case that certain eventive verbs have denotations making reference to result state predications. We adopt this idea and implement it in the following way. Change of state verbs are associated with two denotations: an eventive denotation and a paired eventive-stative denotation. Both denotations involve predicates of eventualities in a logical language. A **paired denotation** has a predicate of events as its first member and a relation between individuals and states as its second member.[14]

For example, a verb like *yoke* has a purely eventive denotation, shown in (19a), as well as a paired denotation, shown in (19b).[15] For the sake of concreteness, we have chosen to associate the arguments of eventive predicates via thematic roles and the arguments of stative predicates via the ordered argument method but this is not essential to our analysis. We assume that meaning postulates regulate the identification of arguments across the two predications.

(19) a. $\lambda y \lambda x \lambda e$ put-yoke-on$(e) \wedge$ Agent$(e, x) \wedge$ Patient(e, y)

   b. $\langle \lambda e$ put-yoke-on$(e), \lambda y \lambda s$ have-yoke-on$(s)(y) \rangle$

---

14 Schematically, it is of the form $\langle \lambda e P(e), \lambda x_1 \ldots \lambda x_n \lambda s Q(s)(x_n) \ldots (x_1) \rangle$.

15 The descriptive term for the state predicate in a paired denotation is determined by the event predicate it is paired with. Thus, if the event predicate is as in (a) below, then the corresponding paired denotation would be as in (b).

a. $\lambda y \lambda z \lambda x \lambda e$ connect-to-with-yoke$(e) \wedge$ Agent$(e, x) \wedge$ Patient$(e, y) \wedge$ Theme(e, z)

b. $\langle \lambda e$ connect-to-with-yoke$(e), \lambda z \lambda y \lambda s$ connected-to-with-yoke$(s)(y)(z) \rangle$

Given this schema for lexical denotations of change of state verbs, we can now characterize the contribution of *-ta*. As a lexical operator, *-ta* applies to a verb with a paired denotation and yields an adjective whose denotation is the stative component of the verb's paired denotation. For instance, applying *-ta* to the verb *yoke* would have the denotation in (20). This is just the stative component of (19b).

(20) $\lambda y\lambda s$ have-yoke-on$(s)(y)$

The eventive component of the meaning of the original predicate is not made available for semantic composition.[16] Any implications about the existence of a prior event of the relevant type resulting in the truth of the stative predication are inferential.

Pairs such as those in (19b) are also projected to the syntax and enter semantic composition, where the arguments of the stative predicate will be saturated.[17] The output will be paired eventive-stative sentence radicals. *-ta* in its function as an aspectual operator applies to such sentence radicals. We identify the meaning of *-ta* with that of the aspectual operator RESPERF, which is shown in (21). RESPERF applied to paired eventive-stative sentence radicals yields the temporal correlate of the stative component. This involves instantiation of the eventive and stative components of the pair via **paired property instantiation**, defined in (22). In words, INST^2 holds between a pair $\langle P, Q\rangle$ and an interval i iff there is an event e of type P and a state s of type Q such that s stands in the result relation with e and i is the time span of s.

(21) RESPERF $= \lambda R\lambda i$ INST$^2(R, i)$ defined only if $R = \langle P, Q\rangle$ with
     $P \subset \mathcal{E}^E$ and $Q \subset \mathcal{E}^S$

(22) **Paired Property Instantiation**
     INST$^2(\langle P, Q\rangle, i) = \exists e\in \mathcal{E}^E \ \exists s\in \mathcal{E}^S \ [P(e) \wedge Q(s) \wedge \text{result}(e, s) \wedge i = \tau(s)]$

We assume that for any event e and state s if result(e, s), then $\tau(e) \prec \tau(s)$, and allow for multiple states, with different time spans, to be related to an event e

---

16 As discussed by Koontz-Garboden (2010), the operation effected by lexical *-ta* as characterized here is non-monotonic. However, the purely stative readings observed in (5a–b) necessitate this move. Koontz-Garboden's particular solution to the semantics of derived statives cannot cover these cases.

17 Applying a paired denotation to an individual argument d results in a paired denotation in which d saturates an argument of its stative component. E.g., for a paired denotation with a two place stative predicate:

$\langle\lambda eP(e), \lambda x\lambda sQ(s)(x)\rangle(d) =_{def} \langle\lambda eP(e), \lambda x\lambda sQ(s)(x)(d)\rangle = \langle\lambda eP(e), \lambda sQ(s)(d)\rangle$

via result, i.e., we do not take result to be functional and can thus avoid having to refer to maximal states. Otherwise, we remain agnostic here on how exactly result should be axiomatized, for instance, whether it involves the notion of causation.

The logical form of sentences with a sentence radical $\langle P, Q \rangle$ would be as in (23).

(23) $\text{TNS}_i(\text{RESPERF}(\langle P, Q \rangle))$

The reference time r specified by tense has to be one of the elements of RESPERF $(\langle P, Q \rangle)$. Given that $r \in \text{RESPERF}(\langle P, Q \rangle)$ only if $r \in Q[i]$ (i.e., the temporal correlate of Q), the characteristic entailment of the resultative perfect that the reference time is included in the time span of the result state is captured.

To illustrate, let us consider a somewhat simplified resultative perfect variant of the Vedic (8a), rendered in English as in (24). Its sentence radical would be as in (25), and application of RESPERF would yield (26). Application of tense to (26) with the reference time set to Now would yield (27).

(24)   *The dolphin has been yoked to the chariot.*

(25) $\langle \lambda e \text{ connect-to-with-yoke}(e), \lambda s \text{ connected-to-with-yoke}(s)(d)(c) \rangle$

(26) $\lambda i \exists e \in \mathcal{E}^E \; \exists s \in \mathcal{E}^S[\text{connect-to-with-yoke}(e) \land \text{connected-to-with-yoke}(s)(d)(c)$
       $\land \text{result}(e, s) \land i = \tau(s)]$

(27) $\exists e \in \mathcal{E}^E \; \exists s \in \mathcal{E}^S[\text{connect-to-with-yoke}(e) \land \text{connected-to-with-yoke}(s)(d)(c)$
       $\land \text{result}(e, s) \land \text{Now} = \tau(s)]$

3.3 From resultative perfect to perfect

For any pair $\langle P, Q \rangle$ and any $i \in \text{RESPERF}(\langle P, Q \rangle)$, there is an interval j of which i is a final subinterval such that j contains an event e of type P which precedes i. In other words, the subset relation in (28) holds for the following two sets of times: the set of times in the temporal correlate of Q and the set of times that are final subintervals of intervals within which P is instantiated non-finally.

(28) $\lambda i \text{ INST}^2(\langle P, Q \rangle, i) \subseteq \lambda i \exists j \text{ NFINST}(P, j, i)$

The expanded distribution of -*ta* in Late Vedic, where it combines with verbs of any kind without restrictions, amounts to the conventionalization of this entailment of the resultative perfect as a new meaning for *-ta*. In Stage II then, *-ta* is polymorphic. It is identified with the aspectual operator RESPERF applying to paired property sentence radicals, as in Stage I, but also with the aspectual operator PERF applying to sentence radicals of the regular, non-paired, type. The meaning of PERF is given in (29).

(29)   PERF $= \lambda P \lambda i \exists j [i \sqsubseteq_{final} j \wedge \text{NFINST}(P, j, i)]$

This is, in effect, the "extended now" analysis of the perfect (McCoard 1978; Dowty 1979; Iatridou, Anagnostopoulou, and Izvorski 2001, among others).[18] If *P* is an eventive or stative sentence radical and the reference time is the time of utterance, the meaning of the sentence would be as in (30): *P* is asserted to be instantiated within intervals preceding Now.

(30) $(\text{PERF}(P))(\text{Now}) = \exists j \exists k \exists e [P(e) \wedge k \prec \text{Now} \wedge \tau(e) \sqsubseteq k \wedge k \sqsubset j \wedge \text{Now} \sqsubseteq_{final} j]$

The existential and universal readings are a consequence of the semantic properties of the predicate *P* to which PERF applies; these determine certain relations between elements of *P* and elements of PERF(*P*). To show how the existential and the universal readings arise, we will consider here only PERF applying to eventive and stative sentence radicals, though the same point can be made for temporal properties as well.

Take an eventive predicate *P*. For any $t \in P[i]$, there is a subset $Sub_t(\text{PERF}(P))$ of PERF(*P*) such that for every $t' \in Sub_t(\text{PERF}(P))$, $t \prec t'$. If *P* is empty, then so will *P*[i] and PERF(*P*). This captures the truth conditions of the existential reading of the perfect.

The figure below illustrates the idea. Let t_1 and t_2 be elements of some *P*[i]. That is, they are the time spans of some events of type *P*. Given that t_1 and t_2 have this property, then there are guaranteed to be non-empty subsets Sub_{t_1} (PERF(*P*)) and Sub_{t_2} (PERF(*P*)) of PERF(*P*).[19] The lines above t_1 represent members of $Sub_{t_1}(\text{PERF}(P))$ and those below t_2 represent members of $Sub_{t_2}(\text{PERF}(P))$. All the

---

18 We take the "extended now" analysis to be as follows:

a. PERF$_{XN} = \lambda P \lambda i \exists j [i \sqsubseteq_{final} j \wedge \text{INST}(P, j)]$

This would allow for the existential reading of the perfect with eventive predicates and both the universal and existential readings with stative predicates. As argued in Iatridou, Anagnostopoulou, and Izvorski 2001, the perfect can have both universal and existential readings with stative predicates, and adverbials can disambiguate between the two.

19 Notice that t_2 itself can be a member of some such subset determined by t_1 and that any member of Sub_{t_2} (PERF(*P*)) will also be a member of PERF(*twice*(*P*)).

members of $Sub_{t_1}(\text{PERF}(P))$ begin no earlier than the right boundary of t_1, and equivalently for $Sub_{t_2}(\text{PERF}(P))$. So if the reference time r is, say, one of the elements of $Sub_{t_1}(\text{PERF}(P))$, then it will be the case that $\text{PERF}(P)(r)$ since $t_1 \prec r$.

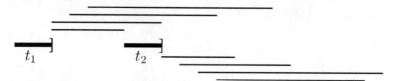

Figure 3: Eventive predicates: existential readings

Take now a stative predicate P that holds over a given time. Given the divisiveness of stative predicates and their temporal correlates,[20] there are $t \in P[i]$ and subsets $Sub_t(\text{PERF}(P))$ of $\text{PERF}(P)$ such that for every $t' \in Sub_t(\text{PERF}(P))$ the convex interval $[t, t']$[21] is itself an element of $P[i]$. If the reference time r happens to be within such a subset of $\text{PERF}(P)$, then the universal reading arises. Otherwise, the existential reading arises. To illustrate this pictorially, let t_1 in Figure 4 be the time span of some state that is a member of a stative predicate P. The lines above t_1 represent some members of $P[i]$, which by the reasoning above are also members of $\text{PERF}(P)$. For a reference time r falling within such a subset of $\text{PERF}(P)$, the universal reading is supported. By contrast, the lines below t_1 represent members of $\text{PERF}(P)$ that are not in $P[i]$. For a reference time r falling within such a subset of $\text{PERF}(P)$, only the existential reading is supported.

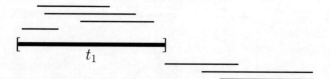

Figure 4: Stative predicates: universal and existential readings

3.4 From perfect to perfective

In the transition from Stage II to Stage III the condition for non-final instantiation is generalized to instantiation and *-ta* is identified with the aspectual operator PERV, whose meaning is given in (31).

---

20 A predicate P is divisive iff its denotation is closed under the relevant subpart relation, such as the subinterval relation for temporal predicates.

21 $[t, t']$ is a convex interval with t as an initial subinterval and t' as a final subinterval.

(31) PERV $= \lambda P \lambda i \exists j\ [i \sqsubseteq_{final} j \wedge$ INST $(P, j)]$

PERV subsumes the readings of PERF and in addition allows for instantiation within the reference time, the hallmark of a perfective reading. As we showed in section 2.5, at Stage III -*ta* is compatible both with the strict perfective reading[22] and with the existential and universal perfect readings.[23] PERV captures all of these kinds of readings.[24] If $i = j$ or if $i \sqsubseteq_{final} j$ and P is instantiated within i, the strict perfective reading arises. This kind of situation is illustrated in Figure 5 restricting attention to e'. Here, the time span of e' is contained within the reference time i, giving us the familiar Reichenbachian semantics for the perfective. Moreover, PERV is also compatible with the perfect reading, as is illustrated in Figure 5 restricting attention to e. In this case, P is instantiated within j but the time-span of e is before i. Thus i is one of the elements of PERF(P).

Figure 5: The generalized perfective

In narratives, sentences with eventive predicates typically advance reference time, so that the following sentence is understood to hold at a later reference time (Kamp 1979; Partee 1984). In this paper we do not work out the dynamics of reference time advancement, but we can assume that in a narrative sequence like that of (12) each sentence is evaluated relative to the reference time set by the context thus far and then resets the reference time to a later time. That reference time is then given as an argument to the temporal abstract obtained by applying PERV to the sentence radical of the following sentence.[25] Suppose that e in Figure 6 is the event of worshipping described in (12c) and that it occurs within the reference time i. Then, the reference time will be advanced to i', where the saying event e' described in (12d) is located. Finally, the reference time is advanced once more to i'', where the going-to-bring-the-goat event e'' described in (12e) is located.

---

22 By this we mean the perfective reading as commonly understood in the literature.

23 The resultative perfect reading is always available, on the condition that the sentence radical has an appropriate paired denotation.

24 This is in contrast to the standard treatments of the perfective, which build on the Reichenbachian $e \sqsubseteq r$ intuition.

25 In this paper we use temporal adverbs as diagnostics for certain readings but we do not provide an analysis of them.

Figure 6: Advancement of reference time

4 Semantic generalization: Implications

We have characterized the meanings of -*ta* as an aspectual operator at the three diachronic stages and demonstrated the semantic relatedness of resultative (RESPERF), perfect (PERF), and perfect+perfective (PERV). This is our answer to question (2a), posed in Section 1. Diachronically, -*ta* undergoes successive generalization of its meaning. This is our answer to question (2b), posed in Section 1. Our proposal rests on the conventionalization of entailed meaning and the generalization of the relation instantiating event descriptions in time. It, therefore, holds promise of application to other instances of this type of cross-linguistic shift.

4.1 Semantic generalization vs. invited inferences

Our semantically-rooted account contrasts with the pragmatic inferencing approach that has been invoked for explaining semantic change (Traugott and Dasher 2002; Eckardt 2006). On this view, pragmatically derived "invited" inferences associated with an expression are diachronically *semanticized* or conventionalized as part of the meaning of that expression. For instance, Eckardt (2006) proposes that the emergence of the prospective aspect in English is the result of the conventionalization of the invited inference of imminent event occurrence available to a transparent *going to V* construction.

On the invited inferences approach, conventionalized meaning is distinct from the original compositionally available meaning and the form may be ambiguous between the diachronically former and latter meanings at some stage. Semantic generalization, by contrast, requires that some element of meaning of the original expression is lost diachronically, resulting in a more general *single* meaning for the expression.

There has been no proposal to date characterizing the trajectory in (1) as involving the conventionalization of some invited inferences. We believe that the lack of such an account is not accidental. Conventionalization of pragmatic inferences is better suited to characterize changes involving the recruitment of lexical categories into the functional domain. The changes of the trajectory in (1), described and analyzed in this paper, involve categories *within* the functional domain. We speculate that the domains of the two types of changes vary along these lines but leave a fuller treatment for further research.

4.2 Motivating semantic generalization

Our account may explain how the diachronic changes involve semantic generalization, but it does not address the motivating factors for the occurrence of each shift. Here we offer some speculative remarks on why the shifts might have occurred. As discussed in Section 2.2, the Old Indo-Aryan finite verbal tense-aspect system (Stage I) contains a number of past referring categories, which overlap with -*ta* in some of their uses. The Aorist expresses the perfective, while the reduplicated Perfect realizes the more general perfect aspect, with stative present readings limited to some predicates. The Imperfect is a neutral past tense, and is often used in narrative contexts and gives rise to an eventive reading (Delbrück 1968; Whitney 1892). In the second stage, the reduplicated perfect generalizes to include the past perfective reading, overlapping in this domain with the Aorist and the Imperfect. By the time of Epic Sanskrit these three past referring categories have become interchangeable and there is an increase in the frequency of the -*ta* form. While this lack of distinction has been well-established in the literature, it is a puzzle why the Imperfect, the Aorist, and the Perfect are interchangeable at the Epic Sanskrit stage. It is conceivable that the writers of the Sanskrit Epics, are, in fact, speakers of a language with a Middle Indo-Aryan (Stage III) type system, characterized by a single perfective form and no further distinctions within the perfective domain. We know that the Middle Indo-Aryan Prakrits were the vernacular languages in the region at least since 300 BCE (based on Aśokan inscriptions). On the other hand, Sanskrit was the learned language of prestige. Middle Indo-Aryan native speakers, whose language was characterized by a single aspectual category that allowed reference to past situations – the -*ta* form – may well have mapped the distinct Vedic paradigms onto this single category, when writing in Sanskrit. This can account for why the three paradigms appear to be undifferentiated in terms of their distribution. It also accounts for the increased frequency in the usage of -*ta* (Avery 1875), an anticipation of the later Middle Indo-Aryan system, where this is the only exponent of the perfective and perfect aspects.

The three finite categories are lost almost entirely by Stage III (Pischel 1981) and their functions taken over by the -*ta* form. At Stage III, -*ta* realizes the complex aspectual category PERV (perfect+perfective) and has the entire range of readings available to the older, lost Perfect and Aorist.

A plausible motivation for this generalization of -ta is the diachronic loss of forms that express perfect and perfective meaning. The semantic shift, thus, may be seen as going hand-in-hand with a morphological change that affects the semantic categories expressed by the broader verbal paradigm of Indo-Aryan. We do not have spontaneous changes in the meaning of -ta but rather these changes are triggered by the need for morphology that can express the semantic categories previously expressed by older forms. This change is, of course, spread over several centuries and must have involved a period over which -ta increased in relative frequency over the Perfect and the Aorist. There is a clear morphological advantage that -ta enjoys over the Perfect and the Aorist: it is built on the root, and constructs an invariant stem that inflects with the set of adjectival endings. The Perfect and Aorist stems involve reduplication and other morphological changes to the root, and the perfect further involves a distinct set of personal endings. The case can be made that the increasing use of -ta is facilitated by its relative lack of morphological complexity and predictable derivation, but that remains a speculative point, and is ultimately orthogonal to the purposes of this paper.

5 Conclusion

Our semantic analysis shows that the trajectory in (1) involves semantic changes that lead to increasingly general aspectual categories, which are arguably part of the universal inventory of functional categories. To the extent that this change is not derived on analogy with any existing patterns in the language, it must be non-exemplar-based in nature. On the other hand, given that the trajectory is robustly attested cross-linguistically, it must be rooted in some (as yet undetermined) universals of grammar. Kiparsky (2012) makes the novel proposal that grammaticalizing changes (at the phonological, morphological, syntactic, as well as semantic levels) can be understood as abstract analogical changes, in which the model for the change comes directly from the structure of universal constraints, rather than from concrete existing patterns. In his words:

> To the extent that there are language-independent constraints defining asymmetries in markedness or complexity, analogy may be driven by those constraints. Analogy can then give rise to patterns which are not instantiated in a parallel exemplar, or even patterns which are not yet instantiated at all. These patterns reflect preferences grounded in UG and/or in pragmatics or perception/production factors. If analogical change is grammar optimization, then the existence of grammaticalization, in this sense, follows as a logical consequence. (Kiparsky 2012: 21)

A more ambitious goal would be to determine the nature of the universal constraints and to specify the language-internal factors that trigger grammaticalization at a particular time. We suggested some factors that might have triggered it in Middle Indo-Aryan. Our proposal makes predictions that can be tested by textual research that traces the changing frequencies of *-ta* and its competitors across time.

Sources

1. BAU: **The Bṛhadāraṇyaka Upaniṣad**. Electronic edition edited by Marcos Albino (corrected by Matthias Ahlborn), available at http://titus.uni-frankfurt.de/texte/etcs/ind/aind/ved/yvw/upanisad/bau/bau.htm.
2. BS: **Baudhāyana-Dharmasūtra**: Electronic version typed and analyzed by Masato Fujii & Mieko Kajihara, available at http://www.cc.kyoto-su.ac.jp/~yanom/sanskrit/dharmas/baudha.dhs.
3. BD: **The Bṛhad-devatā attributed to Śaunaka**: Arthur MacDonell (ed.). (1904). Harvard Oriental Series.
4. RV: **The Ṛgveda**: Electronic edition based on *Die Hymnen des Ṛgveda*, 2nd edition, edited by Th. Aufrecht (1877), entered by H.S. Ananthanarayana, available at http://titus.uni-frankfurt.de/texte/etcs/ind/aind/ved/rv/mt/rv.htm.
5. VH: **Vasudevahiṃḍī of Saṅghadāsagaṇī**: Caturvijaya, Muni and Muni, Puṇyavijaya (eds.). (1930). Atmananda Jainagranthamālā, vol 80–81. Bombay, India: Jaina Atmanandasabha.

References

Alexiadou, Artemis, Monika Rathert & Arnim von Stechow. 2003. Introduction: The modules of perfect constructions. In Artemis Alexiadou, Monika Rathert & Arnim von Stechow (eds.), *Perfect explorations*, vii–xxxviii. Berlin & New York: Mouton de Gruyter.

Alsdorf, Ludwig. 1936. Vasudevahiṃḍī, a specimen of Archaic Jaina Maharastri. *Bulletin of the School of Oriental Studies* 8(2/3). 319–333.

Anagnostopoulou, Elena. 2003. Participles and voice. In Artemis Alexiadou, Monika Rathert & Arnim von Stechow (eds.), *Perfect explorations*, 1–36. Berlin & New York: Mouton de Gruyter.

Avery, John. 1875. Contributions to the history of the verb-inflection in Sanskrit. *Journal of the American Oriental Society* 10. 219–324.

Bloch, Jules. 1965 [1934]. *Indo-Aryan from the Vedas to modern times*, revised by the author and translated from French by Alfred Master. Paris: Adrien-Maisonneuve.

Bubenik, Vit. 1996. *The structure and the development of Middle Indo Aryan dialects*. Delhi: Motilal Banarsidass.

Bybee, Joan, Revere Perkins & William Pagliuca. 1994. *The evolution of grammar. Tense, aspect, and modality in the languages of the world*. Chicago, IL: The University of Chicago Press.

Condoravdi, Cleo & Ashwini Deo. 2009. Aspect shifts in Indo-Aryan. In *Current issues in unity and diversity of languages. Collection of the papers selected from the 18th International Congress of Linguistics*, 2057–2076. Seoul: The Linguistic Society of Korea.

Dahl, Eystein. 2008. *Time, tense and aspect in Early Vedic Grammar: A time-relational approach to the morphosyntax-semantics interface*. Oslo: University of Oslo dissertation.

Dahl, Östen. 1985. *Tense and aspect systems*. Oxford: Basil Blackwell.

Dahl, Östen (ed.). 2000. *Tense and aspect in the languages of Europe*. Berlin & New York: Mouton de Gruyter.

Dahl, Östen & Eva Hedin. 2000. Current relevance and event reference. In Östen Dahl (ed.), *Tense and aspect in the languages of Europe*, 386–401. Berlin & New York: Mouton de Gruyter.

Delbrück, Berthold. 1968 [1888]. *Altindische Syntax*, 2nd edn. Darmstadt: Wissenschaftliche Buchhandlung.

Deo, Ashwini. 2012. The imperfective–perfective contrast in Middle Indic. *Journal of South Asian Linguistics* 5. 3–33.

Deo, Ashwini. 2014. The semantic and pragmatic underpinnings of grammaticalization paths: The progressive and the imperfective. Unpublished manuscript, Yale University.

Dowty, David. 1979. *Word meaning and Montague Grammar*. Dordrecht: Kluwer Academic Publishers.

Eckardt, Regine. 2006. *Meaning change in grammaticalization: An enquiry into semantic reanalysis*. Oxford: Oxford University Press.

Geldner, Karl. 1951. *Der Rig-Veda*. Cambridge, MA: Harvard University Press.

Grassmann, Hermann. 1964 [1872]. *Wörterbuch zum Rigveda*, 4th edn. Wiesbaden: Otto Harrassowitz.

Haspelmath, Martin. 1999. Why is grammaticalization irreversible? *Linguistics* 37(6). 1043–1068.

Heine, Bernd, Ulrike Claudi & Friederike Hünnemeyer. 1991. *Grammaticalization: A conceptual framework*. Chicago, IL: The University of Chicago Press.

Hoffman, Karl. 1967. *Der Injunktiv im Veda*. Heidelberg: Carl Winter.

Hopper, Paul J. & Elizabeth C. Traugott. 2003. *Grammaticalization*. Cambridge: Cambridge University Press.

Iatridou, Sabine, Elena Anagnostopoulou & Roumyana Izvorski. 2001. Observations about the form and meaning of the perfect. In Michael Kenstowicz (ed.), *Ken Hale: A life in language*, 189–238. Cambridge, MA: MIT Press.

Jamison, Stephanie. 1990. The tense of the predicated past participle in Vedic and beyond. *Indo-Iranian Journal* 33(1). 1–19.

Jamison, Stephanie & Michael Witzel. 2002. Vedic Hinduism. Available at http://www.people. fas.harvard.edu/%7Ewitzel/vedica.pdf (accessed 26 February 2014).

Kamp, Hans. 1979. Events, instants, and temporal reference. In Rainer Bäuerle, Urs Egli & Arnim von Stechow (eds.), *Semantics from different points of view*, 376–417. Berlin: Springer-Verlag.

Keith, Arthur B. 1909. *The Aitareya Araṇyaka*. Oxford: Clarendon Press.

Kiparsky, Paul. 1998. Aspect and event structure in Vedic. In Rajendra Singh (ed.), *Yearbook of South Asian languages and linguistics*, vol. 1, 29–61. New Delhi & London: Sage Publications.

Kiparsky, Paul. 2012. Grammaticalization as optimization. In Dianne Jonas, John Whitman & Andrew Garrett (eds.), *Grammatical change: Origins, nature, and outcomes*, 15–51. Oxford: Oxford University Press.

Koontz-Garboden, Andrew. 2010. The lexical semantics of derived statives. *Linguistics and Philosophy* 33(4). 285–324.

Kratzer, Angelika. 2000. Building statives. In Lisa Conathan et al. (eds.), *Proceedings of the 26th annual meeting of the Berkeley Linguistics Society*, 385–399. Berkeley, CA: Berkeley Linguistics Society.

McCoard, Robert W. 1978. *The English perfect: Tense-choice and pragmatic inferences.* Amsterdam: North-Holland Press.

Pancheva, Roumyana & Arnim von Stechow. 2004. On the present perfect puzzle. In Keir Moulton & Matthew Wolf (eds.), *Proceedings of the 43th annual meeting of the North East Linguistic Society*, 469–484. Amherst, MA: GLSA.

Partee, Barbara. 1984. Nominal and temporal anaphora. *Linguistics and Philosophy* 7(3). 243–286.

Piñón, Christopher. 1999. Durative adverbials for result states. In Sonya Bird et al. (eds.), *Proceedings of the 18th West Coast Conference on Formal Linguistics*, 420–433. Somerville, MA: Cascadilla Press.

Pischel, Richard. 1981 [1900]. *A Grammar of the Prākrit languages.* Translated from German by Subhadra Jhā, 2nd rev. edn. Delhi: Motilal Banarsidass.

Renou, Louis. 1925. *La valeur du parfait dans les hymnes védiques.* Paris: Champion.

Schwenter, Scott. A. 1994. The grammaticalization of an anterior in progress: Evidence from a peninsular Spanish dialect. *Studies in Language* 18(1). 71–111.

Schwenter, Scott A. & Rena Torres Cacoullos. 2008. Defaults and indeterminacy in temporal grammaticalization: The 'perfect' road to perfective. *Language Variation and Change* 20 (01). 1–39.

Speijer, Jakob Samuel. 1973 [1886]. *Sanskrit Syntax*, 2nd edn. Delhi: Motilal Banarsidass.

von Stechow, Arnim. 2003. How are results represented and modified? Remarks on Jäger & Blutner's Anti-decomposition. In Ewald Lang, Claudia Maienborn & Cathrine Fabricius-Hansen (eds.), *Modifying adjuncts*, 417–451. Berlin & New York: Mouton de Gruyter.

de Swart, Henriette & Arie Molendijk. 2001. In pursuit of the 'perfect' perfect. Available at: http://www.let.uu.nl/~henriette.deswart/personal/perfect.pdf (accessed 26 February 2014).

Traugott, Elizabeth C. & Richard B. Dasher. 2002. *Regularity in semantic change.* Cambridge: Cambridge University Press.

Wackernagel, Jacob. 1954. *Altindische Grammatik: Die Nominalsuffixe.* Göttingen: Vandenhoeck & Ruprecht.

Whitney, William Dwight. 1885. *The roots, verb-forms, and primary derivatives of the Sanskrit language.* Leipzig: Breitkopf und Härtel.

Whitney, William Dwight. 1889. *Sanskrit Grammar.* Leipzig: Breitkopf und Härtel.

Whitney, William Dwight. 1892. On the narrative use of the imperfect and the perfect in the Brahmanas. *Transactions of the American Philological Association* 11. 5–34.

Witzel, Michael. 1999. Substrate languages in Old Indo-Aryan (R̥gvedic, Middle and Late Vedic). *Electronic Journal of Vedic Studies (EJVS)* 5(1). 1–67.

Anne Breitbarth

10 The development of conditional *should* in English

This paper proposes an account for the development of English "conditional" *should*. It is shown by means of a diachronic corpus study that although *should* already had the conditional meaning in Middle and Early Modern English, *should*-conditionals show an increasing formal tense mismatch between protasis and apodosis over time. The proposed account of the syntax of conditional *should* combines Haegeman's (2010) analysis of conditional clauses with Kempchinsky's (2009) analysis of subjunctives. The diachronic development of conditional *should* is accounted for in terms of Roberts and Roussou's (2003) theory of grammaticalization as upwards reanalysis, combined with a more fine-grained syntactic structure (Cinque 1999). It is argued that *should* shows signs of developing into a conditional marker.

1 Introduction

The present paper deals with an instance of language change at the syntax-semantics interface *par excellence*, namely the development of the "conditional" meaning of the modal verb *should* in English and its incipient grammaticalization as a conditional marker. Like all West Germanic languages, English has a "conditional" use of a modal verb, *should*.[1] This can be illustrated with example (1), where *should* is used in the antecedent of a conditional clause, and does not express a modal, root or epistemic, meaning, but acts more like a marker of "conditionality" (Nieuwint 1989; van der Auwera and Plungian 1998):

(1) *But it shows the immediate chaos that could be triggered if Greece **should** leave the eurozone.*
(http://www.guardian.co.uk/business/2012/may/10/eurozone-crisis-greece-elections [accessed 10 May 2012])

---

1 German uses *sollte(n)* 'should', Afrikaans *sou* 'should', Dutch and Frisian *mocht(en)* 'might', and Southern Dutch (Flemish) *moest* 'must'. The development is furthermore not restricted to West Germanic, cf. Beijering's (2011) study of *må, måtte* and *måste* 'must, may' in Swedish.

Traditionally, the meaning development of modal verbs is viewed as a purely semantic change (e.g. by van der Auwera and Plungian 1998). On the other hand, there are proposals to treat modality in syntactic terms, based on scopal differences between different modal meanings (e.g., Cormack and Smith 2002). The central question the current paper seeks to answer is whether the same constraints, principles and mechanisms that govern syntactic change also apply to semantic change. It will be argued that in the development of conditional *should* in English, given certain assumptions, semantic change and syntactic change are two sides of the same coin. The present paper discusses the constraints, principles and mechanisms involved and proposes an account for the development. This account builds on Roberts and Roussou's (2003) theory of grammaticalization as upwards reanalysis, combined with a more fine-grained syntactic structure as proposed by Cinque (1999).

2 Terminology

Before turning to the development of conditional *should*, I would like to introduce the terminology used in the present paper.

The antecedent (*protasis*) of the conditional construction in (1) is *syndetic*, i.e., marked with the conditional complementizer *if*. The sentence in (1) would be equally grammatical if it lacked a conditional complementizer, that is, if it were *asyndetic*, in which case it would exhibit verb-first word order instead, (2).

(2)   *But it shows the immediate chaos that could be triggered **should** Greece leave the eurozone.*

The type of conditional relation is indicated by the tense and mood of protasis and *apodosis* (the consequent clause). In English, typically, a sequence of tenses holds between them.[2] In (3a), an open or *realis* conditional, in which both condition and consequent are considered possible, the protasis is in present tense, while the apodosis contains the present tense of a modal verb (usually *will*) with an infinitive. (3b) is a *hypothetical* (*irrealis*) conditional. Here, the condition is considered not impossible, but unlikely. The verb form in the protasis is in past (subjunctive),[3] while the form of the verb in the apodosis is *would* (or

---

2 This holds especially in event-conditionals, and less so in inferential or epistemic conditionals (Van den Nest 2010).
3 In English, only *were* is clearly formally distinguished from simple past indicative *was*. In all other verbs, including *should*, past indicative and subjunctive are syncretic.

another modal) with an infinitive. In *counterfactual* conditionals like (3c), the condition formulated in the protasis cannot be fulfilled. The verb in the protasis is in the past perfect, in the apodosis, we find *would* (or another modal) + infinitive perfect.

(3) a. *If Greece leaves the Euro, this will/can trigger immediate chaos.*

   b. *If Greece left the Euro, this would/could trigger immediate chaos.*

   c. *If Greece had left the Euro, this would/could have triggered immediate chaos.*

Conditional *should* is special in that it, albeit formally past (subjunctive), is also able to occur with realis apodoses with *will* + infinitive in Present-Day English. That is, *should* allows a tense mismatch between protasis and apodosis from the point of view of the sequence of tenses, even in event conditionals such as (4), where the sequence of tenses normally encodes the degree of probability of the whole sentence.

(4) **Should** *this year's synod vote for female priests, Bishop Sessford* **will** *not leave the church immediately*
   (BNC: K5G)

It is one of the aims of the present paper to trace the diachronic rise of this possibility and to propose an account for it.

3 Corpus Study

Using a corpus study, the current section traces the development of the conditional use of *should* in English. Although Present-Day English uses only *should* with the conditional meaning in conditional clauses, there is historical variation regarding the modal verbs used with this meaning. In Middle English, *mouen* 'may' (5a) and *moten* 'must' (5b) could have this meaning, besides *shulen* 'shall', (5c).

(5) a. *And* **miȝtest** *þou lacke synne, þen schuldest þou haue God.*
      'And should you lack sin, then you should have God.'
      (CMCLOUD,79.370)

b. *And Vortyger tolde ham, if þat he **moste** bene kyng, as it were þrouȝ tresoun, he wolde make ham richest of þe lande.*
'And Vortyger told him that if he should be king, as it were through treason, he would make him the richest of the land'
(CMBRUT3,48.1447)

c. *and if kniȝtis **schulden** vse the swerd aȝens eny curside men, thei schulden vse it aȝens lordis and prestis principaly, that wolen compelle men, for drede of prisoun and deth, to forsake the treuthe and fredom of Cristis gospel*
'and if knights should/were to use the sword against any cursed men, they should principally use it against lords and priests, who want to compel men, for fear of prison and death, to forsake the truth and freedom of Christ's gospel'
(CMPURVEY,I,43.1884)

As *mocht(en)* 'might' is used as the equivalent of conditional *should* in Dutch, and southern Dutch (Flemish) dialects use *moest(en)* 'must' in this function (e.g., Boogaart 2007), the question of how the 'may' and 'must' modals in the (West) Germanic languages can develop the "conditional" use, and why English (and German) kept the 'should' modal for this purpose, is a highly relevant one. I will defer a more detailed treatment of this question to a separate publication and restrict the focus to English *should* in the current paper.

The data presented in this section are the result of an analysis of Middle, early Modern and Modern English corpora:

(i) Middle English: *Penn-Helsinki Parsed Corpus of Middle English*, second edition (PPCME2) and Middle English Dictionary (MED)
(ii) Early Modern English: *Penn-Helsinki Parsed Corpus of Early Modern English* (PPCEME) and *Parsed Corpus of Early English Correspondence* (PCEEC)
(iii) (older) Modern British English: *Penn Parsed Corpus of Modern British English* (PPCMBE)
(iv) Present-Day British English: *British National Corpus* (BNC).

3.1 Early Modern English

In Early Modern English, as in Middle English, there is a certain variation regarding the choice of the modal in conditionals clauses: Besides *shall/should*, *may/might* is available with a conditional meaning, (6).

(6) a. *if I **mighte** se anie suche inclinacion in you, that leaue to be mercilesse*
         and begynne to be charytable I would then hope wel of you
         (LATIMER-E1-H,23P.47)

    b. *and **may** I find you so fauorable to let me plead my owne case at the*
        bar of your beautie, I doubt not but to vnfold so true a tale as I trust
        will cause you to giue sentence on my side.
        (DELONEY-E2-H,85.486)

Five cases of conditional *may/might* are found in the Early Modern English corpora (PCEEC and PPCEME), besides 131 cases of conditional *shall/should*.[4]

In both asyndetic and syndetic conditional clauses with a form of *shall*, the modal has the "conditional" meaning in virtually all cases, cf. Table 1. Asyndetic conditional clauses are much rarer in the Early Modern English corpora than syndetic ones (only 16% of all conditional clauses with *shall*), but they behave more uniformly: in all of them, the past form *should* is used, while in syndetic conditionals, the modal is in present tense in 28 out of 110 cases (see Table 2 below).

Table 1: Modal meanings of Early Modern English *shall/should* in conditional clauses

	modal meaning	#
asyndetic	conditional	21
syndetic	root	1
	conditional	109
total		131

(7) and (8) are examples for asyndetic and syndetic *shall/should*-conditionals from the Early Modern English corpora, respectively.

(7) *for **should** you weigh it after it were salted, you would be deceiued in the weight*
     (MARKHAM-E2-H,2,113.255)

(8) a. present
         *... with offer that if he **shall** at any tyme be fownd fawtye, he*
         submittith him self to any punishment
         (ELIZ-1570-E2-P2,1.2,278.38)

---

4 *Mouen* 'may' was more frequent in the conditional meaning in Middle English, where I found eight instances of conditional *mouen*, like (5a), vs. five of conditional *shulen* in the PPCME2. Cf. also Van den Nest (2010) on conditional *mouen* in Middle English.

b. past

it were a strange thing if that which accustometh the minde to a
*perpetuall motion and agitation, **should** induce slouthfulnesse*
(BACON-E2-P1,1,10R.114)

There is one instance in which the meaning of *shall* is ambiguous between
"conditional" and a "root" interpretation, (9). The meaning seems to be closer to
'if I **had/were to** speak …' (or 'if it were expected/asked of me to speak') than
to 'if I speak'. The identification of the exact meaning is complicated by the fact
that the conditional marker *if* contributes a conditional meaning itself. Given
that the root meaning is still present somehow, I have opted to classify it as
such, though given the scarcity of such data in the corpus, this example does
not change much with regards to the overall picture.

(9)   *But if I **should** speake of those whiche already be dead, of whom many be*
nowe holy sainctes in heaven, I am very sure it is the farre greater parte of
them that, all the while $they lived, thoughte in his case that waye that I
thinck nowe.
(ROPER-E1-H,95.123)

As mentioned in Section 2, there is usually a sequence of tenses between the
protasis and the apodosis of a conditional sentence in Present-Day English, but
should-conditionals are freer in that they do not need to observe this requirement: *should*, formally past (subjunctive), can be in the antecedent of a realis
conditional, with a present tense modal + infinitive or an imperative of any verb
in the apodosis. In Early Modern English on the other hand, the use of tense on
shall shows a strong tendency to correlate with the type of conditional. As can
be seen in Table 2, all present tense forms of *shall* are found with present tense
modal + infinitive in the apodoses. Past (subjunctive) *should* on the other hand
tends to occur in hypothetical conditionals, though tense mismatches, i.e., realis
conditionals with past (subjunctive) *should* in the protasis, are found in ca. 30%
of all conditionals.[5]

Table 2: The tense of Early Modern English conditional *shall* in different types of conditional

		realis	hypothetical	counterfactual
present	asyndetic	0	0	0
	syndetic	29	0	0
past	asyndetic	5	16	0
		(23.8%)	(76.2%)	
	syndetic	25	54	1
		(31.3%)	(67.5%)	(1.3%)

---

5 The difference between syndetic and asyndetic conditionals is not statistically significant in
this respect (df = 1, p = 0.5975 in Fisher's exact test).

(10a) is an example of a realis conditional with present tense *shalt* (as is [8a]), (10b) is a hypothetical conditional with past (subjunctive) *should*, and (10c) is the one instance of a counterfactual *should*-conditional found in the Early Modern English corpora.

(10)   a.   *and till then, if thou **shalt** think fit, we will sing a Song of Son.*
            (PENNY-E3-H,148.227)

       b.   *yet if one **should** conspire against the whole royal family, when there was no prince of Wales, they would without doubt declare that to be high treason.*
            (BURNETCHA-E3-P2,2,184.181)

       c.   *for if thou **shouldest** haue come, thou couldest not haue got in, because my chamber door was lockt*
            (DELONEY-E2-P1,13.163)

(11) is an example of a conditional sentence with the apparent tense mismatch between protasis and apodosis mentioned above: the past form of *should* in the protasis is matched with a present tense *will* in the apodosis.

(11)   *And lastly, if it **should** miscarry as it seldom doth it will be perceived by Midsummer,*
       (LANGF-E3-H,37.98)

3.2 Modern British English

In the PPCMBE, only syndetic clauses with *shall/should* were found, 112 in total. All instances, whether present or past tense,[6] have the "conditional" meaning, cf. (12a) and (12b), respectively. Other modal verbs are no longer found to express the "conditional" meaning.

(12)   a.   *and if the Plaintiff or Prosecutor **shall** be nonsuit, or forbear further Prosecution, or suffer Discontinuance, or if a Verdict pass against him, the Defendant shall recover treble Costs*
            (STATUTES-171X,5,56.136)

       b.   *But if he **should** refuse it, he could not expect to have it afterwards.*
            (BOSWELL-1776,59.880)

------

6 It should be remarked that 46 of the 47 syndetic realis conditionals with present tense *shall* are from one single text, the *Statutes*. This therefore seems to be a stylistic feature of legal prose at the time.

The instances of a tense mismatch between protasis and apodosis, that is, formally past (subjunctive) *should* in the protasis and a present tense apodosis, have increased from 30% in Early Modern English to 47.7% in Modern British English, as Table 3 shows.

Table 3: The tense of Modern British English conditional *shall* in different types of conditional

		realis	hypothetical	counterfact.
present	asyndetic	0	0	0
	syndetic	47	0	0
past	asyndetic	0	0	0
	syndetic	31	31	3
		(47.7%)	(47.7%)	(4.6%)

Now, formally past (subjunctive) *should* is used in equal measure in realis (13a) and hypothetical (13b) conditionals. It is also used in counterfactual conditionals like (13c), albeit rarely.

(13) a. *and, if any more interior satellites **should** exist, we shall probably not obtain a sight of them*
           (HERSCHEL-1797,34.712)

      b. *if another **should** come in his own Name, you would receive him.*
           (PURVER-NEW-1764,5,40J.371)

      c. *it would have forced the enemy to retire if his attacks **should** have failed*
           (WELLESLEY-1815,860.464)

3.3 Present-Day British English

As the final stage of the development, the situation in Present-Day British English as represented in the BNC was considered. In total, 450 tokens were studied, viz. (a) the first 200 relevant clauses out a search for *should* at the beginning of a clause (". should"), (b) the first 200 relevant clauses out a search for the collocation of *should* following *if* within four words,[7] and all 50 relevant

---

7 The first 200 "relevant" clauses, because the search for *should* at the beginning of a clause also returns V1-questions (e.g., *Should we call the police?*) or elliptical clauses (e.g., *Should've thought about that.*), and the search for *if ... should* also returns indirect questions with deontic *should* (e.g., *I wonder/doubt if I should ...*).

clauses out a search for the collocation of *shall* following *if* within four words.[8] All 400 instances of *should* in conditionals have the "conditional" meaning, while one of the instances of *shall* appears to have a future interpretation, (14).

(14)   *If I can't have her, he thought, I'm damned if he **shall**, either.*
       (BNC: EWH)

The majority of present tense *shall* in syndetic conditionals are from statutory texts and therefore represent the type already seen in the PPCMBE data (12a). This type is exemplified by (15a) from the BNC. (15b) appears to be the only exception from this restriction in text type.[9]

(15)   a.   *If the Buyer **shall** fail to pay for any delivery in accordance with the terms of this contract, the Seller shall be entitled to withhold future deliveries until such payment is made*
            (BNC: J7C)

       b.   *If incoming fire **shall** overload our void shields and damage our Titan, if the feedback dampers **shall** fail too, then a Moderatus will suffer the intense agony of pseudo-injury.*
            (BNC: CJJ)

The correlation between the tense of the modal and the type of conditional in those conditionals in which *shall* and *should* have the "conditional" meaning can be seen in Table 4. There has been a clear shift in the use of formally past (subjunctive) *should*. It is now used in ca. 70% of the cases in the apodosis of realis conditionals, whether they are syndetic or asyndetic. Essentially, the percentages have reversed compared to Early Modern English. *Should* is no longer attested in counterfactual conditionals.[10]

---

8 *Shall* in the beginning of a clause was not searched for given that such a search would only return yes-no-questions with a root meaning of the modal. The only verbs able to appear in verb-first conditionals in Present-Day English are *had, were* and *should* (Van den Nest 2010).
9 Cf. also Van den Nest (2010: 132).
10 Cf. also Nieuwint (1989), according to whom *should* is ungrammatical in counterfactuals:

(i)   ***Should** he have done that, they would have fired him.*

Table 4: The tense of Present-Day British English conditional *shall* in different types of conditional

		realis	hypothetical
present	syndetic	49	0
past	asyndetic	138	62
		(69%)	(31%)
	syndetic	140	60
		(70%)	(30%)

The next section outlines the theoretical assumptions about the syntax and semantics of conditional clauses, and the role of *should* in them, before an account of how *should* could have come to assume this role, historically, in Section 5.

4 Conditional clauses and *should*

According to Bhatt and Pancheva (2006), conditionals are semantically similar to free relatives. Like free relatives, they are definite descriptions, but not of individuals, but of possible worlds, and like free relatives, they are derived by moving a covert operator from the interior of the clause to SpecCP, which functions as the definite binder of the individual variable, (16), in case of conditionals, the world variable w, (17).

(16) *what John bought*
    a. LF: wh_x C^0 John bought x
    b. $\lambda p[p = \exists x[\text{John bought x}]]$
    c. $\iota x[\text{John bought x}]$
       (Bhatt and Pancheva 2006: 654)

(17) *if John arrives late*
    a. LF: OPw C^0 John arrives late in w
    b. $\iota w[\text{John arrives late in w}]$
       (Bhatt and Pancheva 2006: 655)

Haegeman (2010) makes more precise the launch and landing sites of this conditional operator. Based on evidence from English, West Flemish and (Standard) Dutch, she argues that the operator is merged in Cinque's (1999)

Mood$_{\text{irrealis}}$P, a modal/mood projection above circumstantial modals, but below "high" modals (speech act, evaluative, evidential and epistemic modifiers), which are unavailable in conditional clauses. (18) shows the relevant extract from Cinque's functional hierarchy.

(18) Mood$_{\text{speech act}}$ > Mood$_{\text{evaluative}}$ > Mood$_{\text{evidential}}$ > Mod$_{\text{epistemic}}$ > Tense$_{\text{Past}}$ > Tense$_{\text{future}}$ > Mood$_{\text{irrealis}}$ > Mod$_{\text{necessity}}$ > Mod$_{\text{possibility}}$ > Mod$_{\text{volitional}}$ > Mod$_{\text{obligation}}$ > Mod$_{\text{ability/permission}}$
(adapted from Cinque 1999: 76 and 81)

Haegeman (2010: 609–615) argues that West Flemish *moest(en)* 'must' and (Standard) Dutch *mocht(en)* 'might', the equivalents of English conditional *should* in these languages, originate in Mood$_{\text{irrealis}}$. She demonstrates that like high modals such as epistemics (19), conditional *moest* and *mocht* are incompatible with modal complement ellipsis (Aelbrecht 2010), (20), which is fine with root (nonepistemic) modals, (21).

(19) A: *Is   Jan   thuis?*
          be.3SG Jan   home
          'Is Jan at home?'

     B: *Hij **moet**   *(thuis   zijn), zijn fiets   staat   voor.*
          He   must.3SG   home   be   his   bicycle   stand.3SG   in.front
          'He must be, his bicycle is standing in front of the house.'
          (Haegeman 2010: 613)

(20) a. *Hij zal   niet komen, denk ik. Maar als hij*
           he   will.3SG   not   come   think I   but   if   he

           moest   *(komen), ...
           must.PAST.3SG   come
           'He won't come, I think. But if he should come, . . . '

     b. *Hij zal   niet komen, denk ik. Maar **moest***
           he   will.3SG   not   come   think I   but   must.PAST.3SG

           hij *(komen), ...
           he   come
           'He won't come, I think. But should he ...'
           (Haegeman 2010: 613)

(21) *Hij   wilde   niet   komen,   maar   hij   **moest** Ø.*
     He   want.PAST.3SG   not   come   but   he   must.PAST.3SG
     'He did not want to come, but he had to.'
     (Haegeman 2010: 613)

Haegeman argues that in asyndetic conditionals, *moest/mocht* moves to C along with the conditional operator, but stays in Mood$_{irrealis}$ if a conditional complementizer is merged.

I propose to extend Haegeman's analysis to English conditional *should*, with some modifications. Clearly, conditional *should* is not a root modal, as it does not express the bouletic or circumstantial modality *should* expresses outside conditionals, for instance in declaratives (22a) or interrogatives, (22b).

(22) a. *You **should** go to bed now.* ~   'It would be preferable if you went
                                                                        to bed now' /
                                                                        'I want/order you to go to bed now'

      b. **Should** *we call a doctor?* ~   'Do the circumstances require that
                                                                        we call a doctor?'

      c. *If you **should** go to bed now ...*
          ≠ 'If it were preferable for you to go to bed now ...'
          ≠ 'If the circumstances require that you go to bed now ...'
          = 'In case you go to bed now ...'

Conditional *should* can also not be epistemic, given the general unavailability of epistemics in conditionals, cf. (23a).[11] According to Leirbukt (1997), conditional protases typically express a degree of probability, while the locus of epistemic evaluation of this probability is typically the apodosis, hence the felicitousness of (23b).

(23) a. **If he **must** have time, he will help you.*

      b. *If he is sitting in the cafeteria now, he **must** have time.*

---

11 Example (10c) above might look like an example for an epistemic use of *should*, as circumstantial modals do not occur with the perfect infinitive. However, given the incompatibility of epistemic modality with conditionals, (10c) only shows that *should* is a higher modal than circumstantial, it does not prove that it is epistemic.

While *should* can express an epistemic meaning (Copley 2006),[12] (24a), this is not the meaning found in conditionals, (24b).

(24) a. *John **should** be at home by now, unless the train was delayed again.*

b. *If John **should** be at home right now, you could visit him.*

Using epistemic *should* in (24a) means, as Copley (2006: 10) argues, asserting that the proposition expressed is true in the most plausible epistemically accessible world, but that a more informative epistemic state is possible. Conditional *should* in (24b) on the other hand makes no such assertion, in fact, it makes no reference to epistemic states (of the speaker) at all, but to states of the world. Thus quantifying over possible worlds, its semantic contribution seems to be very similar to that of the conditional operator.

These two observations, the fact that conditional *should* does not express bouletic or circumstantial modality and the fact that its meaning cannot be epistemic, suggest that Haegeman's analysis of conditional modals in (dialectal) Dutch as encoding Mood$_{irrealis}$ can possibly be extended to English conditional *should*. Recall that under Cinque's hierarchy of functional projections, root modality is encoded below Mood$_{irrealis}$ and epistemic modality above. Another consideration makes this possibility even more attractive. The meaning contribution of *should* in conditionals is very similar to that of *should* in contexts such as (25).[13]

(25) *If Baden-Powell had had his way, the Boy Scouts might have formed close ties with the Hitler Youth. In 1937, he told the Scouts' international commissioner that the Nazis were "most anxious that the Scouts **should** come into closer touch with the youth movement in Germany."*
(http://www.theatlantic.com/national/archive/2013/01/christopher-hitchens-on-the-mildly-fascist-founder-of-the-boy-scouts/272683/ [accessed 30 January 2013])

Anxious is a predicate that would embed a subjunctive complement in a Romance language such as French, (26).[14]

---

12 I thank an anonymous reviewer for pointing this out.
13 I am grateful to Rachel Nye for drawing my attention to this sort of data.
14 In fact, Haegeman (1986) has proposed that the present subjunctive in complements of predicates of interference (Rau 2009) is in fact an infinitive complement of a silent *should*.

(26) | Cent | cinquante | salaries | à | la | mine | fatiguée | s'étaient |
|------|-----------|----------|---|----|------|----------|-----------|
| hundred | fifty | employees | of | the | look | tired | REFL=were |

retrouvés	à	10 heures	devant	le	vaisseau	amiral	des
found	at	10 hours	before	the	vessel	admiral	of.the

Champs-Elysées.	«On	a	**hate**	que	ça
Champs-Elysées	one	has	hurry	that	this

finisse»,	expliquait	Yaël
finish.SUBJN	explained	Yaël

'One hundred and fifty employees with tired faces found themselves at
10 o'clock in front of the flagship of the Champs Elysées. "We are anxious
for this to be over", explained Yaël.'
(http://www.liberation.fr/economie/2013/05/23/les-gilets-rouges-remportent-
une-bataille_905250 [accessed 19 December 2013])

Furthermore, conditional and subjunctive *should* are semantically similar to
what Leech (1971) has called "putative" *should*, (27).

(27) *It's surprising that she **should** be so late*
      (Bybee 1998: 268)

In both the subjunctive and putative uses, the meaning contribution of *should*
can be characterized as *potentialis*.

These observations are relevant, as they show a similarity between conditionals and subjunctives that goes beyond the superficial. The structure of
subjunctive complements that for instance Kempchinsky (2009) argues for is
strikingly similar to that of conditionals argued for by Haegeman (2010). According to Kempchinsky, there is an operator quantifying over the world variable
in ForceP (an embedded imperative operator in subjunctive complements), an
interpretable world feature introduced in a MoodP between the CP and TP layers
of the clause, and an uninterpretable world feature in Fin, (28).

(28) $V_W \ldots [_{ForceP} Force_{[uW]} [_{FinP} [Fin_{[uW]} OP] [_{IP} (DP) [_{MoodP} [V+T+M_W] [_{TP} \ldots]]]]]$

     selection   checking/Agree
      (Kempchinsky 2009: 1800)

Unlike Kempchinsky's MoodP, the MoodP hosting the world variable under
Haegeman's proposal is Mood$_{irrealis}$, which, if Cinque (1999) is right, is below,
not above the tense projections. From there, the conditional operator moves to
the left periphery where it takes scope over the world variable, (29).

(29)　$[_{CP}$ $[$ C OP_W $]$ $[_{TP}$ $[_{Mood\text{-}irrealisP}$ $[_{Mood\text{-}irrealis}$ *(moest)* $t_W]$ $[_{TP}$ ... $]]]]]$

|_____|

Move

(after Haegeman 2010: 608–609)

I propose a merger of Kempchinsky's (2009) and Haegeman's (2010) proposals to account for *should*-conditionals. I assume that both Fin and Force
bear Kempchinsky's uninterpretable world feature. Unlike subjunctive clauses,
the uninterpretable world feature is not selected by a higher verb in conditional
clauses. I follow Haegeman in assuming that *should* merges in Mood$_{irrealis}$,
below TP(past). I propose that it bears an interpretable world feature and checks
the uninterpretable world features in the left periphery by agreeing with or
moving to Fin. In case no conditional complementizer is merged in Force,
should can move on from Fin to Force, otherwise [uW] in Force is licensed via
Agree (30).

(30)　$[_{ForceP}$ $[$ Force$_{[uW]}$ $[_{FinP}$ $[$ Fin$_{[uW]}$ $[_{TP}$ $[_{Mood\text{-}irrealisP}$ *(should$_{[iW]}$)* ... $]]]]]]$

|_____| |_____|

Agree / Move

As under Haegeman's account, the modal verb moves all the way to C/Force
in asyndetic conditionals. In the next section, I will argue that diachronic
change in the tense of the apodosis can (partly) be understood in terms of an
ongoing upwards reanalysis of conditional *should* from Mood$_{irrealis}$ to Fin along
the lines proposed by Roberts and Roussou (2003) and Roberts (2010, 2012).

5 The grammaticalization of conditional *should*

We have seen in the preceding subsections that *shall/should*, although already
virtually exclusively used in the "conditional" meaning in conditional clauses
in Early Modern English, has undergone a number of changes in this particular
syntactic context. First, it has won out over its earlier competitors, (E)ME *mouen*
'may' and *moten* 'must', which could also express the "conditional" meaning in
older stages of English. Second, it has significantly reduced the connection
between its formal tense and time reference (cf. Roméro 2005). As a consequence, formally past (subjunctive) *should* has become most frequently used
with apodoses with a verb in present or future tense, i.e., there is an ever
decreasing temporal dependency between protases and apodoses in *should-*

conditionals, including in event conditionals.[15] In Section 5.2, I outline a formal account of these two changes based on Roberts and Roussou's (2003) and Roberts' (2010, 2012) theory of grammaticalization as upwards reanalysis.

Another development leading to the rise of conditional *should* is not directly evident from the diachronic corpus data discussed in Section 3, namely the connection between the "lower" bouletic or circumstantial uses of *should/shall* and the "higher" conditional meaning. Comparative evidence shows that "higher" modal meanings, such as epistemic modality, appear later in history than root modality (cf. Diewald 1999 for German and Roméro 2005 for English), and root meanings of modal verbs have in turn developed out of lexical meanings, for instance 'to owe' in case of *shall*.[16] Such a diachronic connection between circumstantial/bouletic, and conditional *should (shall)* is therefore to be expected. I speculate a little more about this connection and a possible account for it in Section 5.3.

Before presenting the account of the development of conditional *should (shall)*, I motivate a syntactic approach to what is traditionally seen as a semantic development in Section 5.1.

5.1 Grammaticalization of modal verbs: semantic changes are syntactic changes

The English modals are already highly grammaticalized even in their non-epistemic uses, and certainly in their epistemic uses in the sense that they have undergone Lehmann's (1995) processes of *attrition* (viz. the loss of their original lexical meanings), *condensation* (restriction of structural scope to bare infinitive), *paradigmaticization* (they constitute a restricted set with highly similar formal properties) and *fixation* (loss of syntactic mobility). In particular the meaning development of modal verbs, which shows repeated attrition, has been analysed as grammaticalization (e.g. by van der Auwera and Plungian 1998), i.e. a development from more lexical ("premodal") to more functional (modal > "postmodal"). The conditional meaning of *should (shall)* discussed in the present paper belongs

---

15 In inferential or speech-act conditionals, independence of the degree of probability of protasis and apodosis is to be expected; cf. Van den Nest 2010.

16 This meaning is still attested in Middle English, as the following quotation from the *Middle English Dictionary* (MED) shows (s.v. *shulen* 1):

(i) *Of his Salerie wiþholde þou nouȝth þat þou* **schalt** *hym with riȝth.*
   'Of his salary you may not withhold anything that you rightly owe him.'
   (*SLeg.OTHist.*[LdMisc 622] 40; c1400[?c1280])

to the "postmodal" meanings in this development (cf. van der Auwera and Plungian 1998: 93; Beijering 2011: 122), besides optative, concessive or evidential.

Evidence for the assumption that the development of higher modal meanings from lower modal meanings and postmodal meanings from modal meanings actually constitute grammaticalization processes comes from studies that have shown that higher modal meanings have appeared historically later than lower modal meanings and postmodal meanings later than modal ones. The development of the 'must' modal in West Germanic is a case in point: it changed from an ability/permission meaning to an obligation meaning, and from there developed the epistemic meaning (Solo 1977; Traugott and Dasher 2002: 122–123). The fact that older modal meanings are not immediately lost, but continue to co-exist with newer ones (for instance, both the root necessity and epistemic necessity meanings of *must* coexist in Present-Day English), giving rise to synchronic gradience, is a common property of grammaticalization processes known as *divergence* (Hopper 1991).

Under a generative approach to understanding language, hierarchical structure is highly important. The principle of compositionality, according to which the meaning of an expression is composed of the meaning of its parts and the way these parts are structurally combined, ensures that meaning corresponds to (hierarchical) structure at least at some level of representation, Logical Form. This connection between hierarchical structure and interpretation is particularly evident under the cartographic approach to syntax (Rizzi 1997; Cinque 1999) that Kempchinsky's (2009) and Haegeman's (2010) proposals adopt, and on which the present analysis is based. The cartographic programme "can be seen as an attempt to 'syntacticize' as much as possible the interpretive domains" (Cinque and Rizzi 2010: 63), and accordingly provides hierarchically ordered structural positions for domains traditionally regarded semantic such as modality.

For the present paper, this means that the basic assumption is that an element with a "more grammaticalized" modal meaning, such as conditional *should* or epistemic *must*, is hierarchically higher than an element with a "less grammaticalized" modal meaning, such as bouletic *should* or deontic *must*. The observed diachronic development from "lower" to "higher" modality therefore corresponds to a structural change from a hierarchically lower to a hierarchically higher position. This is the starting point for Roberts and Roussou's (2003) theory of grammaticalization, which will be applied to conditional *should* in the next subsection.

5.2 The upwards reanalysis of conditional *should*

The aim of the current section is to account for the loss of a sequence of tense between protases with conditional *should* and their apodoses, even where event conditionals are concerned, as in (4), repeated here in (31).

(31) **Should** *this year's synod vote for female priests, Bishop Sessford* **will** *not leave the church immediately*
(BNC: K5G)

I will adopt and adapt Roberts and Roussou's (2003) syntactic approach to grammaticalization, coupled with a more fine-grained clause structure as proposed in the cartographic framework.

The general pattern of change Roberts and Roussou describe is an "upwards reanalysis" of an element as the exponent of a higher functional head, to which it originally moved from a lower position. They write, "the lexical item that formerly realized a lower head has now become the realization of a higher functional head. This can be schematically represented as (...): $[_{XP} Y + X [_{YP} \ldots t_Y \ldots]] > [_{XP} Y = X [_{YP} \ldots Y \ldots]]$" (Roberts and Roussou 2003: 198). This schema is to be read as follows. In an older stage of the language, Y is merged in YP and moves to X. This movement is eventually lost as Y is reanalysed as the new realization of X. This either leads to a lexical split, where the same element can realize X and Y, which is called diversification in the context of grammaticalization, or a new exponent for Y can be found. This upward reanalysis is so common because by assumption, there are economy constraints operative in natural language, and the reanalysed structure is more economical in certain respects. Roberts and Roussou adopt Longobardi's (2001) simplicity metric (32):

(32) A structural representation R for a substring of input text S is simpler than an alternative representation R' iff R contains fewer formal feature syncretisms than R'.
(Roberts and Roussou 2003: 201)

Essentially, in a structure with movement, the moving element is merged with two features, one allowing it to merge in the lower position and one triggering it to move to the higher position. After reanalysis, the formerly moving element has only the feature triggering merge in the higher position.

As seen in the discussion of the corpus data above, conditional *should* tends to not participate in the sequence of tenses normally holding in (event) conditional clauses in the present-day language, and this behaviour has increased significantly since Early Modern English, irrespective of whether we are looking at asyndetic or syndetic conditionals.[17] I take this to indicate that conditional *should* is interpreted in a position above T(past) in such cases.[18] Under Roberts and Roussou's (2003) theory, a very plausible explanation is that the original movement from Mood$_{irrealis}$ to Fin, licensing Fin's uninterpretable world feature, is lost by upwards reanalysis. (33) illustrates how this change works under the proposed analysis.[19]

(33)

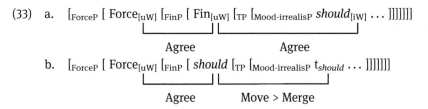

a. [$_{ForceP}$ [Force$_{[uW]}$ [$_{FinP}$ [Fin$_{[uW]}$ [$_{TP}$ [$_{Mood\text{-}irrealisP}$ *should*$_{[iW]}$ ...]]]]]]]

            Agree   Agree

b. [$_{ForceP}$ [Force$_{[uW]}$ [$_{FinP}$ [*should* [$_{TP}$ [$_{Mood\text{-}irrealisP}$ t$_{should}$ ...]]]]]]]

            Agree   Move > Merge

Given that Mood$_{irrealis}$ is above the projections for root modality under Cinque's (1999) account, the question arises how root (bouletic or circumstantial) *should* could have become an expression of Mood$_{irrealis}$. Although these changes are difficult to pin down just relying on the historical corpora available, as the "conditional" meaning was already present in (Early) Modern English, I will at least offer some speculations in the next subsection.

---

17 Note that this is different for all other modal verbs for as far as they can be used in conditional protases at all. While outside conditional clauses, the "core" modal verbs (Mortelmans, Boye, and van der Auwera 2009) no longer express a temporal distinction, even if they historically do, like *can/could* or *may/might*, they do seem to still be subjected to the sequence of tenses in conditional clauses, as seen in (i), while conditional *should* does not.

(i) a. *If I could help him, I would do it.*
  b. **If I could help him, I will do it.*
  c. *If I can help him, I will do it.*
  d. **If I can help him, I would do it.*

Might is in fact not possible in regular hypothetical conditionals at all (iia), only in premise conditionals (iib), in which protasis and apodosis have independent degrees of probability and therefore need not obey the sequence of tenses.

(ii) a. **If I **might** add an opinion, I would/will do so.*
  b. *If I **might** add an opinion, he's not the brightest.*

As for other modals, it is well-known that *would* is ungrammatical in conditional protases in any case. With *must*, it is not possible to see what tense it is.

18 For a similar argument concerning the syntax of epistemic modals, see Erb (2001).

19 In terms of Kempchinsky's (2009) account of subjunctives, this change can be compared to a change from a Romance-style subjunctive with a dependency between Mood and Fin, and subjunctive morphology on the verb in Mood, to a Balkan-style system, with a special subjunctive complementizer in Fin.

5.3 The semantic development of conditional *should* and its syntactic analysis

Traugott (1985: 290–291) observes that typologically, "[o]ne main lexical source for markers of the protasis is words of modality, especially epistemic modality (the modality of possibility and doubt)". Although the input to the development of the conditional meaning of *should* is not likely epistemic, as argued in Section 4 above, *should* is a modal verb, and as will be argued in the current section, the modality of possibility is a plausible input meaning, and there are signs that *should* is well on its way to becoming a conditional marker. In the present section, I take a closer look at the semantic changes likely involved in the development of conditional *should*, arguing that it involves semantic abstraction. This is a typical feature of grammaticalization processes, equalling Lehmann's (1995) attrition, or decrease in paradigmatic weight. I also argue that it is more plausible that such abstraction involves small steps rather than radical reduction of meaning components. I will then extend Roberts and Roussou's (2003) and Roberts' (2010, 2012) account of the grammaticalization of modal verbs, in particular *must*, to conditional *should (shall)*.

In search of the possible "input" meaning conditional *shall/should* might have developed from, let us briefly look at the uses of *shulen* 'shall' in Middle English. Besides the original lexical meaning 'to owe', (34), for instance, the *Middle English Dictionary* (MED) lists a number modal uses of *should/shall* for that period, which can roughly be grouped as bouletic (35), future (36), and (hypothetical) possibility (37). Furthermore, the MED lists what we have called subjunctive uses of *shulen* in Section 4 above, such as (38).

(34) *for3eue me þat I **schal**.*
'forgive me what I owe'
(*Vices & Virtues* [2] [Hnt HM 147]; c1450 [c1400])

(35) *Ech of hem **sholde** helpen oother In meschief, as a suster **shal** the brother.*
'Each of them should help the other in hardship as a sister shall [help] her brother.'
(Chaucer *CT.Mch.* [Manly-Rickert] E.1454; c1395)

(36) a. *This sorghfull king was so bestad That he **schal** nevermor be glad.*
'This sorrowful king was so distressed that he shall never be glad anymore'
(Gower *CA* [Frf 3] 2.1304; a1393)

b. *ȝe ne wite noth wat* **schal** *befalle.*
    'You don't know what will happen.'
    (*NPass.* [Cmb Gg.1.1] 30; a1325[?c1300])

c. *Nous serrons, uous serrez ... we* **chall** *be, ȝe* **chall** *be.*
    '(French) we shall be, you shall be ... (English) we shall be,
    you shall be.'
    (*Paston* 1.153; c1450–54)

(37) a. *I promysyd...To be her protectour in aduersyte That to theym* **shuld**
         fall opon the see.
         'I promised to be her protector in (any) adversity that might befall
         them at sea.'
         (*Ass.Gods* [Trin-C R.3.19] 124; c1500[?a1475])

     b. *Ihc wene þat ihc* **schal** *leose Þe fiss þat ihc wolde cheose.*
        'I suppose that I might lose the fish that I wanted to choose'
        (*Horn* [Cmb Gg.4.27] 39/663; c1300[?c1225])

     c. *Hu* **sulde** *oninan [read: on man]... so manige sunes bigeten?*
        'How could a man (possibly) beget so many sons?'
        (*Gen.& Ex.* [Corp-C 444] 2179; a1325[c1250])

(38) a. *I hope þat þou* **shuldist** *fynde grete comfort in such deuoute wordis.*
         'I hope that you (will/may) find great comfort in such devote words.'
         (*Tree & Fruits HG* [McC 132] 32/4; c1460)

     b. *I am not so hardy ... For to desire that ye* **shulde** *love me.*
        'I am not so presumptuous to desire that you (should) love me'
        (Chaucer Comp.L.(Benson-Robinson) 85; a1500(c1370))

     c. *I prayed hym to, He* **shulde** *besette myn herte*
        'I prayed him that he (should) occupy my heart'
        (Chaucer BD [Benson-Robinson] 772; c1450[1369])

As argued above, there is reason to assume that the conditional and subjunctive meanings overlap. The possibility meaning in rhetorical questions seen
in (37c) is very similar to the use of German *sollte(n)*, the cognate of English
should, in cases such as *Sollte sie wirklich krank sein?* 'Could she really/actually
be ill?', which Diewald (1999: 202, note 32) explicitly compares to the conditional use that *sollte(n)* has in German as well. Note that the possibility ex-

pressed by *shuld* in (37) is not bouletic, but hypothetical.[20] This suggests the possibility meaning as a very likely "input" meaning to the development of conditional *should/shall*. Both the possibility and the subjunctive/conditional meanings lack the element of "speaker's control" that the bouletic necessity and future meanings share (Haegeman 1981), in Early Modern English as well as in the present-day language, (39)–(40).[21]

(39)　*The tenant's adviser **should**, therefore, insist that the requirement be that the tenant **shall** have "reasonably" performed his covenants.*
　　　(BNC: J6R)

(40)　*For convenience of reference I **shall** call this idea of transgression humanist.*
　　　(BNC: A6D)

　　　The future meaning seen in (36) and (40) might therefore be a separate development starting from an earlier lexical split. Given the presence of an element of "speaker's control" in this use, it is more likely to have developed directly out of the bouletic meaning of *shall/should*. The element of speaker's control is not found in the conditional use of *shall/should*, not even in the Early Modern English data (Section 3.1).[22] In the only example in my Early Modern English data with what seems to be a bouletic reading in a conditional clause, (9), *should* has an interpretation similar to *be to* (cf. Lee 2006; Kayne 2012).

　　　As indicated in Section 4 above, however, modal verbs are not only subject to semantic changes, diachronically. Different modal meanings correlate with different syntactic positions in terms of LF scope. I will therefore apply Roberts and Roussou's approach to grammaticalization as upwards reanalysis, expanded with Cinque's hierarchy of modality projections, as sketched for *must* by Roberts

---

20 Note that the use of *shulen* in (37a) is in fact rather similar to the conditional use in that it appears in a relative clause modifying a (determinerless) noun with a free choice interpretation. This seems to be close to "generalising relative clauses" or irrelevance/concessive conditionals with *wh…(so)ever*, which express a condition that is irrelevant for the apodosis (cf. Haspelmath and König 1998; Lühr 1998; Leuschner 2000), and which also use "conditional" *should* already in Middle English:

(i)　*Who so euer **schall** schede mannus blode, þe blode of hym schall be sched.*
　　　'whoever should sheds a man's blood, the blood of this person shall be shed'
　　　(WBible[1] [Bod 959] Gen.9.6; a1382)

21 That the element of "speaker's control" is preserved in the use of *shall* as a future auxiliary is evident in its (prescriptive) restriction to first person singular or plural.
22 Cf. Van den Nest (2010), who approaches the meaning of conditional *should* (and its German equivalent *sollte*) as *Schicksalhaftigkeit* 'fatefulness', indicating the lack of control by any participant.

(2010, 2012), to the development of *should* as an expression of $Mood_{irrealis}$, translating the semantic changes discussed in the present subsection into syntactic changes upward through this hierarchy.

Combining a more fine-grained functional hierarchy with the grammaticalization approach of Roberts and Roussou (2003) has the advantage of capturing two properties often connected to grammaticalization, namely synchronic gradience of grammatical categories and diachronic gradualness of category changes. Although Roberts (2010: 47, note 3) is careful to hedge that the correlation between gradience and gradualness is not straightforward, Roberts and Roussou's (2003: 36) statement that "much of the allegedly continuous or cline-like nature of grammaticalization is due to multiple 'lexical splits'; [whereby] the different readings attributed to a single lexical item correspond to different positions in which it may be merged in the clause structure" is able to cover both synchronic gradience and diachronic gradualness. Multiple lexical splits lead to the association of the affected element(s) to different functional heads, giving rise to gradience. In case of *shall/should*, the old lexical meaning ('owe') continued to exist in Modern English, while the modal could also (already) be associated with higher functional heads.

According to Roberts and Roussou (2003), the grammaticalization of the English modals is the loss of movement to T, with direct merger of the verb in that position, (41)–(42).

(41) $[_{TP}$ T $[_{vP}$ v $[_{VP}$ V $]]]$
      epistemic modals   dynamic modals   lexical verbs
      (adapted from Roberts and Roussou 2003: 47)

(42) English modals:
    i.   Structural change: $[_{TP}$ V+T $[_{vP}$ t_V TP]] > $[_{TP}$ T VP]
    ii.   Parametric change: T^{*}_{Move} > T^{*}_{Merge}
    iii.   Cause: loss of infinitive marker
    (Roberts and Roussou 2003: 195)

(42) says that the earlier movement of the modal verb from V to T was lost, causing T to be realized (symbolized by the asterisk, T*) by Merge instead of Move, as a result of the loss of the infinitival marker. Roberts (2010, 2012) proposes to merge Roberts and Roussou's (2003) Minimalist proposal with Cinque's (1999) cartography of functional projections (cf. [18] above), to achieve a more fine-grained account of the development of modal verbs, and briefly sketches how this may work for the development of *motan>must* as an upwards reanalysis from $Mod_{ability/permission}$ to $Mod_{obligation}$ and from there, $Mod_{epistemic}$.

The development of conditional *shall/should* can be captured in an analogous fashion, building on the synchronic polysemy, or gradience, of *shall/should* at different stages of English. More detailed research would have to confirm that these meanings are indeed also diachronically ordered. If they are, *should/shall* would undergo the steps of upwards reanalysis through Cinque's hierarchy of modal heads seen in (43):

(43)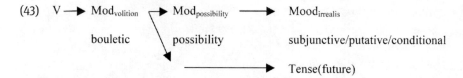

Although Roberts and Roussou (2003) and Roberts (2010, 2012) are not very specific about the details, the development can be thought of as follows. Assuming the meaning components of certain modal meanings, such as "control" (by a force present in the discourse such as the speaker or an unidentified external source), "posteriority", "hypotheticity", or "potentiality", can be equated with their features, as would be a natural extension of the cartographic approach, semantic abstraction can be understood as loss or reanalysis of semantic features associated with lexical items. In the case at hand, the abstraction from posteriority to potentiality is one example. The bouletic meaning expresses speaker's control and posteriority, with speaker's control being the more prominent feature. The prominence of the features is reversed in the future meaning. In the hypothetical possibility meaning, the posteriority component is reanalysed as hypotheticity, as posteriority identifies an event as unrealized. In case of the subjunctive and conditional meanings, the hypotheticity is reanalysed as potentiality.

The abstraction process itself may be cognitive; the meanings might for instance be in subset or metaphorical relations, such as posteriority > unrealized event = hypotheticity. But as Roberts and Roussou in the quote above state, "different readings attributed to a single lexical item correspond to different positions in which it may be merged in the clause structure", and different modal meanings demonstrably have different scopal properties, pointing to different hierarchical positions. It can therefore be assumed that movement to higher positions becomes possible as a consequence of the semantic abstraction. This movement may at first be optional, but the co-existence of (pre-/post-)modal meanings that show little overlap in their meaning components indicates that we really are dealing with a lexical split after an upward reanalysis: the old item continues to be merged low, the new one is directly merged high, without movement from a lower position.

A potential problem is the locality of the relations between these positions, cf. also Roberts (2012: 359; note 5). For instance, on Cinque's hierarchy, $Mod_{necessity}$ intervenes between $Mod_{possibility}$ and $Mood_{irrealis}$, and $Tense_{future}$ is several functional heads removed from $Mod_{volitional}$. The question is why a higher head should be able to attract an element across a number of intervening heads without creating intervention effects, that is, it needs to be explained why the element undergoing the grammaticalization in question does not go through a stage at which it is first-merged in an intermediate position, given Cinque's hierarchy. Roberts proposes to distinguish substantive functional features (e.g. Asp or Mod) from formal functional features (e.g. [v] or [φ]). The former make up the functional hierarchy, under the bare-phrase-structure view (Chomsky 1995) that "[e]ach head can be simply seen as a feature that is able to autonomously merge into the structure, creating and labelling a category consisting of itself and its structural (presumably selected) complement" (Roberts 2012: 356). The latter trigger Agree and Move relations. In principle, locality of Agree and Move does not have to be given up if it can be appropriately relativized.

The present proposal also offers an account for *should/shall* winning out over its earlier competitors *mouen* 'may' and *moten* 'must' for the conditional meaning (Section 3.1). As I argued above that the development of conditional *should* is an instance of grammaticalization, this process can be identified as Lehmann's (1995) *obligatorification*, or decreased paradigmatic variability. Initially, any modal verb in $Mood_{possibility}$, that is, with compatible feature content, could move to $Mood_{irrealis}$ and thus license the world feature in Fin. ME *mouen*, for instance, had a "weakened" possibility meaning (besides the root dynamic meaning), according to the MED, "in which the ability or potentiality becomes mere possibility, or is made contingent upon something else". The dictionary quotes examples such as those in (44).

(44) a. *Þou **myȝtest** han ben a greth lording.*
          'You might have been a great ruler.'
          (*St.Alex.*[1] [LdMisc 108] 71/511; a1350)

    b. *Heþen þow **mayt** gangen to late.*
          'You may go too late from here'
          'Perhaps/possibly you are going too late from here'
          (*Havelok* [LdMisc 108] 845; c1300)

That is, both *shulen > shall* and *mouen > may* were arguably available to move from $Mod_{possibility}$ in Middle English and Early Modern English in conditional clauses. In addition to the hypothetical possibility use, however, *shulen* had its subjunctive or potentialis use, which *mouen* lacked. The fact that potential *shulen* in Modern English was restricted to certain types of embedded clauses points at Cinque's Mood$_{irrealis}$ as the "stepstone" for the grammaticalization of the conditional use of *shulen > shall/should*. As this head is closer to the target position above Tense than Mod$_{possibility}$ on Cinque's hierarchy, the movement to be reanalysed in the upwards reanalysis had to cover a shorter distance, which under considerations of economy, recognized as playing an important role in all recent formal approaches to grammaticalization (Roberts and Roussou 2003; van Gelderen 2011), is expected to be preferred, (45).

(45) [$_{CP}$ ... [$_{FinP}$ ... [$_{TP}$ ... [$_{Mood-irrealisP}$ ... [$_{Mod-possP}$ ... [...]]]]]]

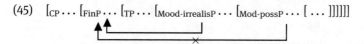

The final observation that could be made on the basis of the diachronic data in Section 3 is that there is a significant diachronic increase in the number of cases with a "tense mismatch" between the protasis and the apodosis in that in the present-day language, formally past (subjunctive) *should* is used most frequently in the protasis of realis conditionals. Historically, it was used more frequently in the protasis of hypothetical conditionals, as expected given that normally, a sequence of tenses holds between protasis and apodosis. I propose to analyse this observation as a sign that *should* is established as a new conditional marker. This process has not come to its conclusion yet, as the modal still takes an infinitival complement, and hence heads the clause. Once it becomes a C-element, one would expect that the verb that was originally selected by the modal *should* show finite morphology. This may, however, be a protracted process. Estonian for instance expresses negation by an invariant negative auxiliary that has historically lost all its finiteness features (unlike other Uralic languages, such as Finnish or North Sámi, where the negative auxiliary still inflects for person and number), followed by the infinitive of the main verb. That is, the loss of finiteness features on the grammaticalizing auxiliary has not (yet) led to the expression of person and number on the lexical verb in Estonian. Under the cartographic approach, finiteness is represented high, in the lowest head of the C-domain (Rizzi 1997). This is above the domain of mood and modality in Cinque's hierarchy. It is therefore theoretically not impossible for a head being reanalysed from Mood$_{irrealis}$ to a head in the C-domain to continue to express finiteness information. There are, however, indications that this process may have progressed further in certain varieties of English, such as spoken American usage. Trousdale (2012) quotes examples from internet forums such as (46).

(46) **Should** *Obama* <u>*gets*</u> *the nomination, my vote goes to John McCain* ...
      (Trousdale 2012: 173)

Crucially, the lexical verb (*gets*) is finite in (46), pointing at *should* coming to be used simply as a conditional marker on a par with *if*, possibly modelled on *say* (as in *say Obama gets the nomination* ...; Trousdale 2012). Clearly, this reanalysis can happen first in asyndetic conditionals in which no other overt conditional marker is present and in which the verb fronting to the initial position can with Haegeman (2010) be understood as the modal moving along with the covert conditional operator from Mood$_{irrealis}$ to its scope position in the C-domain.

6 Conclusion

In the present paper, I have presented evidence from three periods of English for the development of the conditional use of the modal *shall/should*. While available already in Early Modern English (and, in fact, Middle English, which was not systematically researched), we witnessed a number of changes in the use of conditional *shall/should*. The use of present tense *shall* was restricted to a certain text type, viz. statutory texts, after Early Modern English. In consequence, formally past (subjunctive) *should* extends its use also to protases of realis conditionals. While in Early Modern English, only 30% of these used *should*, compared to 70% of the protases of hypothetical conditionals, the percentages were found to be essentially reversed in Present-Day British English. I argued in Section 5 that this is the result of the ongoing grammaticalization of *should* as a new pure conditional marker.

I further proposed a formal syntactic analysis of conditional *shall/should* and presented an account of the most likely grammaticalization path leading to the present-day syntactic position of conditional *shall/should*. Assuming that hierarchical syntactic structure is motivated by compositionality, that is, LF-scope requirements, I argued in Section 5 that the syntax and semantics of the conditional modal change in lockstep. Semantically, the meaning of the modal is subject to attrition or abstraction of its meaning components. Syntactically, different modal meanings are associated with different hierarchical positions. The rise of new (post)modal meanings was described as upwards reanalysis in consequence of an economy principle preferring direct merge over re-merge (movement) (Roberts and Roussou 2003; van Gelderen 2011). Semantic change in a modal verb therefore is tightly connected to syntactic change.

Sources

[BNC]
(1980s–1993)
The British National Corpus, version 3 (BNC XML Edition). 2007. Distributed by Oxford University
    Computing Services on behalf of the BNC Consortium. http://www.natcorp.ox.ac.uk/
    [Searched with the web interface of Brigham Young University: http://corpus.byu.edu/bnc/]
[MED]
(1100–1500)
Middle English Dictionary, online version. http://quod.lib.umich.edu/m/med/
[PCEEC]
(ca. 1410–1681)
Parsed Corpus of Early English Correspondence, parsed version. 2006. Annotated by Ann Taylor,
    Arja Nurmi, Anthony Warner, Susan Pintzuk & Terttu Nevalainen. Compiled by the CEEC
    Project Team. York: University of York & Helsinki: University of Helsinki. Distributed
    through the Oxford Text Archive. http://www-users.york.ac.uk/~lang22/PCEEC-manual/
[PPCEME]
(1500–1710)
Kroch, Anthony, Beatrice Santorini & Ariel Diertani. 2004. *Penn-Helsinki Parsed Corpus of Early
    Modern English*. http://www.ling.upenn.edu/hist-corpora/PPCEME-RELEASE-2/index.html
[PPCMBE]
(1700–1914)
Kroch, Anthony, Beatrice Santorini & Ariel Diertani. 2010. *Penn Parsed Corpus of Modern
    British English*. http://www.ling.upenn.edu/hist-corpora/PPCMBE-RELEASE-1/index.html
[PPCME2]
(1150–1420)
Kroch, Anthony & Ann Taylor. 2000. *Penn-Helsinki Parsed Corpus of Middle English*, second
    edition. http://www.ling.upenn.edu/histcorpora/PPCME2-RELEASE-3/index.html

References

Aelbrecht, Lobke. 2010. *The syntactic licensing of ellipsis*. Amsterdam & Philadelphia: John
    Benjamins.
van der Auwera, Johan & Vladimir A. Plungian. 1998. Modality's semantic map. *Linguistic Typology*
    2. 79–124.
Beijering, Karin. 2011. Semantic change and grammaticalization: The development of modal
    and postmodal meanings in Mainland Scandinavian *må, måtte* and *måste*. *Nordic Journal
    of Linguistics* 32(2). 105–132.
Bhatt, Rajesh & Roumyana Pancheva. 2006. Conditionals. In Martin Everaert & Henk van Riems-
    dijk (eds.), *The Blackwell companion to syntax*, vol. 1, 638–687. Oxford: Blackwell.
Boogaart, Ronny. 2007. Conditionele constructies met *moest(en)* en *mocht(en)* in Belgisch-
    Nederlands en Nederlands-Nederlands. *Neerlandistiek.nl* 2007(07.05). http://www.meertens.
    knaw.nl/neerlandistiek/ (accessed 23 June 2014).

Bybee, Joan. 1998. "Irrealis" as a grammatical category. *Anthropological Linguistics* 40. 257–271.

Chomsky, Noam. 1995. Bare phrase structure. In Gert Webelhuth (ed.), *Government and binding theory and the Minimalist Program*, 383–439. Oxford: Blackwell.

Cinque, Guglielmo. 1999. *Adverbs and functional heads.* Oxford: Oxford University Press.

Cinque, Guglielmo & Luigi Rizzi. 2010. The cartography of syntactic structures. In Bernd Heine & Heiko Narrog (eds.), *The Oxford handbook of linguistic analysis*, 51–65. Oxford: Oxford University Press.

Copley, Bridget. 2006. What should 'should' mean? Ms., CNRS, Université Paris VIII. http://copley.free.fr/copley.should.pdf (accessed 13 January 2014).

Cormack, Annabel & Neil Smith. 2002. Modals and negation in English. In Sjef Barbiers, Frits Beukema & Wim van der Wurff, *Modality and its interaction with the verbal system*, 133–163. Amsterdam & Philadelphia: John Benjamins.

Diewald, Gabriele. 1999. *Die Modalverben im Deutschen. Grammatikalisierung und Polyfunktionalität.* Tübingen: Niemeyer.

Erb, Marie Christine. 2001. *Finite auxiliaries in German.* Tilburg: Tilburg University dissertation.

van Gelderen, Elly. 2011. *The linguistic cycle: Language change and the language faculty.* Oxford: Oxford University Press.

Haegeman, Liliane. 1981. Modal *shall* and speaker's control. *Journal of English Linguistics* 15. 4–9.

Haegeman, Liliane. 1986. The present subjunctive in contemporary British English. *Studia Anglica Posnaniensia* 17. 61–74.

Haegeman, Liliane. 2010. The movement derivation of conditional clauses. *Linguistic Inquiry* 41. 595–621.

Haspelmath, Martin & Ekkehard König. 1998. Concessive conditionals in the languages of Europe. In Johan van der Auwera (ed.), *Adverbial relations in the languages of Europe*, 563–640. Berlin: Mouton de Gruyter.

Hopper, Paul. 1991. On some principles of grammaticization. In Elizabeth Closs Traugott & Bernd Heine (eds.), *Approaches to grammaticalization*, vol. 1, 17–36. Amsterdam & Philadelphia: John Benjamins.

Kayne, Richard S. 2012. Comparative syntax and English *Is to.* Unpub. ms., New York University.

Kempchinsky, Paula. 2009. What can the subjunctive disjoint reference effect tell us about the subjunctive? *Lingua* 119. 1788–1810.

Lee, Felicia. 2006. "Have to" and "be to". Paper presented at the *25th West Coast Conference on Formal Linguistics*, University of Washington Seattle, 28–30 April. http://depts.washington.edu/lingweb/events/wccfl25/abstracts/LeeF.html (accessed 13 January 2014).

Leech, Geoffrey. 1971. *Meaning and the English verb.* London: Longman.

Lehmann, Christian. 1995. *Thoughts on grammaticalization: A programmatic sketch.* 2nd. edn. München: Lincom.

Leirbukt, Oddleif. 1997. Dimensions of epistemicity in English, German and Norwegian conditionals. In Toril Swan & Olaf Jansen Westvik (eds.), *Modality in Germanic languages: Historical and comparative perspectives*, 49–74. Berlin & New York: Mouton de Gruyter.

Leuschner, Torsten. 2000. '..., wo immer es mir begegnet ... – wo es auch sei.' Zur Distribution von 'Irrelevanzpartikeln' in Nebensätzen mit w-*auch / immer. Deutsche Sprache* 28. 342–356.

Longobardi, Giuseppe. 2001. Formal syntax, diachronic minimalism, and etymology: The history of French *chez. Linguistic Inquiry* 32(2). 275–302.

Lühr, Rosemarie. 1998. Der Finitheitsfaktor als sprachtypologischer Parameter. *Historische Sprachforschung* 111. 347–368.

Mortelmans, Tanja, Kasper Boye & Johan van der Auwera. 2009. Modals in the Germanic languages. In Björn Hansen & Ferdinand de Haan (eds.), *Modals in the languages of Europe*, 11–70. Berlin & New York: Mouton de Gruyter.

Nieuwint, Pieter. 1989. *Should* in conditional protases. *Linguistics* 27. 305–318.

Rau, Jennifer. 2009. Modalverben in Komplementsätzen von Einflussprädikaten. *Linguistische Berichte* 219. 271–290.

Rizzi, Luigi. 1997. The fine structure of the left periphery. In Liliane Haegeman (ed.), *Elements of grammar*, 281–337. Dordrecht: Kluwer.

Roberts, Ian. 2010. Grammaticalization, the clausal hierarchy and semantic bleaching. In Elizabeth Traugott & Graeme Trousdale (eds.), *Gradience, gradualness, and grammaticalization*, 45–73. Amsterdam & Philadelphia: John Benjamins.

Roberts, Ian. 2012. Diachrony and cartography: Paths of grammaticalization and the clausal hierarchy. In Laura Brugé, Anna Cardinaletti, Giuliana Giusti, Nicola Munaro & Cecilia Poletto (eds.), *Functional heads. The cartography of syntactic structures*, vol. 7, 351–367. Oxford: Oxford University Press.

Roberts, Ian & Anna Roussou. 2003. *Syntactic change. A minimalist approach to grammaticalization*. Cambridge: Cambridge University Press.

Roméro, Céline. 2005. *The syntactic evolution of modal verbs in the history of English*. Paris: Université Paris III – La Sorbonne Nouvelle dissertation. http://www-sop.inria.fr/miaou/tralics/thesis/thesis.html (accessed 13 January 2014).

Solo, Harry J. 1977. The meaning of **motan*. A secondary denotation of necessity in Old English? *Neuphilologische Mitteilungen* 78(3). 215–232.

Traugott, Elisabeth Closs. 1985. Conditional markers. In John Haiman (ed.), *Iconicity in syntax*, 289–307. Amsterdam & Philadelphia: John Benjamins.

Traugott, Elisabeth Closs & Richard B. Dasher. 2002. *Regularities in semantic change*. Cambridge: Cambridge University Press.

Trousdale, Graeme. 2012. Grammaticalization, constructions and the grammaticalization of constructions. In Kristin Davidse, Tine Breban, Lieselotte Brems & Tanja Mortelmans (eds.), *Grammaticalization and language change. New reflections*, 167–198. Amsterdam & Philadelphia: John Benjamins.

Van den Nest, Daan. 2010. *Emergenz und Grammatikalisierung von V1-Konditionalen. Ein Rekonstruktionsversuch am Beispiel des Deutschen und Englischen*. Gent: Universiteit Gent dissertation.

Katerina Chatzopoulou

11 The Greek Jespersen's cycle: Renewal, stability and structural microelevation[1]

This paper examines the diachronic development of the Greek negator system, NEG1 and NEG2, and highlights major changes that take place at the syntax-semantics interface for the case of each negator, based on qualitative and quantitative evidence from three major stages of vernacular Greek (Attic Greek, Koine Greek, Late Medieval Greek). The contrast between NEG1 and NEG2 is explained in terms of sensitivity of NEG2 *mē* to nonveridicality: NEG2 is a polarity item in all stages of the Greek language, an element licensed exclusively in nonveridical environments in the sense of Giannakidou (1998). The developments observed in the history of Greek negation are shown to agree with current generative perspectives on syntactic change (Roberts and Roussou 2003; van Gelderen 2004), not only for the case of the Greek NEG1, which provides an instance of Jespersen's cycle in the sense of Chatzopoulou (2012, 2013a), but also for the more subtle transformations of NEG2, described here as structural microelevation on the Cinque (1999) hierarchy.

1 Introduction

The Greek language maintains a contrast between two negators, NEG1 and NEG2, in complementary distribution throughout its history, as part of its inheritance from Proto-Indo-European (Fowler 1896; Moorhouse 1959; Joseph 2002; Fortson 2010). This paper examines the diachronic development of the Greek negator system and highlights major changes that take place at the syntax-semantics interface for the case of each negator, based on qualitative and quantitative evidence from three major stages of spoken Greek (Attic Greek, Koine Greek, Late Medieval Greek).[2] The developments observed in the history of Greek negation are shown to agree with current generative perspectives on syntactic change (Roberts and Roussou 2003; van Gelderen 2004), not only for the case of the Greek NEG1, which provides an instance of Jespersen's cycle in

---

1 Some parts of this paper have also appeared in an earlier version in Chatzopoulou (2013a, 2013b).

2 See the Sources for the list of texts examined from each stage.

the sense of Chatzopoulou (2012, 2013a), but also regarding the more subtle transformations of NEG2, described here as structural microelevation on the Cinque (1999) hierarchy.

The contrast between NEG1 and NEG2 is explained in terms of sensitivity of NEG2 *μη* /me:/ to nonveridicality: NEG2 is a polarity item in all stages of the Greek language, an element licensed exclusively in nonveridical environments in the sense of Giannakidou (1998), such as imperatives, interrogatives, conditionals, optatives among others, while it diachronically appears also in uses which are not always negative, e.g., as question particle (Chatzopoulou and Giannakidou 2011; Chatzopoulou 2011, 2012). NEG1 on the other hand is the standard negation of the language in each stage in the sense of Payne (1985); it is the default form of sentential negation, which is diachronically unmarked in terms of nonveridicality.

Table 1: The two negator contrast from Proto-Indo-European to Standard Modern Greek.

	NEG1		NEG2
Proto-Indo-European	*ne	vs	*me_{H1}
Homeric Greek	u:(k^{[h]})	vs	me:
Classical Greek	u:(k^{[h]})	vs	me:
Koine	u(k)	vs	mi
Late Medieval	u(k) (or [u]dhén)	vs	mi (or midhén)
Modern Greek	dhe(n)	vs	mi(n)

Focusing on the developments that took place after Homeric Greek – although connections have been made also between the Proto-Indo-European *ne and the Greek NEG1 *ού(κ)* or *ούχ* /u:(k^{[h]})/[3] – only NEG1 provides an instance of *negator renewal* (the term belongs to van der Auwera 2010), in that the Homeric and Classical Greek *u:(k^{[h]})* is gradually replaced in its sentential negation function by the former indefinite *ούδέν* /udhén/ (*u.dh[e].én* morphologically: not.even.one), which resulted to Modern Greek *δεν* /dhe(n)/ (Horrocks [1997] 2010; Rijksbaron 2012). The corresponding nonveridical indefinite *μηδέν* /midhén/ (*mi.dh[e].én* morphologically: not.even.one) underwent a similar stage in replacing NEG2 *mē* in some of its negative functions in Late Medieval Greek, yet this development was interrupted and NEG2 *mē* remained the nonveridical

---

3 The origin of NEG1 *ού(κ)* /u:(k)/ is unknown, although an etymology has been proposed by Cowgill (1960), supported more recently in Beekes (1995, 2010) and Joseph (2005: 43), that NEG1 *ού(κ)* /u:(k)/ comes from a pre-Greek phrase *ne oiu kwid with the original meaning 'not ever in my life' from *ne (Proto-Indo-European NEG1), *oiu ('life', 'age') and *kwid ('something'), see also van Gelderen (2011: 300). Pre-Greek developments are at this point beyond our investigation.

negator of Standard Greek until today.[4] Therefore, in the transition from Attic Greek to Koine and then Medieval, the Greek NEG2 endured only predictable phonological alterations, such as loss of contrastive vowel length and raising (Horrocks 2010): *me: > mi*. Yet these changes were not reflected in the orthography and NEG2 would be conservatively transcribed as *μη* until the Modern Greek stage.[5]

This paper is structured as follows. In Section 2 the transformations of the Greek NEG1 are discussed in connection to Jespersen's cycle: the Greek NEG1 provides an instance of Jespersen's cycle in the understanding of Chatzopoulou (2012, 2013a), through the semantic bleaching and structural elevation of intensified predicate negation to plain propositional. This change is described as upward structural micromovement and immediately falls from van Gelderen's (2004) Late Merge Principle, agreeing also with Roberts and Roussou's (2003) approach on endogenous syntactic change as up-the-tree movement. In Section 3 the developments of the Greek NEG2 are presented, for which Jespersen's cycle was not completed: NEG2 *mē* was not replaced by the former NEG2 indefinite *μηδέν* /midhén/ in any of its uses (see Table 1). The diachrony of NEG2 *mē*, however, provides two instances of parameter resetting by the Late Medieval stage: (i) the inability of NEG2 *mē* to co-occur with morphological imperatives (loss of True Negative Imperatives), and (ii) the ban of NEG2 *mē* from the conditional antecedent. The first resetting points to a syntactic status shift from phrase to head, which is expected according to van Gelderen's (2004) Spec-to-Head Principle of diachronic change. For the second resetting I present an explanation that assumes further microelevation of NEG2 *mē* on the Cinque (1999) hierarchy by Late Medieval Greek following Chatzopoulou (2012, 2013b). Section 4 summarizes the paper.

2 The Greek Jespersen's cycle and the transformations of NEG1

The diachrony of Greek negation, regarding the transformations of NEG1, deviates from the traditional understanding of Jespersen's cycle in that at no point in its

---

[4] In dialectal Greek, namely in Romeyka, *midhen* survives as a kind of propositional negation particular to conditional antecedents (see Chatzopoulou and Sitaridou 2014).

[5] In Standard Modern Greek an euphonic [n] appears both in sound and spelling, and NEG2 *mi* surfaces as *min*, if NEG2 is followed by a word that begins with a vowel, e.g., *mi fíghis* 'don't go', but *min érthis* 'don't come'. The presence of a nasal coda in NEG2 *mi* is also detectable when NEG2 *mi* is followed by a voiceless stop, which becomes voiced, e.g., *tréhis* 'you run', but *mi dréhis* 'don't run' (see Malikouti-Drachman 1993, 2001 and Arvaniti 2007 for discussion).

attested history did sentential negation in Greek manifest a doubling stage: the addition of a second element, which after a point is required for the expression of negation, as was the case in French (Bréal 1897; Clarke 1904; Horn 1989; Detges and Waltereit 2002; Godard 2004), English (Horn 1989; Frisch 1997; Mazzon 2004; Wallage 2005, 2008), Dutch/Flemish (Hoeksema 1997; Zeijlstra 2004; Breitbarth and Haegeman 2008), German (Jäger 2008; Breitbarth 2009), Egyptian (Gardiner 1904), Old Norse (van Gelderen 2008), Arabic and Berber (Lucas 2007) among numerous other languages (see van der Auwera 2010). It is, however, obvious that the history of the Greek language indeed provides evidence of negator renewal.

(1) ταῦτα   δ'   οὐκ   ἐβούλοντο   ATTIC GREEK (5th–4th c. BC)
    tauta   *d'*   ***u:k***   *ebu:lonto*
    these   2P   NEG1   want.ind.past.3sg
    'They didn't want these.'   NEG1 *u:(k)*
    (Demosthenes, *De pace* 21.4)

(2) ουδέν   σε   θεωρούμεν   LATE MEDIEVAL (12th c. AD)
    udhén   *se*   *theorúmen*
    NEG1   you.ACC   see.PRES.IND.1PL
    'we do not see you.'   NEG1 *(u)dhén*
    (*Digenis Akritis* 111)

(3) Δεν   σε   βλέπω   STANDARD MODERN GREEK
    dhen   *se*   *vlépo*
    NEG1   you.ACC   see.INP.1SG
    'I do not see you.'   NEG1 *dhen*

This is a fact already pointed out in Willmott (2013), although studies on grammaticalization and language change have included Greek in the Jespersen's cycle discussion (Roberts and Roussou 2003; Roussou 2007). Following Chatzopoulou (2012, 2013a) I present here a broader description of the Jespersen's cycle phenomenon, which accommodates not only for Greek, but for other atypical negator renewal manifestations as well. The proposed approach abstracts away from the morphosyntactic and phonological particulars of the phenomenon and explicitly places its regularities in the semantics/pragmatics. This is an intuition already present in the literature (Horn 1989; van Kemenade 2000; Roberts and Roussou 2003; Kiparsky and Condoravdi 2006; van Gelderen 2011; de Cuypere 2008; van der Auwera 2009, 2010), which nevertheless has not received a formal description.

2.1 Jespersen's cycle traditionally and the atypicality of Greek: no doubling stage

The term Jespersen's cycle (after Jespersen 1917) was first used by Östen Dahl in his (1979) paper "Typology of sentence negation" to refer to the process by which the expression of negation in a language tends to increase and decrease in complexity over time in regular ways. French is the prototypical example of a language that exhibits such a development and is typically mentioned in all studies throughout the Jespersen's cycle literature, being among the three languages of Jespersen's original corpus. Below are examples from the proto-typical case of French, while negation in English (Horn 1989; Frisch 1997; Wallage 2005 among others), German (Jäger 2008; Breitbarth 2009) and Dutch (Hoeksema 1997; Zeijlstra 2004; van der Auwera 2005, 2006, 2010; Breitbarth and Haegeman 2008) has gone through similar transformations.

(4) *Il* ***ne*** *peut*   *venir* *ce*   *soir.*   STAGE I   OLD FRENCH
   Il ***ne*** *peut* ***pas*** *venir* *ce*   *soir.*   STAGE II   MIDDLE FRENCH
   Il   *peut* ***pas*** *venir* *ce*   *soir.*   STAGE III MODERN COLLOQUIAL
   he NEG can   NEG come this evening
   'He can't come tonight.'
   (van der Auwera 2009: 39)

Jespersen's observation regarding the tendency for regular renewal of the expression of negation in a language (in particular regarding the French *ne...pas*) has been preceded not only by Antoine Meillet's seminal work on grammaticalization (1912: 393–394), but also by Alan H. Gardiner (1904, cf. van der Auwera 2008), who discusses the origin of negators in Egyptian and Coptic in relation to the French negator transformations. However, the negator renewal path in the languages that both Gardiner and Jespersen studied was morpho-syntactic, in that the languages under discussion (Egyptian, English, French, Danish) manifested a doubling stage: the addition of a second element (an indefinite or minimizer), that after a point was required for the expression of plain sentential negation and eventually assumed the function of plain sentential negation itself. This had a permanent effect in the understanding of Jespersen's cycle. As a result, Jespersen's cycle is generally described in the literature as a diachronic multistage process that involves three main stages, as recently as de Swart (2010: 114), whose description of each stage is given relatively to the position of the verb in (5).

(5) Preverbal expression of sentential negation STAGE I
Discontinuous expression of sentential negation STAGE II
Postverbal expression of sentential negation STAGE III

According to the traditional description for Jespersen's cycle Greek is problematic in that it does not have a Stage II, which is the stage of discontinuous negation, or even independently of discontinuity, the stage of doubling (Willmott 2013, Chatzopoulou 2013a). The Attic Greek NEG1 *u:(k[h])* was gradually replaced in Late Medieval by NEG1 *οὐδέν* /udhén/ (Horrocks 2010; Rijksbaron 2012), see (6) and (7), and the same happened to NEG2, although to a lesser extent, see (8) and (9), as NEG2 *μηδέν* /midhén/ did not eventually replace the former NEG2 *mē* in any of its uses.

(6) (...) τοῖς   φίλοις   αὐτῶν   οὐ   θεωροῦσιν   ATTIC GREEK
      tois   *p^hilois*   *auto:n*   **u:**   *t^heo:ru:sin*
      the.DAT   friends.DAT   their.GEN   NEG1   look.PRES.IND.3PL
      'they do not observe (the misfortunes) of their friends.'
      (Isocrates, *Epist 6 Ad filios Jasonis* 12.9–10)

(7) οιμέν   αδέλφιν   μας   καλόν,   ουδέν
      oimén   *adhélfin*   *mas*   *kalón,*   **udhén**
      alas   sibling.VOC   our.GEN   good.ACC   NEG1

      σε   θεωρούμεν   LATE MEDIEVAL
      se   *theorúmen*
      you.ACC   see.PRES.IND.1PL
      'Alas, our dear sibling, we do not see you.'
      (*Digenis Akritis* 111)

(8) μὴ   ψεῦσον (...)   τῆς   ἐπιούσης   ἐλπίδος.   ATTIC GREEK
      me: *pseuson*   *te:s*   *epiu:se:s*   *elpidos*
      NEG2   falsify.AOR.IMP   the.GEN   sum.PRPCPL.FEM.GEN   hope.GEN
      'Do not prove wrong the hope that comes from this.'
      (Aristophanes, *Thesmophoriazusae* 870)

(9) το   αδέλφιν   μας   το   άρπαξες,   μηδέν
      to   *adhélfin*   *mas*   *to*   *árpakses,*   **midhén**
      the   sibling   our   which   abduct.PP.2SG   NEG2

      μας   το   στερέψης.   LATE MEDIEVAL
      mas   *to*   *sterépsis*
      our   it   deprive.PNP.2SG
      'Do not deprive us from our sibling that you took away.'
      (*Digenis Akritis* 130)

An explanation for the lack of a Stage II comes from the fact that Greek, being a non-strict negative concord language, according to Giannakidou's (1998) typology, at least until the end of Koine (3rd c. AD), employed two syntactic strategies of negative reinforcement (10). On a par with other non-strict negative concord languages like Italian and Spanish (cf. Zanuttini 1991; Laka 1990; Herburger 2001), in Greek, the negators of Attic Greek and Koine were generally required, in case the n-word was postverbal, (11), (13), and dropped, if the n-word was preverbal, (12), (14).

(10)   NEGATIVE REINFORCEMENT STRATEGY 1:   NEG verb N-WORD
       NEGATIVE REINFORCEMENT STRATEGY 2:   N-WORD verb

(11)   *oὐ*   *πέπονθεν*   *oὐδέν*   ATTIC GREEK
       u: pepont^{h}en   **u:den**
       NEG1   suffer.PRES-PERF.3SG   NEG1-thing
       'Nothing happened to him.'
       (Aristophanes, *Pax* 1256)

(12)   *oὐδὲν*   *πέπονθεν*   ATTIC GREEK
       u:den   pepont^{h}en
       NEG1-thing   suffer.PRES-PERF.3SG
       'Nothing happened to him.'
       (Isocrates, *In Call.* 4.5)

(13)   *μὴ*   *νῦν*   *ἔτι*   *εἴπης*   *μηδέν.*   ATTIC GREEK
       mε: ny:n   eti   e:pe:is   **mε:den**
       NEG2   now   more   say.AOR.SUBJ.2SG   NEG2-thing
       'Do not say anything more.'
       (Sophocles, *Elena* 324)

(14)   *μηδὲν*   *λέγε* (...)   ATTIC GREEK
       mε:den   lege
       NEG2-thing   say.PRES.IMP.2SG
       'Do not say anything (...)'
       (Plato, *Symposium* 214.d.6)

After the significant decline of negative concord structures during the Hellenistic Greek period and the strong preference of NEG1 and NEG2 indefinites for preverbal position (see Chatzopoulou 2012), strategy 2 (N-WORD verb) was further stabilized as the dominant strategy for negative reinforcement. As a

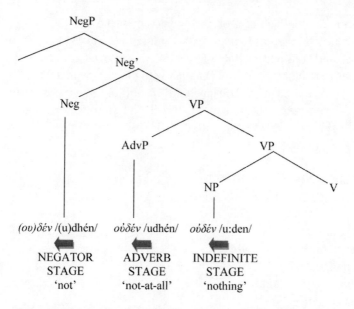

Figure 1: The structural microelevation of the Greek NEG1 indefinite.

result, it was strategy 2 that gave rise to the negators NEG1 *οὐδέν* /udhén/ and NEG2 *μηδέν* /midhén/ of Late Medieval Greek, through the bleaching and re-analysis of the former negative indefinites and a discontinuous stage of sentential negation did not occur. This development, at least regarding the Greek NEG1, for which the cycle was completed, is reminiscent of that of the Latin *non*, which deviates from prototypical Jespersen's cycle patterns in a similar way: Latin did not exemplify a discontinuous negation stage either. Latin *non* resulted from the merging of the weak negator *nĕ* (see van der Auwera 2010) and *œnum* which was the word for 'one' in Early Latin (later *unum, ne + œnum > non*), an etymology that has been assigned to *non* already in Jespersen (1917: 14–15). The fact that neither Greek nor Latin manifested a Stage II in the traditional Jespersen's cycle description, among other factors, may relate to underived word order in Stage I: both Greek and Latin were primarily SOV languages (Ebeling 1902; Devine and Stephens 1994; Taylor 1994; Deligianni 2011 for Greek). The potential correlation of Jespersen's cycle with word order in a language, a hypothesis already entertained in Vennemann (1974) and Harris (1976, 1978), is discussed also in de Cuypere (2008: 230) towards the conclusion that in OV languages with preverbal negators, such as Attic Greek and Latin, discontinuous negation does not eventually occur.

Figure 1 provides a visualization of the grammaticalization path of the Greek NEG1 indefinite as structural microelevation (described also as upward lexical micromovement in Chatzopoulou 2012, 2013a). This agrees with Roberts and Roussou's (2003) and Roberts' (2010) general approach to grammaticalization as *up-the-tree movement*, as well as van Gelderen's (2004) Late Merge Principle, that lexical elements diachronically prefer structurally higher positions.

2.3 Other negator renewal pathways: no doubling stage and tripling stage strategies

Negator renewal paths that deviate in one way or another from the traditional understanding of Jespersen's cycle have been identified crosslinguistically. Two are of particular relevance, as the approach for Jespersen's cycle proposed in Chatzopoulou (2012, 2013a) is inclusive of these as well: (i) the case in which propositional negation has its origin in a verbal head and, as a result, there is no doubling or syntactic discontinuity effect; (ii) the case where negation is reinforced for a second time with no loss of phonological material from the previous form resulting in a tripling negator stage.

A path for negator renewal mostly attested outside the Indo-European language family is the one where sentential negation originates from former verbs and in particular verbs that have some inherent negative property, e.g., 'to lack', 'to fail', 'to not exist', 'to refuse' (Givón 1978; Payne 1985; Croft 1991; Heine and Kuteva 2002; Miestamo 2003; van der Auwera 2006 and van Gelderen 2008, 2011). Chinese is one prototypical such language. Sentential negation *mei* in Modern Chinese, used with predicates of inherent perfectivity, comes from the Old Chinese verb *mo* 'to die' with a predictable change in the vowel (Lin 2002; see also Djamouri 1991, 1996 and Pulleyblank 1995, cited in van Gelderen 2011: 320).

(15)   *Yao*   *Shun*   *ji*   ***mo*** (...)   OLD CHINESE
       Yao   Shun   since died
       'Since Yao and Shun died (...)'
       (Mengzi, Tengwengong B, cited in Lin 2002: 5)

(16)   *Yu*   *de*   *wang*   *ren*   ***mei***   *kunan*   EARLY MANDARIN
       wish   PRT   died   person not.be suffering
       'If you wish that the deceased one has no suffering'
       (*Dunhuang Bianwen*, cited in Lin 2002: 5–6).

(17)   *Wo* ***mei*** *you*   *shu.*   MODERN CHINESE
       I   NEG exist book
       'I don't have a book.'
       (van Gelderen 2008: 199)

Numerous such languages have been identified that manifest this pattern, with degrees of variation in the details, e.g., several Athabaskan languages, among the Koyukon, Lower Tanana and Chipewyan (van Gelderen 2008: 222–223), Australian aboriginal languages, e.g., Nunggubuyu (Croft 1991: 11), some varieties of Berber (see Mettouchi 1996; Chaker 1996) and the Tagalog *huwag* prohibitive marker (see Croft 1991: 15). In a significant number of these cases, there is a correlation of the negator that comes from a verbal head with perfectivity or telicity in general, in that at some point in its history it carried perfective aspect marking (see van Gelderen 2008; Givón 2000) or it placed restrictions on the predicates it could co-occur with, again in terms of perfectivity, either lexical or grammatical.

Another major strategy for negator renewal in a language, which again deviates from the traditional morphosyntactic description of Jespersen's cycle, is the case where a language that already has syntactically discontinuous negation enters the cycle for the second time by adding a third element, which with time bleaches to plain sentential negation without any loss of phonological material from the previous stage. Such a development results in a structure that can allow for three elements in the expression of plain propositional negation. Multiple such examples have been attested crosslinguistically in Bantu, e.g., in Kanincin, a dialect of Ruund (Devos, Kasombo Tshibanda, and van der Auwera 2010), and Austronesian languages, e.g., in Lewo, a Vanuatu language (Early 1994a, 1994b; van der Auwera 2006; Crowley 2006; Vossen and van der Auwera 2012), and it is even found in European languages, e.g., in dialects of Dutch/Flemish (van der Auwera and Neuckermans 2004), as well as in Dego Italian (Manzini and Savoia 2005). Below is an example of a prohibitive structure attested in Lewo. The basic negative pattern required the embracing structure *ve...re*. However, the prohibitive *toko* (which is of verbal origin, 'to desist') can be further added, resulting in a *ve...re toko* negator without traces of emphasis.

(18) **Ve**   *a-kan*   **re**   **toko!**   LEWO (AUSTRONESIAN)
NEG1   2SG.eat   NEG2   NEG3
'Do not eat it!'
(Early 1994b: 76)

The tripling stage negator is a situation that would have occurred, for instance in French, if the *ne...pas* construction had been reinforced through another lexical element prior to the loss of *ne* from the pattern in actual language. This of course was not the case for French, nor was it for English, German and Standard Dutch or any of the other typical Jespersen's cycle languages. But clearly, it is a typological possibility that, similarly to the developments of Greek, is not predicted by the text book account for Jespersen's cycle.

2.4 A broader definition for Jespersen's cycle

In spite of the differences in the details, the point where all the aforementioned Negative cycles meet is the bleaching of intensified predicate negation to plain propositional and based on this observation, I propose the definition in (19), (cf. Chatzopoulou 2012, 2013a).

(19)   Jespersen's cycle definition:
   Formalization I (broad)
   Negator renewal through the semantic bleaching and structural elevation
   of intensified predicate negation to plain propositional, further
   re-intensified by morphological, syntactic, prosodic or other means.
   Formalization II (includes traditional Jespersen's cycle, Greek, Latin and
   tripling stage languages)
   If X is a negative expression, either syntactically continuous or
   discontinuous, and α a variable of quantities (as of individuals, amounts
   or times) Jespersen's cycle goes through the following stages:
   STAGE I $[\![X]\!] = \lambda P_{<d, \, <\alpha, \, t>>}. \, \lambda\alpha. \, [\forall d > 0. \, \neg P(d)(\alpha)]$
   (intensified predicate negation)

   STAGE II $[\![X]\!] = \lambda p. \, \neg p$ (plain propositional negation)

This definition reflects a view that labels what has so far been described as emphatic negation as *intensified negation* (see also Mustajoki and Heino 1991; Hammond 2005), that is, plain negation with the addition of an intensifier (morphological or syntactic) with an understanding for intensification in the sense of Romero (2007): intensity is a qualitative or quantitative gap between *two states* relative to a phenomenon. In the formalization provided in Formalization II of the definition, X is used as a structurally and compositionally opaque element, which can stand either for the French *ne...pas*, or the Greek *udhén*, the Chinese *mei* or the three co-occurring negators attested. The link between negation and intensity agrees with Bolinger's (1972) observation that gradeability can have crosscategorial relevance and is not just a property of adjectives (a view preceded in Sapir 1944). The proposed definition focuses on the emphatic/intensified form of negation that eventually bleaches to plain sentential negation and identifies two stages: one in which the element is emphatic and one in which it is not.

   Predicate negation in Formalization I of the definition refers to a negative element either (i) from within the verb phrase (VP), which can be either the complement of the verb (as in French, Dutch, German, English, Greek, Latin) or the verb itself (as in Chinese, Athabaskan, Semitic and Austronesian and languages in general in which the negator is of verbal origin) or (ii) immediately above the VP, as in the case of a negative adverb (e.g., *never* in African American Vernacular, cf. van Gelderen 2008, and possibly Homeric and Attic Greek NEG1 *oὐ(κ)* /uː(k)/).

The two forms of definition Part II are truth-conditionally equivalent, something which may facilitate the eventual generalization of intensified negation as plain propositional. The difference is that in the case of emphatic/intensified negation the X element explicitly negates a whole set of entities or quantities or times that are introduced through a scale evoking lexical property. This means that a scale evoking element is morphologically encoded in Stage I, e.g., in the case of Greek it is the lexical element *en* 'one' in *udhén* combined also with *dhe* 'even', which brings this result. The process of bleaching in the transition from Stage I to Stage II involves the loss of scalar reference: at Stage II a scale is no longer evoked and only the standard of comparison or scalar endpoint gets interpreted (see Chatzopoulou 2012: 285–290 for discussion and Deligianni *forthcoming*; also Lee 2011 for Jespersen's cycle bleaching as loss of scalar reference).

3 The Greek NEG2: Stability and change

Although the Greek NEG2 persisted in function and form for the most part, the exact distribution of the Greek NEG2 *mē* has not remained the same from Classical Greek to Late Medieval and Modern Greek. The prototypical use of NEG2 *mē* in prohibition has remained most frequent among its functions in each stage (see Table 2 unembedded directives). There are, however, subtle changes that point to a syntactic status shift: from phrase in Classical Greek to head by the Late Medieval stage.

3.1 NEG2 as a negative polarity item

The distribution of the Greek negative particles, NEG1 and NEG2, especially for Ancient Greek (Homeric, Classical and Koine), has been the object of investigation for scholars since the late 18th century and throughout the 19th and 20th centuries (Hoogeveen [1769] 1782; Anton 1824; Franke 1832; Goodwin 1889; Jannaris 1897; Kühner and Gerth 1898; Smyth 1920; among many others, see for full overview and discussion Gerö 1997). More recently Philippaki-Warburton and Spyropoulos (2004) have linked the use of NEG2 in all Greek (whether with finite or non-finite forms) to deontic modality, while Willmott (2008, 2013), brings into the discussion the notion of irrealis in connection to the Greek NEG2. In Chatzopoulou and Giannakidou (2011) and Chatzopoulou (2011, 2012) the regulating factor that explains the distribution of NEG1 and NEG2 in Greek is identified by the notion of (non)veridicality. The theory of (non)veridicality (Giannakidou 1998) is a detailed formal account of the pretheoretical notion of irrealis, in a way that singles out the unifying property in various elements with limited distribution crosslinguistically – e.g., the English *any* – described as negative polarity items (Buyssens 1959; Klima 1964; Jackendoff 1969; Baker 1970; Ladusaw 1979; Zwarts 1986, 1995; Dowty 1994; Giannakidou 1998 are only part of the extensive previous literature on polarity). One such negative polarity item proves to be the Greek NEG2 in all the history of the language. (Non)veridicality is formally defined as a property of propositional operators (definition from Giannakidou 2006: 589).

(20) (Non)veridicality for propositional operators
  (i) A propositional operator F is veridical iff Fp entails or presupposes that p is true in some individual's epistemic model ME(x); otherwise F is nonveridical.
  (ii) A nonveridical operator F is antiveridical iff Fp entails that *not p* in some individual's epistemic model: $Fp \rightarrow \neg p$ in some ME(x)

(21) Definition for polarity items
  A linguistic expression α is a polarity item iff:
  (i) The distribution of α is limited by sensitivity to some semantic property β of the context of appearance; and
  (ii) β is (non)veridicality.

A function F is veridical if Fp entails or presupposes that p is true in some individual's epistemic model: the set of possible worlds compatible with a person's beliefs or anchored to an individual (cf. the *individual anchor*; Farkas 1992). A veridical operator entails the truth of p in all worlds in the model, while a nonveridical operator expresses uncertainty: there are some worlds w where p is true, and some worlds w' where it is not. In other words, veridical operators reflect the speaker's certainty and commitment to the truth of the proposition which is uttered, whereas nonveridical operators reflect uncertainty and lack of commitment.

It is important to note that the (non)veridicality theory of polarity poses no categorical restrictions on the elements that depend on it (Giannakidou 1998: 2–3, 93–95). Clearly negation itself can be a polarity item, in that it can exhibit an allomorph conditioned by the semantic environment in terms of the property of (non)veridicality. This is actually quite common from a crosslinguistic perspective (see van der Auwera and Lejeune 2005; van der Auwera 2006).[6] Furthermore, the fact that NEG2 *mē* maintains both negative and non-negative functions in each stage (as complementizer and as question particle, see also Joseph and Janda 1999 for an approach on the Greek NEG2 in Modern Greek *mē* as a morphological constellation) means that the unifying property of NEG2 is not negativity, but nonveridicality. Representative examples of the uses of NEG2 in the history of Greek are given below.

(22) *μὴ*   *πολλῶν*   *ἐπιθύμει*   1st c. AD
      mi   *polón*   *epithými*
      NEG2   many.GEN   desire.PRES.IMP.2SG
      'Do not desire many things.'   directive → NONVERIDICAL
      (Epictetus, *Dissertationes ab Arriano digestae* 3.9.22.5)

(23) *μὴ*   *φοβηθῇς*   *τὸν*   *θάνατον*   *παρὰ μητρὸς*   *κατάραν.*   12th c. AD
      mi   *fovithís*   *ton*   *thánaton* *pará mitrós*   *katáran*
      NEG2   fear.PNP.2SG the.ACC death.ACC   but   mother.GEN curse.ACC
      'Do not fear death, but a mother's curse.'   directive → NONVERIDICAL
      (*Digenis Akritis* 2)

(24) *εἰ* *μὴ*   *τις*   *κωλύσει*
      e: **mε:** *tis*   *ko:lyse:*
      If   NEG2   someone stop.FUT.IND.3SG
      'if someone doesn't stop (him).'   protasis of conditional → NONVERIDICAL
      (Demosthenes, *Philippica* 1 43.6)

(25) *πειρατέον* *μὴ*   *ἐλλείπειν.*   ATTIC GREEK
      pe:rateon **mε:** *elle:pe:n*
      try.GDV   NEG2   fall-short.PRES.INF
      'I must try my best to be adequate.'   scope of deontic[7] → NONVERIDICAL
      (Plato, *Symposium* 196d 6)

---

6 According to van der Auwera and Lejeune's (2005) study, 327 languages from a corpus of 495 languages worldwide maintain a negator which is particular to prohibition, while the same negator in these languages can appear in other nonveridical environments as well, see also Honda (1996).

7 The Attic Greek gerundive is a kind of verbal adjective with inherent deontic modality semantics.

(26) οὐ   ζῶμεν   ὡς   ἥδιστα
      u: *zo:men*   *ho:s*   *hε:dista*
      NEG1   live.PRES.IND   as   pleasant.SUPERL

      μὴ   λυπούμενοι;   ATTIC GREEK
      mε: *lypu:menoi*
      NEG2   sadden.MP.PRES.PCPL.MASC.NOM
      'Do we not live as happily if we are not saddened?'
                                    conditional pcpl → NONVERIDICAL
      (Euripides, *Fragmenta Antiopes* 14.5)

(27) μὴ   πάντες   ἀπόστολοι;   μὴ   πάντες   προφῆται;   1st c. AD
      mi   *pántes*   *apóstoli?*   *mi*   *pántes*   *prophíte?*
      NEG2   all   apostles.NOM   NEG2   all   prophets.NOM
      'Are all apostles? Are all prophets?'   question particle → NONVERIDICAL
      (Novum Testamentum, *Ad Corinthios* I 12.29.1–30.2)

(28) Μην   εἴδατε   τον   ἄντρα   μου τον
      min   *ídhate*   *ton*   *ándra*   *mu ton*
      NEG2   see.PP.2PL   the.ACC   husband.ACC   my the.ACC

      Λούκα   Καλιακούδα;   18th c. AD
      Lúka   *Kaljakúdha*
      Lukas.ACC   Kaljakudhas.ACC
      'Did you happen to see my husband, Lukas Kaliakudas?'
                                    question particle → NONVERIDICAL
      (Fauriel (1824–1825), 1.118)

(29) δέδοικα   μὴ   τἀναντία
      dedoika   *mε:*   *tanantia*
      fear.PRES.IND.1SG   NEG2   the.opposite

      πράττοντες   φανῶμεν·   ATTIC GREEK
      prattontes   *pʰano:men*
      do.PRES.PCPL.NOM   seem.SUBJ.1PL
      'I fear that we may seem to have pursued the opposite'
      (Isocrates, *Archidamus* 51.1–2)   scope of *timendi* → NONVERIDICAL

(30) Ο   Γιάννης φοβάται   μην   αρρωστήσει.   STANDARD MODERN GREEK
      o   *Jánis*   *fováte*   *min*   *arostísi*
      the   Janis   fear.INP.3SG   NEG2   get.sick.PNP.3SG
      'John is afraid that he may get sick.'   scope of *timendi* → NONVERIDICAL

Table 2 summarizes the uses of NEG2 *mē* and the development of each use in three major stages of spoken Greek (Attic Greek, Koine, Late Medieval) on samples of over 1000 negators (NEG1+NEG2) per chronological stage.[8]

Table 2: The distribution of NEG2 *mē* in Attic Greek, in Koine and in Late Medieval Greek

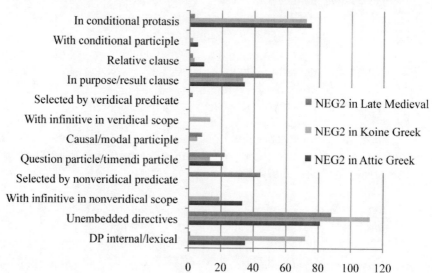

3.2 NEG2 developments by Late Medieval Greek

There are two changes in the distribution of NEG2 *mē* by the Late Medieval stage that take place at the syntax-semantics interface and can be described as parameter resettings: (i) NEG2 *mē* can no longer negate morphological imperatives, and (ii) NEG2 *mē* is no longer licensed in the conditional protasis. The explanation proposed in Chatzopoulou (2012, 2013b) points to a syntactic status shift of NEG2 *mē* from specifier to head, a change which is not unexpected, according to one of van Gelderen's (2004) economy principles of grammaticalization, the Specifier-to-Head Principle.

3.2.1 Loss of True Negative Imperatives

The availability of negative morphological imperatives, referred to as True Negative Imperatives or simply prohibitives, is a parameter according to which

8 The list of selected works from each stage is given in the Sources.

languages can vary (Joseph and Philippaki-Warburton 1987; Zanuttini 1991, 1997a, 1997b; Rivero 1994; Rivero and Terzi 1995; Tomić 1999; Han 2000, 2001; Zeijlstra 2004, 2006). In the history of Greek, True Negative Imperatives (TNIs) were available both in Attic Greek (31) and in Hellenistic Koine (32), although surrogate forms through the subjunctive were also attested.

(31) μὴ   φάθι   ATTIC GREEK
     mɛː: **pʰatʰi**
     NEG2   speak.IMP.2SG
     'Don't speak (Say 'no').'   TRUE NEGATIVE IMPERATIVE
     (Plato, *Gorgias* 501d 9)

(32) μὴ   πολλῶν   ἐπιθύμει   KOINE GREEK
     mi polón   epithými
     NEG2 many.GEN   desire.PRES.IMP.2SG
     'Do not desire many things.'   TRUE NEGATIVE IMPERATIVE
     (Epictetus, *Dissertationes ab Arriano digestae* 3.9.22.5)

By Late Medieval Greek, such structures are nearly unattested in spoken language and only the surrogate forms are possible, using either the perfective non-past or the imperfective non-past forms of the verb. The examples below present instances of negative directives formed by combining NEG2 *mē* with the perfective non-past of *fováme* 'I fear' in (33). (34) and (35) provide examples from Standard Modern Greek, where we can actually provide negative evidence on the unavailability of True Negative Imperatives in (34) and the standard way to form a negative directive in (35) through the perfective non-past and optionally the *να* /na/ particle.

(33) μὴ   φοβηθῆς   τὸν   θάνατον παρὰ μητρὸς   κατάραν.   12th c. AD
     mi   **fovithis** ton   thánaton pará mitrós   katáran
     NEG2 fear.PNP.2SG the.ACC death.ACC but mother.GEN curse.ACC
     'Do not fear death, but a mother's curse.'
                                 SURROGATE FORM (TNI UNAVAILABLE)
     (*Digenis Akritis* 2)

(34) *Μην   ἔλα.   STANDARD MODERN GREEK
     min éla
     NEG2   come.IMP.2SG
     'Don't come!'   TNIs UNAVAILABLE

(35) *(Να)*   *μην*   *ἑρθεις/ἑρχεσαι*   STANDARD MODERN GREEK
      (na)   **min**   *érthis/érhese*
      (subj)   NEG2   come.PNP/INP.2SG
      'Don't come/be coming.'   SURROGATE (IM)PERFECTIVE NON-PAST

Several analyses have been proposed on this parameter of crosslinguistic variation, the (un)availability of True Negative Imperatives, which clearly is a parameter that can be reset even in the diachrony of a single language, as has already been observed in Italian (Zanuttini 1997a; Zeijlstra 2006) and Welsh (Willis 2013). However, in both Italian and Welsh this change co-occurs with a change of the negator, whereas in Greek there was no directly noticeable change in the form of NEG2 *μη* /mi/. Yet all three cases relate to Jespersen's cycle developments, which for the Greek NEG2 though are not as obvious. The analysis I propose agrees with those of Zeijlstra (2006) and Willis (2013) in connecting the loss of true negative imperatives to the syntactic status of the negator. I adopt the account of Rivero (1994) and Rivero and Terzi (1995) on the (un)availability of True Negative Imperatives, generally supported also in Zeijlstra (2004) and further enriched in Zeijlstra (2006), as appropriate for the case of Greek (but see Zanuttini 1991, 1997a; Han 2000, 2001; Postma and van der Wurff 2007 for alternative approaches). The analysis of Rivero (1994), Rivero and Terzi (1995) links the (un)availability of True Negative Imperatives to the hierarchical structure of functional projections and the syntactic status of the negative marker (see also Giannakidou 1998: 52–55 on the unavailability of True Negative Imperatives in Modern Greek). In languages that form imperatives through V-to-C movement – as is Standard Modern Greek and Late Medieval – True Negative Imperatives cannot emerge, if there is an overt negator of head status that blocks head movement. A surrogate form is employed instead, whose morphology does not require movement to C, like the Late Medieval perfective non-past or the subjunctive *να* /na/ (former *ἵνα* /ina/) particle that is already base generated in a position higher than negation after the formal restructuring of the mood system in Hellenistic-Roman times (see Lightfoot 1979: 288–294; Chatzopoulou 2012: 179–184).

The analysis proposed by Rivero (1994) and Rivero and Terzi (1995) explains the unavailability of True Negative Imperatives in Late Medieval Greek, provided that NEG2 *mē* is now a head in its preverbal prohibitive function. This also agrees with Zeijlstra's (2004, 2006) analysis, who generally adopts Rivero's (1994) and Rivero and Terzi's (1995) view, but also discusses counter arguments. Zeijlstra (2006) explicitly links the unavailability of True Negative Imperatives in a language to the head status of the negator: 'every language that bans TNIs exhibits an overt negative marker X⁰' (Zeijlstra 2006: 405).

3.2.2 The phrasal status of the Attic Greek NEG2

Regarding the phrasal status of NEG2 in Attic Greek two diagnostic tests are presented here (cf. also Chatzopoulou 2013b and Chatzopoulou 2012: 90–97 for a more detailed account of the phrasal status of both NEG1 and NEG2 in Attic Greek). The Attic Greek NEG2 (a) responds positive to the *why no(t)?* test, introduced as a diagnostic for syntactic status in Merchant (2006), and takes XP position in other elliptical constructions (relative clauses, disjunctions, conditionals), and (b) it can be postposed: NEG2 can occasionally follow the verb or verbal form, if the latter is under focus.

(a) According to the *why no(t)?* test (Merchant 2006) only negators of phrasal status are grammatical in a *why NEG?* construction. NEG2 is found in this construction in Attic Greek.

(36) *Ἀρχοντές   εἰσιν,   ὥσθ᾽   ὑπεικτέον·   τί   μή;*
      *arkʰontes   e:sin   o:stʰ   hype:kteon   ti   **mɛ:***
      rulers   are.3PL   therefore submit.GVD   how   NEG2
      'They are rulers, so we must submit. How could we not?'
      (Sophocles, *Ajax* 668)

Given that the wh-item τί /ti/ is a phrase that occupies the specifier of a higher phrase, its complement can only be another phrase.

(37) [$_{XP}$ [τί] [$_{XP}$ μή]]
      [$_{XP}$ [*why*] [$_{XP}$ NEG2]]

The phrasal nature of the Attic Greek NEG2 is also supported by its presence in elliptical constructions that involve disjunction, conditionals and relatives clauses. This is actually a variant of the previous test, described as *Whether TP or no(t)?*, also discussed in Merchant (2006).

(38) *[...]   πότερον   χρή   με   λέγειν   ἤ   μή.*
              *poteron   kʰrɛ: me   lege:n   ɛ: **mɛ:***
              which-of-the-two must   me   talk.PRES.INF   or   NEG2
      '(I have come in order to decide) whether I should speak or not.'
      (Demosthenes, *Exordia* 19.1–2)

(39) *ἐπερωτῶντας (...) ὅ τι   τε   χρὴ   ποιεῖν   καὶ   ὅ τι   μή*
      *epero:to:ntas   hoti   te   kʰrɛ: poie:n   kai   hoti   **mɛ:***
      ask.PCPL.MASC.PL   what   and.ENC must do.PRES.INF and.PROC what NEG2
      'Asking (the gods) both what should be done and what (should) not'
      (Xenophon, *Oeconomicus* 5.19.5–20.1)

(b) Although the general tendency is that both NEG1 and NEG2 precede the negated category, postposing of the negator in Attic Greek was also possible. In the case of focusing of the verb or verbal form through a Wackernagel clitic like μὲν /men/ or δέ /de/, the negator could appear after the negated category following the clitic. Such clitics have been analyzed as focus particles in Arad and Roussou (1997).

(40) ἀρκεῖν   ἔοικέ   σοι   παθεῖν,   δρᾶσαι
      arke:n   eoike   soi   patʰe:n   dra:sai
      suffice.PRES.INF   seem.PRES.3S   you.DAT   suffer.PRES.INF   act.AOR.INF

      δὲ μή.
      de mε:
      2P NEG2
      'You are, it seems, content to suffer and make no return.'
      (Euripides, *Rhesus* 483)

Based on what we have seen so far and in combination with the reasoning of Rivero (1994) and Rivero and Terzi (1995) the unavailability of true negative imperatives in Late Medieval Greek is readily explained, provided that NEG2 *mē* is now a head in its preverbal prohibitive function. Figure 2 presents the phrasal status of NEG2 in Classical and Koine Greek, while figure 3 shows the head status of NEG2 in Late Medieval Greek.

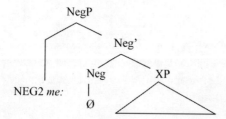

Figure 2: The phrasal status of NEG2 in Classical and Koine Greek.

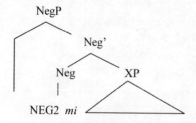

Figure 3: The head status of NEG2 in Late Medieval Greek.

The transformation of lexical elements from phrases to heads is a phenomenon with crosslinguistic representation in language diachrony, as shown in van Gelderen's (2004) study *Grammaticalization as Economy*, preceded in van Gelderen (2001). The principle of diachronic change that supports the Phrase-to-Head transformation of the Late Medieval Greek negators is the Head Preference Principle from van Gelderen (2004: 11) presented in (41) below.

(41)   Head Preference or Spec-to-Head Principle:
       Be a head, rather than a phrase

This is a structure minimizing principle widely attested, e.g., in the case of English auxiliaries, in the demonstrative *that* to complementizer and determiner, the crosslinguistic formation of determiners from pronouns (Heine and Kuteva 2002; Wood 2003), adverbs to complementizers (see van Gelderen 2011 for a full overview), while it also offers a syntactic explanation for Jespersen's cycle in Greek: *udhén* (phrase in Attic Greek) > *(u)dhen* (head in Late Medieval and Modern Greek), and in many other languages.

3.3 The ban of NEG2 from the conditional antecedent

One more change that is already settled in Late Medieval Greek is the fact that NEG2 no longer appears in the conditional protasis, neither in its former form *μη* /mi/, nor in its novel, but temporary variant *μηδέν* /midhén/. Only NEG1 is generally licensed in the conditional antecedent, either as *οὐ(κ)* /u(k)/, *οὐδέν* /udhén/ or *δεν* /dhen/. Examples (42) through (44) contain representative cases.

(42) *«Καλῶς   ἦλθες,   νεώτερε, ἂν   οὐκ   εἶσαι   προδότης».*
     *Kalós   ílthes   neótere, an   **uk**   íse   prodhótis*
     Well   come.PP.2SG   younger, if   NEG1 be.INP.2SG traitor
     'Welcome, younger one, if you are not a traitor.'
     (*Digenis Akritis* 651)

(43) *εἰ δὲ καὶ οὐ   θέλεις   νὰ   ἐλθης,   ἰδοὺ ἐγὼ ὑπαγαίνω.*
     *i   dhe ke   **u**   thélis   na   elthis   idhú eghó ipaghéno*
     if 2P   and NEG1 want.INP.2SG SUBJ come.PNP.2SG here I   go.INP.1SG
     'And if you do not want to came, here I am going.'
     (*Digenis Akritis* 1005)

(44) καὶ   ἂν   οὐδὲν   ἔλθῃς   τὸ   γοργόν,   κατέβην   ἔχω   εἰς   Μάγγε
     ke   an   **udhén**   élthis   to   ghorghón   katévin   echo   is   Máge
     and   if   NEG1   come.PNP.2SG   the   soon,   go.PNP.1SG   FUT   to   Mage
     'And if you do not come soon, I will go to Mage (…).'
     (*Digenis Akritis* 288)

Table 3: Negator distribution in the conditional protasis in Attic Greek, in Koine and Late Medieval Greek

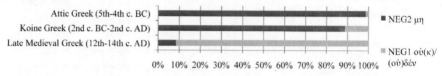

Table 3 depicts the distribution of NEG1 and NEG2 in the conditional protasis in Late Medieval Greek compared to those of the previous stages, Classical Greek and Hellenistic Koine. NEG2 *mē* is attested in conditionals in Late Medieval, but to a very limited extent. The change in the distribution of NEG1 and NEG2 from Attic Greek to Koine is not statistically significant (p-value = 0.1939), while the change from Koine Greek to Late Medieval is significant (p-value < 10^{-15}). This use of NEG2 *mē* is no longer productive and would not survive in Standard Modern Greek.

3.3.1 An explanation: upward reanalysis of NEG2 on Cinque's (1999) hierarchy

The unavailability of NEG2 in the conditional protasis during Late Medieval Greek (although other polarity items are still licensed in that environment) possibly relates to a repartitioning of labor between NEG1 and NEG2 that must have taken place during the Early Medieval stage. The picture that emerges for the use of NEG2 *mē* in Late Medieval Greek – as well as for the stages to follow – is that NEG2 *mē* became an element that correlates to the C position (see also Giannakidou 2009), in contributing illocutionary force (as in the case of prohibition, interrogation and introducing *verba timendi* complements). The conditional protasis does not offer such a position for NEG2 *μη* /mi/. The C position in conditionals is filled by the *ἂν* /an/ or the *εἰ* /i/ conditional particles that now compete with NEG2 *mē* and are in complementary distribution. This is a fact that describes the situation in Standard Modern Greek as well. Only NEG1 *δεν* /dhen/ can appear in the conditional protasis in Standard Modern Greek, as presented in the example below.

(45) *Av δεν /*μην   έρθει,   θα στεναχωρεθώ.* STANDARD MODERN GREEK
   An **dhen** / **min érthi   tha stenakhorethó*
   If   NEG1/*NEG2 come.PNP.3SG FUT be.sad.PNP.1SG
   'If s/he doesn't come, I will be sad.'
                 ONLY NEG1 IN THE CONDITIONAL PROTASIS

One reason for this may be that NEG2, apart from its shift in syntactic status (from phrase to head), may also have reanalyzed as relating to a higher position within C, in its expanded form according to Cinque's (1999) cartographic approach. NEG2 seems to have elevated to a position where it competes with the conditional particle both in Late Medieval (*àv* /an/ or the *εἰ* /i/) and in Standard Modern Greek (*αv* /an/). This transition agrees with both Roberts and Roussou's (2003) up-the-tree movement and van Gelderen's (2004) Late Merge Principle.

(46) The upward reanalysis of the Greek NEG2 on Cinque's hierarchy
      (for conditionals)

Mood$_{SpeechAct}$ Mood$_{Evaluative}$ Mood$_{Evidential}$ Mod$_{Epistemic}$ T(Past) T(Future) **Mood$_{Irrealis}$**
Mod$_{Necessity}$ Mod$_{Possibility}$ Asp$_{Habitual}$ Asp$_{Repetitive(I)}$ Asp$_{Frequentative(I)}$ Asp$_{Celerative(I)}$ Mod$_{Volitional}$
Mod$_{Obligation}$ Mod$_{Ability/Permission}$ Asp$_{Celerative(II)}$ T(Anterior) Asp$_{Terminative}$ Asp$_{Continuative}$
Asp$_{Perfect(?)}$ Asp$_{Retrospective}$ Asp$_{Proximative}$ Asp$_{Durative}$ Asp$_{Generic/progressive}$ Asp$_{Prospective}$
Asp$_{SgCompletive(I)}$ Asp$_{PlCompletive}$ Voice Asp$_{Celerative(II)}$ Asp$_{SgCompletive(II)}$ Asp$_{Repetitive(II)}$
Asp$_{Frequentative(II)}$ Asp$_{SgCompletive(II)}$

The Mood$_{Irrealis}$ is clearly akin to nonveridicality in its purest form: deprived from all additional connotations, such as speech act, evaluativity, evidentiality, etc. Furthermore, a movement from Mood$_{Irrealis}$ to Mood$_{SpeechAct}$ has recently been claimed to be involved in the synchronic derivation of conditionals in general (Danckaert and Haegeman 2012). The relevance of Danckaert and Haegeman's claim with respect to the upward reanalysis of NEG2 from a position that merely indicates irrealis (in Classical and Koine Greek) to the locus of illocutionary force is clear if we consider it along with Roberts and Roussou's (2003) understanding of grammaticalization as "loss of movement" (loss of synchronic movement; the elements get permanently reanalyzed as originating in their former landing site, cf. also van Gelderen 2004). Therefore, the loss of NEG2 from the conditional protasis may be a result of the diachronic elevation of the family of uses of NEG2 to a syntactic position in which the conditional particles are already hosted. The other functions of NEG2 *mē* (as a particle introducing *yes/no* questions and complementizer selected by *timendi* predicates) were already in that position (see also Willmott 2008, who provides a mapping for the uses of NEG2 in connection to Cinque's hierarchy), as was NEG2 in its prohibitive use.

(47)   The upward reanalysis of the Greek NEG2 family on Cinque's hierarchy

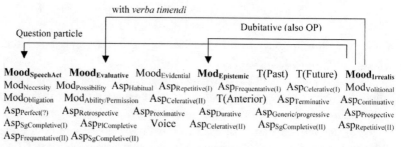

The *micro-* part of "micromovement" captures the gradualness of the changes described, which is in agreement with outlooks on grammaticalization and language change that highlight the gradual nature of the phenomenon (Lichtenberk 1991; Hopper and Traugott [1993] 2003; Lehmann 2004; Lightfoot 2005; but see Lightfoot 1999 for language change as "catastrophic"). This can easily be captured through the notion of mismatch between semantic and syntactic representations (or modules, see Sadock 1991, 2012; Sadock and Schiller 1993). Yet even within the generative perspective, the position that a minimalist outlook on syntactic change can only be abrupt (described also as "saltational") and not incremental, as suggested in Kinsella (2009: 91–92), has been recently dismissed in Clark (2012), while Roberts (2010, 2012), as well as Traugott and Trousdale (2010), discuss such *micro*-operations and support a view on language change as involving a number of *micro*-steps that can eventually have a *macro* effect.

4 Summary

The examination of the history of negation in Greek by definition places this study within the Jespersen's cycle literature. However, the exact developments of NEG1 and NEG2 do not properly fall under Jespersen's cycle in the traditional understanding. Making some room in the literature not just for Greek, but for a significant number of other languages, is more than a matter of terminology. It is an attempt to define a semantic phenomenon – as is grammaticalization in general (cf. Lightfoot 1999; Heine and Kuteva 2002) – in semantic terms, in a way that is consistent, accessible across different linguistic fields to the extent possible, and captures the regularity in the phenomenon of negator renewal, in a way that is not universal, but still broader than the traditional morphosyntactic account. Both NEG1 and NEG2 underwent Jespersen's cycle in the proposed sense by the Late Medieval stage. Yet only the novel form of NEG1 *(ου)δέν* /(u)dhén/ would be generalized and make it to Standard Modern Greek. NEG2 *μη* /mi/ – a reflex of the Proto-Indo-European reconstructed form *me_{h1} (Moorhouse 1959; Joseph 2002) – remained stable, but not unaffected. Two subtle transformations of NEG2 *mē* by Late Medieval Greek were discussed: the loss of True Negative Imperatives and the ban of NEG2 from the conditional antecedent. The Greek data were shown to further verify generative outlooks on syntactic change, while also an explanation was provided regarding the ban of NEG2 from the conditional antecedent, which assumes further elevation of NEG2 *mē* on the Cinque (1999) hierarchy.

Sources

ATTIC GREEK (5TH–4TH CENTURY BC)

Aristophanes, *Lysistrata, Ranae* (Aristophanes. *Acharnenses, Equites, Pax, Aves, Lysistrata, Thesmophoriazusae, Ranae, Plutus*: Coulon, V. and M. van Daele. 1967. Aristophane, Paris: Les Belles Lettres)

Euripides, *Alcestis, Hippolytus* (Euripides. Murray, G. 1902. *Euripidis fabulae*. Oxford: Clarendon Press)

Lysias, *In Eratosthenem, In Agoratum, De caede Eratosthenis* (Lysias with an English translation by W.R.M. Lamb, M.A. Cambridge, MA, Harvard University Press; London, William Heinemann 1930)

Plato, *Respublica IV* (Plato. *Platonis Opera*, ed. John Burnet. Oxford University Press. 1903)

KOINE GREEK (1ST CENTURY BC-1ST CENTURY AD)

Strabo, *Geographica VI-VIII* (Meineke, A. 1877. *Strabonis geographica*, vol. 1–3. Leipzig: Teubner)

Greek New Testament (synoptic gospels: *Secundum Mattheum, Secundum Marcum, Secundum Lucam, Novum Testamentum Graece cum apparatu critico*. 1956. *curavit* D. Eberhard Nestle, *novis curis elaboravit* D. Erwin Nestle *adiuvante* D. Kurt Aland, 22nd edn., Stuttgart: Württembergische Bibelanstalt)

Epictetus, *Dissertationes ab Arriano digestae III* (Schenkl, H. 1916. *Epicteti dissertations ab Arriano digestae*. Leipzig: Teubner)

LATE MEDIEVAL GREEK (12TH–14TH CENTURY AD)

Digenis Akritis (Escorial manuscript, *Digenis Akritis*. Alexiou, S. 1985. *Vasileios Digenis Akritis kai to Asma tou Armouri*. Athina: Ermis)

Livistros and Rodamne (Vatican version, *Livistros and Rodamni (version b)*. Lendari, T. 2007. *Livistros and Rodamne: The Vatican version*. Athina: MIET)

Imperios and Margarona (*Imberios and Margarona*. E. M. Jeffreys and M. J. Jeffreys. 1983. *Popular literature in Late Byzantium*. London: Variorum Reprints)

Chronicle of Moreas (*Chronicle of Morea*. Kalonaros, P. P. 1940. *To Hronikon tou Moreos*. Athina: Dimitrakos)

Ptoholeon (*Ptoholeon*. Kehagioglou, G. 2011. *Ptoholeon*. Thessaloniki: MIET)

References

Anton, C. Theophilus. 1824. De discrimine particularum *οὔ et μή* brevis dissertatio. *Archiv für Philologie und Pädagogik* 1. 481–488.

Arad, Maya & Anna Roussou. 1997. Particles and C-positions in Classical Greek. Unpub. ms. University College London & University of Wales, Bangor.

Arvaniti, Amalia. 2007. Greek phonetics: The state of the art. *Journal of Greek Linguistics* 8. 97–208.

van der Auwera, Johan. 2005. Prohibitives: Why two thirds of the world's languages are unlike Dutch. In Paul Dekker & Michael Francke (eds.), *Proceedings of the Fifteenth Amsterdam Colloquium*, 25–30. Amsterdam: University of Amsterdam, ILLC.

van der Auwera, Johan. 2006. Why languages prefer prohibitives. 外国语 [*Wai guo yu – Journal of Foreign Languages*] 161. 2–25.

van der Auwera, Johan. 2008. Gardiner's cycle. Unpub. ms. Universiteit Antwerpen.

van der Auwera, Johan. 2009. The Jespersen cycles. In Elly van Gelderen (ed.), *Cyclical change*, 35–71. Amsterdam & Philadelphia: John Benjamins.

van der Auwera, Johan. 2010. On the diachrony of negation. In Larry R. Horn (ed.), *The Expression of Negation*, 73–101. Berlin & New York: de Gruyter Mouton.

van der Auwera, Johan & Ludo Lejeune. 2005. The prohibitive. In Martin Haspelmath, Matthew Dryer, David Gil & Bernard Comrie (eds.), *World atlas of language structures*, 290–293. Oxford: Oxford University Press.

van der Auwera, Johan & Neuckermans, Annemie. 2004. Een Oost-Vlaamse driedubbele negatie [An East Flemish triple negation]. In Sjef Barbiers, Magda Devos & Geert de Schutter (eds.), *Dialectsyntaxis in bloei* [Dialectsyntax in bloom] (Theme issue *Taal en Tongval* 15–16). 143–157. Gent: Koninklijke Academie voor Nederlandse Taal- en Letterkunde.

Baker, Carl L. 1970. Double negatives. *Linguistic Inquiry* 1(2). 169–186.

Beekes, Robert Stephen Paul. 1995. *Comparative Indo-European linguistics. An introduction.* Amsterdam & Philadelphia: John Benjamins.

Beekes, Robert Stephen Paul. 2010. *Etymological dictionary of Greek.* Leiden: Brill.

Bolinger, Dwight. 1972. *Degree words.* The Hague: Mouton.

Bréal, Michel. 1897. *Essai de sémantique. Science de significations.* Paris: Hachette. [Engl. trans. by Henry-Nina Cust, *Semantics: Studies in the science of meaning*, London: Henry Holt & Company, 1900.]

Breitbarth, Anne. 2009. A hybrid approach to Jespersen's cycle in West Germanic. *Journal of Comparative Germanic Linguistics* 12(2). 81–114.

Breitbarth, Anne & Liliane Haegeman. 2008. Not continuity, but change: Stable stage II in Jespersen's cycle. Unpub. ms. University of Cambridge & Université de Lille III.

Buyssens, Edward. 1959. Negative contexts. *English Studies* 40. 163–169.

Chatzopoulou, Katerina. 2011. Negation beyond fate. Paper presented at the *10th International Conference on Greek Linguistics* (ICGL 10), Democritus University of Komotini, Greece, September 1–4.

Chatzopoulou, Katerina. 2012. *Negation and nonveridicality in the history of Greek.* Chicago, IL: University of Chicago dissertation.

Chatzopoulou, Katerina. 2013a. Re(de)fining Jespersen's cycle. *University of Pennsylvania Working Papers in Linguistics* 19(1). 31–40. http://repository.upenn.edu/pwpl/vol19/iss1/5/ (accessed 4 November 2013).

Chatzopoulou, Katerina. 2013b. The history of the Greek NEG2: Two parameter resets linked to a syntactic status shift. *Journal of Historical Syntax* 2(5). 1–47.

Chatzopoulou, Katerina & Anastasia Giannakidou. 2011. Negator selection in Attic Greek is a polarity phenomenon. Poster presented at the *13th Diachronic Generative Syntax Conference* (DiGS XIII), University of Pennsylvania, Philadelphia, PA, June 2–5.

Chatzopoulou, Katerina & Ioanna Sitaridou. 2014. Negator selection in Romeyka conditionals: Jespersen's cycle for NEG2. Paper presented at the *16th Diachronic Generative Syntax Conference* (DiGS XVI), Hungarian Acadamy of Sciences, Budapest, July 3–5.

Chaker, Salem. 1996. Quelques remarques préliminaires sur la négation en berbère. In Salem Chaker & Dominique Caubet (eds.), *La négation en berbère et en Arabe Maghrébin*, 9–22. Paris: Harmattan.

Cinque, Guglielmo. 1999. Adverbs and functional heads: A cross-linguistic perspective. Oxford: Oxford University Press.

Clark, Brady. 2012. Syntactic theory and the evolution of syntax. Presentation at the *Language Variation and Change Workshop*, University of Chicago, Chicago, IL, May 4.

Clarke, Charles C. 1904. The actual force of the French *ne*. *Modern Philology* 2. 279–287.

Cowgill, Warren. 1960. Greek *ou* and Armenian *oč*. *Language* 36(3). 347–50.

Croft, William. 1991. The evolution of negation. *Journal of Linguistics* 27. 1–27.

Crowley, Terry. 2006. *Nese: A diminishing speech variety of Northwest Malakula (Vanuatu)*. Canberra: Australian National University.

Dahl, Östen. 1979. Typology of sentence negation. *Linguistics* 17. 79–106.

Danckaert, Lieven & Liliane Haegeman. 2012. Conditional clauses, main clause phenomena and the syntax of polarity emphasis. In Peter Ackema, Rhona Alcorn, Caroline Heycock, Dany Jaspers, Jeroen Van Craenenbroeck & Guido Vanden Wyngaerd (eds.), *Comparative Germanic syntax. The state of the art*, 133–167. Amsterdam & Philadelphia: John Benjamins.

de Cuypere, Ludovic. 2008. *Limiting the iconic: From the metatheoretical foundations to the creative possibilities of iconicity in language*. Amsterdam & Philadelphia: John Benjamins.

de Swart, Henriëtte. 2010. *Expression and interpretation of negation* (Studies in Natural Language and Linguistic Theory 77). Dordrecht: Springer.

Deligianni, Efrosini. 2011. Pragmatic factors that determine main constituent order in Greek: A diachronic consideration. In Elisa Kitis, Nikolaos Lavidas, Nina Topintzi & Tasos Tsangalidis (eds.), *Selected Papers from the 19th International Symposium on Theoretical and Applied Linguistics*, 163–173. Thessaloniki: Monochromia.

Deligianni, Efrosini. forthcoming. The interaction between Jespersen's cycle and scalarity in Greek. In Maj-Britt Mosegaard Hansen & Jaqueline Visconti (eds.), *The diachrony of negation*. Amsterdam & Philadelphia: John Benjamins.

Detges, Ulrich & Richard Waltereit. 2002. Grammaticalization vs. reanalysis: A semantic-pragmatic account of functional change in grammar. *Zeitschrift für Sprachwissenschaft* 21. 151–195.

Devine, Andrew & Lawrence Stephens. 1994. *The prosody of Greek speech*. Oxford: Oxford University Press.

Devos, Maud, Michael Kasombo Tshibanda & Johan van der Auwera. 2010. Jespersen cycles in Kanincin: Double, triple and maybe even quadruple negation. *Africana Linguistica* 16. 155–181.

Djamouri, Redouane. 1991. Particule de negation dans les inscriptions sur bronze de la dynastie des Zhou. *Cahiers de Linguistique – Asie Orientale* 20(1). 5–76.

Djamouri, Redouane. 1996. Comptes rendus-Pulleyblank. *Cahiers de Linguistique – Asie Orientale* 25(2). 289–298.

Dowty, David. 1994. The role of negative polarity and concord marking in natural language reasoning. In Mandy Harvey & Lynn Santelmann (eds.), *Proceedings from Semantics and Linguistic Theory (SALT) IV*, 114–144. Ithaca, NY: CLC Publications, Cornell University.

Early, Robert. 1994a. Lewo. In Peter Kahrel & René van den Berg (eds.), *Typological studies in negation*, 65–92. Amsterdam & Philadelphia: John Benjamins.

Early, Robert. 1994b. *A grammar of Lewo, Vanuatu.* Canberra: Australian National University dissertation.

Ebeling, Heinrich L. 1902. Some statistics on the order of words in Greek. In *Studies in honor of Basil L. Gildersleeve*, 229–240. Baltimore, MD: Johns Hopkins University Press.

Farkas, Donka. F. 1992. On the semantics of subjunctive complements. In Paul Hirschbühler & Konrad Koerne (eds.), *Romance languages and modern linguistic theory*, 69–104. Amsterdam & Philadelphia: John Benjamins.

Fortson, Benjamin. W. 2010. *Indo-European language and culture: An introduction.* 2nd edn. Chichester, U.K. & Malden, MA: Wiley-Blackwell.

Fowler, Frank Hamilton. 1896. *The negatives of the Indo-European languages.* Chicago, IL: The University of Chicago Press.

Franke, Friedrich. 1832. *De particulis negantibus linguae graecae commentatio.* Part 1. *Annalium scholasticorum particula undetricesima qua publicata ad examina in Gymnasio Electorali Hasso-Schaumburgo*, Rinteln.

Frisch, Stefan A. 1997. The change in negation in Middle English: A NegP licensing account. *Lingua* 101. 21–64.

Gardiner, Alan H. 1904. The word ⸗ ⸗. *Zeitschrift für Ägyptische Sprache und Altertumskunde* 41. 130–135.

van Gelderen, Elly. 2001. Phrases, heads, grammaticalization and economy. *International Conference on Historical Linguistics*, published in *Journal of Comparative Germanic Linguistics* 7.1(2004): 59–98.

van Gelderen, Elly. 2004. *Grammaticalization as economy.* Amsterdam & Philadelphia: John Benjamins.

van Gelderen, Elly. 2008. The negative cycle. *Linguistic Typology* 12(2). 195–243.

van Gelderen, Elly. 2011. *The linguistic cycle: Language change and the language faculty.* Oxford: Oxford University Press.

Gerö, Eva-Carin. 1997. *Negatives and Noun Phrases in Classical Greek: an investigation based on the Corpus Platonicum.* Frankfurt/M. & Berlin: Peter Lang.

Giannakidou, Anastasia. 1998. *Polarity sensitivity as (non)veridical dependency.* Amsterdam & Philadelphia: John Benjamins.

Giannakidou, Anastasia. 2006. *Only*, emotive factives, and the dual nature of polarity dependency. *Language*, 82(3). 575–603.

Giannakidou, Anastasia. 2009. The dependency of the subjunctive revisited: Temporal semantics and polarity. *Lingua* 120. 1883–1908.

Givón, Talmy. 1978. Negation in language: Pragmatics, function, ontology. In Peter Cole (ed.), *Syntax and Semantics 9: Pragmatics*, 69–112. New York: Academic Press.

Givón, Talmy. 2000. Internal reconstruction: As method, as theory. In Spike Gildea (ed.), *Reconstructing grammar*, 107–159. Amsterdam & Philadelphia: John Benjamins.

Godard, Danièle. 2004. French negative dependency. In Francis Corblin & Henriëtte de Swart (eds.), *Handbook of French semantics*, 351–390. Stanford, CA: CSLI Publications.

Goodwin, William Watson. 1889. *Syntax of the moods and tenses of the Greek verb.* New York: Macmillan.

Hammond, Lila. 2005. *Serbian: An essential grammar.* London & New York: Routledge.

Harris, Martin. 1976. A typological approach to word order change in French. In Martin Harris (ed.), *Romance syntax: Synchronic and diachronic perspectives*, 33–53. Salford: University of Salford.

Harris, Martin. 1978. *The evolution of French syntax.* London: Longman.

Han, Chung-Hye. 2000. *The structure and interpretation of imperatives: Mood and force in universal grammar.* New York: Garland.

Han, Chung-Hye. 2001. Force, negation and imperatives. *The Linguistic Review* 18. 289–325.

Heine, Bernd & Tania Kuteva. 2002. *World lexicon of grammaticalization.* Cambridge: Cambridge University Press.

Herburger, Elena. 2001. The negative concord puzzle revisited. *Natural Language Semantics* 9. 289–333.

Hoeksema, Jack. 1997. Negation and negative concord in middle Dutch. In Danielle Forget, Paul Hirschbühler, France Martineau & María Luisa Rivero (eds.), *Negation and polarity: Syntax and semantics*, 139–158. Amsterdam & Philadelphia: John Benjamins.

Honda, Isao. 1996. *Negation: A cross-linguistic study.* Buffalo, NY: The State University of New York dissertation.

Hoogeveen, Hendrik. 1782 [1769]. *Doctrina Particularum Graecarum.* revised by Christian G. Schütz, Leipzig: Dessau.

Hopper, Paul J. & Elizabeth Closs Traugott. 2003 [1993]. *Grammaticalization*, 2nd edn. Cambridge: Cambridge University Press.

Horn, Larry R. 1989. *A natural history of negation.* Stanford, CA: CSLI Publications.

Horrocks, Geoffrey. 2010 [1997]. *Greek: A history of the language and its speakers*, 2nd edn. Malden, MA: Wiley-Blackwell.

Jackendoff, Ray. 1969. An interpretive theory of negation. *Foundations of Language* 5. 218–241.

Jäger, Agnes. 2008. *History of German negation.* Amsterdam & Philadelphia: John Benjamins.

Jannaris, Antonius N. 1897. *An historical Greek grammar.* London: MacMillan.

Jespersen, Otto. 1917. *Negation in English and other languages.* Copenhagen: A. F. Høst.

Joseph, Brian D. 2002. Balkan insights into the Syntax of *me: in Indo-European. In Mark Southern (ed.), *Indo-European perspectives* (Journal of Indo-European Studies Monograph Series 43), 103–120. Washington, DC: Institute for the Study of Man.

Joseph, Brian D. 2005. Some ancient shared metaphors in the Balkans. *Acta Studia Albanica* 2 (2). 43–46.

Joseph, Brian D. & Richard D. Janda. 1999. The Modern Greek negator *mi(n)(-)* as a morphological constellation. In Giórgios Babiniótis & Amalía Mózer (eds.), *Greek linguistics '97: Proceedings of the 3rd International Conference on the Greek Languages*, 341–351. Athens: Eliniká Grámata.

Joseph, Brian D. & Irene Philippaki-Warburton. 1987. *Modern Greek.* London: Croom Helm.

van Kemenade, Ans. 2000. Jespersen's cycle revisited: Formal properties of grammaticalization. In Susan Pintzuk, George Tsoulas & Anthony Warner (eds.), *Diachronic syntax: Models and mechanisms*, 51–75. Oxford: Oxford University Press.

Kinsella, Anna. 2009. *Language evolution and syntactic theory.* Cambridge: Cambridge University Press.

Kiparsky, Paul & Cleo Condoravdi. 2006. Tracking Jespersen's cycle. In Mark Janse, Brian D. Joseph & Angela Ralli (eds.), *Proceedings of the 2nd International Conference of Modern Greek Dialects and Linguistic Theory*, 172–197. Mytilene: Doukas.

Klima, Edward. 1964. Negation in English. In Jerry A. Fodor & Jerrold J. Katz (eds.), *The structure of language*, 246–323, Englewood Cliffs, NJ: Prentice Hall.

Kühner, Raphael & Bernhard Gerth. 1898/1904. *Ausführliche Grammatik der griechischen Sprache. II: Satzlehre.* 2 vols. Hannover: Hahn.

Ladusaw, William. 1979. *Polarity sensitivity as inherent scope relations.* Austin, TX: University of Texas dissertation.

Laka, Itziar. 1990. *Negation in syntax: On the nature of functional categories and projections.* Cambridge, MA: MIT dissertation.

Lee, Chungmin. 2011. Middle English negative concord: How it competed with negative polarity. Paper presented at *10th Medieval English Studies Symposium* (MESS 10), Poznań, Poland, November 19–20.

Lehmann, Christian. 2004. Theory and method in grammaticalization. *Zeitschrift für Germanistische Linguistik* 32: 152–187.

Lichtenberk, Frantisek. 1991. On the gradualness of grammaticalization. In Elizabeth Closs Traugott and Bernd Heine (eds.), *Approaches to grammaticalization*, vol. 1, 37–80. Amsterdam & Philadelphia: John Benjamins.

Lightfoot, David W. 1979. *Principles of diachronic syntax.* Cambridge: Cambridge University Press.

Lightfoot, David W. 1999. *The development of language: Acquisition, change, and evolution.* Oxford: Blackwell.

Lightfoot, David W. 2005. Can the lexicalization/grammaticalization distinction be reconciled? *Studies in Language* 29. 583–615.

Lin, Nina Yuhsun. 2002. A corpus-based study on the development of Mandarin negative marker 'mei'. Paper presented at *35th International Conference on Sino-Tibetan Languages and Linguistics*, Arizona State University, Tempe, November 9–10.

Lucas, Christopher. 2007. Jespersen's cycle in Arabic and Berber. *Transactions of the Philological Society* 105(3). 398–431.

Malikouti-Drachman, Angeliki. 1993. New approaches to some problems of Greek phonology. In Irene Philippaki-Warburton, Katerina Nicolaidis & Maria Sifianou (eds.), *Themes in Greek linguistics*, 33–44. Amsterdam & Philadelphia: John Benjamins.

Malikouti-Drachman, Angeliki. 2001. Greek phonology: A contemporary perspective. *Journal of Greek Linguistics* 2. 187–243.

Manzini, Maria Rita & Leonardo M. Savoia. 2005. *I dialetti italiani e romanci. Morfosintassi generativa* [The dialects of Italian and Romance. Generative morphosyntax], 3 vols. Alessandria: Edizioni dell'Orso.

Mazzon, Gabriella. 2004. *A history of English negation.* London: Pearson Longman.

Meillet, Antoine. 1912. L'évolution des formes grammaticales. *Scientia (Rivista di Scienza)* 12 (26.6). 130–148.

Merchant, Jason. 2006. 'Why no(t)?'. *Style* 40(1/2). 20–23.

Mettouchi, Amina. 1996. La négation dans les langues du Maghreb: Synthèse. In Salem Chaker & Dominique Caubet (eds.), *La négation en Berbère et en Arabe Maghrébin*, 177–195. Paris: Harmattan.

Miestamo, Matti. 2003. *Clausal negation: A typological study.* Helsinki: University of Helsinki dissertation.

Moorhouse, Alfred C. 1959. *Studies in the Greek negatives.* Cardiff: University of Wales Press.

Mustajoki Arto & Hannes Heino. 1991. *Case selection for the direct object in Russian negative clauses.* Part II: *Report on a statistical analysis* (Slavica Helsingiensia 9). Helsinki: University of Helsinki.

Payne, John. R. 1985. Negation. Language typology and syntactic description. In Timothy Shopen (ed.), *Clause structure*, vol. 1, 197–242. Cambridge: Cambridge University Press.

Philippaki-Warburton, Irene & Vassilis Spyropoulos. 2004. A change of mood: The development of the Greek mood system. *Linguistics* 42(2). 791–817.

Postma, Gertjan & Wim van der Wurff. 2007. How to say *no* and *don't*: Negative imperatives in Romance and Germanic. In Wim van der Wurff (ed.), *Imperative clauses in generative grammar*, 205–49. Amsterdam & Philadelphia: John Benjamins.

Pulleyblank, Edwin. 1995. *Outline of Classical Chinese grammar.* Vancouver, BC: University of British Columbia Press.

Rijksbaron, Albert. 2012. Does Ancient Greek have a word for 'No'? *Journal of Greek Linguistics* 12(1). 140–160.

Rivero, María Luisa. 1994. Negation, imperatives and Wackernagel effects. *Rivista di Linguistica* 6(1). 39–66.

Rivero, María Luisa & Arhonto Terzi. 1995. Imperative, V-movement and logical mood. *Journal of Linguistics* 31. 301–332.

Roberts, Ian. 2010. Grammaticalization, the clausal hierarchy and semantic bleaching. In Elizabeth Closs Traugott & Graeme Trousdale (eds.), *Gradience, gradualness and grammaticalization*, 45–73. Cambridge: Cambridge University Press.

Roberts, Ian. 2012. Towards a parameter hierarchy for verb-movement: Diachronic considerations. Paper presented at the *34th Annual Meeting of the Deutsche Gesellschaft für Sprachwissenschaft* (DGfS), Frankfurt, March 6–9.

Roberts, Ian & Anna Roussou. 2003. *Syntactic change. A minimalist approach to grammaticalization.* Cambridge: Cambridge University Press.

Romero, Clara. 2007. Pour une définition générale de l'intensité dans le langage. *Travaux de Linguistique* 54. 57–68.

Roussou, Anna. 2007. Minimalism and diachronic syntax: The development of negative expressions. In Eleni Agathopoulou, Maria Dimitrakopoulou & Despoina Papadopoulou (eds.), *Proceedings of the 17th International Symposium on Theoretical and Applied Linguistics – Festschrift for Prof. E. Panagopoulos*, 11–27. Thessaloniki: Monochromia Publishing.

Sadock, Jerry M. 1991. *Autolexical syntax: A theory of parallel grammatical representations.* Chicago, IL: The University of Chicago Press.

Sadock, Jerry M. 2012. *The modular architecture of grammar.* Cambridge: Cambridge University Press.

Sadock, Jerrold M. & Eric Schiller. 1993. The generalized interface principle. In Katharine Beals et al. (eds.), *Papers from the 29th Regional Meeting of the Chicago Linguistic Society* (CLS 29), 391–402. Chicago, IL: Chicago Linguistic Society.

Sapir, Edward. 1944. Grading: A study in semantics. *Philosophy of Science* 11(2). 93–116.

Smyth, Herbert W. 1920. *Greek grammar.* Cambridge, MA: Harvard University Press.

Taylor, Ann. 1994. The change from SOV to SVO in Ancient Greek. *Language Variation and Change* 6. 1–37.

Tomić, Olga M. 1999. Negation and imperatives. *Catalan Working Papers in Linguistics* 7. 191–206.

Traugott, Elizabeth Closs & Graeme Trousdale. 2010. Gradience, gradualness and grammaticalization: How do they intersect? In Elizabeth Closs Traugott & Graeme Trousdale (eds.), *Gradience, gradualness and grammaticalization*, 19–44. Amsterdam & Philadelphia: John Benjamins.

Vennemann, Theo. 1974. Topics, subjects, and word order. From SXV to SVX via TVX. In John M. Anderson and Charles Jones (eds.), *Historical linguistics*, 339–376. Amsterdam: North Holland.

Vossen, Frens & Johan van der Auwera. 2012. Multiple exponence of standard negation in Austronesian. Paper presented at the *12th International Conference of Austronesian Linguistics*, Bali, July 2.

Wallage, Phillip. 2005. *Negation in Early English: Parametrization and grammatical competition*. Heslington, York: University of York dissertation.

Wallage, Phillip. 2008. Jespersen's cycle in Middle English: Parametric variation and grammatical competition. *Lingua* 118. 643–674.

Willis, David. 2013. The history of negation in the Brythonic Celtic languages. In David Willis, Anne Breitbarth & Christopher Lucas (eds.), *The history of negation in the languages of Europe and the Mediterranean*, vol. 1: *Case studies*, 239–298. Oxford: Oxford University Press.

Willmott, Jo. 2008. Not in the mood: Modality and negation in the history of Greek. Paper presented at the *29th Annual Meeting of the Department of Linguistics*, Thessaloniki, May 2008 and at the *Conference on Continuity and Change in Grammar*, Cambridge, March 2008.

Willmott, Jo. 2013. Negation in the history of Greek. In David Willis, Anne Breitbarth & Christopher Lucas (eds.), *The history of negation in the languages of Europe and the Mediterranean*, vol. 1: *Case studies*, 299–340. Oxford: Oxford University Press.

Wood, Johanna. 2003. *Definiteness and number*. Tempe, AZ: Arizona State University dissertation.

Zanuttini, Raffaella. 1991. *Syntactic properties of sentential negation: A comparative study of Romance languages*. Philadelphia, PA: University of Pennsylvania dissertation.

Zanuttini, Raffaella. 1997a. *Negation and clausal structure*. Oxford: Oxford University Press.

Zanuttini, Raffaella. 1997b. Negation and verb movement. In Liliane Haegeman (ed.), *The new comparative syntax*, 214–245. London & New York: Longman.

Zeijlstra, Hedde H. 2004. *Sentential negation and negative concord*. Amsterdam: Universiteit van Amsterdam dissertation.

Zeijlstra, Hedde. H. 2006. The ban on true negative imperatives. In Olivier Bonami & Patricia Cabredo Hofherr (eds.), *Empirical Issues in Syntax and Semantics 6*, 405–424. Paris: CSSR.

Zwarts, Frans. 1986. *Categoriale Grammatica en Algebraïsche Semantiek. Een onderzoek naar negatie en polariteit in het Nederlands*. Groningen: Rijksuniversiteit Groningen dissertation.

Zwarts, Frans. 1995. Nonveridical contexts. *Linguistic Analysis* 25. 286–312.

Subject index